Sustaining Cities

ENVIRONMENTAL PLANNING AND MANAGEMENT IN URBAN DESIGN

Josef Leitmann

McGraw-Hill

New York San Francisco Washington, D.C. Auckland Bogotá
Caracas Lisbon London Madrid Mexico City Milan
Montreal New Delhi San Juan Singapore
Sydney Tokyo Toronto

Library of Congress Cataloging-in-Publication Data

Leitmann, Josef
Sustaining cities : environmental planning and management in urban design / Josef Leitmann.
p. cm.
Includes index.
ISBN 0-07-038316-2
1. City planning—Environmental aspects—Study and teaching. 2. Urban ecology—Study and teaching. I. Title.
HT165.5.L45 1999
307.1'2—dc21 99-17193
CIP

McGraw-Hill
A Division of The ***McGraw-Hill*** *Companies*

2 3 4 5 6 7 8 9 0 DOC/DOC 9 0 4 3 2 1 0 9

ISBN 0-07-038316-2

The sponsoring editor for this book was Wendy Lochner, the editing supervisor was Caroline R. Levine, and the production supervisor was Sherri Souffrance. This book was set in Matt Antique by North Market Street Graphics.

Printed and bound by R. R. Donnelley & Sons Company.

This book is printed on recycled, acid-free paper containing a minimum of 50% recycled, de-inked fiber.

**To Joseph Rafael, Alessandra Sumiko and Nicolas Makoto—
may they be a part of sustaining cities in their century.**

Contents

List of Tables

Foreword

Municipal governments in Europe and North America first established the modern practice of urban environmental planning and management (EPM) when they took the lead to provide sewerage infrastructure and waste collection services to their residents. These measures provided dramatic improvements in quality of life to millions of inhabitants. Yet, in the twentieth century, the word *environment* became associated with the protection of "wild" nature. As exporters of human wastes into the natural environment, cities were often cited as pariahs by modern environmentalists.

Many of these environmentalists relied heavily on central government regulation, as opposed to local controls, in an effort to protect the environment. At the same time, as cities grew, central governments and international donors invested most heavily in rural development projects and in futile efforts to stop rural-to-urban migration. Indeed, early preparations for the 1992 United Nations Earth Summit were initially biased towards rural development and nature protection. But that Summit, persuaded by a coalition of mayors and urbanists, including Dr. Leitmann and his colleagues at the World Bank, succeeded in refocusing public attention on the environmental problems and opportunities of cities.

The reality is that our societies are decentralizing. More than 65 countries are engaged in formal processes of government decentralization or devolution. This global trend reflects the fiscal withdrawal of central governments as agents in solving many societal problems, but it also reflects the common sense efficiency of addressing problems at the local level. In essence, sustainable development is a rejection of the top-down, centralized approaches that imposed so many expensive and failed "solutions" on communities in both capitalist and socialist societies throughout the Cold War era.

In response to these global forces, we are witnessing an explosion in urban EPM activities. Dozens of new international city networks have been established in recent years to support sustainable urban development. The world's major environmental organizations have cast aside the "city-as-problem" paradigm and have focused on opportunities to reduce environmental stresses through ecological urban development.

These efforts have served as laboratories to address the fundamental challenges of urban EPM. How can local communities assume control of local development trends that are driven by global forces? How can the diverse interests and perspectives that exist in urban communities be factored into local environmental strategies? How can communities maintain commitment to long-term environmental goals while they respond to the daily challenges of rapid urban growth? How can municipalities apply the traditional instruments of local government to reduce the resource demands of societies?

In preparing *Sustaining Cities,* Joe Leitmann has reviewed the experiences of these real-life laboratories and distilled their lessons into a general urban EPM framework. This framework will serve as a practical guide to urban planners, engineers, managers, politicians, and activists to devise locally appropriate EPM approaches for their cities.

Dr. Leitmann points out the challenges of urban EPM. Among these challenges is the fact that, having been ignored for so many decades, many world cities are struggling to simply apply the EPM measures instituted by New York and London in the nineteenth century. But there are tremendous opportunities. Cities can vastly increase the economic and ecological efficiency of a society. For example, in a world where motor vehicles are a major pollution source and health risk, urban design can bring us closer to our schools and work places, and reduce the demand for mobility. Cities provide the concentrations of resources required to support public transit, district heating and cooling, recycling programs, and many other measures that can allow us to reduce human consumption of natural resources.

Ironically, the cities that have been so vilified as a human scourge on earth today provide our best hope for achieving balance between nature's requirements and humanity's aspirations. *Sustaining Cities,* in essence, guides us to claim our cities, plan them, develop their potential, and, indeed, treat them with the intensity of care deserving of our homes. In this regard, *Sustaining Cities* is a concrete, practical contribution to one of the great human challenges of the twenty-first century. I hope that its lessons are widely studied and applied.

Jeb Brugmann
SECRETARY GENERAL
International Council for Local
Environmental Initiatives

Acknowledgments

In writing this text, I stand on the shoulders of a plethora of practitioners and researchers, many of whom I count as colleagues and friends. In particular, I would like to thank my son, Joseph Rafael Leitmann-Santa Cruz, and my wife, Reiko Niimi, for suggesting improvements in the writing and for enduring the writing process; Gordon McGranahan (Stockholm Environment Institute) for an insightful review of much of the text; Carl Bartone (World Bank) and David Satterthwaite (International Institute of Environment and Development) for supportive reviews of the book outline; David Edelman (Centre for the Urban Environment) for helpful comments concerning organization of the book; Jeb Brugmann (International Council for Local Environmental Initiatives), Szilard Fricska (UN Centre for Human Settlements), Gunnar Eskeland (World Bank), Pratibha Mehta (UN Development Programme), Carl Heinz-Mumme (World Bank), Peter Newton (Commonwealth Scientific and Industrial Research Organization—Australia), Leslie Roberts (World Resources Institute), Teresa Serra (World Bank), Jitu Shah (World Bank), Hari Srinivas (Urban Environmental Management Research Initiative), Jorge Daniel Taillant (World Bank), Dominique van der Mensbrugghe (Organization for Economic Cooperation and Development), and Kate White (Urban Ecology) for providing helpful information in a timely fashion; Wendy Lochner, my editor at McGraw-Hill, for her efficiency, responsiveness, and pragmatic advice; and Ahmed Abunomay (Middle East Technical University) for assistance with photographs and illustrations.

This book was written in 1998 while I was a visiting professor of city and regional planning in the Faculty of Architecture at the Middle East Technical University in Ankara, Turkey. I would like to thank Tansi Senyapili, chair of the City and Regional Planning Department, for persevering in hiring me and then giving me the time and space to think and write. Thanks are also due to the upper division and graduate students who participated in the two courses I gave on urban environmental planning and management where much of the structure and material for this book was tested.

Josef Leitmann

Abbreviations

BOD	Biochemical oxygen demand
C	Centigrade
CBD	Central business district
CEMSAP	Calcutta Environmental Management Strategy and Action Plan
CFC	Chlorofluorocarbon
cm	centimeter
CO	Carbon monoxide
CO_2	Carbon dioxide
COD	Chemical oxygen demand
DALY	Disability-adjusted life year
EIA	Environmental impact assessment
EMAS	Ecomanagement and audit scheme
CNG	Compressed natural gas
GDP	Gross domestic product
GIGO	Garbage in, garbage out
GIS	Geographic information system
GNP	Gross national product
GTZ	German technical cooperation
ha	hectare
ICLEI	International Council for Local Environmental Initiatives
ISO	International Standards Organization
kg	kilogram

KIP	Kampung Improvement Program
l	Liter
LEAP	Local environmental action planning
LPG	Liquefied petroleum gas
m	meter
m^2	square meter
m^3	cubic meter
MCMA	Mexico City Metropolitan Area
MEIP	UNDP/World Bank Metropolitan Environmental Improvement Programme
NA	not applicable
NGO	Nongovernmental organization
NO_x	Nitrogen oxides
ODA	United Kingdom Overseas Development Administration
OECD	Organization for Economic Cooperation and Development
PRA	Participatory rapid appraisal
SCP	UNCHS/UNEP Sustainable Cities Programme
SEA	Strategic environmental assessment
SO_2	Sulfur dioxide
TSP	Total suspended particulates
UMP	UNDP/UNCHS/World Bank Urban Management Programme
UN	United Nations
UNCHS	United Nations Center for Human Settlements
UNDP	United Nations Development Programme
UNEP	United Nations Environment Programme
UNESCO	United Nations Educational, Scientific, and Cultural Organization
USEPA	United States Environmental Protection Agency
USAID	United States Agency for International Development
WHO	World Health Organization
WRI	World Resources Institute

CHAPTER 1

Introduction

Chapter Outline

- Textbook objectives and structure
- User's guide
- Why bother about cities and sustainability?
  - The world and its environmental concerns are urbanizing.
  - Range and severity of problems in richer and poorer cities
  - Cities as solutions
- Summary of key conclusions and messages
- References

The future will be predominantly urban, and the most immediate environmental concerns of most people will be urban ones.

—BRUNDTLAND COMMISSION (WCED 1987, 255)

Textbook Objectives and Structure

The title of this book has two meanings. In a rapidly urbanizing world, we need to plan and manage our cities in order to sustain them (*sustaining* as a verb). Thus, sustaining cities is an imperative. Taken another way, "sustaining cities" is a goal (*sustaining* as an adjective). We should strive for urban areas that contribute to local, regional, and global sustainable development.

Mayors, city organizations, and the urban management community rediscovered the importance of the links between cities and the environment in the early 1990s. Their successful lobbying led to the inclusion of chapters on local problems and initiatives as part of the 1992 Earth Summit's "Agenda 21." Academia, nongovernmental organizations, and aid agencies followed suit with research, publications, training courses, and even professional degrees for urban environmental planning and management. However, no publication has yet assembled this wealth of theoretical and applied material in a textbook that can be used to meet the growing demand for academic and professional training.

Thus, this text has been designed to meet the needs of two audiences: academics and professionals. Academically, the structure and exercises have been prepared to support an upper division or master's level course in city and regional planning, environmental engineering, civil engineering, public administration, management, political science, architecture, or landscape architecture. Professionally, sections of the text can be used as resources for city planners and managers, housing and urban development agencies, land and real estate developers, aid agencies, and community organizers. The content can be applied to lower-income cities as well as wealthier ones. Each chapter contains many examples drawn from both the developed and developing world. There is a slight weighting to cases from poorer countries and cities because (1) the world's urbanizing population is increasingly located in cities of the developing world and (2) in the past there has been a bias of information transfer that has downplayed what industrialized cities can learn from less-developed ones.

The objectives of this publication are to:

- Increase awareness about the urban dimension of the environmental challenge and the environmental dimension of urban development
- Improve understanding of the underlying causes of priority urban environmental problems
- Draw preliminary conclusions about where cities stand in the debate over sustainable development

- Present a proven planning framework and strategic approach for addressing the environmental issues confronting and caused by cities
- Provide guidance about practical tools that can be used for urban environmental analysis and planning
- Compile options that urban managers can use on a day-to-day basis for tackling environmental issues
- Assemble a compendium of good practice to provide students and managers with references as to what has worked around the world
- Derive general lessons that have been learned about planning and managing the urban environment
- Pose questions that might guide future research
- Offer a set of resources on where to turn for help, more information, and training

The textbook is organized into three parts:

1. *Cities and Sustainability.* Part 1 (Chapters 2 to 4) reviews past thinking about the urban environment, assesses key problems and their underlying causes, and looks at responses to whether urban development can be sustained.
2. *Planning to Sustain Cities.* Part 2 (Chapters 5 to 7) provides an urban environmental planning framework, tools for analysis and planning, and the elements of urban environmental strategies and action plans.
3. *Managing to Sustain Cities.* Part 3 (Chapters 8 and 9) outlines options for managing urban environmental problems and presents intensive as well as extensive examples of good practice.

A concluding Chapter 10 draws practical lessons for planning and managing, and reviews what we still need to know. Annexes provide resources for assistance, information, and training, and urban environmental data for major cities of the world.

User's Guide

This text can be approached in different ways, depending on whether you are a student or teacher, urban manager, researcher, or community organizer. Students and teachers can use the entire text as a course resource. In fact, the book has been structured to serve as the basis for a semester-long course on urban environmental planning and management. Urban managers may want to focus on the analysis of key problems and their causes (Chapter 3) as well as Parts 2 and 3 on planning and management approaches. Researchers may be more interested in past thinking about the urban environment (Chapter 2), different approaches to urban sustainability (Chapter 4), tools for analysis and planning (Chapter 6), potential research topics (Chapter 10), and the references at the end of each chapter. Community organizers can draw on information about key problems and their causes (Chapter 3), the participatory nature of the planning framework (Chapter 5), examples of good practice from other cities (Chapter 9), and resources for help and information (Annex B). Examples of how the text might help different users is provided in Table 1-1.

Why Bother About Cities and Sustainability?

We are on the verge of an urbanized world. As we begin the twenty-first century, about half of the world's population is living in cities and towns. (At the beginning of the twentieth century, less than 10 percent of the world was urban.) Cities are increasingly where the world's population, including the poorest people, reside. At the same time, urban areas are more and more the engines of national and regional economic growth. Thus, they are the world's chief consumers of resources and generators of waste, and, consequently, its leading sources of environmental problems.

A brief look at an "average" city in the world depicts some of these traits (see Box 1-1 for details). The average city (1996 data) is estimated to hold 1.5 million people and is growing at a rate at which its population will double in under 25 years. Residentially, average population density is relatively high, and almost one-third of the housing does not comply with local regulations.

Table 1-1 How the Text Can Help Different Users

User	Needs	Text resources
Teacher, student, or researcher	Framework and information for a course that covers the urban environment	• Framework for organizing university course (Table of Contents) • Theoretical genesis of thinking about the urban environment (Chapter 2) • References and exercises for course work and research (at the end of each chapter) • Conceptual frameworks for understanding problems, underlying causes, and solutions (Chapters 3 and 5) • Questions to guide future research (Chapter 10) • Information about academic and other institutions that offer training (Annex C)
Urban manager	Successful options for addressing urban environment issues through day-to-day city operations	• Helpful analysis of underlying causes of urban environmental issues (Chapter 3) • Options to deal with specific types of city-level environmental problems (Chapter 8) • Examples of what has worked in other cities and lessons learned (Chapter 9) • Resources for more information and assistance (Annex B)
Mayor, city councillor, or community organizer	Meet commitment to address urban pollution, health, and ecosystems	• How to organize a participatory process to prioritize problems and identify options (Chapter 5) • Preparation and implementation of an urban environmental management strategy and action plans (Chapter 7) • Lessons from other cities about what has worked (Chapter 9)

Thirty percent of households are classified as poor. The top fifth of households receives over ten times the income of the bottom fifth. Almost 7 children out of 100 die before the age of five. About half of households do not have sewerage connections; a third are not connected to a water supply system; and almost a third do not have their garbage collected on a regular basis. Nearly two-thirds of the city's wastewater (including sewage) is dumped into receiving bodies without treatment.

This section will look at two compelling reasons why we should bother with cities and sustainability. First, the rapid pace of urbanization is directly linked to a number of key local, regional, and international environmental concerns. Second, these environmental concerns are important and have serious economic, health, and ecological consequences that will only increase in magnitude as urbanization proceeds. A more detailed

BOX

As part of the Habitat II preparation process, urban indicators were developed by the United Nations Centre for Human Settlements (UNCHS) and solicited from cities around the world. Indicators were received from 236 cities in 109 countries by 1996. These cities do not constitute a representative sample of the world's urban areas because they were self-selected by the participating countries. As there is no comprehensive database for the cities of the world, this limited sample is the best available source for drawing a profile of the world's "average" city. Demographic, economic, and urban environmental indicators are as follows:

DEMOGRAPHY
City size = 1.5 million people
Population growth rate = 3.1% per year
Population density = 154 people per hectare
Female-headed households = 21% of all households

ECONOMY
City product = U.S.$4411 per capita
Number of poor households = 30% of all households
Income disparity = 10.7*

URBAN ENVIRONMENT
Child mortality rate = 67 per 1000 live births
Households with:
water connections = 66%
sewerage = 51%
solid waste collection = 69%
electricity = 77%
telephone = 37%
access to clean water = 84%
Infrastructure expenditure = $96/person/year
Water consumption = 165 liters/capita/day
Percent of wastewater treated = 38%
Solid waste generated = 0.33 tons/capita/year
Automobile ownership = 133 per 1000 population
Average travel time to work = 35 minutes
Illegal housing = 31% of housing stock

* The top income quintile earns 10.7 times the lower income quintile.

Box 1-1 The world's average city?

SOURCES: UNCHS 1996; Flood 1997.

examination of key urban environmental problems, including their underlying causes, can be found in Chapter 3.

The World and Its Environmental Concerns Are Urbanizing

Since 1950, the world's urban population has risen from under 300 million to over 2.6 billion persons. The population of urban areas is currently growing at 2.4 percent annually, over three times as fast as the 0.7 percent rate for rural areas. Over 60 million people are added to urban populations each year—more than 1 million per week. By the year 2030, 61 percent of the world's population will live in cities and towns (UN 1997). An estimated 90 percent of this increase will occur in cities of the developing world. Figure 1-1 indicates how urbanization differs according to geographic area; it suggests that Africa and Asia are urbanizing most quickly.

In the early 1990s, half of the world's urban population was located in 394 cities, each containing over half a million inhabitants. By the beginning of the twenty-first century, there will be

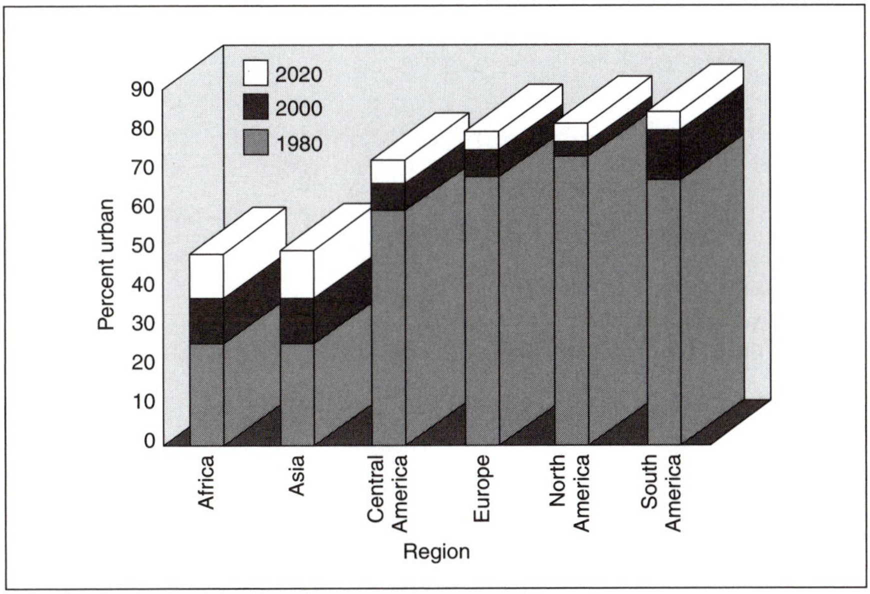

Figure 1-1 Percentage of population residing in urban areas, 1980–2020.

SOURCE: UN 1996.

over 500 cities of this size, containing 53 percent of all urban dwellers (Bartone et al. 1994). The number of megacities (those with populations over eight million) rose from just 2 (New York and London) in 1950 to 23 in 1995, with 17 located in the developing world. By 2030, the number is projected to grow to 36, with 23 of these megacities located in Asia (WRI et al. 1998). World population, therefore, will shift from being predominantly rural to predominantly urban.

Poverty is also becoming urbanized. In 1988, about a quarter of the developing world's absolute poor were thought to be located in cities. By the turn of the century, urban areas will hold half of the Third World's poor (WRI et al. 1996). Even this enormous transition in the location of poor people may be an underestimate (Sattherwaite 1997). In North America and Western Europe, most of the people and most of the poor have been urban since the beginning of the twentieth century.

Urban growth and economic development driven by the higher productivity of households and enterprises than in rural areas translate into higher wages and increased job opportunities for urban dwellers. As cities grow, productive activities tend to concentrate in urban centers, so city residents generate a disproportionate share of gross domestic product (GDP). Globally, city product per capita is about 10 percent higher than national GDP per capita; this disparity can reach higher than 40 percent in Latin American and Caribbean cities (Auclair 1998). About 80 percent of GDP growth in the developing world between 1991 and 2000 was expected to have originated in cities and towns, with higher productivity in cities rather than in the countryside, and higher productivity in large cities than in small towns (Bartone et al. 1994). The Organization for Economic Cooperation and Development (OECD) concludes that cities are similarly important in the industrialized world and for the global economy:

> *. . . urban areas are the principal centres for new jobs formation and for new or expanding economic opportunities. It is through an increasingly inter-linked system of cities, smaller urban centres and rural settlements that world production, trade and communications take place (Shachar in OECD 1995, 119).*

Increasing productivity, however, has not eliminated the massive problems of poverty and environmental degradation in cities.

Throughout the history of urban settlements, cities have always had special relationships with the environment. Box 1-2 groups the links between cities and ecosystems into three phases. Serious environmental consequences of urbanization became significant only following the Industrial Revolution, as city dwellers were more exposed to concentrated wastes, and resources to sustain the urban population were increasingly imported from other regions. Since the 1950s, the city/environment relationship has entered a third phase, with rapid population growth and globalization of the economy. Cities are at the center of the global flow of resources and wastes, and environmental problems generated by cities are experienced at the local, regional, and global levels. The current nature of this relationship is more fully described in the following section.

BOX

***Phase One—Early Urbanization* (3000 B.C.–1800 A.D.). Daily energy consumption per capita: 26,000 kcals.**

This phase began five thousand years ago in Mesopotamia, followed by locations in China and India. More productive agricultural techniques generated surpluses that could support nonagricultural concentrations of people. Settlement density increased, along with the incidence of communicable diseases. Social divisions increased and became more extreme as occupational specialization accelerated and wealth became increasingly concentrated. Diets often came to rely on single staples (e.g., rice, wheat, maize, potatoes) which increased vulnerability to disease and famine. The size and number of cities in an area were dependent on their power to extract food and other surpluses from rural populations without long-term environmental degradation.

***Phase Two—Urban Industrialism* (1800 A.D.–1950 A.D.). Daily energy consumption per capita: 50,000 kcals.**

This phase began two hundred years ago with the Industrial Revolution in Europe and North America. Energy consumption, especially fossil fuels, increased rapidly with mechanization of production. Cities grew rapidly in size and in their share of total population. Nutrient cycles were disrupted; for example, nitrogenous human wastes that normally would have been recycled were lost, largely to rivers and oceans. The urbanized population was increasingly exposed to various urban wastes and pollutants. Many cities grew by appropriating the carrying capacity of other regions and by exporting their wastes.

***Phase Three—Global Interdependence* (1950 A.D.–present). Daily energy consumption per capita: 300,000 kcals.**

Cities are nodal points for large and globally interconnected flows of resources, wastes, goods and services, financial capital, and labor. Environmental problems are local, regional, and global in scale, with cities increasingly contributing to global environmental damage.

Box 1-2 Phases of urban/ecosystem relations.

SOURCE: Adapted from Haughton and Hunter 1994, 2–3; Stren et al. 1992, 9–17.

Range and Severity of Urban Environmental Problems

The challenge of rapid urbanization is to absorb urban growth while solving the environmental and social equity problems arising from economic and physical concentration. The most critical urban environmental problems, known as the "brown agenda," can be roughly categorized into two groups: those concerns relating to environmental health, and those relating to industrialization. Environmental health problems are linked to inadequate shelter and services (lack of a safe water supply, sanitation, and drainage; inadequate solid waste management; use of low-grade domestic fuels; health risks from overcrowding; and the occupation and degradation of environmentally sensitive lands). Problems of industrialization include uncontrolled emissions from factories and mobile sources, accidents linked to congestion, and improper disposal of hazardous wastes. The costs of these problems fall most heavily on the urban poor in terms of poor health, lower productivity, and reduced income and quality of life. Brown problems, then, are those of pollution and environmental risks faced by the current generation and their children; they are primarily local and urban in nature.

This set of environmental issues can be contrasted with "green" problems, which involve natural resource management across generations. They are primarily global or transnational and rural in nature, such as global warming, ozone depletion, loss of biodiversity, and pollution of international waters. However, this brown/green distinction can be a false dichotomy. Cities are often the most important sources of greenhouse gases and the key users of ozone-depleting substances. Urban demand for natural resources, and disposal of urban-generated wastes, can accelerate habitat destruction and loss of biodiversity. Cities account for many of the land-based sources of marine pollution. Thus, solving urban environmental problems can help reduce the brown problems of environmental health and industrialization as well as some of the green problems.

The range of urban environmental challenges varies according to income level and spatial level of impact. Problems of urban wastes and pollution are inextricably linked to poverty and productivity as well as broader macroeconomic performance. Residents of lower-income cities typically face a different mix of problems than people in wealthier urban areas. Also, within a city, the poor are typically more exposed to and affected by urban environmental insults. Finally, problems can occur at different spatial levels, from the household or workplace to the global level.

Figure 1-2 roughly illustrates the spatial and economic range of urban environmental problems. Low-income cities (area A),

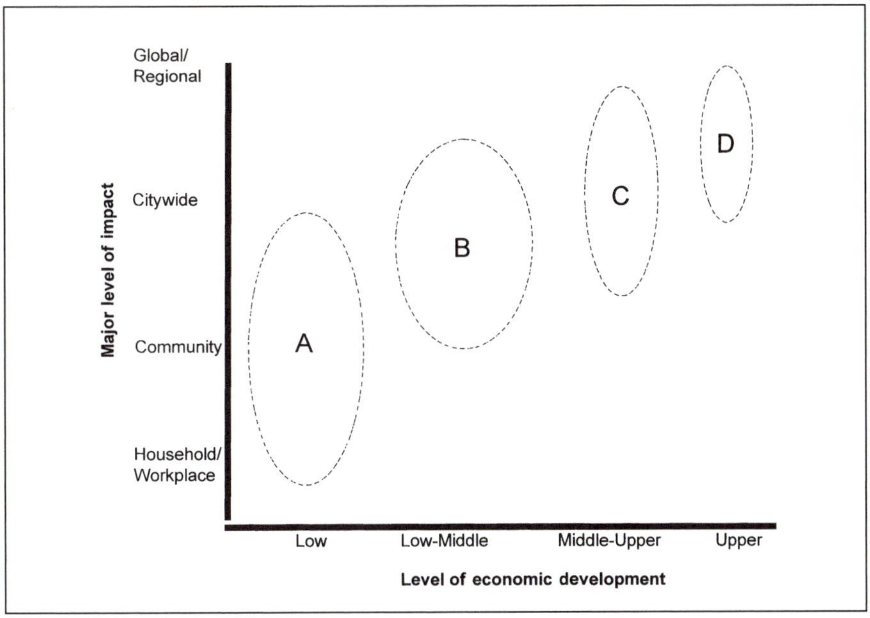

Figure 1-2 Brown problems by levels of spatial impact and economic development.
SOURCE: Adapted from Pugh 1996, 155; Bartone et al. 1994, 15, 19; Smith Whitelegg, and William 1998, 14–17.

with city products below $650 per capita annually, are characterized by low coverage and poor quality of water supply and sanitation; inadequate drainage and frequent flooding; infrequent solid waste collection; water pollution from poor sanitation; ambient and indoor air pollution from low-quality fuels; low emission of greenhouse gases per capita; open dumping and mixing of solid wastes, with recycling by the informal sector; no hazardous waste management; uncontrolled land development and pressure from squatter settlements; and recurrent natural and man-made disasters with loss of life and property damage. Low- to middle-income cities (area B), with city products of $650 to $2500 per capita per year, experience low access to water supply and sanitation by urban poor; inadequate drainage with occasional flooding; moderate coverage of solid waste collection; water pollution from untreated municipal sewage; ambient air pollution from industrial and vehicular emissions; low but growing greenhouse gas emissions per capita; mostly uncontrolled landfills; serious problems with and little capacity for hazardous waste management; ineffective land use controls; and recurrent disasters with some loss of life and property damage. Middle-income cities (area C), with city products of $2500 to $6500 per person each year, have generally reliable water supply and sewerage; reasonable drainage and solid waste collection; severe water pollution problems from industrial and municipal discharges; severe ambient air pollution from industries and vehicles; rapidly increasing output of greenhouse gases per capita; semicontrolled landfills; severe problems but growing capacity for hazardous waste management; some environmental zoning for land management; and high risk from industrial disasters. Higher-income cities (area D), with city products of more than $6500 per capita each year, are characterized by good water supply, with some concern for trace pollutants; good sanitation, drainage, and solid waste collection; high levels of effluent treatment to reduce water pollution; ambient air pollution primarily from vehicles; very high output per capita of greenhouse gases; controlled landfills with incineration and/or resource recovery; a shift in emphasis from treating to preventing hazardous wastes; regular use of environmental zoning; and good

Table 1-2 Urban Environmental Indicators by Level of Economic Development

	City Product Quintile				
Indicator	**Very low**	**Low**	**Medium**	**Higher**	**High**
City product (U.S.$/capita/year)	151	376	914	2968	17,716
Poor households (% of total)	46	35	31	38	19
Child mortality (% dying before 5)	12.3	7.4	6.7	3.1	2.3
Percent of households connected to:					
water	29	51	76	93	98
sewerage	9	26	56	83	91
solid waste collection service	34	51	74	94	99
electricity	38	65	93	96	99
Access to clean water (% of houses)	66	76	90	97	99+
Wastewater treated (%)	9	23	34	52	79
Infrastructure expenditure (U.S.$/person/year)	16	15	48	136	421
Housing in compliance with regulations (% of households)	43	53	73	86	96

SOURCE: Flood 1997.

emergency response capacity for natural and human disasters.

This typology is borne out by recent United Nations Centre for Human Settlements (UNCHS) statistics on urban indicators as summarized in Table 1-2. As an example of the environmental health burden, children in the poorest cities are five times more likely to die before they reach the age of five than are children in the wealthiest cities. The majority of households in the low- and very-low-income cities are not connected to the water supply, sewerage, and solid waste collection networks. In part, this reflects a 10 percent drop between 1990 and 1994 in the population with access to adequate sanitation in African and Latin American cities (Brown et al. 1998). Comprehensive sewage treatment appears to be a luxury that only the wealthiest cities pay for. The deficiency of these services is further illustrated by the low per capita expenditure on infrastructure for all but the wealthiest quintile of cities. Half or more of the housing in the two lowest-income quintile groups is illegal in some way (location, density, nature of construction, etc.). Nearly half of the residents in the poorest cities are in poverty themselves, compared to less than one-fifth in the wealthiest urban areas. A study by the Population Council concludes that the quality of life in many developing cities is worse than in rural areas (Brockerhoff and Brennan 1997).

In summary, the poorest cities are most affected by environmental health problems that are largely contained within city

(a)

(b)

Figure 1-3 Urban environment in Singapore (*a*) and Sana'a, Yemen (*b*).

Figure 1-4 Explosive health risk in Soweto, South Africa.

boundaries. As city incomes rise and their economies become more developed, poorer residents face a "double-whammy" of (1) unresolved environmental health problems and (2) pollution from rapid industrialization that has impacts stretching from the household to the regional level. Urban areas at the top of the eco-

Figure 1-5 Wealth and poverty within a city: Jakarta, Indonesia.

nomic ladder have largely resolved their basic environmental health problems and are more plagued by sophisticated pollution and waste problems that are citywide to global in nature.

The range of urban environmental problems within a city is also experienced differently depending on the residents' income levels. For a variety of reasons, the poor are most affected by environmental risks in cities. The first reason has to do with location. The neighborhoods or areas where poor people can afford to live are often undesirable pieces of real estate because they are located near industrial areas, are exposed to high levels of air pollution and/or water pollution, and/or may be more subject to damage by natural hazards. Second, poor communities often lack the political power to pressure government for a cleaner environment or to obtain environmental services such as a clean and reliable water supply, sanitation, waste collection, and drainage. Finally, the poor often cannot afford coping mechanisms to mitigate negative environmental impacts (e.g., using pumps to evacuate flood waters, taking vacations out of the city during severe air pollution days, or drinking bottled water).

The brown problems are manifest in cities throughout the world. Global estimates of their severity are few and far between, but those estimates that do exist indicate the problems are significant. The 1993 *World Development Report* estimates that nearly 340 million disability-adjusted life years are associated with poor household environments; improving household environmental quality could result in nearly 80 million disability-free years of human life (see Table 1-3). Globally, the health costs of urban particulate air pollution approach $100 billion annually (Litvin 1998). Pearce and Warford (1995) estimate that the costs for pollution problems alone in developing countries exceed 5 percent of the gross national products.

At the national level, specific urban environmental problems can impose heavy human and economic costs. Air and water pollution in China were estimated to cost $54 billion in 1995 alone, equivalent to 8 percent of GDP. If during the same year ambient urban air pollution had been reduced to meet China's Class 2 air quality standards, 178,000 deaths (7 percent of all urban deaths) and over 4.5 million restricted-activity days could have been

Table 1-3 Disease Burden Associated with Poor Household Environments, 1990

Disease	Environmental problem	Burden (millions of DALYs* per year)	Burden avoidable by feasible actions
Tuberculosis	Crowding	46	5
Diarrhea	Sanitation, water supply, hygiene	99	40
Trachoma	Water supply, hygiene	3	1
Tropical cluster	Sanitation, solid waste disposal, disease vectors breeding around home	8	2
Intestinal worms	Sanitation, water supply, hygiene	18	7
Respiratory infections	Indoor air pollution, crowding	119	18
Chronic respiratory diseases	Indoor air pollution	41	6
Respiratory tract cancers	Indoor air pollution	4	<1
All of the above		338	79

* DALY = disability-adjusted life year
SOURCE: World Bank 1993.

BOX

Poor urban air quality has had three key impacts in Australia's cities:

1. ***Human health effects.*** **The health costs of poor air quality are estimated to range between A$3.0 and 5.3 billion each year.**
2. ***Damage to materials and buildings.*** **Degradation and loss of property is estimated to cost the Australian economy about 1 percent of GDP per year (roughly the same magnitude as the health costs of air pollution).**
3. ***Urban amenity impacts.*** **These are harder to quantify but easy to perceive. Urban photochemical smog that lowers visibility and reduces perceived quality of life can damage a city's image and its efforts to attract investments and tourism.**

Box 1-3 Impacts of urban air pollution in Australia.
SOURCE: Newton 1997.

avoided (World Bank 1997). Overall, air pollution in Chinese cities is estimated to annually cause 130,000 to 200,000 deaths from chronic obstructive pulmonary disease, 25,000 to 50,000 deaths from coronary heart disease, 14,000 to 20,000 deaths from lung cancer, and 3000 to 16,000 deaths from childhood pneumonia—potentially over 10 percent of all urban mortality (Florig 1997). The health benefits of better air quality in Chinese cities are estimated to have a value equivalent to 20 percent of annual urban income (World Bank 1997). In a more developed country (Australia), air pollution alone costs the economy 2 percent of GDP in human health effects, as well as damage to materials and buildings (see Box 1-3).

The following are only a few examples of city-specific impacts:

- *Cairo, Egypt.* This city has one of the highest concentrations of particulate matter of any large city, exceeding U.S. standards by a factor of nearly 10. If concentrations in Greater Cairo were reduced to the U.S. standard, an estimated 11,000 deaths a year could be avoided. Lead levels in the blood of Cairo residents are five times higher than in large cities of the industrialized world, causing an average 3.75 IQ points to be lost per child (USAID 1995).
- *Asian cities.* Traffic congestion imposes high economic losses each year on many Asian cities, for example, $293 million in Hong Kong, $272 million in Bangkok, $154 million in Seoul, and $68 million each in Kuala Lumpur and Jakarta (Shin et al. 1997).
- *Mexico City, Mexico.* Abnormally high levels of suspended particulates have caused an average of 2.4 lost work days per person and 6,400 deaths every year; lead exposure may contribute to as much as 20 percent of the incidence of hypertension in adults, and 29 percent of all children have unhealthy lead levels in their blood. Annual health costs from air pollution are estimated to exceed $1.5 billion (Eskeland 1992; Margulis 1992).
- *Accra, Ghana.* In this capital city, as in all of Ghana, 70 percent of health care expenditures (including productivity losses and health resource costs such as doctors, nurses, technicians, administration, equipment, and drugs) have been linked to environment-related diseases (Convery and Tutu 1990).
- *Jakarta, Indonesia.* More than $50 million is spent each year by households to boil impure water—the equivalent of 1 percent of the city's gross domestic product (World Bank 1992).

Each city has its own mix of these problems, which shift over time with economic fluctuations and other changes. In cities where effective management controls are not established, however, ever-increasing amounts of waste and pollution accompany-

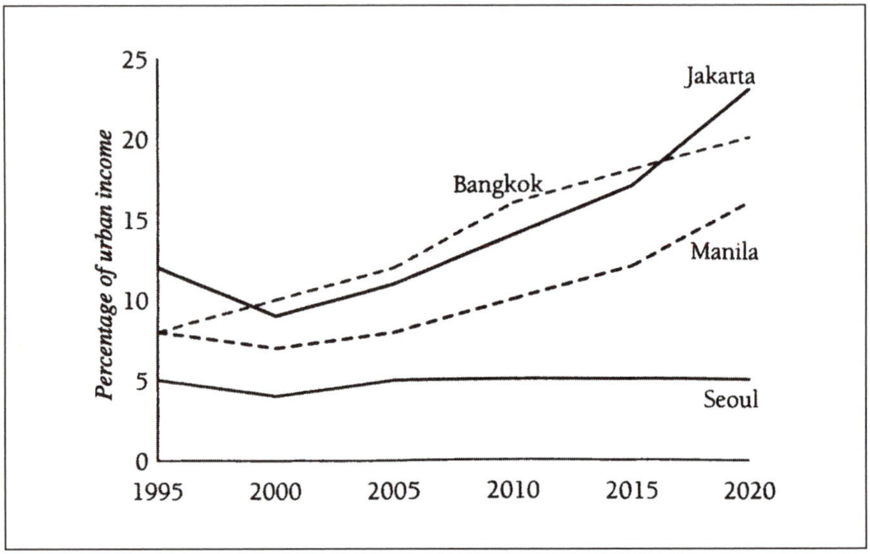

Figure 1-6 Air pollution costs in business-as-usual scenario.
SOURCE: World Bank 1997, 17.

ing rapid population growth and industrialization will seriously constrain urban productivity and economic development.

The forecast for continued urban demographic and economic growth does not bode well for the urban environment in many cities. For example, the cost of air pollution alone in Chinese cities is expected to reach $104 billion in 2020 under a business-as-usual scenario (World Bank 1997). Figure 1-6 suggests that rapidly growing Asian cities will incur significant and increasing costs related to air pollution. A similar situation may be in the making for other environmental problems; for example, the global volume of urban waste is expected to quadruple by 2025 (Sanio 1998).

The sum of this evidence has not gone unnoticed. At the beginning of the chapter, mention was made of the inclusion of cities in the UN's Agenda 21 document. A review of nearly 40 national environmental action plans concludes that urban environmental problems can be serious constraints on sustainable development (Bernstein 1995). Urban issues are the priority, if not the sole focus, of environmental strategies that the World Bank has helped to develop in Brazil, China, and Thailand. In Europe, The Nether-

(a)

(b)

Figure 1-7 Air quality: An unusually clear day in Bangkok, Thailand (*a*) and business as usual in Cairo, Egypt (*b*).

lands developed a municipal environmental policy at the national level as early as 1990.

Cities as Solutions

These trends and litany of problems paint a dismal picture. Cities may increasingly be the causes and the victims of environmental ills. However, cities also have the resources to prevent and cure their environmental problems. Compared to rural areas, cities can tap more in the way of:

Financial capital. As the key producers of national goods and services, urban areas concentrate personal and corporate income which can be taxed or channeled into investments in environmental management.

Human capital. Cities are generally where a country's intellectual and scientific communities are located. Research facilities, universities, and consulting firms also have urban addresses. Thus, the brainpower for analyzing and solving environmental problems is city-based.

Social capital. Urban areas contain a wealth of nonprofit, local organizations and networks such as neighborhood associations, women's investment circles, and citizen-interest groups. These social relationships can be the base of voluntary participation in resolving urban environmental problems.

The concentration of money, brains, and organization in cities also results in a higher effective demand for environmental quality. This can lead to pressure on government and the private sector for remedial and preventive action.

The concentration of people and production also gives cities some comparative advantages over dispersed settlements in rural areas. Higher population densities result in lower costs per household and per business in providing urban infrastructure and social services such as education and health care. The volume and concentration of waste present a greater opportunity for recycling and reuse, and cities also represent much of the market for recyclables. Cities also reduce per capita demand for land: In most countries, cities consume less than 1 percent of the national territory. The world's entire urban population would fit into an area of 200,000 km^2 (roughly the size of Senegal or Oman) at European residential urban densities. Finally, cities offer an opportunity for reducing industrial and transport-related pollution. Waste process heat can be used for heating in colder climates. Public transport, walking, and cycling are much more feasible at the higher densities found in cities (UNCHS 1996).

Summary of Conclusions and Recommendations

The major messages of this book are (1) that the world's population as well as the nature of environmental problems are rapidly urbanizing, and (2) that successful approaches can be used to plan for and manage this new reality at the dawn of the twenty-first century. Specific conclusions are:

- Past thought has tended to downplay or ignore the significance of environmental issues in urban development or to view cities solely as parasites on the natural environment (see Chapter 2).
- Urban environmental problems can be better defined as poor access to basic environmental infrastructure and services, pollution from urban wastes and emissions, resource losses, environmental hazards, and global environmental impacts. They vary according to spatial scale of impact, a city's surrounding ecosystems, its economic level of development, and the institutional setting. The underlying causes of these problems are lack of public awareness, inadequate governance, poor policies, and insufficient knowledge (Chapter 3).
- There is no such thing as a sustainable city. The important question is not whether cities can be sustained but how they can better contribute to overall sustainable development (Chapter 4).
- The classic approach to dealing with urban environmental problems—impact assessment—needs to be replaced by a strategic framework that encompasses informed consultation, strategy development, and implementation of action plans (Chapter 5).
- Analytical and planning tools exist and are being used to support all stages of this strategic framework (Chapter 6).

- Processes and procedures exist for developing local environmental action plans (LEAPs). Recent experience indicates that a learning curve is being achieved in producing and implementing strategies and action plans (Chapter 7).
- Managing environmental problems in a city on a day-to-day basis requires mobilizing public support and participation, improving governance, and choosing appropriate policy instruments (Chapter 8).
- Cities can draw on an abundance of good practice to improve access to infrastructure and services, to control or reduce pollution, to sustainably consume resources, to build capacity for environmental planning, and to minimize risks and protect natural areas (Chapter 9).
- Principles and practical lessons for sustaining cities in the twenty-first century can be drawn from existing experience and thinking—but important knowledge gaps still remain to be filled (Chapter 10).

References

Auclair, Christine. 1998. Taking the pulse of cities. *Urban Age* 6(1): 21–24.

Bartone, Carl, Janis Bernstein, Josef Leitmann, and Jochen Eigen. 1994. Toward environmental strategies for cities: Policy considerations for urban environmental management in developing countries. Urban Management Programme Policy Paper No. 18. Washington, D.C.: World Bank.

Bernstein, Janis. 1995. The new urban challenge in national environmental strategies. Environmental Management Series Paper No. 12. Washington, D.C.: World Bank.

Brockerhoff, Martin, and Ellen Brennan. 1997. *The poverty of cities in the developing world.* New York: Population Council.

Brown, Lester, Michael Renner, and Christopher Flavin. 1998. *Vital signs 1998: The environmental trends that are shaping our future.* Washington, D.C.: Worldwatch Institute.

Convery, F. J., and K. A. Tutu. 1990. Evaluating the cost of environmental degradation in Ghana. Report prepared for the Ghana Environmental Protection Council, Accra.

Eskeland, Gunnar. 1992. The objective: Reduce pollution at low cost. *Outreach* No. 2, World Bank Country Economics Department, Washington, D.C.

Flood, Joe. 1997. Urban and housing indicators. *Urban Studies* 34(10): 1635–1665.

Florig, H. Keith. 1997. China's air pollution risks. *Environmental Science and Technology* 31(6): 274–279.

Litvin, Daniel. 1998. Yellow skies, smarting eyes. *The Economist,* March 21.

Margulis, Sergio. 1992. Back-of-the-envelope estimates of environmental damage costs in Mexico. Policy Research Working Paper 824. Washington, D.C.: World Bank.

Newton, Peter. 1997. Re-shaping cities for a more sustainable future: Exploring the link between urban form, air quality, energy and greenhouse gas emissions. Report of Task Group 6 for the Inquiry into Urban Air Pollution in Australia. Melbourne: Australian Academy of Technological Sciences and Engineering.

Pearce, David, and Jeremy Warford. 1995. *World without end: Economics, environment and sustainable development.* New York: Oxford University Press.

Pugh, Cedric (ed.). 1996. *Sustainability, the environment and urbanization.* London: Earthscan Publications, Ltd.

Sanio, Michael. 1998. Waste not, want not. *Urban Age* 6(1): 18–20.

Sattherwaite, David. 1997. Urban poverty: Reconsidering its nature and scale. *IDS Bulletin* 28(2): 9–33.

Shachar, Arie. 1995. Sustainable urban development and urban planning and policies. In OECD (Organization for Economic Cooperation and Development). *Urban policies for an environmentally sustainable world.* Paris: OECD.

Shin, Euisoon, et al. 1997. Valuating the economic impacts of urban environmental problems: Asian cities. UMP Working Paper Series No. 13. Washington, D.C.: World Bank.

Smith, Maf, John Whitelegg, and Nick Williams. 1998. *Greening the built environment.* London: Earthscan Publications, Ltd.

Stren, Richard, Rodney White, and Joseph Whitney (eds.). 1992. *Sustainable cities: Urbanization and the environment in international perspective.* Boulder: Westview Press.

UN (United Nations). 1996. *World urbanization prospects* (1996 revision). UN Population Division, New York: United Nations.

———. 1997. *Urban agglomerations 1996*. UN Population Division, New York: United Nations.

UNCHS (United Nations Centre for Human Settlements). 1996. *An urbanizing world: Global report on human settlements 1996*. London: Oxford University Press.

———. 1996. Housing and urban indicators. Report of the Secretary-General No. A/CONF.165/CRP.2.

USAID. 1995. Ranking risks in Cairo: Air pollution poses worst environmental threat. *EnviroNet,* Project in Development and the Environment (PRIDE), Washington, D.C.: PRIDE.

World Bank. 1992. *World development report 1992: Environment and development*. New York: Oxford University Press.

———. 1993. *World development report 1993: Investing in health*. New York: Oxford University Press.

———. 1997. *Can the environment wait? Priorities for East Asia*. Washington, D.C.: World Bank.

WRI (World Resources Institute), UN Environmental Programme, UN Development Programme and the World Bank. 1996. *World resources 1996–97: The urban environment*. New York: Oxford University Press.

———. 1998. *World resources 1998–99: Environmental change and human health*. New York: Oxford University Press.

PART

I

CITIES AND SUSTAINABILITY

CHAPTER 2

Thinking About the Urban Environment

Chapter Outline

- The environment in urban literature
- Cities in environmental theory
- Synthesis
  - Thinking about urban ecology
  - Sustainable development
  - The Earth Summit, local Agenda 21, and Habitat II
- Other theoretical perspectives
- Theoretical issues
- Resources and exercises for further thought
- References

On the one hand, cities were exalted as the intelligent creation of civilized man and were sharply distinguished from the products of unreflective nature. Yet, they also manifested an astonishing order within their vast complexity, and demonstrated a capacity for growth and self-regulation that resembled the working of nature itself. . . . From time to time, the balance between these ideas—the city as man-made; the city as natural—has shifted back and forth in response to changing experiences of urban life and changing assumptions about man and his place in nature.

—GRAEME DAVISON, HISTORIAN (Fraser and Sutcliffe 1983, 349)

The Environment in Urban Literature

Throughout time, urban thinkers, primarily in the disciplines of urban planning, geography, and sociology, have used the environment as a metaphor for understanding macrolevel relationships in and between cities. As Graeme Davison notes, "From Aristotle's *Politics* to the Chicago School and beyond, social theorists have likened cities to bodies or organisms; dissected them into constituent organs, such as 'heart,' 'lungs,' and 'arteries'; and charted their growth and decay" (Fraser and Sutcliffe 1983, 349).

"Cities as natural systems" was the dominant paradigm of urban researchers in Great Britain in the late eighteenth and early nineteenth centuries. This theme reappeared from time to time up through the 1960s, with the vogue for using systems analysis in an attempt to model urban dynamics, beginning with Brian Berry's influential 1964 article, "Cities as systems within systems of cities." In the 1970s the systems approach to urban analysis declined under a barrage of criticism for being too limited, too formal, and too simplistic (Melosi 1993). The natural systems analogy returned in the 1980s in a more sophisticated guise, with Manuel Castells arguing: "Cities are living systems, made, transformed and experienced by people. Urban forms and functions are produced and managed . . . by the historical relationship between human consciousness, matter, energy and information" (Castells 1983, xv).

Figure 2-1 Water and urban development: Public water supply, Fez, Morocco.

Another strain of urban thinking about the environment comes from the negative health effects of urbanization and the Industrial Revolution. The problems of industrialization in nineteenth-century Europe and North America gave rise to urban/industrial thinkers such as Jane Adams,

Florence Kelly, and Alice Hamilton. The Progressive Era in the United States (1880–1920s) was particularly concerned about the intersection of health, environment, and politics. Subsequently, concern about the city's health and environment was expressed by urbanists in the Regional Planning Association of America, the Tennessee Valley Authority, and the British "garden cities" movement (1920s–1930s) (Pezzoli 1997).

A third perspective on the environment in urban literature has to do with the relationship between cities and nature. Ibn Khaldun, writing in the fourteenth century, noted several natural resources that were essential for the planning of towns (Khaldun, cited in Kjellen and McGranahan 1997). Two more recent urbanists focused on cities and the natural environment. Patrick Geddes introduced ecological concerns into the new field of urban planning at the turn of the twentieth century in Scotland. He believed in an organic approach to city planning, stressing "the harmonious relationships between city and region, between city and environment, and of land uses within cities, as well as the role of planning to achieve harmony where it did not exist" (Melosi 1993, 18). Geddes even commented on environmental problems in colonial cities: While visiting the city of Indore in India during the First World War, he decried, "Instead of the nineteenth-century European city panacea of 'Everything to the Sewer!' . . . the right maxim for India is the traditional rural one of 'Everything to the Soil' [thus creating] a verdant and fruitful garden environment" (Geddes in Hall 1988, 244–245). British utopian Ebenezer Howard, author of the 1898 book *Garden Cities of To-morrow,* argued that cities that married town and countryside would help stem the rapid pace of urbanization in England and create a healthier environment that would produce better citizens. His ideas were to influence the British new towns program, the American Greenbelt towns of the 1930s, and private developments like Reston and Columbia in the United States (Knack 1998).

QUOTES

. . . these illusions (of independence from nature) encouraged habits of predation or parasitism that eventually undermined the whole social and economic structure, after having worked ruin in the surrounding landscape and even in far-distant regions (Mumford 1961, 144).

Lewis Mumford, the preeminent urban historian (as well as a student of Geddes and author of the introduction to the

1946 edition of Howard's book), continued the focus on the urban/nature relationship in his work. He linked the rise and fall of cities to the urban displacement of nature. He also paid particular attention to the environmental and other impacts of the coming of the railroad to cities in the nineteenth century: ". . . the railroad carried into the heart of the city not merely noise and soot but the industrial plants and the debased housing that alone could thrive in the environment it produced" (Mumford 1961, 461). For the twentieth century, he replaced railroads with automobiles, noting that "we have sold our urban birthright for a sorry mess of motor cars" (Mumford 1961, 509), partly because of demand for private transportation and partly due to the suburbanization of housing.

More recently, urbanists have taken up the theme of the city's relationship with nature and begun to move away from a focus on "built form," where urban structures are treated as independent from nature. For example, in *Good City Form,* Kevin Lynch (1984) defines people and cities as natural phenomena which must be understood as part of an integrated, living community (McCarney 1995).

So, city planners, geographers, and sociologists have treated the environment in three different ways. The mainstreams of thought have been:

- *Cities as natural systems.* The workings of cities and the relations between cities can be partly understood by thinking of them as living organisms.
- *Cities as victims of the Industrial Revolution.* Cities are where the bulk of industrialization has taken place, and their residents are most exposed to the negative health effects of poor sanitation and industrial pollution.
- *Cities as integral parts of nature.* Cities should be designed to incorporate natural features, and when they fail to do so they risk collapse.

Cities in Environmental Theory

Environmental literature initially focused on the ecological impact of only two human activities: natural resource extraction and agricultural production. (Natural resource economics, which began in the 1930s, helped societies think about the optimal rate of extracting renewable and nonrenewable resources, while the ecological implications of agriculture have long been a focus of environmentalists.) This neglect of urban areas can be traced to a strain of thinking that dates from the era of philosopher Jean-Jacques Rousseau: Natural, rural areas are where the environment takes place; they are good and pristine; cities are evil and irrelevant. This romantic view of "paradise lost" could be found in mid-nineteenth-century painting (e.g., Cole, Church, and Bierstadt), poetry (Longfellow, Whitman, and Bryant), and literature (Emerson, Thoreau, and Hawthorne). The text that revolutionized thinking about the environment, focusing on humanity's impact on nature rather than vice versa, was George Marsh's *Man and Nature, or Physical Geography As Modified by Human Action,* which focused on problems of deforestation, overgrazing, and erosion. A 1955 conference, "Man's Role in Changing the Face of the Earth," had a primarily rural focus except for contributions by Mumford and Paul Sears (Platt 1994). More recently, cities and the "built environment" were even consciously excluded from study by some environmental historians in the 1980s (Melosi 1993). Even U.S. Vice President Al Gore's *Earth in the Balance* (1992) has no focused discussion of cities and the environment.

When ecologists did recognize the existence of cities, they were usually concerned with resource flows. One popular approach was to study the flow and transformation of energy through the urban ecosystem. Patrick Geddes first studied "urban energetics" to analyze the evolution of cities by tracing energy flows (Geddes 1915). More recently (over the last 30 years) the study of energy flows, ecosystems, and human systems was championed by Howard Odum (1971, 1983). Cities and economies were seen as part of the process of entropy where energy devolved from more useful to less useful forms. Georgescu-Roegen (1971) commented on how industrialism resulted in a shift from dependence on solar energy to use of nonrenewable resources (metals and fossil fuels), enabling resource-intensive forms of urban development (summarized in Pezzoli 1997). Thus, cities were able to exist by extracting natural resources (low entropy) from the environment and

BOX

The environmental literature has tended to view urban areas as purely detrimental agents that consume resources and spew wastes. Consider the following quotes:

- **Great cities are biologically parasites in their use of vital resources, air, water, and food, in urban metabolism. The bigger the cities, the more these systems demand from the surrounding countryside and the greater the danger of damaging the natural environment "host" (Douglas 1983, 11).**
- **[The city is] an overgrown organ which takes all the food, so much food it can no longer perform its proper function: and cancer is a lethal illness (Friedman 1984, 48–49).**
- **. . . the big city is nothing else than a highly organized consumer department of the natural ecosystem. . . . As opposed to the natural ecosystem, the urban one satisfies its material—and energy—demands almost fully from sources outside the system, and its products and wastes are similarly taken away from within the system (Borhidi 1988, 14).**
- **The city is a parasite on the natural and domesticated environments, since it makes no food, cleans no air, and cleans very little water to a point where it could be reused (Odum 1989, 17).**
- **[Cities are] overgrown monstrosities with gluttonous appetites for material goods and fast declining carrying capacities. . . . Only catastrophe awaits such a system of disharmony (Mayur 1990, 37–38).**

Box 2-1 Cities as environmental parasites.

SOURCES: White 1994; Haughton and Hunter 1994; McCarney in Stren 1995.

dumping wastes (high entropy) back into the environment (Daly 1991). An unfortunate outcome of these perspectives is that cities came to be viewed in the environmental literature as parasites (see Box 2-1 for entertaining quotes).

In 1976, the first U.N. Conference on Human Settlements was held in Vancouver, Canada. Though the environment was a sideshow at the conference, some environmentalists used the opportunity to draw attention to urban issues. Notably, Barbara Ward, head of the International Institute for Environment and Development, prepared a special volume for the conference that drew attention to cities, the environment, and natural resources (Ward 1976). This was followed by the inclusion of an urban chapter in her 1979 work, *Progress for a Small Planet.*

The year 1987 marked a watershed for how cities came to be treated by mainstream environmentalists. The Brundtland Commission issued its pivotal report, *Our Common Future,* a document that not only recognized the critical interaction between cities and the environment but also squarely focused on problems of environmental infrastructure and health in urban areas of the developing world. In that same year, environmental groups began to discover the city. For example, the Worldwatch Institute issued its first urban-focused paper (Brown and Jacobson 1987), which considered the environmental consequences of urban population growth, energy needs, food supply, and nutrient recycling. The focus of most environmental thinkers, though, was still on the rural environmental impact of urbanization.

Table 2-1 Environmental Paradigms and Their Views of Cities

Paradigm	General characteristics	View of cities
Environmental protection	Key theme = trade-offs between environment and economic growth; strongly anthropocentric; key issues = health impacts of pollution	Strong functional separation; emphasis on hygiene, basic services, and household environmental quality
Resource management	Key theme = sustainability as main constraint for growth; moderately anthropocentric; key issues = resource conservation, poverty, population growth	Resource conservation and waste minimization; concentrated city structure with boundaries to contain urban growth; reducing urban ecological footprint
Ecodevelopment	Key theme = codeveloping humans and nature; more ecocentric; key issues = minimizing ecological disturbances and global impacts	Resource management views + urban greening; self-reliance measures such as urban agriculture; returning urban land to its former "natural" state
Deep ecology	Key theme = antigrowth, equal existence rights for all species; biocentric; key issues = ecosystem collapse from rapid human population growth and consumption patterns	End urbanization; dismantle cities and replace with self-reliant villages using appropriate technologies; negative population growth

SOURCE: Modified from Naess 1992, 15.

Further progress in environmental thinking about cities is included in the following section on synthesis. A summary of how the main subsets of environmental thinking (environmental protection, natural resource management, ecodevelopment, and deep ecology) view cities is contained in Table 2-1. As a counterpoint to Box 2-1, it is interesting to note that some environmentalists are now thinking about the positive environmental dimensions of cities, as depicted in Box 2-2.

Synthesis

Thinking About Urban Ecology

The theoretical origins of applying ecological principles to city planning can be traced back to Robert E. Park's 1916 paper entitled "The city: Suggestions for the investigation of human behavior in the urban environment." Using ecological principles, Park and his students at the University of Chicago defined cities as essentially natural environments (Melosi 1990). The approach

BOX

Making room for the city can allow more room for preservation of natural systems because:

- **Human activity can be contained in cities that are located in ecologically resilient regions**
- **Supplying people in cities with food, fiber, water, energy, and minerals is easier and less environmentally damaging than meeting the needs of a similar but dispersed rural population**
- **It is easier to protect natural areas from human activity by surrounding cities with interface ecosystems that produce high yields of food and fiber or that absorb and process human waste, than to do so in the countryside**
- **More space can be designated as wilderness if humans are supplied from high-yield ecosystems than from unmanaged ecosystems (Lugo 1996)**

In addition, cities can improve the quality of both the human and the natural environment via:

- **Lower per capita costs of providing treated water, sewers and drains, and solid waste collection than in rural areas**
- **More potential for resource conservation, reclamation, recycling, and reuse**
- **Less land use per capita due to higher population densities than in the countryside**
- **Greater human interaction and thinking about solving environmental problems**
- **A higher standard of living and greater demand for environmental quality**
- **A concentration of financial resources that can be tapped to invest in environmental protection and rehabilitation**

Box 2-2 Cities can be good for the environment.

SOURCES: Lugo 1996; Mitlin and Satterthwaite 1994.

was again advocated more than 50 years later when Ian McHarg's *Design with Nature* was published in 1969. McHarg advocated analyzing a city within its surrounding natural system and pursuing ecosystem-based planning. He also illustrated how overlay mapping (a precursor of geographic information systems) could be used to analyze urban environmental issues and identify environmentally sensitive areas within cities that should be protected.

In his classic work on ecology, Howard Odum (1969) defines an ecosystem as a community of biological organization that interacts with its physical environment to achieve a stable (mature) state where maximum biomass and symbiotic interactions are maintained per unit of available energy flow. Key ecosystem concepts include:

- Energetics (ratios of production/respiration, production/standing biomass, and biomass/unit of energy flow; new yields; food chains)
- Structure (organic matter, inorganic nutrients, species diversity, biochemical diversity, hierarchies)
- Life history (niche specialization, size of organisms, life cycles)
- Nutrient cycling (mineral cycles, exchange rates, water flows, role of waste)
- Overall homeostasis (internal symbiosis, nutrient conservation, robustness, entropy, information)

Figure 2-2 Preserving natural ecology in urban Singapore.

These attributes will differ depending on whether an ecosystem is in a developmental or mature stage. "Young" systems are characterized by production, growth, and quantity, while mature systems exhibit protection, stability, and quality.

During the 1970s, some of these ecosystem concepts were applied to urban settings, including:

- *Urban metabolism.* Between 1972 and 1975, a major study was conducted on resource and energy flows in Hong Kong (Boyden et al. 1981). Summary results are presented in Figure 2-3.
- *Resource-conserving urbanism.* Richard Meier and a group at the Lawrence Berkeley Laboratory in California applied ecosystem analysis to study resource flows in Third-World cities, based on thinking pursued by Meier since the early 1970s (Meier at al. 1981).

- *Ecological cities.* A nonprofit organization, Urban Ecology, was founded in California in 1975 to "rebuild cities in balance with nature" (Roseland 1997, 197).
- *Man and the Biosphere (MAB).* In 1975, UNESCO initiated a range of studies to consider cities as ecological systems. These included analyses of energy flows, urban food production and forestry, ecological models for city planning, vegetation and urban climate, and use of plants to indicate changes in the urban environment (Celecia 1996).

Efforts to synthesize ecological and urban planning approaches slowed somewhat in the 1980s, but useful refinements were made. The United Nations Development Programme (UNDP) and the World Bank initiated an Integrated Resource Recovery and Waste Recycling Project to promote improved resource and waste management in cities (Bartone 1986). The United Nations Environment Programme (UNEP) and UNCHS collaborated to develop a set of environmental guidelines for settlements planning and management (UNEP and UNCHS 1987). Jorge Hardoy and David Satterthwaite (1984) noted that the range and diversity of urban environmental problems should be analyzed at different geographical scales. In the United States, the Institute for Local Self-Reliance was founded to apply a number of ecological principles in urban development (Morris 1986). Eco-city architects and ana-

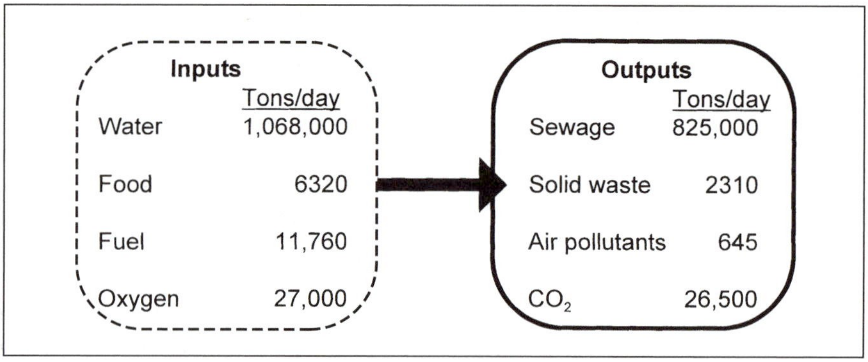

Figure 2-3 Simple input-output analysis for Hong Kong, 1972 (based on population of 5.5 million).

SOURCE: Modified from White 1994, 45.

lysts (Calthorpe, Arkin, Lovins, Register) carried on Ian McHarg's work with practical recommendations for resource-conserving urbanism, ecological design principles, and use of renewable energy sources (Pezzoli 1997). One of the major debates that emerged from this decade was to what extent cities should strive for self-sufficiency (see Box 2-3).

The early 1990s saw a resurgence of interest in synthesized thinking, such as considering cities as ecosystems (Brugmann and Hersh 1991), and applying the principle of carrying capacity to urban development (Whitney 1990). Some of the more important ideas that have emerged from this synthesis include:

- *Input-output analysis.* A city's relationship with its natural environment can be partially understood by measuring flows of food, energy, information, and wastes.

BOX

E. F. Schumacher, author of the appropriate technology text *Small Is Beautiful* (1974), best summarizes the argument for self-sufficiency: "Production from local resources for local needs is the most rational way of economic life, while dependence on imports from afar and the consequent need to produce for export to unknown and distant people is highly uneconomic and justifiable only in exceptional cases and on a small scale" (p. 49). Mainstream economists, beginning with Adam Smith and David Ricardo, would disagree by stressing that trading between entities with comparative advantages improves the welfare of all concerned.

Beginning in the 1980s, urban ecologists like Peter Calthorpe and renewable energy advocates like Amory Lovins argued for communities that are designed to conserve energy and other resources. The underlying assumption of their work is that sustainability can largely be achieved at the local level as environmental impact is largely a factor of local population, consumption or economic activity per capita, and material or energy flow per unit of economic activity. One critic of this view notes that it does not recognize the globalization of the economy: "While today's economic activity is concentrated in the world's urban/industrial regions, few, if any, of these regions are ecologically self-contained" (Pezzoli 1997, 570).

Jane Jacobs (1984) accepts that cities are the key nodes of the global economy and that external trade is a hallmark of a healthy city economy. She notes that competition with imported goods and services stimulates a city's economy to develop local substitutes. Cities that are too strongly oriented toward export *or* self-sufficiency tend to decline, but those that are engaged in the global economy while seeking to competitively substitute for imports will enjoy healthier economic development (Haughton and Hunter 1994).

Morris (1986) refined the debate by advocating for self-reliance instead of self-sufficiency. Urban self-reliance focuses on improving the efficiency of resource use, recovery and recycling of wastes, and shifting from nonrenewable to renewable resources while accelerating global integration for the exchange of information, culture, and knowledge.

Box 2-3 The self-sufficiency versus globalization debate.

BOX

The *marais* system of vegetable production helped to provide Paris with a significant proportion of its fresh food while transforming a transportation pollution problem into an asset during the second half of the nineteenth century. Horses, the main source of power for the city's transportation system, produced about one million tons of stable manure each year. The city's sewage system was also a source for irrigated agriculture. These wastes were used in intensive horticulture to produce an annual yield of 110,000 tons of high-value salads, other vegetables, and fruits.

The crops sold for about ten times the cost of the manure. Their volume was equivalent to 50 kg per capita annually, or more than current levels of consumption of these foods. A surplus existed that allowed for exports to London. Surplus growing medium was also produced that was used to increase the production area by an average of 6 percent a year. *Maraichage* is now the French term used for all types of market gardening.

The *marais* system declined in the early twentieth century due to (1) the replacement of the horse by the automobile; (2) conversion of agricultural land in the city to higher-value uses; and (3) increased competition from other growing areas, facilitated by improved transportation.

Box 2-4 Closed-loop production in nineteenth-century Paris.

SOURCES: Stanhill 1977; UNDP 1996.

- *Nutrient recycling.* Urban wastes should be viewed as resources that can be reused by the surrounding ecosystem as well as the urban economy. An example from nineteenth-century Paris of this "closing the loop" is presented in Box 2-4.
- *Diversity-resilience relationship.* Cities that have more diversified systems (e.g., for using resources, transporting people, or disposing of wastes) will be more successful at responding to sudden changes such as price increases.
- *Environmental versus city boundaries.* The environmental niche that a city occupies almost never coincides with the boundaries used for urban political, administrative, and statistical purposes.
- *Young versus mature cities.* Cities are akin to ecosystems in that young (developing) cities tend to emphasize production, growth, and quantity, while mature (developed) cities are concerned with protection, stability, and quality.
- *Carrying capacity.* The ability of a city's surrounding environment to generate resources and assimilate wastes is affected by urban systems and will affect urban quality of life.
- *Elegance and synergy.* Multiple problems can be solved with a single solution, and the interaction of individual actions can create an outcome that is larger or qualitatively different than the sum of the parts.
- *Urban metabolism.* Many of these applications can be brought together at the city level by conceptually understanding the interactions between resource flows, urban transformation processes, waste streams, and quality of life (see Figure 2-5 for an illustration).

Figure 2-4 Agricultural production in Los Angeles, California. (Ron Milam.)

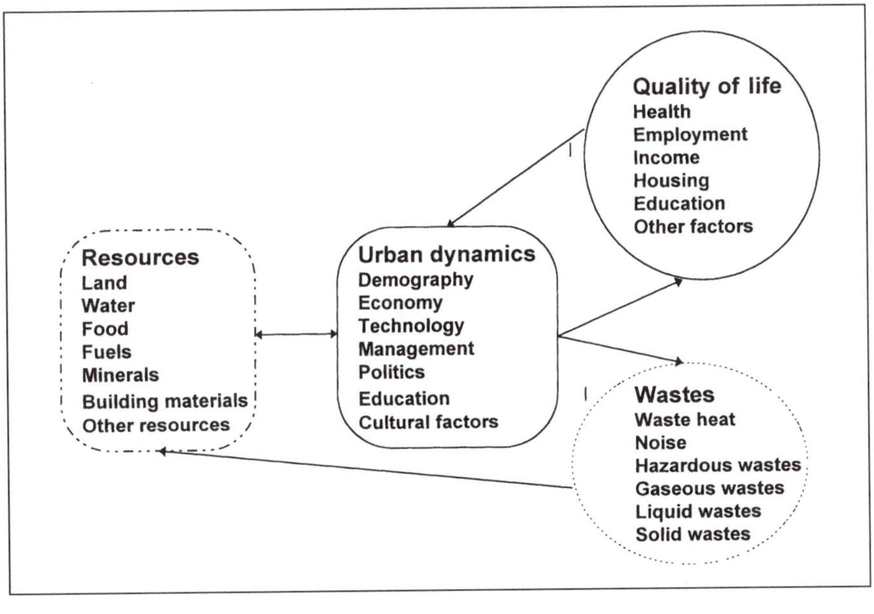

Figure 2-5 Urban metabolism diagrammed.

SOURCE: Modified from Newton 1997.

Urbanists who use these synthesized concepts primarily seek to apply carrying capacity analysis, ecological footprint assessments (see Chapter 4 for details), environmental impact assessments (see Chapter 5 for evaluation), bioregional planning, and protection of critical natural habitats as the means for integrating ecological principles in urban development.

Sustainable Development

The concept of sustainable development has many roots, which have been traced in excellent older (Lele 1991) and newer (Pezzoli 1997) analyses of its genesis. The purpose of this section is not to summarize the vast literature on sustainability but rather to briefly review when cities entered the sustainability debate. Specific definitions and applications of urban sustainability can be found in Chapter 4.

Although the roots of sustainable development can be traced back to the 1974 United Nations Conference on Trade and Development's Cocoyoc Declaration, and even as far back as a 1962

Figure 2-6 1992 Earth Summit was held in Rio de Janeiro, Brazil.

UN declaration on natural resources and economic development, urban environmental issues did not enter into thinking about the concept until much later. It was the World Commission on Environment and Development (the Brundtland Commission) in its report, *Our Common Future* (WCED 1987), that generated perhaps the most popular definition of the term and clearly linked cities to sustainability.

In the Brundtland Commission's report, *sustainable development* is defined as "development that meets the needs of the present without compromising the ability of future generations to meet their own needs" (WCED 1987, 43). There are dozens if not hundreds of competing definitions, but this one is sufficiently comprehensive (and at the same time vague enough) to be widely accepted. The commission also listed "urban challenges" as one of the priority issues for sustainable development, along with population growth, food security, biodiversity, energy use, and industrial production. The sustainability challenges listed for cities focused on deficiencies in environmental services such as potable water, sanitation and waste management, and housing and transportation.

The next formal milestone for thinking about cities and sustainable development was the 1992 United Nations Conference on Environment and Development (UNCED or Earth Summit) in Rio de Janeiro. As indicated in the previous sections, a good deal of thinking about the urban environment occurred between 1987 and 1992. However, early preparatory documents indicated that UNCED would focus on green and global issues that were neither people- nor city-centered. A coalition of cities, international city organizations, national governments, nongovernmental organizations (NGOs), academics, and donor agencies mobilized to lobby the United Nations (UN) and raise the profile of urban issues prior to the conference. This occurred from within, as several UN agencies made environmental sustainability part of their urban policies (World Bank 1991; UNDP 1991), and from outside, via widely attended conferences on sustainable urban development, including those in Toronto (1991) and Curitiba (1992). Additional support was provided by policy documents from organizations of developed countries such as the European Union's 1990 green paper on the urban environment and the Organization for Economic Cooperation and Development (OECD) publication, *Environmental Policies for Cities in the 1990s* (OECD 1990). The results of these efforts are presented in the text that follows.

The Earth Summit, Local Agenda 21, and Habitat II

The *Earth Summit's Agenda for Change,* commonly known as Agenda 21, is a program of action containing 40 chapters and hundreds of recommendations for moving countries towards sustainable development in the twenty-first century. References to urban issues are scattered throughout the text, as indicated in Box 2-5. There is no unifying urban framework in the document, and urban issues are mentioned in many of the chapters but under varied headings, such as poverty, human health, land management, drinking water, wastes, NGOs, and business and industry.

Despite these weaknesses, two chapters in Agenda 21 emerged from the efforts of the coalition to raise the profile of urban issues. Chapter 7, on sustainable human settlements, covers a range of issues that include the role of rapid urbanization; access to affordable, tenured land by the urban poor; availability of environmental infrastructure and services; environmentally sound construction and transportation; development of secondary cities; natural disaster management; and capacity building. Chapter 28 underlines the key role of local authorities in making sustainable development happen. It calls on local governments to consult key stakeholders and arrive at a consensus on local strategies for achieving the objectives of Agenda 21.

The call for developing and implementing local Agenda 21s added to an ongoing movement for supporting environmental management at the local level. Some key programs for providing such support; their implementing organizations; and their year of inception are:

- Healthy Cities Program, World Health Organization (1986)
- Metropolitan Environmental Improvement Programme, United Nations Development Programme (UNDP)/World Bank (1989)

BOX

A. *Provision of adequate shelter for all.* Adopt/strengthen national shelter strategies, including legal protection against unfair eviction from homes or land; provide shelter for the homeless and the urban poor; seek to reduce rural-urban drift by improving rural shelter; introduce resettlement programs for displaced persons; develop multinational cooperation to support the efforts of developing countries.

B. *Improve human settlement management.* Improve urban management; strengthen urban data systems; encourage intermediate city development.

C. *Promote sustainable land use planning and management.* Develop national land inventory and classification system; create efficient and accessible land markets, with land registers, etc.; encourage public-private partnerships in managing the land resource; establish appropriate forms of land tenure; develop fiscal and land use planning solutions for a more rational and environmentally sound use of the land resource; promote access to land for the urban poor; adopt comprehensive land use strategies; encourage awareness of the problems of unplanned settlements in vulnerable areas.

D. *Ensure integrated provision of environmental infrastructure (water, sanitation, drainage and solid waste management).* Introduce policies to minimize environmental damage; undertake environmental impact assessments; promote policies to recover infrastructure costs while extending services to all households; seek joint solutions where issues cross localities.

E. *Develop sustainable energy and transport systems in human settlements.* Develop and transfer technologies that are more energy-efficient and involve renewable resources; improve urban transport systems.

F. *Encourage human settlement planning and management in disaster-prone areas.* Promote a culture of safety; develop predisaster planning; initiate postdisaster reconstruction and rehabilitation planning.

G. *Promote sustainable construction industry activities.* Encourage greater use of local natural materials and greater energy efficiency in design and materials; strengthen land use controls in sensitive areas; encourage self-help schemes.

H. *Meet the urban health challenge.* Develop municipal health plans; promote awareness of primary health care; strengthen environmental health services; establish city collaboration networks; improve training; adopt health impact and EIA procedures.

Box 2-5 Urban dimensions of Agenda 21.

SOURCE: Quarrie in Haughton and Hunter 1994, 298–299.

- Sustainable Cities Programme, UN Centre for Human Settlements (UNCHS) (1990)
- Environment Component, UNDP/World Bank/UNCHS Urban Management Programme (1990)
- Local Agenda 21 Initiative, International Council for Local Environmental Initiatives (1991)
- Urban Environmental Training Materials Program, GTZ (German technical cooperation) (1991)
- Local Initiative Facility for Urban Environment, UNDP (1992)
- Local Initiatives for the Environment Program, European Union (1992)
- Sustainable Cities Project, European Union (1993)
- Capacity Building for the Urban Environment, Institute for Housing and Urban Development Studies (1994)
- Sustainable Cities Initiative, U.S. Agency for International Development (1994)
- Public-Private Partnerships Programme for the Urban Environment, UNDP (1994)

These and other international support activities are more fully described in Annex A on resources.

At the municipal level, cities around the world responded to UNCED's challenge to develop local Agenda 21s. Many were initiated and prepared locally without help from the programs listed above. According to a comprehensive survey (ICLEI 1997), more than 1800 local governments in 64 countries were involved in developing environmental strategies by the beginning of 1997. Nearly a thousand municipalities in 43 countries had completed or made important progress in their activities, while almost 900 municipalities were just getting started. Most of the local authorities were calling their efforts "Local Agenda 21," but in a number of cities and towns a different name was used or the process was being supported by an international assistance program.

Over four-fifths of the known local Agenda 21 activities are concentrated in just 11 countries (Australia, Bolivia, China, Denmark, Finland, Japan, The Netherlands, Norway, Republic of Korea, Sweden, and the United Kingdom). These countries all have national local Agenda 21 campaigns and they involve nearly 1500 local governments. Ten other countries (Brazil, Colombia, Germany, Greece, Ireland, Malawi, Peru, South Africa, Turkey, and the United States) have recently started national campaigns or programs.

An evaluation of this international movement to prepare local Agenda 21s (ICLEI 1997) identified a set of universal elements for the success of local sustainable development planning:

- *Multisectoral participation* in the planning process, where a group of local stakeholders acts as the coordination and policy body to prepare a long-term sustainable development action plan
- *Consultation* with community groups, NGOs, the private sector, religious leaders, government agencies, professional groups, and unions to create a shared vision and to identify proposals and priorities for action
- *Participatory assessment* of local social, economic, and environmental conditions and needs
- *Target-setting* through negotiations among key stakeholders in order to achieve the vision and goals set forth in the action plan
- *Monitoring and reporting procedures,* including local indicators, to measure progress and to allow participants to hold each other accountable for implementing the action plan.

At the final big UN conference of the century, the 2nd UN Conference on Human Settlements (Habitat II or City Summit), nations, local governments, and NGOs strongly endorsed sustainable urban development. Thinking about the urban environment at this conference was supported by UNCHS's *Global Report on Urban Settlements* (UNCHS 1996a) and a joint report on the urban environment by the World Resources Institute, UNEP, UNDP, and the World Bank (WRI et al. 1996). The conference

Figure 2-7 Stamps commemorating Habitat II in Istanbul, Turkey.

ended with the approval of the *Habitat Agenda* that organizers of Habitat II described as "a guide for the development of sustainable human settlements in the world's cities, towns and villages into the first two decades of the next century" (UNCHS 1996b). The conference also endorsed the *Istanbul Declaration on Human Settlements*. Paragraph 10 of the declaration begins with the following commitment to urban environmental management:

> *In order to sustain our global environment and improve the quality of living in our human settlements, we commit ourselves to sustainable patterns of production, consumption, transportation and settlement development, pollution prevention; respect for the carrying capacity of eco-systems and the preservation of opportunities for future generations.*

However, the conference has been criticized as having been long on broad commitments but short on the specifics of how to achieve sustainable urban development (Cohen 1996). The conference documents particularly lack guidance on national and international frameworks for urban sustainability, the relationship of cities with global environment issues, and the transfer of environmental costs from wealthier cities to poorer regions (Satterthwaite 1997). Thus, it did not succeed in translating the Earth Summit's commitment to sustainable development into practical approaches for urban planning and management.

Other Theoretical Perspectives

The centralization of population in great cities is itself an unfavorable influence. All putrefying vegetable and animal substances give off gases decidedly injurious to health, and if these gases have no free way of escape, they inevitably poison the atmosphere, . . . [the poor] are obliged to throw all offal and garbage, all dirty water, often all disgusting drainage and excrement into the streets, being without other means of disposing of them; they are thus compelled to infect the region of their own dwelling.

—FRIEDRICH ENGELS, 1844 (quoted in Litvin 1998)

The Engels quote indicates that, at least in many poorer neighborhoods and cities, not much has changed in the past 150 years. It also suggests that other disciplines besides the ecological sciences and urban studies have something to say about environmental problems in cities. The fields of sociology, public health, and governance have touched on urban environmental issues in an important way.

Sociologists concerned with poverty and gender issues have thought about the urban environmental dimension of their work. Some poverty analysts, narrowly defining "environment" to mean only green issues, have argued that the urban poor do not have the luxury of being concerned with environmental issues (e.g., Wekwete 1992). However, those analysts who have encompassed the brown agenda of problems (e.g., Wratten 1995; Moser 1996; McGranahan, Songsore, and Kjellen 1996) have highlighted problems of the urban poor's access to basic environmental services and the deterioration of those services during times of economic crisis. Gender analysts have noted that women and children are usually most exposed to urban environmental risks, and that women often play a critical role in community organizing and maintaining networks that can help solve local environmental problems (Lee-Smith and Trujillo 1992; Moser 1989; Moser and Peake 1995).

Concern about urban environmental quality was one of the founding forces of the public health movement. In nineteenth-century Europe, a great debate raged about how to deal with sanitary problems in the continent's rapidly urbanizing and industrializing cities. Sir Edwin Chadwick pioneered work in England during the 1830s and 1840s on the relationship between public health and the physical urban environment; his work inspired similar studies in the United States (Platt 1994). Another early scientific breakthrough was John Snow's discovery in 1834 of the link between cholera and contaminated drinking water in London (Hamlin 1990). In fact, modern urban government and city planning have their roots in public health (see Box 2-6). The public health field has continued to focus on sanitation and hygiene, while expanding to include the importance of both adequate quantities and quality of drinking water; health problems caused by ambient and indoor air pollution; the relationship between urban overcrowding and disease transmission; exposure to accidents in homes, communities, and workplaces; and the greater environmental health risk faced by low-income households. Globally, the World Health Organization (WHO) has expanded its Healthy Cities Program for more than a decade, and its new director, Gro Harlem Brundtland (former head of the World Commission on Environment and Development), is steering the organization more toward urban environmental health problems (*The Economist* 1998). More information on the use of public health approaches for urban environmental analysis can be found in Chapter 6.

BOX

During the Industrial Revolution, city populations were doubling or tripling within two or three decades. Manchester's population increased six times in less than sixty years (between 1774 and 1831). New York City grew ninefold between 1800 and 1850. City governments could not keep up with these changes and failed to provide adequate infrastructure and waste removal services. Average life expectancies in the newly industrialized cities were often under 30 years, and fell below 18 years for the lowest income groups.

Cholera epidemics that swept through European and North American cities in the nineteenth century produced a public outcry for action. The emerging public health field called for improving water supplies and public action to hygienically remove excreta and other urban wastes as ways of combating disease. Because of the health threat posed by epidemics and the risk that wealthier citizens and businesses might permanently flee the city, businesses and households overcame their reluctance to pay for improved water supply and sanitation. These forces helped redirect the focus of city governments and their planners on environmental infrastructure and public health needs.

Box 2-6 Public health and urban development in the nineteenth century.

Source: UNCHS 1996a, 132.

Governance is about the relationship between the state (government) and society (the governed). In an earlier guise, the fields of public administration and policy stressed the importance of urban management for solving environmental problems in the city. This included a focus on the institutional capacity of municipalities to pay for and deliver environmental services, and to use the right mix of regulatory and incentive policies. Lack of focus could result in nonmarket failure and ensuing environmental problems, as outlined in Box 2-7. More recently, governance theorists have posited that many urban environmental problems are a result of poor governance, and they cite the following causes: inadequate public participation; lack of awareness and access to information; covert decision-making processes; unaccountable decision-makers; and lack of political will (McCarney 1995; Sivaramakrishnan 1995).

QUOTES

Good governance is epitomized by a transparent process; a bureaucracy imbued with a professional ethos; an executive arm of government accountable for its actions; a strong civil society participating in public affairs; and all behaving under the rule of law (World Bank 1994).

Theoretical Issues

Two main theoretical challenges emerge from this summary of thinking about the urban environment. The first is that environmental issues in cities are generally studied by individual disciplines, while the problems themselves tend to be multidisciplinary. Ecologists focus on natural systems within cities or on natural systems that are affected by urban development. Environmental and civil engineers look at problems from an infrastructural perspective. Sociologists consider the interactions between people, poverty, and the urban environment. Governance specialists look at how the relationship between the state and civil society leads to different environmental outcomes in cities. Public health experts concentrate on arresting the transmission of disease

BOX

Urban environmental problems can be caused by noneconomic as well as market forces. Government intervention may result in unintended consequences that create or worsen conditions. Some of these nonmarket failures include:

- **Lack of feedback on the quality of outputs, combined with an absence of competition, that results in high costs and poor quality of environmental infrastructure and services provided by municipal utilities**
- **Political pressure to focus on potentially suboptimal short-term solutions, when many environmental problems require sustained investments and management over the long term**
- **Standard procedures, budget rules, and civil service regulations that substitute for efficiency or equity objectives, and lead to distortion in the pricing and distribution of environmental goods and services such as water, sanitation, and solid waste management**
- **Corruption and abuse of power that lead to the inequitable distribution of services and other benefits, with results similar to the above**

Box 2-7 Nonmarket failure and the urban environment.
SOURCE: Adapted from Wolf 1983.

by pathogens and vectors in the urban environment. However, issues such as the supply of clean drinking water cut across these disciplines and involve problems such as watershed management, appropriate infrastructure, access in low-income neighborhoods, pricing policies and affordability, and household hygiene behavior. The first challenge, then, is to find ways for different disciplines to work together to understand and solve the many urban environmental problems that are multidisciplinary.

A second issue is that much of the thinking about the urban environment has been done in developed countries and has often been biased toward the concerns of industrialized cities. One outcome of this bias is that greater attention has been paid to chemical agents in the air than to pathogens in the water, food, air, and soil that are responsible for infectious and parasitic diseases more often found in cities of the developing world (Hardoy et al. 1992). Similar biases can be found regarding emphases on hazardous as opposed to municipal waste management, protection of parks and natural reserves as opposed to support for urban agriculture, and minimization of industrial accidents as opposed to management of natural hazards. Many of the latter problems usually have been solved in industrialized cities, while both sets of problems are often faced by lower-income urban areas. The second challenge, then, is to think about which types of problems are most important in a particular locality, and to identify solutions that work, regardless of whether they come from the North or the South.

Resources and Exercises for Further Thought

Resources

THE ENVIRONMENT IN URBAN LITERATURE

The Melosi articles (1990, 1993) and the volume edited by Platt et al. (1994) are good surveys that trace the history of how urban thinkers have treated the environment, particularly in the United States.

CITIES IN ENVIRONMENTAL THEORY

Pezzoli (1997) and McCarney (1995) provide preliminary information on this topic. However, a full review of the literature has yet to be done.

SYNTHESIS

For more information on urban energetics and an application, see: Huang, Shu-li. 1998. Urban ecosystems, energetic hierarchies, and ecological economics of Taipei metropolis. *Journal of Environmental Management* 52:39–51.

For a collection of essays and experiences on urban ecology, see: Gordon, David (ed.). 1990. *Green cities: Ecologically sound approaches to urban space.* Montreal: Black Rose Books.

The Lele (1991) and Pezzoli (1997) articles are good surveys of early and more recent thinking about sustainable development. Web sites that provide ongoing information about sustainable development include those of the International Institute for Sustainable Development (http://iisd1.iisd.ca), the Earth Council's Earth Network for Sustainable Development (http://www.ecouncil.ac.cr); and environmental organizations involved with sustainability (http://www.webdirectory.com/Sustainable_Development/).

A plain-language summary of Agenda 21 appears in: Centre for Our Common Future. 1993. *The Earth Summit's agenda for change.* Geneva: Centre for Our Common Future.

Documents from both the Earth Summit and the Habitat II meetings are available on-line at http://www.igc.apc.org/habitat/un-proc/index.html.

At least two reviews of the urban environmental literature have identified work on bringing urban and environmental perspectives together. They are: Brantly and Barr (1992) and Chowdury and Furedy (1994).

Extensive and more recent bibliographic references are available in UNCHS (1996a) and WRI et al. (1996).

OTHER THEORETICAL PERSPECTIVES

Hunter and Haughton (1994) and McCarney (1995) include useful summaries of other disciplinary views that have contributed to an understanding of urban environmental issues.

Exercises for Further Thought

1. To what extent did views that cities were corrupt, criminal, and contaminated influence the initial rural focus of environmental thinking?
2. Compare arguments that urban areas are environmental parasites, environmental benefactors, or both.
3. Why is there no consensus in the environmental community about how to treat cities?
4. What are the environmental consequences of self-sufficient, self-reliant, and globally interdependent cities?
5. Which principles of ecology are not relevant for cities, and why?
6. Why did the synthesis of urban and ecological thinking only occur in the latter half of the twentieth century?
7. Besides the *marais* system in Paris, list historical cases that exemplify "closing the loop" between resources and wastes.
8. How successful were urbanists in raising the profile of cities at the 1992 Earth Summit?
9. Why is there no standard definition of sustainable development?
10. What is the utility of the sustainable development concept for cities?
11. Why was the 1996 Habitat II conference less focused on concrete means of achieving sustainable urban development?
12. What have other disciplines besides sociology, public health, and political science (governance) contributed to thinking about the urban environment (e.g., economics and environmental engineering)?
13. How might the problems of disciplinary focus and bias toward the concerns of wealthier cities be overcome?

References

Bartone, Carl. 1986. Recycling waste: The World Bank project on resource recovery. *Development* 4: 35–39.

Berry, Brian L. 1964. Cities as systems within systems of cities. *Regional Science Association Papers* 13: 147–163.

Borhidi, A. 1988. Some ecological and social features of big cities. *Cities and ecology,* Vol. 2. Moscow: Center of International Projects of the USSR State Commission for Science and Technology.

Boyden, Stephen, S. Millar, K. Newcombe, and B. O'Neill. 1981. *The ecology of a city and its people: The case of Hong Kong.* Canberra: Australian National University Press.

Brantly, Eugene, and Pamela Barr. 1992. Bibliography of urban environmental literature. Prepared for USAID. Research Triangle Park: Research Triangle Institute.

Brown, Lester, and Jodi Jacobson. 1987. The future of urbanization: Facing the ecological and economic constraints. Worldwatch Paper No. 77. Washington, D.C.: Worldwatch Institute.

Brugmann, Jeb, and Robert Hersh. 1991. *Cities as ecosystems: Opportunities for local government.* Toronto: International Council for Local Environmental Initiatives.

Castells, Manuel. 1983. *The city and the grassroots: A cross-cultural theory of urban social movements.* Berkeley: University of California Press.

Celecia, John. 1996. Towards an urban ecology. *Nature & Resources* 32(2): 3–6.

Chowdury, Tasneem, and Christine Furedy. 1994. Urban sustainability in the Third World: A review of the literature. Institute of Urban Studies/Issues in Urban Sustainability No. 5. Winnipeg: University of Winnipeg.

Cohen, Michael. 1996. Habitat II: A critical assessment. *Environmental Impact Assessment Review* 16(4–6): 429–434.

Davison, Graeme. 1983. The city as a natural system: Theories of urban society in early nineteenth-century Britain. In Derek Fraser and Anthony Sutcliffe (eds.). 1983. *The pursuit of urban history.* London.

Geddes, Patrick. 1915. *Cities in evolution.* London: Williams and Norgate.

Georgescu-Roegen. 1971. *The entropy law and the economic process*. Cambridge: Harvard University Press.

Goode, David. 1990. Introduction: A green renaissance. In David Gordon (ed.). *Green cities: Ecologically sound approaches to urban space*. Montreal: Black Rose Books.

Hall, Peter. 1988. *Cities of tomorrow: An intellectual history of urban planning and design in the twentieth century*. Cambridge, Mass.: Blackwell, quoting Patrick Geddes. 1918. *Town planning towards city development: A report to the Durbar of Indore*. Indore: Holkore State Printing Press.

Hamlin, C. 1990. *A science of impurity: Water analysis in nineteenth century Britain*. Bristol: Adam Hilger.

Hardoy, Jorge, and David Satterthwaite. 1984. Third World cities and the environment of poverty. *Geoforum* 15(3).

Hardoy, Jorge, Diana Mitlin, and David Satterthwaite. 1992. *Environmental problems in Third World cities*. London: Earthscan.

Haughton, Graham, and Colin Hunter. 1994. *Sustainable cities*. London: Jessica Kingsley Publishers, Ltd.

ICLEI (International Council for Local Environmental Initiatives). 1997. *Local Agenda 21 survey: A study of responses by local authorities and their national and international associations to Agenda 21*. Toronto: ICLEI.

Jacobs, Jane. 1984. *Cities and the wealth of nations: Principles of economic life*. Harmondsworth: Penguin.

Kjellen, Marianne, and Gordon McGranahan. 1997. Urban water—Towards health and sustainability. Contribution to the Comprehensive Assessment of the Freshwater Resources of the World. Stockholm: Stockholm Environment Institute.

Knack, Ruth. 1998. Garden cities: Ebenezer had a point. *Planning* 64(6): 4–8.

Lee-Smith, Diana, and Catalina Trujillo. 1992. The struggle to legitimize subsistence: Women and sustainable development. *Environment and Urbanization* 4(1): 77–84.

Lele, Sharachandra. 1991. Sustainable development: A critical review. *World Development* 19(6).

Litvin, Daniel. 1998. Dirt poor. *The Economist,* March 21, pp. 3–5.

Lugo, Ariel. 1996. Making room for the city. *Nature & Resources* 32(2): 8.

Lynch, Kevin. 1984. *Good city form.* Cambridge: MIT Press.
Marsh, George. 1965. *Man and nature.* Cambridge: Harvard University Press.
McCarney, Patricia. 1995. Four approaches to the environment of cities. In Richard Stren with Judith K. Bell (eds.). *Perspectives on the city,* Urban Research in the Developing World, Vol. 4. Toronto: Centre for Community and Urban Studies, University of Toronto.
McGranahan, Gordon, Jacob Songsore, and Marianne Kjellen. 1996. Sustainability, poverty and urban environmental transitions. In Cedric Pugh (ed.). *Sustainability, the environment and urbanization.* London: Earthscan Publications, Ltd.
McHarg, Ian. 1969. *Design with nature.* Garden City: Doubleday.
Meier, Richard, Sam Berman, Tim Campbell, and Chris Fitzgerald. 1981. *The urban ecosystem and resource-conserving urbanism in Third World cities.* Berkeley: Lawrence Berkeley Laboratory and University of California.
Melosi, Martin. 1990. Cities, technical systems and the environment. *Environmental History Review* 14(1–2): 47–64.
———. 1993. The place of the city in environmental history. *Environmental History Review* 17(2): 1–23.
Mitlin, Diana, and David Satterthwaite. 1994. *Global Forum 1994: Cities and sustainable development.* London: International Institute for Environment and Development.
Moser, Caroline. 1989. Gender planning in the Third World: Meeting practical and strategic gender needs. *World Development* 17(11): 1799–1826.
———. 1996. Confronting crisis: A comparative study of household responses to poverty and vulnerability in four poor urban communities. Environmentally Sustainable Development Studies and Monographs Series No. 8. Washington, D.C.: World Bank.
Moser, Caroline, and Linda Peake. 1995. Seeing the invisible: Women, gender and urban development. In Richard Stren with Judith K. Bell (eds.). *Perspectives on the city,* Urban Research in the Developing World, Vol. 4. Toronto: Centre for Community and Urban Studies, University of Toronto.
Morris, David. 1986. The city as nation. *Development* 4: 72–76.

Mumford, Lewis. 1961. *The city in history: Its origins, its transformations, and its prospects.* San Diego: Harcourt Brace and Company.

Naess, P. 1992. Urban development and environmental philosophy. Rapporteur paper to the ECE Research Conference, Ankara, Turkey, 29 June (reproduced by UN Economic Commission for Europe, Geneva, HBP/SEM.47/R.1).

Newton, Peter. 1997. Re-shaping cities for a more sustainable future: Exploring the link between urban form, air quality, energy and greenhouse gas emissions. Report of Task Group 6 for the Inquiry into Urban Air Pollution in Australia. Melbourne: Australian Academy of Technological Sciences and Engineering.

Odum, Howard. 1971. *Environment, power, and society.* New York: John Wiley & Sons.

———. 1983. *Systems ecology.* New York: John Wiley & Sons.

———. 1969. The strategy of ecosystem development. *Science* 164: 262–270.

OECD (Organization for Economic Cooperation and Development). 1990. *Environmental policies for cities in the 1990s.* Paris: OECD.

Pezzoli, Keith. 1997. Sustainable development: A transdisciplinary overview of the literature. *Journal of Environmental Planning and Management* 40(5): 549–574.

Platt, Rutherford. 1994. Introduction and overview. In Rutherford Platt, Rowan Rowntree, and Pamela Muick. *The ecological city: Preserving and restoring urban biodiversity.* Amherst: University of Massachusetts Press.

Roseland, Mark. 1997. Dimensions of the eco-city. *Cities* 14(4): 197–202.

Schumacher, E. F. 1974. *Small is beautiful: A study of economics as if people mattered.* London: Abacus.

Sivaramakrishnan, K. C. 1995. Overview—Urban environmental governance. In Ismail Serageldin, Michael Cohen, and K. C. Sivaramakrishnan (eds.). The human face of the urban environment. *Proceedings of the 2nd Annual World Bank Conference on Environmentally Sustainable Development,* September 19–21, Washington, D.C.

Stanhill, G. 1977. An urban agro-ecosystem: The example of nineteenth-century Paris. *Agro-Ecosystems* 3: 265–284, September.

The Economist. 1998. Repositioning the WHO. May 9, 79–81.

UNCHS. 1996a. *An urbanizing world: Global report on human settlements 1996*. London: Oxford University Press.

———. 1996b. Habitat II press release. Issued June 3 in Istanbul, Turkey.

UNDP (United Nations Development Programme). 1991. *Cities, people & poverty: Urban development cooperation for the 1990s*. UNDP Strategy Paper. New York: UNDP.

UNEP (UN Environment Programme) and UNCHS (UN Centre for Human Settlements). 1986. *Environmental guidelines for settlements planning and management*. Volumes 1–3. Nairobi: UNEP and UNCHS.

Ward, Barbara. 1976. *The home of man*. New York: W. W. Norton and Co.

———. 1979. *Progress for a small planet*. Harmondsworth (UK): Penguin Books.

WCED (World Commission on Environment and Development). 1987. *Our common future*. Oxford: Oxford University Press.

Wekwete, Kadmiel. 1992. Africa. In Richard Stren, Rodney White, and Joseph Whitney (eds.). *Sustainable cities: Urbanization and the environment in international perspective*. Boulder, Colo.: Westview Press.

White, Rodney. 1994. *Urban environmental management: Environmental change and urban design*. Chichester: John Wiley & Sons.

Whitney, Joseph. 1990. The carrying capacity concept and sustainable urban development. Paper presented to the Working Group on Analytical Approaches to Urban Environmental Issues, September 17–21, East-West Center, Honolulu, Hawaii.

Wolf, Charles. 1983. *Public expenditures and policy analysis*. Chicago: Markham.

World Bank. 1991. *Urban policy and economic development: An agenda for the 1990s*. Washington, D.C.: World Bank.

Wratten, Ellen. 1995. Conceptualizing urban poverty. *Environment and Urbanization* 7(1).

WRI (World Resources Institute) et al. 1996. *World resources 1996–97: The urban environment*. New York: Oxford University Press.

CHAPTER 3

Understanding Problems, Characteristics, and Underlying Causes

Chapter Outline

- Key problem areas
  - Access to environmental infrastructure and services
  - Pollution from urban wastes and emissions
  - Resource losses
  - Environmental hazards
  - The global dimension
- Conditions influencing the urban environment
- Underlying causes of urban environmental degradation
- Resources and exercises for further thought
- References

This chapter develops a framework for understanding urban environmental issues by answering three questions: (1) what are the key problem areas?; (2) what are the special characteristics of the urban environment that make it different from other spatial levels of analysis?; and (3) what are the underlying causes of urban environmental degradation? Problems of the urban environment generally fall into one of four categories: inadequate access to environmental infrastructure and services; pollution from urban wastes and emissions; resource losses; or environmental hazards. These may often occur within a city or an urbanized region, but they may also have a global dimension that should not be ignored. A number of factors help to shape the characteristics of urban environmental issues. These include: economic forces, demographic factors, natural and spatial considerations, and the institutional setting. A city's environmental characteristics can become problematic as a result of one or more underlying causes—a lack of public awareness and participation, inadequate governance, poor policies, and/or insufficient knowledge.

Key Problem Areas

The key environmental problems that face cities can be grouped in four categories: (1) problems of access to environmental infrastructure and services; (2) problems of pollution from urban wastes and emissions; (3) problems of resource degradation; and (4) problems of environmental hazards. The first and the last problems are generally under control or less prevalent in cities of the developed world; lower-income urban areas often face all four sets of problems. Also, these problems do not occur discretely. They can occur simultaneously, and interaction between different problem types can intensify existing environmental impacts and even create new ones. For example, inadequate drainage (an "access" problem), solid waste disposal in existing drains (a "waste" problem), a tropical rainstorm (a "hazards" problem), and sea-level rise (a "global" problem) may combine to intensify the loss of life and property associated with flooding.

Access to Environmental Infrastructure and Services

The most critical urban infrastructure and services from an environmental perspective are water and sanitation systems, solid waste management, drainage, and transportation. A set of important environmental problems occurs, mostly with health consequences, when people do not have adequate access to these facilities or when their quality is poor. Electricity is not included in this presentation as it is usually not provided by municipalities; however, access to electricity can be important for improving indoor air quality.

WATER AND SANITATION

An estimated 280 million city dwellers around the world do not have access to safe drinking water near their homes, and 590 million urban residents do not have access to adequate sanitation (UNCHS 1996). Although 70 percent of the urban population has access to some form of sanitation, only about 40 percent are connected to sewers (WHO 1992).

Figure 3-1 Access to water in a Delhi, India, slum.

In poorer cities, the pollutant that takes the highest toll on health is human waste (Hardoy and Satterthwaite 1992). The World Health Organization estimates that 3.2 million children under the age of five die each year in the developing world from diarrheal diseases, largely because of poor sanitation, contaminated drinking water, and related problems of food hygiene; an estimated 2 million fewer of these children would die if all people had access to adequate water and sanitation facilities (World Bank 1992). Evidence also suggests that the quantity of available water is equally important, if not more important, than water quality (Cairncross and Feachem 1993). Infectious and parasitic diseases linked to water quality and quantity are the third leading cause of productive years being lost to health problems in the developing world (World Bank 1993). Diarrheal death rates are typically about 60 percent lower among children who live in households with adequate water and sanitation facilities than among those in homes without such facilities (World Bank 1992).

MUNICIPAL SOLID WASTE COLLECTION

From one-half to two-thirds of household solid waste in lower-income cities is not collected (WRI 1996). At the same time, solid waste management consumes 20 to 40 percent of municipal budgets in poorer cities (UNCHS 1996). Uncollected waste is then informally dumped and/or burned in neighborhoods. This situation provides a breeding ground for disease-carrying pests and causes localized air pollution. The lack of basic solid waste services in crowded, low-income neighborhoods is an important contributor to disease among the poor, though much less so than the pathogens associated with poor water and sanitation. In wealthier cities, collection rates improve and approach 100 percent; however, the volume grows and the waste composition changes, creating disposal problems that are discussed later in this chapter.

DRAINAGE

Inadequate storm water drainage has a number of negative impacts. Flooding that is exacerbated by poor drainage can result in death due to drowning, or burial in landslides or collapsing houses. Flooding results in economic harm through property damage, road congestion, disruption of public services, and lost employment. In many poorer cities, sewage and sullage (gray water) are removed by drains. Flooding can spread wastewater in communities, with resulting detrimental health effects. Standing water, resulting from poorly drained rainwater, provides ideal conditions for outbreaks of insect-borne diseases.

PUBLIC TRANSPORTATION

Insufficient access to safe and reliable transportation can be a major environmental problem. Increasing motorization, poorly functioning public transportation, badly maintained roads, lack of walkways and cycle paths, poor traffic management, and lack of enforcement and education all contribute to traffic congestion, road accidents, and air pollution, with associated health and economic losses. The cost of road accidents in developing countries, two-thirds of which occur in urban areas, is as high as 1 to 2 percent of GDP, reflecting high fatality and injury rates and property damage (WHO 1989).

Pollution from Urban Wastes and Emissions

City-based activities generate pollution that affects water, air, and the land. This section briefly reviews the sources, levels, and impacts of urban air pollution, water pollution, and wastes that affect more than one environmental medium. Problems of land degradation are mostly covered in the subsequent discussion on resource losses.

AIR POLLUTION

Some 1.1 billion people live in cities with air pollution levels that exceed healthful limits. An estimated 300,000 to 700,000 premature deaths could be avoided each year if particulate matter was reduced to the average yearly level that the World Health Organization considers safe; this is equivalent to 2 to 5 percent of all urban deaths in cities where particulate pollution is excessive (WRI 1996). Ambient or outdoor air pollution, closely linked to energy use (see multimedia effects in a subsequent unit), is an increasingly serious problem in cities with poor ventilation and high rates of motorization, industrialization, and/or coal use. The problem is expected to become especially severe in large, developing cities, where vehicle fleets and related emissions are expected to grow 5 to 10 percent annually. In Chinese cities alone, an additional 850,000 premature deaths will occur each year if policies to tackle urban air pollution are not implemented (World Bank 1997). Air quality in developed cities has largely improved over the last 20 years; the greatest remaining threat is increased vehicle use due to urban sprawl (WRI 1996). Transport-related pollution is due to vehicle emissions, dust from unpaved roads, and poorly planned land use patterns. These and other environmental impacts of motorization are listed in Box 3-1. Exposure to outdoor air pollution can result in an increase in breathing problems, hypertension, respiratory disease, heart attacks, strokes, and death. Nonhealth effects of ambient air pollution include damage to buildings, monuments, crops, and vegetation.

BOX

Perhaps the most important technological change affecting cities has been the motorized vehicle. It is incontestable that cars have greatly increased urban mobility and productivity. They have also taken a serious toll on the environment:

- **In OECD countries, motorized transportation is responsible for half of atmospheric lead emissions, 80 percent of all benzene emissions, and almost half of total hydrocarbons in urban areas.**
- **In heavily polluted cities like Athens and Mexico City, motor vehicles account for 83 percent of air pollution.**
- **Air-conditioning for cars comprises 10 percent of global CFC-12 demand.**
- **An estimated 80 to 85 percent of urban nitrous oxide emissions are deposited outside of the city boundaries.**
- **Motorized transport is associated with high accident and death tolls, and can deter cycling and walking as alternative forms of transport.**
- **Congestion costs are high: Average traffic speeds are 7 to 8 km/hour in Athens, 18 km/hour in Paris, and 20 km/hour in London.**
- **Private automobile transport is land-intensive: In U.S. and Australian cities, road supply per capita is three to four times as high as in European cities and seven to nine times higher than in Asian cities.**
- **In OECD countries, the social costs of road transport are estimated at 2.0 to 2.4 percent of GDP for accidents, 0.4 percent for air pollution, and 0.1 percent for noise.**

Box 3-1 Motorization and the urban environment.

SOURCE: Haughton and Hunter 1994, 97–98.

Indoor air pollution is a problem of particular concern in developing cities. Smoke from the combustion of biomass indoors contributes to respiratory tract infections that cause an estimated four million deaths annually among infants and children (World Bank 1992). The problem is aggravated by high-density and poorly ventilated housing, the presence of primary and secondary cigarette smoke, and the use of toxic pesticides in the home. Health effects include respiratory infections that can lead to permanent lung damage and heart failure. Another problem of indoor air pollution is worker exposure to toxic emissions from small manufacturing enterprises that are often household-based. The key consideration from a public health perspective is the cumulative exposure of individuals to air pollutants from all urban sources—ambient, household, and occupational (Smith 1993).

WATER POLLUTION

Sources of water pollution in cities include municipal and industrial discharges. In developing cities where sewerage connections exist and some treatment occurs, operational difficulties are common, and desired effluent quality is not achieved. In Cairo, for example, 70 percent of the city is connected to the public sewer system, but only 15 percent of the collected wastewater is fully treated. Of the remainder, 25 percent is partially treated and 60 percent is dumped as raw sewage via open canals to a lake and then to the sea (Grenon and Batisse 1989). Most domestic sewage in poorer cities is deposited directly on land or into surface waters, posing serious public health risks, particularly to children.

The problem of inadequate domestic wastewater disposal is

Figure 3-2 Industrial water pollution in Quatzalcoalcos, Mexico.

often compounded by industrial discharges. Industries that discharge untreated effluents directly into surface waters or on land contribute to pollution of both surface and ground water resources. In Karachi and Lahore, for example, industries annually discharge 35 tons of suspended solids, 376 tons of dissolved solids, 2 tons of ammonia, and 1.5 tons of arsenic oxide into a local stream. These discharges can make water unsuitable for irrigation and livestock consumption (World Bank 1991). Industries that release effluents into municipal sewers can damage infrastructure, interfere with effective treatment, and, as was the case in Guadalajara, even contribute to a disastrous explosion. Industrial pollution of water resources can also raise the cost of treatment for industrial and drinking water.

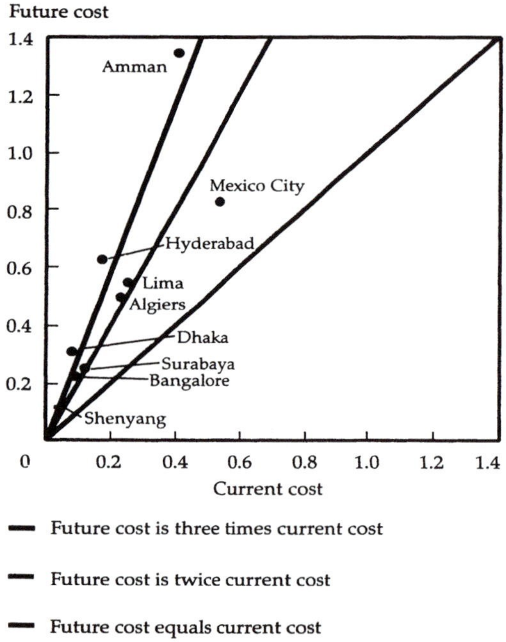

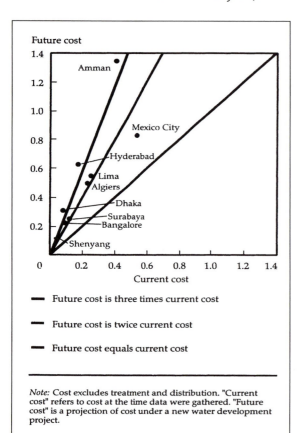

Note: Cost excludes treatment and distribution. "Current cost" refers to cost at the time data were gathered. "Future cost" is a projection of cost under a new water development project.

Figure 3-3 The high cost of developing new sources of water supply.

SOURCE: World Bank 1992.

Pollution of surface waters (streams, rivers, lakes, and coastal and marine waters) can lead to health problems from direct contact with untreated water or consumption of contaminated seafood. Economic impacts include revenue losses from depleted fisheries and declining tourism, and increased costs of water treatment and supply. Untreated urban sewage has resulted in declining fish catches in the rivers and estuaries around cities in India, China, the Philippines, Venezuela, and Senegal (WRI 1996). When sources of water supply become degraded, cities must invest in developing alternatives. The unit cost of water from new water development projects can double or even triple, as indicated by Figure 3-3. In Lima, Peru, upstream pollution has raised treatment costs by about 30 percent, while Shanghai has had to move its water intake more than 40 kilometers upstream at a cost of around $300 million due to pollution (World Bank 1992).

MULTIMEDIA PROBLEMS

As the term suggests, multimedia problems cut across more than one environmental medium (air, water, and land). For example, solid waste that is collected in poorer cities is often disposed of improperly; waste that is placed in open dumps or dumped in water bodies then ends up contaminating ground and surface waters. Leachates from open dumps can also contaminate surrounding soils with heavy metals. Spontaneous combustion of solid waste at uncontrolled landfills and improper incineration can contribute to air pollution. Improper solid waste disposal can result in fatal accidents, as well: during a seven-week period in 1993, collapsing solid waste dumps killed 39 people in Istanbul and 22 in San Salvador.

Poorly managed hazardous wastes are another threat to several environmental mediums. Industries and health facilities that dispose of toxic and clinical wastes in city sewers or landfills may end up polluting sources of drinking water as well as contaminating soil used for urban agriculture. Small-scale and cottage industries, which can account for a significant portion of a city's emission of hazardous wastes, can increase local water and

Figure 3-4 Improper solid waste disposal in Abidjan, Côte d'Ivoire.

air pollution. Human exposure to these wastes—whether through inhalation, ingestion, or absorption through the skin—can result in short-term health problems and long-term irreversible chronic diseases or genetic mutations affecting future generations.

Energy use also impacts on more than one environmental medium. The supply and demand of virtually every type of fuel generate environmental externalities. On the supply side, the extraction and conversion of energy resources for urban use can have various impacts, such as deforestation from fuelwood harvesting or the disruption of watersheds and communities to make way for hydropower projects. On the demand side, human health is affected largely because of exposure to emissions resulting from fuel combustion. A secondary impact is the generation of heat that can raise average temperatures in cities by 5 to 10°C. These effects are dynamic: As economic development occurs, the structure of a city's energy balance changes and environmental effects shift accordingly (Leitmann 1991). Within cities, the severity of environmental impact is very much related to land use: Urban form and density affect energy consumption for travel, heating, and cooling, while landscaping influences microclimatic conditions (OECD 1993).

BOX

In *Bellamy's Europe* (1976), David Bellamy notes:

> **Whenever you walk in Venice, not far beneath your overheated feet is one of over 22 million wooden stakes, the majority of which are as sound as the day they were driven into the soft silts of the lagoon. The reason for their long lasting service is that the lagoon muds are, and presumably always have been, deficient in oxygen... tourists and local inhabitants should rejoice in the fact that the waters of Venice are polluted. All the time there is excess organic matter pouring through the canals, the water will be bung full of bacteria thriving on the products of decay and in so doing using up the oxygen dissolved in the water and that helps protect the all important piles.**

Box 3-2 When are urban wastes good?

Source: Cited in Hough 1995, 33.

Resource Degradation

Urban land development can damage surrounding ecosystems in two ways. First, construction on sensitive land can lead to habitat loss; hillsides, floodplains, wetlands, coastal areas, and forests are particularly susceptible. For example, most of Singapore's mangroves were reclaimed for urban development, resulting in the disappearance of coastal prawn ponds and fish traps that used to provide abundant harvest (Chia 1979). In many poor cities, illegal settlements are built on environmentally sensitive land, which both degrades land ecosystems and exposes residents to risks such as floods, landslides, and fires. Second, conversion of productive land to urban uses can intensify environmental pressure on remaining lands. In one decade in the United States (1982–1992), 2.1 million hectares of forests, 1.5 million hectares of cultivated cropland, 945,000 hectares of pastureland, and 775,000 hectares of rangeland were converted to urban uses (WRI 1996). In this situation, timber, crop, and livestock production on remaining land can become more intense and environmentally damaging.

Resource extraction represents a second category of resource degradation. Groundwater is an important source of drinking water for many cities. Improper disposal of urban and industrial wastes can contaminate groundwater. Overextraction, or withdrawing more water than is naturally recharged, can also damage aquifers. Together, pollution and overextraction can lead to the permanent loss of an aquifer as a source of high-quality drinking water. Groundwater depletion can also cause land subsidence that undermines buildings, damages infrastructure, and exacer-

Figure 3-5 Land reclamation destroyed mangroves in Singapore.

bates the impact of flooding. Watershed degradation can occur far from the city when major water supply or hydropower projects are built to meet urban demand, or when firewood and charcoal are produced in an unsustainable fashion.

Downstream urban pollution is another source of resource degradation. For example, in the United States, ozone from primarily urban sources is responsible for most of crop-yield losses due to air pollutants. Ozone from Los Angeles has also been implicated in tree loss that has threatened a nearby national forest (WRI 1996).

Cultural and historical heritage constitutes another resource that is subject to deterioration and loss in urban areas. This resource consists of archaeological and paleontological sites, historic and religious monuments, architecture, and natural wonders. Important historic structures or areas can be lost during public or private urban development efforts such as reconstruction of a city's historic center, densification of existing real estate, construction of a metro system, or preparation of major infrastructure works. As city centers shift, historic neighborhoods and sites may be neglected and left to deteriorate. Air and water problems, combined with inadequate infrastructure and maintenance, can also accelerate decay of valued buildings and monuments (e.g., aquifer depletion that causes subsidence can damage buildings, while acid rain accelerates the decay of the built environment).

Environmental Hazards

Environmental hazards come from natural and human sources, as well as from interaction between the two. Many cities are subject to significant loss of life and property from natural events such as earthquakes, floods, wildfires, tropical storms, mud slides, and volcanic eruptions. For example, the average annual loss from earthquakes in Turkey, mostly in urban areas, is estimated at 0.8 percent of GNP (SPO 1998). Damage from the 1988 flooding in the Rio de Janeiro metropolitan region was estimated at over $900 million, and the 1998 flooding in Wuhan left 200,000 people stranded while causing an estimated $480 million in damage.

Figure 3-6 Traffic accidents as a source of risk: Bali, Indonesia.

Human sources of environmental risk in cities include accidents caused by industries, municipal facilities, traffic, and fires. Perhaps the most notorious urban industrial accident was the 1984 isocyanate gas disaster in Bhopal that claimed thousands of lives and led to the destruction of a swath of homes and industrial facilities. The death toll from this gas leak was exacerbated by the failure to control settlement around the chemical plant. In 1992, powerful explosions caused by liquid hexane being dumped into Guadalajara's municipal sewer system killed over 200 people, injured 1000 others, and damaged homes, streets, and commercial buildings. Traffic accidents claim thousands of lives in some of the world's largest cities each year. The situation is particularly striking in developing cities, which usually have fewer cars per capita but higher accident rates. In India, for example, there are more fatalities each year from road accidents than in the United States, though India has only one-twentieth as many motorized vehicles (UNCHS 1996). The loss of life and property from fires that are intentionally or accidentally set plagues virtually every city in the world; the problem is worsened by the insufficient pre-

Figure 3-7 Drainage canal clogged with waste in Tunis, Tunisia.

ventive measures (e.g., public education and enforced building codes) and low emergency-response capacity (e.g., inadequate fire-fighting capability and medical facilities) characteristic of developing cities.

Human actions can deepen and widen the impact of many natural hazards. Loss of life and property from earthquakes is heightened when unsafe buildings are constructed in areas of high seismic activity or when cities are unprepared to handle emergencies. Similarly, the damage from flooding is intensified when people settle in floodplains, when drainage is inadequate, or when uncollected solid waste is disposed of in existing drains. An example of this interaction is provided in Box 3-3.

The Global Dimension

While many of the environmental effects of urban areas tend to be local, cities can have important consequences for environmental problems of a global nature and can also be seriously affected by global problems. Examples include:

- *Greenhouse gases.* Cities consume 80 percent of the world's fossil fuels (Girardet 1996). Consequently, cities such as Canberra, Chicago, and Los Angeles have carbon dioxide emissions that are 6 to 9 times greater per capita than the world's average and 25 times (or more) than poorer cities such as Dhaka (UNCHS 1996). One estimate suggests that 40 percent of total CO_2 emissions in North America come from 50 metropolitan areas (WRI 1996).
- *Sea level rise.* If cities are a primary contributor to global warming, they can also be its victim. Most U.S. coastal cities, Buenos Aires, Rio de Janeiro, London, St. Petersburg,

Lagos, Bombay, Bangkok, and Sydney are among the places that would be seriously affected by flooding due to a rise in sea levels (Girardet 1996).

- *Climate change.* Projections of the impact of changing global climate on European cities suggest that Berlin will experience a warmer and wetter climate that could exacerbate smog and acid rain, that Volgograd could suffer from spring flooding and summer dust storms, and that Liverpool could be affected by malfunctioning sewers due to the impact of increased rainfall on its tidal river (Deelstra 1993).
- *Pollution of international waters.* Land-based sources of marine pollution have been an important cause of degrading international waters. Urban wastes usually constitute the major component of these land-based sources. Examples of such pollution are given in Box 3-4.

BOX

In 1995, heavy rains caused floods that killed 63 people in slum areas of Izmir, Turkey's third-largest city. A detailed analysis concluded that the damage was primarily due to poorly functioning drains and culverts that were blocked with solid waste.

Three human activities worsened the impact of this disaster: (1) poor people seeking low-cost housing constructed illegal dwellings in riverbeds that were inundated during the heavy rains; (2) solid waste collection was inadequate, so residents dumped their garbage in nearby drains; and (3) drains were poorly maintained, which allowed the waste to accumulate to the point where the drains could not function properly.

Box 3-3 How human and natural forces interact to worsen flooding.

SOURCE: SPO 1998.

Finally, although the areas of primary concern are physically more remote, even the issue of preservation versus destruction of biodiversity on this planet has two important urban dimensions. First, much of the demand for resources and products that in turn leads to threats to plant and animal species comes from the urban economy. Second, the political, financial, and intellectual support for protecting biodiversity is usually based on cities. Just think how many pro-wildlife, pro-park, and other environmentally oriented groups have their headquarters and membership bases in urban areas.

Conditions Influencing the Urban Environment

Urban environments differ from rural settings for a number of different reasons. On average, cities tend to have poorer air quality, less ultraviolet radiation, more fog, greater cloudiness, more precipitation, higher temperatures, less humidity, and lower wind velocities than surrounding rural areas (see Table 3-1 for comparison). Important factors influence these and other environmental characteristics that make cities different. These include (1) economic factors (the impact of growth, level of development, macroeconomic links, the poverty dimension); (2) demographic and social factors; (3) natural and spatial factors (key ecosystems, land use); and (4) the institutional setting (key actors, jurisdictional arrangements, cross-sectoral features). These conditions constitute critical forces that help shape specific urban environments.

BOX

Much of land-based pollution that affects international waters comes from cities. For example:

- ***Mediterranean Sea.*** **This sea receives a largely untreated sewage load of 30 to 50 million tons annually from 120 coastal settlements, along with discharges from 170 refineries and chemical plants. Industrial pollution primarily originates from heavily urbanized areas such as those around Barcelona, Marseilles, Genoa, and Athens. Urban-based pollution has accelerated problems with destruction of wetland habitats, damage to breeding grounds of endangered species, and an increase in "red tides." Health hazards and ecological damage now affect 25 percent of the Mediterranean coastline.**
- ***Seto Sea.*** **The shoreline of this sea, located along the southern edge of Japan, contains major cities like Osaka and Hiroshima that have experienced rapid population and industrial growth. Excessive inflows of organic pollution and nutrients have contributed to frequent and extensive "red tides" that have degraded fisheries.**
- ***New York Bight.*** **This shallow marine area 19 km off the New York/New Jersey coast is the world's most intensive ocean dumping site for dredge spoils, industrial wastes, and sewage sludge. Some 8.6 million tons of waste are dumped into the area off the mouth of the Hudson River each year. An estimated 105 km^2 of seabed is covered by black sludge containing high levels of bacteria, long-lived viruses, toxic metals, and organic compounds. Storms have caused some of this sludge to move inland, contaminating Long Island and New Jersey beaches and shellfish beds, and resulting in disease outbreaks among people consuming raw shellfish.**

Box 3-4 Urban-based pollution of international waters.
SOURCE: Haughton and Hunter 1994, 178–179.

Economic Factors

ECONOMIC GROWTH AND THE URBAN ENVIRONMENT

A simplistic model of the relationship between economic growth and the urban environment would suggest that, as cities become wealthier, they consume more resources and throw out more waste. Thus, economic growth should lead to greater environmental degradation from higher resource use and higher waste generation per capita. However, the evidence shows that this is only partially true.

As cities grow economically (as measured by per capita income), they do produce more municipal waste and carbon dioxide emissions per person. However, urban concentrations of particulate matter decrease with growing wealth, as do sulfur dioxide emissions (after a period of increase). Importantly, the percentage of the population with access to safe drinking

Table 3-1 Environmental Differences Between Urban and Rural Areas

Environmental factor	In urban areas
Air quality:	
• Particulate matter	10 times greater
• Carbon dioxide	10 times greater
• Sulfur compounds	5 times greater
Ultraviolet radiation at ground level	15–20% less
Fog	30–100% greater
Cloudiness	5–10% greater
Precipitation	5–15% greater
Annual mean temperature	0.7–1.5°C higher
Humidity	5–10% less
Mean wind speed	10–30% less

SOURCES: Trefil 1994, 13; Haughton and Hunter 1994, 132–133.

water and adequate sanitation increases dramatically with economic growth (World Bank 1992). This more complicated picture can be understood if we add some additional information to the simplistic model.

Consumption and waste do increase with economic growth. At the same time, as cities become richer, they have more financial, technological, and human resources available to solve certain problems, and a more educated and wealthier population that increasingly demands a better quality of life. Thus, citizens demand (and can increasingly pay for) piped water, sewerage, and air that does not contain health-threatening pollutants such as fine particulates, sulfur dioxide, and lead. Municipal and sometimes national governments sooner or later respond to this demand, and, with higher revenues from economic development, they obtain the resources to provide water, remove wastes, and clean the air for more of the urban population. Benefits also extend beyond the wealthy and educated classes to a broader group of citizens. Production of municipal solid waste and emissions of carbon dioxide increase on a per capita basis partly because of greater consumption of energy and other resources, and partly because these are externalities that usually do not directly affect the health and well-being of urban residents in the short term.

LEVEL OF DEVELOPMENT AND THE RISK TRANSITION

Information in the previous text and in Chapter 1 (see Figure 1-2 and Table 1-1) indicates that the severity and composition of urban environmental problems change according to a city's level of development. The poorest cities are most affected by environmental health problems that are largely contained within city boundaries. As city incomes rise and their economies become more developed, residents face a "double-whammy" of (1) unresolved environmental health problems and (2) pollution from rapid industrialization that has impacts stretching from the household to the regional level. Urban areas at the top of the economic ladder have largely resolved their basic environmental health problems and are more plagued by pollution and waste problems that are citywide to global in nature and require more sophisticated responses.

Another way of understanding this relationship is to think in terms of a "risk transition" (Smith 1990). As cities develop eco-

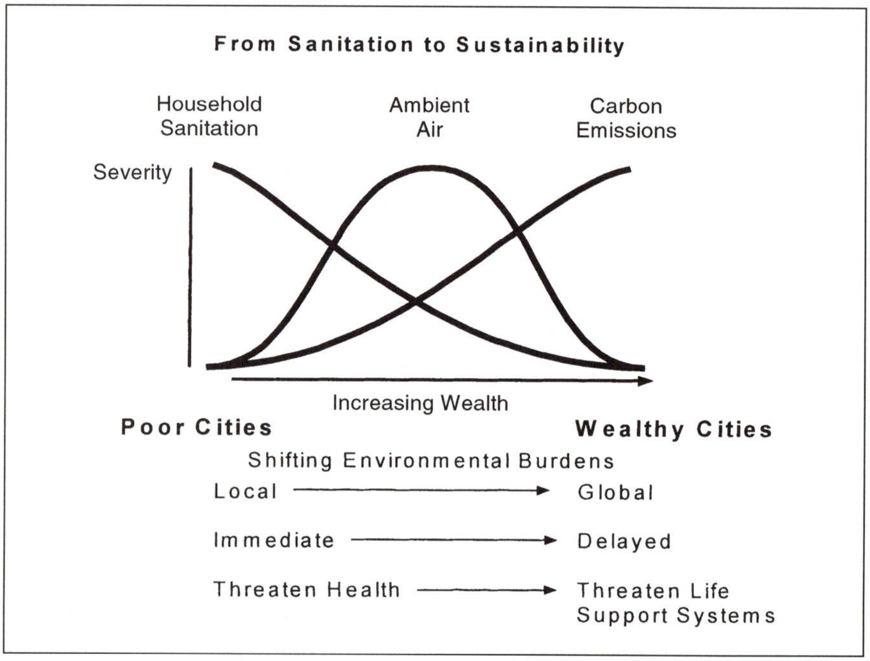

Figure 3-8 The urban environmental transition in cities.

SOURCE: McGranahan et al. 1999.

nomically, the nature of environmental risks faced by their populations undergoes a transition. This is graphically shown in Figure 3-8. In the poorest cities, household sanitation problems are most severe; they are also local, immediate, and health-threatening. As cities develop economically, household sanitation improves but ambient air quality deteriorates and carbon dioxide emissions begin to grow. In the wealthiest cities, household sanitation is usually excellent and air quality has improved, but emissions of greenhouse gases continue to rise; in these cities, problems are more global in nature, have a delayed impact, and threaten life-support systems.

THE MACROECONOMIC DIMENSION

Macroeconomic conditions (e.g., exchange, interest and inflation rates, pricing and fiscal policies, and subsidies) can have important environmental consequences at the city level. For example, in countries with an unstable investment climate or high inflation, there may be overinvestment in real estate and construction. Accelerated consumption of land and construction of buildings can have a number of negative environmental impacts in cities:

- Increased pressure to develop environmentally sensitive lands
- More rapid conversion of agricultural land
- Heightened pressure on existing environmental infrastructure and services
- Greater environmental impacts from construction, both in terms of demand for resources and generation of waste
- Densification of existing neighborhoods, resulting in more environmental health problems

In poorer cities, increased demand for land will lead to higher land prices (in the absence of increased supply). This, in turn, will make urban land less affordable to the poor and can increase the incidence of squatting with its attendant environmental problems (building on environmentally sensitive land, low access to basic services, low-quality construction with vulnerability to hazards). Overinvestment or speculation in housing construction may have

Figure 3-9 Asian economic crisis: Jakarta, Indonesia.

the opposite effect by increasing the housing stock, reducing prices, increasing affordability, and decreasing squatting.

URBAN POVERTY/ENVIRONMENT DYNAMICS

Poverty interacts with the urban environment in two ways: (1) the actions of low-income groups have consequences for the environment; and (2) the poor are disproportionately affected by many environmental problems. Briefly, some of the effects of poor groups on the urban environment are:

- *Migration.* In developing countries, it is often the rural poor who migrate to cities and accelerate urban population growth. This accelerated growth threatens the ability of municipalities to provide environmental services as well as to collect and treat wastes.
- *Squatting.* Lack of disposable income combined with dysfunctional land markets in many developing cities often result in the growth of illegal settlements. Often, these settlements are located on land that is environmentally sensitive or hazard-prone. The development of irregular settlements also

makes it difficult to efficiently provide squatters with access to environmental services and infrastructure.

- *Lack of options*. When services and infrastructure are not available or are too costly (see following text), then low-income households and neighborhoods may be forced to act in ways that harm the environment and themselves. For example, if solid waste is not regularly collected, it may be dumped or burned, contributing to the spread of disease vectors, air pollution, and flooding.

The poor are the ones most seriously affected by a range of urban environmental problems. Foremost among the environmental concerns of the urban poor are health problems resulting from a substandard living environment that does not protect them from human excreta and other wastes, indoor air pollution, or natural hazards. Intraurban studies confirm that the mortality and morbidity from gastrointestinal and respiratory infections and malnutrition are significantly higher for the urban poor than for other urban residents.[1] So too are the resulting costs of health care and productivity losses. The urban poor include several especially vulnerable groups: children, women, adolescents, cottage industry workers, the disabled, and the elderly. These groups are particularly exposed because they lack the economic ability to invest in mitigating measures and pay for services, are not knowledgeable about alternatives, and do not have the political strength to push for environmental improvements (Bartone et al. 1994). They also tend to spend more time at home, where exposure to polluted water, poor indoor air quality, disease vectors, crowded conditions, and poor sanitation may be the most severe (McGranahan,

[1] See, for example, Carolyn Stephens. 1996. Healthy cities or unhealthy islands? The health and social implications of urban inequality. *Environment and Urbanization* 8(2): 9–30; Gordon McGranahan and Jacob Songsore. 1994. Wealth, health and the urban household: Weighing environmental burdens in Accra, Jakarta, and Sao Paulo. *Environment* 36(6): 4–11, 40–45; Bradley et al. 1992. A review of environmental health impacts in developing country cities. Urban Management Program Discussion Paper No. 6, Washington, D.C.: World Bank; Jorge Hardoy and David Satterthwaite (1992); and Harpham et al. (eds.). 1988. *In the shadow of the city: Community health and the urban poor.* Oxford: Oxford University Press.

Songsore, and Kjellen 1996). In industrialized countries, this inequitable exposure to environmental risks has helped spawn the "environmental justice" movement.

A key observation is that the poor often pay more than the wealthy do for a less hygienic and more irregular water supply, poorer sanitation, and dirtier sources of energy. For example, studies in several cities show that when the regular water supply fails to reach the poor, the peri-urban poor pay private vendors ten to twenty times more for lower-quality water than those living in areas served by public piped water supplies. The increased costs of services, health care, and productivity losses, however, are only partial indicators of the economic impacts on the poor; these elements cannot adequately measure the costs of human suffering and lowered quality of life.

Demographic Factors

Rapid population growth poses an especially significant challenge to the environment in the cities of developing countries. As a city grows, there is a greater concentration of people, industries, commerce, vehicles, energy consumption, water use, waste generation, and other environmental stresses. Cities that are doubling every 10 to 20 years must rapidly mobilize their resources if they are to manage and mitigate the impacts of these stresses.

The scale of the problem can often exceed the capacity of local government to collect, treat, and dispose of municipal sewage and solid wastes; the capacity of authorities to control dangerous wastes and emissions; and the capacity of nature to assimilate all of these wastes. An analogous scale problem exists on the input side as a result of the concentrated resource consumption taking place in urban areas. Urban demand for fossil fuels, water, food, minerals, timber and fuelwood, and other resources often impacts on distant peoples, watersheds, and forests (Bartone et al. 1994). These problems can exist for large and megacities, where the magnitude of resource consumption and waste generation is enormous and the jurisdictional situation is often complex. They can also affect smaller and medium-sized cities that may not have the capacity or the resources to respond to rapid changes in population and the nature of environmental problems.

Natural and Spatial Factors

Two key conditions that affect the nature of the urban environment are (1) the features of the ecosystem(s) where a city is located, and (2) the patterns of land use. In Chapter 1, another spatial aspect of the urban environment was mentioned that will not be examined in detail here: Urban environmental problems occur at different spatial scales (from the household/workplace level to the global level). This is an observation that should be kept more in mind when we move to the sections on planning and managing.

ECOSYSTEM EFFECTS

The ecosystem(s) surrounding a city can have important consequences for the nature and degree of the environmental problems it faces. Factors include the geography, topography, vegetation, and climate where a city is located. For example, London has not suffered from malaria because it is not located in a tropical ecosystem where the mosquito vector can thrive. And air pollution in Mexico City and Los Angeles is intensified as a result of natural and climatological features in those cities that produce thermal inversions (WRI 1996).

(a)

(b)

Figure 3-10 Ecosystems, Abidjan, Côte d'Ivoire.

Some major ecosystem types and their implications for the urban environment are:

- *Coastal systems*. Thirty-six of the world's 100 largest cities are located along coasts and estuaries. These cities are more subject to certain natural risks like flooding and severe storms, as well as saline intrusion in depleted aquifers. Urban development can result in destruction of wetlands and other critical marine habitats, shoreline erosion, beach pollution, and marine pollution with subsequent eutrophication, fish kills, and shellfish contamination.

- *River basins.* Most noncoastal cities are located along rivers. These areas face problems of upstream and downstream water quality and quantity. Settlements built along riverbanks are at risk from flooding. Cities linked to lake ecosystems can provoke eutrophication from domestic and industrial discharges.
- *Arid regions.* Many cities are located in arid or semiarid climates. For example, 60 percent of the urban population in Latin America is located in such zones, which contain only 5 percent of the region's water resources. Critical problems include: competition between cities, industries, and agriculture for limited water resources; increased vulnerability of the limited water supply to pollution; and accelerated deforestation in cities where fuelwood and charcoal are important in the energy balance.
- *Humid tropical areas.* Heat and humidity in these areas provide the conditions for the outbreak of communicable diseases and pests. Tropical coastal areas are often susceptible to severe storms and routine flooding.
- *Cold climates.* Cities with cold winters often have seasonal air pollution problems from energy use for heating. This is particularly true where coal is the main heating fuel, as in China, Eastern Europe, and Turkey. Power plant waste and cold weather also affect the composition and decomposition of solid waste in winter.
- *Mountainous zones.* Cities built in mountain basins and on slopes can be affected by erosion, landslides, and flash floods. Altitude and temperature also affect the efficiency of internal combustion engines, the formation of emissions such as ozone, and the rate at which natural wastes can be assimilated (Bartone et al. 1994).

The built environment in a city also constitutes a sort of ecosystem which can affect air quality, wind speed, and water management. For example, some of the differences between the river flow downstream of an urbanized catchment and that of an equivalent rural catchment are:

- A greater percentage of rainfall becomes surface runoff, so that average discharge into the river is increased.
- The lag time between rainfall and increased river discharge is reduced, as is the time to peak river discharge.
- There are increased peak flood discharges.
- Discharges are decreased at times of low flow, reflecting the reduced contribution of groundwater.
- Water quality is degraded through effluent discharges and pollutants running off of impermeable surfaces (Haughton and Hunter 1994, 171).

THE ROLE OF LAND USE

Urban land use decisions are critical determinants of environmental quality. At some point in their existence, most cities have experienced distortions in land markets. Poorly functioning land markets, combined with ineffective land management policies and practices, have resulted in: degradation of environmentally fragile lands (e.g., wetlands and coastal resources); occupation of hazard-prone areas (e.g., steep slopes, floodplains, and vacant land adjacent to polluting industries or waste disposal sites); air pollution; congestion and accidents; and the loss of cultural/historical resources, open space, and prime agricultural land. Some examples appear in Box 3-5.

BOX

Urban form, density, and the way that cities use land all have important effects on the environment. Consider the following evidence:

- **Changing the shape, size, residential density, layout, and location of activities in cities can yield energy savings of up to 150 percent.**
- **Studies show that low-density cities use twice as much energy as high-density cities, even when controlling for climate and income differences.**
- **Each resident in most low-density Canadian cities emits around 20 metric tons of CO_2 a year on average, while in higher-density Amsterdam the equivalent figure is 10 metric tons.**
- **Low-density urban development in Australia has been associated with accelerated conversion of farmland for roads and housing; more impermeable surfaces and urban runoff; increased water consumption for gardening; higher energy consumption for heating and cooling single-story detached homes; high per capita fuel consumption and vehicular emissions due to low use of public transport and greater distances traveled; and low recycling rates due to relatively higher costs of collection.**
- **Increasing the percentage of people traveling by public transport is usually easier in higher-density, compact cities. Increased reliance on public transport can yield major energy savings and reductions in air pollution. In Tokyo, 15 percent of commuters drive to work, compared to 90 percent in Los Angeles.**
- **Urban agriculture is an important land use in some cities. Fourteen of China's 15 largest cities are virtually self-sufficient in food production.**

Box 3-5 Urban land use and the environment.

SOURCE: Haughton and Hunter 1994, 13, 85.

By failing to consider land use planning as an integral part of a transport strategy, many developing country cities have allowed automobile traffic to shape their growth and development (Kenworthy and Laube 1996). Excessive amounts of land dedicated to traffic circulation can lead to problems with drainage, runoff, limited absorption, and flooding, as well as traffic congestion, pollution, accidents, and noise. In Warsaw, for example, the master plan envisaged expanding the city to a distance of more than 70 kilometers to protect residents from exposure to automotive emissions. The right-of-way between buildings on main thoroughfares was increased to 180 meters. The implementation of this plan, however, substantially increased air pollution from automobiles. Conversely, inadequate road space can result in congestion, accidents, and an increase in exposure to air pollution, as is the case in Bangkok.

Figure 3-11 Conflicting land uses in Fez, Morocco.

Density and spatial patterns of development also have important implications for various environmental outcomes. For example, high-density development can achieve economies of scale in infrastructure provision, but impose higher costs associated with congestion (e.g., the rapid spread of communicable disease due to crowding, or increased incidences of accidental injuries) if the development is not well-planned and provided with adequate infrastructure. Lower-density development outside of the central city means reduced congestion in residential areas, but higher costs for infrastructure provision and, in the absence of adequate public transport, higher levels of air pollution from automobile traffic. The concentration of industry in relatively few locations is another factor that imposes serious environmental consequences. In the metropolitan areas of Bangkok, Lima, Mexico City, Manila, and Sao Paulo, for example, industrial pollution, including the impacts of poorly managed hazardous wastes, imposes serious health impacts in the areas of the country where there are the highest concentrations of population (Bartone et al. 1994).

Land use controls that can protect populations and sensitive resources as well as enhance environmental quality also can exacerbate environmental degradation and the vulnerability of low-income populations to hazards. For example, enhancing the urban environment by requiring excessive amounts of land for recreation, community facilities, and rights-of-way within subdivisions results in the consumption of excessive amounts of urban land. In the state of Madhya Pradesh in India, land-use regulations resulted in residential standards that were affordable to only the wealthiest 20 percent of households. The victims of the Bhopal accident had been forced to live in squatter settlements located near the Union Carbide factory because they could not afford such formal housing (or the transport costs associated with living outside the city).

Similarly, the imposition of properly enforced development restrictions on hazard-prone lands may substantially reduce the supply of developable land in a city and therefore increase the cost of available land for housing. Unless the government or private sector can provide alternative affordable sites for housing development, the increase in land prices will either push the poor to outlying areas where they will be even further away from employment opportunities and urban services, or excessively increase the density of accessible inner-city areas. By contrast, if the development restrictions are not enforced, the very delineation of hazard-prone areas will direct the poor to them because these areas are often the only ones available for squatter settlement in accessible locations.

Institutional Setting

A number of institutional factors influence urban environmental outcomes in cities. First, the composition, interests, relative power, and interactions of stakeholders are important. Next, the relationship of jurisdictions to key environmental problems in a city has serious consequences. Finally, the degree to which intersectoral coordination exists will affect how cross-media environmental problems are managed.

ROLES AND CONCERNS OF KEY STAKEHOLDERS

To a large extent, the nature of urban environmental problems is determined by the interaction of numerous public, private, not-for-profit, and household stakeholders, each group having its own interests and patterns of behavior. The varied and sometimes conflicting actions and viewpoints of these actors can add to other constraints on planning and implementing environmental programs. Some of the most influential stakeholders who can have an important effect on creating problems as well as solving them include:

- *Environmental protection agencies,* who should be responsible for setting environmental regulations and standards and for monitoring and enforcement. Most often they are relatively weak bodies with only coordination functions.
- *Planning agencies,* who are often unfamiliar with environmental analysis and information, or how to use them, in local development planning.
- *Politicians,* particularly at the local level, who are usually preoccupied with maintaining their power and influence and take a short-term view when allocating resources. Unless there are vocal constituencies pressing for improvements in local environmental conditions, needed political commitment to solving environmental problems may be absent.
- *Sector agencies,* who tend to have little experience in collaborating with each other, disregard the interrelationships between projects, and promote infrastructure and development projects that often lack basic environmental considerations. Local environmental service agencies are often inefficient and particularly ineffective in providing needed services to the most vulnerable groups.
- *Local communities and community-based organizations,* who are acutely aware of the impacts of environmental problems at the household and neighborhood level, but usually have

little opportunity to participate in the preparation of urban infrastructure or industrial projects that affect them, and even less in setting agendas for environmental protection and pollution control.

- *Private and informal sector enterprises,* who generally are concerned about the constraints placed on their activities by environmental regulations and the corresponding costs, particularly when regulations are not applied evenhandedly. At the same time, the business community does not wish to be perceived as the environmental villain and should be coopted into the search for solutions. Further, both formal and informal waste management enterprises can play an important role in the delivery of local environmental services, but they rarely are employed in formal public service provision.
- *Nongovernmental organizations,* who can be effective agents for building local awareness and mobilizing community action as well as for voicing local concerns, including those affecting the disadvantaged, in political forums and the media.
- *The news media,* which can itself play an independent role in voicing concern for the environment and documenting the status of groups affected by environmental conditions, provided, of course, that it has the political freedom and professional sense of responsibility to do so.
- *The scientific and academic community,* which often sets its agenda for environmental research and monitoring on the basis of its own scientific interests without giving due thought to the needs of vulnerable populations. Because valuable information on the environment often is published in scientific journals in abstruse language, the scientific community should ensure that data are translated into a form suitable for use by environmental policy makers, planners, managers, and the media.
- *Support agencies,* either at higher levels of government or internationally, may in some cases give high priority to the environment and poverty reduction. Only recently have

> many recognized that urban areas are critical to overall national development but suffer from severe environmental and poverty problems (Bartone et al. 1994).

These concerns, along with the cultural constraints, social context, and political dynamics of cities, help us to understand the process of degradation in a particular city, and to evaluate the full costs of impacts and likely benefits of alternative measures for prevention, mitigation, and improvement. Such interdisciplinary studies also contribute to the development of the overall institutional framework for urban environmental management and the development of institutional capacity to conduct environmental analyses and design locally appropriate interventions.

JURISDICTIONAL FACTORS

Ideally, levels of responsibility and decision making should correspond to the scale of an environmental problem. However, actual jurisdictional arrangements usually do not adhere to this principle. For example, municipal authorities are normally responsible for solid waste management, but their usually inadequate approaches to disposal have important spillover effects for neighboring jurisdictions within a region or metropolitan area.

A second jurisdictional factor is that urban institutions are often not the only stakeholders with the power to address environmental problems within their jurisdictions. For example, leaded gasoline may be causing health problems in a particular city, but the authority to regulate fuel composition usually rests with the national government. Thus, cities usually cannot solve many of their environmental problems by themselves but must enter into partnerships with different levels of government, with the private sector, and with the community.

A third jurisdictional element concerns cities that have grown into metropolitan areas. Environmental problems that have causes or impacts beyond a single city's boundaries need to be solved by multiple jurisdictions. This can be problematic when, as in the case of metropolitan Los Angeles, there are over 100 local governments. In democratic societies, different political parties are often in charge of adjacent cities; this can complicate relations between individual cities or between cities and an overarching metropolitan authority, and limit their ability to solve mutual problems. Similar problems exist when there are political differences between cities and regional or central authorities.

CROSS-SECTORAL ISSUES

Managing the urban environment requires both policy makers and managers to take into account the complex cross-media effects of urban pollution. Any plans to improve one environmental medium (air, water, or land), therefore, should consider the potential effects of that intervention on other media. For example, sewage treatment plants may clean up the flow of wastewater but at the same time produce large quantities of sludge that will have to be disposed of safely on land. Similarly, emission standards that require the installation of scrubbers will create additional burdens for land disposal. In light of cross-media effects, relevant jurisdictions and institutions should carefully coordinate their activities to ensure that problems are effectively addressed. Failure to do so can result in both cross-media pollution problems as well as a loss of resources spent on ineffective actions, for example, investments in surface drainage without parallel improvements in solid waste collection and disposal, or the development of a sewage treatment plant without parallel control of industrial pollution (Bartone et al. 1994).

Underlying Causes of Urban Environmental Degradation

Urban environmental problems have immediate causes that are relatively easy to identify. However, there are also underlying causes that are the driving forces behind long-term environmental degradation in cities. Examples of the two types of causes as they apply to problems of urban groundwater appear in Table 3-2. Too often, researchers and practitioners focus on the immediate culprits because they are evident and sometimes easier to address. This can result in a Band-Aid approach that does not resolve the situation. Attention must be paid to the underlying causes of

Table 3-2 Immediate and Underlying Causes of Urban Groundwater Problems

Problem	Immediate cause	Underlying cause
Degradation or loss of high-quality water resource	Overabstraction by industries and households	• Unclear property rights • Pricing policy does not cover full costs • Weak monitoring and enforcement capacity
Contamination	Excessive subsurface contaminant load from municipal, residential, and industrial discharges	• Insufficient knowledge about groundwater regime • Lack of public awareness about water quality issues • Inadequate regulations governing discharges
Damage from rising water table beneath the city	Leakage from water supply system and infiltration from on-site sanitation units	• Lack of cross-sectoral coordination • Inadequate public participation and political will

SOURCE: Adapted from Foster, Lawrence, and Morris 1998, 36.

urban environmental issues; these include lack of public awareness and participation, inadequate governance, poor policies, and insufficient knowledge.

Lack of Public Awareness and Participation

People must be aware of the existence and consequences of the environmental risks that they and their children face in order to assess whether such problems should be a priority concern. Once citizens are concerned, their participation is essential so that decision-makers in the public and private sectors can be made aware of their concerns. If the public does not actively demand improvements in urban environmental quality, such changes will be low on the agendas of politicians and businesses.

Urban citizens need to be educated about local environmental quality; the health, economic, environmental, and other consequences of major problems; the effects of existing policies and practices; and available options for change. However, in many countries, environmental awareness is not part of the regular education system. In other instances, well-prepared environmental education or public awareness programs can be undermined by the media, which tends to sensationalize environmental issues rather than focus on the real priorities (Bartone et al. 1994). Some local and national governments conceal environmental information from their citizenry for fear that it will reveal inadequacies in governance or that it will give their cities a bad reputation which perhaps would hurt investment or tourism.

Awareness is only part of the equation. If citizens know about environmental issues but cannot effectively participate to express their concerns, then local environmental matters may be ignored. In the absence of public pressure to address urban environmental degradation, the easiest government response may be inaction. Alternatively, political leaders may focus on the most visible issues and immediate causes. Typically, they then seek to solve problems with short-term solutions that may yield results before the next election but may not address underlying causes. This can result in lack of attention to high-priority problems that have little political payoff because they require long-term investment or because they spill over to another political jurisdiction. For example, building or expanding a sewerage system to solve critical sanitation problems can be an expensive and lengthy process, so it is rarely championed by government leaders. A final impediment is that environmentally damaging activities may be controlled by powerful interests (members of the local elite, a state enterprise, or a multinational corporation); without public support, it may be difficult to muster the political will to take on such heavyweights.

When there is public participation in urban environmental management, there is a greater likelihood that priority problems will be identified, relevant options will be formulated, and effective interventions will be implemented. Experience suggests that stakeholder participation improves the performance of development interventions (Isham, Narayan, and Pritchett 1994). More specifically, the joint evaluation of urban conditions by experts *and* decision-makers *and* stakeholders affected by problems within a city yields more comprehensive and more acceptable results than a purely expert-driven approach (Leitmann 1993; UNCHS 1997). Some earlier examples of how public awareness and participation

BOX

Mexico City. Residents had long suffered from air pollution due to outdoor burning at the Santa Cruz Meyehualco dump. Then, in the spring of 1981, after toxic gray clouds drifted 20 miles to the richest suburbs, there was a major outcry and the government began studying plans to move the dump and build a garbage processing plant.

Cordoba, Spain. A communist mayor was elected in large part because he focused his campaign on pollution in the Guadalquivir River and capitalized on widespread antipollution sentiment among noncommunist voters.

Athens. Andreas Papandreou was elevated from opposition leader to prime minister of Greece in 1981 partly because he was able to build on a grassroots movement in Athens that was protesting air and water pollution in the city and placing the blame on the former government.

Jundiai, Brazil. In response to growing public concern about pollution of the Jundiai River, the mayor organized the Jundai Front in order to lobby state and federal authorities to take action.

Box 3-6 Examples linking awareness and participation.
SOURCE: Leonard 1985, 280–281.

can stimulate action on the urban environment are offered in Box 3-6.

Inadequate Governance

Good governance, as defined in the previous chapter, is a relationship between the people and their government that is characterized by transparent processes, a professional bureaucracy, an executive branch that is accountable for its actions, and a strong civil society that participates in public affairs, all of which occurs under the rule of law. Governance can become inadequate and worsen urban environmental problems when any one of these characteristics is absent. The following are examples of how this might occur:

- *Lack of transparency.* Citizens may not be aware of how decisions about their environmental quality are made, or they may not be provided with key information about environmental quality. This limits their awareness about problems and how they can take action to solve them.
- *Institutional capacity.* A city may not possess a professional bureaucracy because institutional capacity is low (i.e., the people, money, and organizational skills required for professionalism are missing). This can result in an administration that is unable to cope with problems or, worse still, deepens and expands problems because of corruption.
- *Limited accountability.* If decision-makers are not accountable for their handling of urban environmental problems, they have less incentive to take action. Citizens then may not be able to voice their concerns in one of the most effective ways—through the ballot box.
- *Minimal participation.* As was previously noted, when people cannot participate in the process of environmental plan-

> ning and management, decisions may be left to experts and politicians who may not share the public's priorities, and there may be little public enthusiasm for effectively implementing these decisions.

In addition, urban environmental governance may be hampered by the problems of jurisdictional complexity and lack of intersectoral coordination that were discussed in the previous section.

Inadequate governance is an especially significant underlying cause in cities of the developing world. Effective environmental planning and management are often difficult for several reasons. First, many developing cities are faced with substantial infrastructure backlogs. When environmental awareness in the United States and Europe grew in the 1960s, the basic infrastructure and management systems were already in place. Thus, the challenge in poorer cities is much greater. Second, developing countries tend to have much more centralized governments. This limits the ability of local governments to raise revenues, make decisions, and modify procedures that affect the urban environment because the locus of power is often with higher levels of government. Third, many developing nations do not have fully representative governments. Even the increasing democratization of the 1990s in several countries has not worked its way down to the local level. Without the strong pressures of citizen groups and nongovernmental organizations, governments may not feel compelled to address environmental concerns (Hardoy and Satterthwaite 1991). Finally, Third World governments are often relatively active participants in the economy. State enterprises are usually worse polluters than their private sector counterparts and are the most difficult to control since they can avoid environmental regulations. Also, the private sector is less likely to be involved in the provision and management of environmental services. Box 3-7 provides an example of this situation from Jamaica.

Poor Policies

The ability to solve urban environmental problems can be hampered by inadequate regulatory policies, unclear property rights, and inefficient economic policies. Few countries and cities have comprehensive and realistic environmental laws and regulations.

BOX

From the mid-nineteenth century until the 1950s, the St. James Parish Council was responsible for urban services in the city of Montego Bay, Jamaica. Over the last four decades, it—like other parish councils in Jamaica—has lost responsibility for urban water and sewer systems to the National Water Commission; for electricity provision to the Jamaica Power Service; much planning authority to the Town and Country Planning Department of the national government; and main roads to the Ministry of Public Works.

As a result, the St. James Parish Council has also lost many sources of income. It collects and receives extremely little revenue (about $800,000 in 1992, or about $7 per capita). Eighty-five percent of this comes from transfers from the central government. Of this revenue, 25 percent goes to wages, salaries, and pensions; 50 percent to street lighting fees paid to the Jamaica Power Service; and most of the remainder to maintaining parish council buildings. Virtually no funds are left over for new infrastructure investment.

Central government agencies are responsible for water, sewers, electricity, and solid waste management. Although they have invested significant sums in Montego Bay (it is a prime tourist destination and source of foreign exchange), the central government has neither a mandate nor a vision for successfully reconciling economic development with local environmental management.

Box 3-7 Weakness of local authorities in Jamaica.

SOURCE: Ferguson 1996, 178.

Typically, pollution control legislation does not assign clear jurisdiction, funding, and power for monitoring and enforcement. Steps for issuing new regulations and standards to reflect changing situations and new knowledge are not spelled out. Excessive and inconsistent regulations and standards that are too costly, politically unacceptable, or bureaucratically unmanageable can deter progress in environmental management. In many cases, though, significant progress could be achieved through existing laws and regulations if there were sufficient monitoring and enforcement (Bernstein 1991).

Inappropriate urban land use regulations often account for the location of low-income people in environmentally sensitive areas as well as the loss of ecologically and culturally important resources. Land use regulations are often unaffordable, difficult to implement, or unenforceable. Sometimes, land regulation results in land development standards that artificially reduce the supply and raise the price of land by requiring excessive amounts of land for government facilities, traffic circulation, or open space. In some cities, governments have not developed effective land use policies, laws, and standards that regulate development in environmentally sensitive areas or that guide urban growth away from areas that need to be managed and protected (Bernstein 1993).

The absence of clear property rights can create a range of urban environmental problems. An obvious example is that when water rights are unclear, the extraction of groundwater for municipal and industrial purposes can lead to unsustainable extraction, with ensuing problems of land subsidence, aquifer contamination, and saline intrusion. Another important aspect of this underlying cause, particularly in poorer cities, is the lack of clear land tenure. Inadequate registration of land titles or a plain lack of tenure deeply affects the attitude of residents in illegal areas toward the environment. Without secure tenure, people have little incentive to invest in building maintenance, infrastructure upgrading, or protecting themselves from floods, earthquakes, or other hazards. In addition, without clear property rights, squatters cannot use their land and dwellings as collateral to obtain formal credit for these and other investments (Bartone et al. 1994).

Bad economic policies include distorted pricing of urban services, energy, and other natural resources; ineffective taxes; and wasteful subsidies. Underpricing of land, water, energy, and food promotes excessive use of scarce resources and undercuts attempts at resource management. In Algeria, Egypt, Turkey, and Yugoslavia, for example, water prices are usually 20 percent of marginal costs (World Bank 1993). Industries and households consequently use much more water than is needed for essential

Figure 3-12 Energy overexploitation in Sana'a, Yemen.

purposes. This results in: (1) the need to build larger supply systems and treatment plants; (2) generation of excess wastewater that is often discharged untreated into surface waters; and (3) faster depletion of existing water supplies, triggering the need to invest in developing new sources.

Underpricing and inefficient tax collection create a situation where urban services cannot recover the costs of providing water, sewerage, or solid-waste management. This usually results in the deterioration of services since utilities cannot maintain and repair their networks. It also limits the ability to expand services since no capital is available for investment. The result is often that poor neighborhoods receive inadequate or no infrastructure and services, while the political power of wealthier settlements ensures that they receive whatever subsidized services that can be provided. This situation can also result in increased dependence of local service providers on transfers and bailouts from the central government.

Poorly devised subsidies, interest rates, trade policies, and exchange rates can also contribute to urban environmental degradation. Subsidies on energy were estimated at $230 billion per year in developing countries alone and accounted for an estimated 10 percent of excess greenhouse gas emissions (World Bank 1992). Artificially high interest rates for housing finance can stimulate unregulated informal production of dwellings that are more vulnerable to natural disasters. Protective tariffs can encourage the production of highly polluting vehicles, industrial processes, and products, as was the case in the former Soviet Union and socialist Eastern Europe. Currency instability or lack of convertibility can lead to overinvestment in real estate and construction, exacerbating land shortages and demand for natural resources used in building.

Insufficient Knowledge

Lack of knowledge about the existence, extent, impact, and costs of urban environmental problems can make it difficult to achieve public consensus about what should be a priority. Even if a problem can be established as a priority, an understanding of how to solve it may be lacking. Many authorities do not have information on the scope and impact of environmental problems on human health, the urban economy, or surrounding ecosystems. Data on environmentally sensitive land, vulnerable populations, and the capacities of existing infrastructure and services are often not available. Without this knowledge, it is difficult to engage in effective land use planning, infrastructure management, and hazard mitigation.

This underlying cause is particularly pronounced in cities of the developing world. A global review of urban research in developing countries, supported by the Ford Foundation (Stren 1994–95), found that the urban environment was a priority topic in virtually every region for the urban research agenda in the 1990s. However, there was little evidence that such research was actually being conducted and disseminated: only 2 to 3 percent of all urban research had an environmental focus. To make matters worse, education programs in the Third World that cover the scientific, technical, and managerial aspects of the urban environment are often weak, outdated, or nonexistent. This results in a shortage of professionals who can develop the necessary knowledge for managing the environmental problems of cities (Bartone et al. 1994).

Figure 3-13 Inadequate water supply in Malatya, Turkey.

Applying the Framework: Slums in Turkey

As part of the International Decade for Natural Disaster Reduction, the World Bank, UNDP, and UNCHS collaborated on a study entitled *Disaster Prevention and Mitigation in Metropolitan Areas*. Environmental degradation and disaster vulnerability in Turkey's informal settlements were the subjects for one case study within this collaboration (Parker, Kreimer, and Munasinghe 1995). The case study consists of ten articles that cover four cities, legal and institutional issues, disaster prevention and mitigation measures, hazardous and solid waste problems, coastal issues, earthquakes, and general lessons about vulnerability and sustainability. These articles contain a wealth of useful material that can be very hard to summarize. The framework developed in this chapter for grouping environmental problems and identifying

Table 3-3 Applying the Framework to Environmental Problems in Turkish Slums

Problem area	Underlying causes
A. Access to environmental infrastructure and services	
1. Improper solid waste management (illegal dumping; accidents in Istanbul and Izmir)	1. Inadequate regulations; weak institutional capacity; insufficient knowledge; cross-sectoral (wastes and drainage) relations; poor policies for land market and waste control
2. Water supply (access, leakage and waste, theft)	2. Poor policies for water pricing, conservation, and groundwater use; ineffective regulatory system for planning and infrastructure
B. Pollution from urban wastes and emissions	
1. Water pollution (wastewater, agricultural runoff)	1. Weak technical and financial capacity; insufficient knowledge about extent, costs, and risks of water pollution; subsidized agricultural chemicals
2. Hazardous wastes (industrial and medical; water and health effects)	2. Lack of public awareness; inadequate regulations; weak institutional capacity
3. Air pollution	3. Pricing policy for unleaded fuel; weak monitoring and enforcement capacity; lack of knowledge about indoor air pollution, lead effects, and unmeasured pollutants
C. Resource degradation	
1. Coastal zone degradation (environmental and economic impacts)	1. Unenforceable regulations; unclear property rights; jurisidictional complexity
D. Environmental hazards	
1. Earthquakes (improperly constructed housing in earthquake-prone zones)	1. Poor land market policies; unenforceable regulations; poor regulations; weak institutional capacity; lack of awareness about risks

underlying causes was used to sort out and summarize this material, as presented in Table 3-3. This framework allows for a more concise statement of key problems and a better understanding of what is driving environmental degradation and vulnerability to disasters in Turkish slums.

Resources and Exercises for Further Thought

Resources

The framework used in this chapter is drawn from Carl Bartone, Janis Bernstein, Josef Leitmann, and Jochen Eigen (1994). The author is grateful for being a part of the team that developed this conceptual approach to understanding urban environmental problems.

Exercises for Further Thought

1. With so many types of potential environmental problems, what criteria and procedures can cities use to set priorities?
2. Should cities in the developing world devote scarce resources to improving their population's access to environmental infrastructure and services, or should these resources be invested in more traditional forms of economic development?
3. If urban wastes and emissions have such serious human health effects, why aren't citizens and politicians making their control a top priority?
4. If cities expanded the provision and improved the management of environmental infrastructure and services, which problems would become less severe? Which would persist?
5. What are the implications of multimedia problems for the way that city governments are organized?

6. Besides the example in Box 3-2, can you think of instances where urban environmental problems might also be resources?
7. Is the loss of life and property from environmental hazards a "necessary evil" to stimulate public outcry and government response to urban environmental issues?
8. If cities are intrinsically linked to global environmental problems, can global issues be resolved without the participation of local governments?
9. Beyond meteorological data (Table 3-1), what are other key environmental differences between urban and rural areas?
10. Are there examples of poor cities that have succeeded in managing the "double whammy" of environmental health problems and rapid industrialization?
11. Are the urban poor more the victims or the causes of certain environmental problems?
12. What key factors result in environmental injustice?
13. To what extent are family planning and control of rural-urban migration solutions to urban environmental degradation?
14. If urban land markets were improved, which environmental problems would diminish in importance and why?
15. How might institutional problems of participation, jurisdiction, and cross-sectoral coordination be overcome?
16. Why do analysts and decision-makers tend to focus on the immediate rather than the underlying causes of urban environmental degradation?
17. How can cities move from poor to good governance? What difference might the transition make for the urban environment?
18. Apply the "problem area" and "underlying cause" framework to a case study in order to better understand a city's urban environmental dynamics.

References

Bartone, Carl, Janis Bernstein, Josef Leitmann, and Jochen Eigen. 1994. Toward environmental strategies for cities: Policy considerations for urban environmental management in developing countries. UMP Policy Paper No. 18. Washington, D.C.: World Bank.

Bellamy, David. 1976. *Bellamy's Europe*. London: British Broadcasting Corporation.

Bernstein, Janis. 1991. *Alternative approaches to pollution control and waste management: Regulatory and economic instruments*. UMP Discussion Paper No. 3. Washington, D.C.: World Bank.

———. 1993. *Land use considerations in urban environmental management*. UMP Discussion Paper No. 12. Washington, D.C.: World Bank.

Cairncross, Sandy and Richard Feachem. 1993. *Environmental health engineering in the tropics: An introductory text*. Chichester: John Wiley & Sons.

Chia, Lin Sien. 1979. Coastal changes, marine pollution, and the fishing industry in Singapore. In Aida Librero and William Collier (eds.), *Economics of aquaculture, sea-fishing and coastal resource use in Asia*. Manila: Philippine Council for Agriculture and Resources Research.

Deelstra, Tjeerd. 1993. The quest for sustainability in urban development and design. In Ministry of the Environment (Finland) and City of Helsinki, *The European city today: The Helsinki round table on urban improvement strategies*. Vantaa: Kajoprint Oy.

Ferguson, Bruce. 1996. The environmental impacts and public costs of unguided informal settlement: The case of Montego Bay. *Environment and Urbanization* 8(2): 171–193.

Foster, Stephen, Adrian Lawrence, and Brian Morris. 1998. Groundwater in urban development: Assessing management needs and formulating policy strategies. Technical Paper No. 390. Washington, D.C.: World Bank.

Girardet, Herbert. 1996. *The Gaia atlas of cities: New directions for sustainable urban living*. London: Gaia Books Ltd.

Grenon, Michel, and Michel Batisse. 1989. *Futures for the Mediterranean basin—The Blue Plan*. New York: Oxford University Press.

Hardoy, Jorge, and David Satterthwaite. 1991. Environmental problems of Third World cities: A global issue ignored? *Public Administration and Development* 11: 341–361.

———. 1992. *Environmental problems in Third World cities: An agenda for the poor and the planet*. London: International Institute for Environment and Development.

Haughton, Graham, and Colin Hunter. 1994. *Sustainable cities*. London: Jessica Kingsley Publishers, Ltd.

Hough, Michael. 1995. *Cities and natural processes*. New York: Routledge.

Isham, Jonathan, Deepa Narayan, and L. Pritchett. 1994. Does participation improve performance? Establishing causality with subjective data. Policy Research Working Paper No. 1357. Washington, D.C.: World Bank.

Kenworthy, Jeffrey, and Felix Laube. 1996. Automobile dependence in cities: An international comparison of urban transport and land use patterns with implications for sustainability. *Environmental Impact Assessment Review* 16(4–6): 279–308.

Leitmann, Josef. 1991. Energy-environment linkages in the urban sector. UMP Discussion Paper No. 2. Washington, D.C.: World Bank.

———. 1993. Rapid urban environmental assessment: Lessons from cities in the developing world. Volume I: Methodology and preliminary findings. UMP Discussion Paper No. 14. Washington, D.C.: World Bank.

Leonard, Jeffrey. 1985. Politics and pollution. In Jeffrey Leonard (ed.) *Divesting nature's capital: The political economy of environmental abuse in the Third World*. New York: Holmes and Meier.

McGranahan, Gordon, Pedro Jacobi, Marianne Kjellen, Jacob Songsore, and Charles Surjadi. 1999. *Citizens at risk: From sanitation to sustainability*. London: Earthscan Publications, Ltd.

McGranahan, Gordon, Jacob Songsore, and Marianne Kjellen. 1996. Sustainability, poverty and urban environmental transitions. In C. Pugh (ed.). *Sustainability, the environment and urbanization*. London: Earthscan Publications, Ltd.

Newton, Peter. 1997. Re-shaping cities for a more sustainable future: Exploring the link between urban form, air quality, energy and greenhouse gas emissions. Report of Task Group 6 for the Inquiry into Urban Air Pollution in Australia. Melbourne: Australian Academy of Technological Sciences and Engineering.

OECD (Organization for Economic Cooperation and Development). 1993. *Cities and the environment*. Paris: OECD.

Parker, Ronald, Alcira Kreimer, and Mohan Munasinghe (eds.). 1995. Informal settlements, environmental degradation and disaster vulnerability: The Turkey case study. Washington, D.C.: International Decade for Natural Disaster Reduction and World Bank.

Smith, Kirk. 1993. Fuel combustion, air pollution exposure, and health: The situation in developing countries. *Annual Review of Energy and Environment* 18: 529–566.

———. 1990. The risk transition. *International Environmental Affairs* 2(3): 227–251.

SPO (State Planning Organization). 1998. *Turkey: National environmental action plan*. Ankara: SPO.

Stren, Richard. 1994–1995. *Urban research in the developing world*. Vols. 1 (Asia), 2 (Africa), and 3 (Latin America). Toronto: Centre for Urban and Community Studies.

Trefil, James. 1994. *A scientist in the city*. New York: Doubleday.

UNCHS (UN Centre for Human Settlements). 1996. *An urbanizing world: Global report on human settlements*. London: Oxford University Press.

———. 1997. Urban indicators programme phase two: 1997–2001. Programme document. Nairobi: UNCHS.

WHO (World Health Organization). 1989. New approaches to improve road safety. Technical Report Series 781. Geneva: WHO.

———. 1992. *The international drinking water supply and sanitation decade: review of decade progress*. Geneva: WHO.

World Bank. 1991. *Urban policy and economic development: An agenda for the 1990s*. Washington, D.C.: World Bank.

———. 1992. *World development report 1992: Development and the environment*. New York: Oxford University Press.

———. 1993. *World development report 1993: Investing in health*. New York: Oxford University Press.

WRI (World Resources Institute) et al. 1996. *World resources 1996–97: The urban environment*. New York: Oxford University Press.

CHAPTER 4

Can Urban Development Be Sustained?

Chapter Outline

- Differing views of urban sustainability
    - Reducing ecological footprints
    - Sustaining the production of wealth
    - Resolving critical problems
- Case studies of Las Vegas and Mexico City
- Are cities sustainable?
- The case for urban environmental planning and management
- Resources and exercises for further thought
- References

Differing Views of Urban Sustainability

How one views urban sustainability depends on how one perceives the relationship between cities and sustainable development. There are at least three different viewpoints on how to determine whether urban areas are proceeding along a sustainable path of development: (1) assessing an "ecological footprint"; (2) calculating a broader measure of wealth; and (3) evaluating critical problem areas. The approach, conclusions, strengths, and weaknesses of each method are outlined in the text that follows.

Minimizing Ecological Footprints

An urban "ecological footprint" is simply the total amount of the earth's surface needed to support a given city's level of consumption and absorb its waste products. The developers of this concept, William Rees and Mathis Wackernagel, compare a city to a large animal grazing in a meadow and pose the ecological footprint as a question: "How large a pasture is necessary to support that city indefinitely—to produce all its 'feed' and to assimilate all its wastes sustainably?" (Wackernagel and Rees 1995). In other words, the ecological footprint is a geographical measure of an urban population's demand on natural capital.

The surface area that makes up a footprint is a sum of all land required to supply resources and absorb wastes, wherever that land may be on earth. For example, residents of a Chinese city may require provincial land for a reservoir to supply water and for forests to absorb the carbon dioxide that they produce. They may rely on coal mines in other provinces for their heating and industrial energy. Their footprint can also extend beyond their borders, perhaps to North American grain fields to supply feed for

Figure 4-1 Rural effect of urban footprints: Fuelwood supply in Baluchistan, Pakistan.

the livestock that they consume or to coastal fisheries in Thailand for some of their seafood consumption. The sum of all this land and surface water directly related to resource consumption and waste absorption becomes the city's ecological footprint. Information regarding the footprint generated by Vancouver, British Columbia, appears in Box 4-1.

BOX

Calculations indicate that the average Canadian requires at least 4.3 hectares of land to support present consumption levels, including 2.3 hectares for assimilation of carbon dioxide. The 1991 population of Vancouver was 472,000 and the city covered an area of 11,400 hectares. The average Canadian also requires 0.7 hectares of marine surface area to meet demand for seafood. Thus, Vancouver's total footprint is:

472,000 x (4.3 hectares + 0.7 hectares)
= 2.36 million hectares

Another way of looking at the footprint is that Vancouver requires more than 200 times its geographic size to support its level of consumption and waste generation. This ratio becomes less dramatic if one considers the Lower Fraser Basin, the watershed that encompasses Vancouver. The basin has a population of 1.78 million, a land area of 555,000 hectares, and an ecological footprint (including marine surface area) of 8.9 million hectares, or 16 times the basin's physical area.

Box 4-1 Vancouver's ecological footprint.
SOURCE: Rees 1997.

Two key concepts underlie ecological footprint analysis. The first is that sustainable development is primarily about whether we use natural capital in a sustainable manner. The developers of the footprint approach prefer a definition known as *strong sustainability:* "Each generation should inherit an adequate per capita stock of natural capital assets no less than the stock of such assets inherited by the previous generation" (Costanza and Daly 1992). Second, they believe in intragenerational global equity, or the "fair earthshare" as they call it. There are an estimated 8.9 billion hectares of ecologically productive land on earth; if this is allocated to the 1995 population of 5.8 billion, then each person's fair earthshare is 1.5 hectares. The implication is that global equity will be served to the extent that individuals alter their consumption and waste habits so that each person's footprint approaches the global average.

The major conclusions that can be drawn from footprint analysis are:

- *Urban "self-sufficiency" is impossible.* A city cannot live off of its physical area. Its residents would be impoverished, starve, or suffocate on their own wastes if they tried to do so.
- *Geographical location does not equal ecological location.* Because no city lives within its geographical means, a city's ecological reach will always be larger than (and will not coincide with) its administrative boundaries.

- *The wealthy have bigger footprints within a city.* In Santiago, Chile, the ecological footprint of the highest income quintile was estimated to be 16 times greater than that of the lowest quintile (Wackernagel 1998).
- *Globalization can increase urban vulnerability.* Footprint analysis demonstrates that cities are dependent on distant sources for food, water, energy, and other resources. This raises a city's vulnerability to global climate change, trade restraints, competition, and price fluctuations.
- *Urban form and technology choice have important environmental impacts.* Increased urban density (high-rise apartments instead of single-family homes) reduces the footprint components associated with housing type and urban transportation by 40 percent (Walker 1995).
- *Cities create ecological benefits, as well as costs.* Cities incorporate economies of scale that reduce the cost per capita of providing services and infrastructure as well as collecting and recycling or treating wastes. Higher population density reduces per capita demand for residential land.

The strengths of the footprint method lie in its measurability. The approach allows one to quantify a particular definition of sustainable development. Once a city's footprint has been measured, it can be compared with those of similar cities to identify differences and their causes. A city's footprint can also be regularly drawn and compared over time to determine whether it is growing on a per capita basis (becoming less sustainable) or shrinking (becoming more sustainable). The components of the footprint can also be examined to determine which are most significant. Policymakers can then focus on

BOX

One option for reducing a city's ecological footprint is to shift from fossil fuels to renewable sources of energy. However, increased reliance on renewables will also increase the footprint of these energy sources if consumption continues at current levels.

Photovoltaics. **The average energy in sunlight in the United States is about 177 watts per square meter. A photovoltaic cell 2 meters on each side would be required to power a single 100-watt light bulb at current levels of conversion efficiency. A huge land surface area would thus be required to meet even a fraction of American energy demand.**

Wood energy. **A moderately well-insulated U.S. house needs about five cords of deadwood for heating in an average winter. In the hardwood forests of the northeastern United States, an acre produces one cord of deadwood on a sustainable basis. So, each house requires about five acres of forest to meet heating needs on a renewable basis. Scaling up to a city level, a 30-story apartment building would need something on the order of 600 acres of forest to meet its heating needs.**

Box 4-2 Urban energy footprints.

Source: Trefil 1994, 107.

reducing those activities, factors, and technologies that are the major contributors to the footprint. See Box 4-2.

First definition of urban sustainability: Cities with relatively lower or decreasing ecological footprints per capita are more sustainable.

The ecological footprint method is hobbled by a number of limitations. It assesses only the natural capital dimension of sustainability, and does not deal directly with economic and social development. Thus, a city's footprint may be small or getting smaller, but its population might also be getting impoverished, less healthy, and less literate. Next, the footprint approach is a snapshot of a situation and does not recognize ecological, technological, and price changes. It is also descriptive: The approach gives us a total surface area—an area used per capita and the ratio of urban area to total ecological use area—but it does not tell us what to do. Finally, the approach has some methodological weaknesses. Only one type of land use for waste products is typically calculated as part of the footprint (land area required as a CO_2 sink) so the calculation probably underestimates reality. Also, the magnitude of the ratio of city size to ecological use area can be misleading. The Vancouver ratio of 1 to 200 (Box 4-1) is cause for concern; casting a wider net by using the Lower Fraser Basin yields a perhaps less worrisome ratio of 1 to 16.

Sustaining the Production of Wealth

Traditional measures of urban development have focused on assessing and comparing flows of produced assets. *Produced assets* are the goods and services created by a geographical unit, such as a city, usually over the course of a year. By this measure, cities with higher per capita incomes were classified as more developed. This measurable but simplistic indicator of development has been criticized for several reasons:

- *Counting "goods" and "bads" equally.* Both positive goods and services as well as negative ones (e.g., cleaning up a polluted river, responding to crime, or repairing people and vehicles after car crashes) are counted and contribute to income growth.

- *Disregarding equity.* An economy can appear to be healthy according to GDP growth but this "progress" may be at the expense of the poor getting poorer. GDP is distribution-neutral, yielding no information about the critical issues of equity and poverty.
- *Ignoring changes in natural capital.* Traditional calculations of domestic product do not value changes in the stock of natural resources (e.g., from depletion or new discoveries).
- *Not accounting for changes in human resources.* An economy's present and future productivity is intrinsically related to the quality of its human resource base, but this is not reflected in the flow calculations of produced assets.
- *Failing to value noncountable economic activities.* Domestic product calculations like GDP are based on available statistics and usually do not account for potentially important economic activities like goods and services produced by the informal sector, volunteer work, and household labor.

Figure 4-2 New York City: Wealthy but with a big footprint.

At the national level, there have been attempts to correct some of these problems by developing "green" macroeconomic accounts that value natural capital and remove negatives such as the costs of pollution; using purchasing power parity (PPP) to better reflect the true value of local currencies; and incorporating estimates of the economic contribution of the informal sector.

Most recently, the World Bank has developed a broader measure of wealth that improves on the classic calculation of domestic product. *Wealth* is defined as the sum of an economy's produced assets, natural capital, and human resources. These individual components are defined as follows:

- *Produced assets.* Human-made capital is calculated using the perpetual inventory model (initial capital stock plus gross domestic investment less depreciation). All produced assets, except machinery and equipment, are valued using PPP exchange rates.
- *Natural capital.* International market prices, adjusted to represent the rent portion of the traded price, are used to value a subset of natural capital that consists of agricultural land, pasture lands, forests, protected areas, metals and minerals, and coal, oil, and natural gas. Nonrenewable resources are priced in present-value terms using a 4 percent discount rate.
- *Human resources.* This is the most difficult component to estimate. A calculation is used to estimate the returns to human resources, produced assets, and urban land with a given population or age distribution and the current labor force. This is a proxy that helps reflect the economic consequences of investments in health, education, and nutrition.

To date, this new methodology has been applied to national economies (World Bank 1997). Results of the wealth per capita calculation, on a regional basis, are presented in Table 4-1.

Table 4-1 Wealth per Capita by Region, 1994

Region	Total wealth* (U.S.$/capita)	Human resources (U.S.$/capita)	Produced assets (U.S.$/capita)	Natural capital (U.S.$/capita)
North America	326,000	249,000	62,000	16,000
Pacific OECD	302,000	205,000	90,000	8,000
Western Europe	237,000	177,000	55,000	6,000
Middle East	150,000	65,000	27,000	58,000
South America	95,000	70,000	16,000	9,000
North Africa	55,000	38,000	14,000	3,000
Central America	52,000	41,000	8,000	3,000
Caribbean	48,000	33,000	10,000	5,000
East Asia	47,000	36,000	7,000	4,000
E/Southern Africa	30,000	20,000	7,000	3,000
West Africa	22,000	13,000	4,000	5,000
South Asia	22,000	14,000	4,000	4,000

* Totals may not add up due to rounding errors.

SOURCE: World Bank 1997.

A number of lessons have been learned in the course of developing and applying this new measurement of wealth:

- Human resources are the single largest component of wealth, accounting for between 40 and almost 80 percent of the total in all regions.
- Investments in produced assets are a necessary part of expanding wealth, but there must be simultaneous investment in human capital.
- Natural capital is important regionally, comprising more than 10 percent of total wealth in the Caribbean, East and Southern Africa, the Middle East, South Asia, and West Africa.
- Natural resources are particularly important in low-income countries, making resource and environmental management an important part of development.

These conclusions underlie a new paradigm of economic development that emphasizes investment in human resources and environmental management, along with growth in produced assets.

The main strength of the wealth approach is that it can be used to develop a measurable definition of sustainable development: *Wealth per capita should be the same, if not larger, from generation to generation* (*or from year to year*) (Serageldin 1996). Methodologically, the wealth approach overcomes some of the key drawbacks of assessing economic progress based on measurements of per capita income: (1) The value of the stock of natural capital is incorporated; (2) the contribution of human capital is recognized; and (3) the more accurate PPP exchange rate is used where appropriate.

On the negative side, the wealth approach is very much a work in progress that has not yet been applied to calculate the wealth of cities. Some of the weaknesses of the approach are: (1) Data limitations prevent all natural capital from being valued; (2) "bads" such as defensive and preventive environmental expenditures are still counted as part of produced assets; and (3) the problems of equity and noncountable economic activity are not solved. A conceptual difficulty would be how to assess a city's share of national natural capital. This could be overcome by using the city/national ratio of produced assets as the percentage of natural capital linked to a particular city. Or, one could assess the value of natural capital used by a city through the ecological footprint approach.

Second definition of urban sustainability: Cities that create nondeclining wealth per capita are on a sustainable path.

Efforts to measure developmental sustainability have concluded that one must move beyond the traditional assessment of produced assets (GDP per capita) to include valuations of both natural and human capital. This approach, currently being applied at the country level, yields a broad view of a nation's wealth instead of only its income. It can help explain why two countries with similar endowments of natural capital may have very different growth paths and levels of well-being, and have quite different levels of overall environmental quality. And it can be used to determine whether a country is moving toward or away from a sustainable development path.

Reducing Key Environmental Impacts

A third conceptual approach for assessing the sustainability of cities has been developed by a longtime observer of the urban environment, David Satterthwaite of the International Institute for Environment and Development. He argues that cities by themselves cannot be sustainable, but that their pattern of development has an impact on the overall sustainability of development. A framework is then needed that can be used to assess the environmental performance of cities as an overall measure of their contribution to sustainable development.

Satterthwaite's framework consists of five broad categories of environmental action for gauging urban environmental performance:

1. *Controlling infectious and parasitic diseases.* These include gastrointestinal illnesses linked to inadequate water supply, sanitation, drainage, and waste collection; acute respiratory infections and tuberculosis from air pollution and overcrowding; and the various diseases transmitted by insect and animal vectors.

2. *Reducing chemical and physical hazards.* This involves natural and human-induced risks that affect people in the household, at the workplace, and throughout the city.
3. *Achieving a high-quality urban environment.* This is defined as the amount and quality of open space per person, and the degree to which natural and cultural heritage are protected.
4. *Minimizing the transfer of environmental costs.* These are the external costs of pollution from both resource use and waste disposal that affect people and ecosystems surrounding a city.
5. *Moving toward sustainable consumption.* This means ensuring that the city's consumption of goods and services minimizes environmental impacts on natural capital and present as well as future generations (e.g., through use of clean technologies, renewable resources, and recycling).

These categories fit within a modified version of the Brundtland Commission's definition of sustainable development: *meet-*

Figure 4-3 Improving sanitation in Accra, Ghana.

ing the needs of the present without compromising the ability of future generations to meet their own needs. The first three categories concern environmental activities that affect the ability of urban residents to meet their needs and take place within city boundaries. The last two involve environmental effects that affect present as well as future generations and occur beyond the city's jurisdiction. Cities that contribute to sustainable development should "ensure that the needs of the people within their boundaries are addressed while minimizing the transferring of environmental costs to other people or ecosystems or into the future" (Satterthwaite 1997, 1682).

Data can be collected for each of the five categories. This might include mortality and morbidity rates for environmental health problems; health and economic costs of natural and human-induced hazards; green space per capita; extraurban impacts of gaseous, liquid, and solid wastes; and rates of resource recovery. Such information can then be compared with that from other cities, regions, and nations, or from one year to the next for the same city. Then, a judgment can be made as to whether an urban area's aggregate environmental performance is following a more or less sustainable path.

The central conclusions that Satterthwaite draws from this approach are:

- The first three categories are part of the urban "sanitary revolution" that began in Europe and North America in the nineteenth century, and which persists today in many lower-income cities.
- Jurisdictional problems normally arise when assessing and responding to the problem of transfer of environmental costs.
- National and international action will probably be required to encourage urban residents to adopt more sustainable consumption habits.
- The documents emanating from the 1996 Habitat II Conference do not provide clear guidance for pursuing sustainable development at the city level because they contain few specific actions relating to the categories listed above.

QUOTES

A sustainable city is one in which its people and businesses continuously endeavor to improve their natural, built and cultural environments at neighborhood and regional levels, whilst working in ways which always support the goal of global sustainable development (Haughton and Hunter 1994, 27).

The strengths of Satterthwaite's approach are that (1) it focuses on tangible problem areas where measurements can be developed, options identified, and actions taken; (2) it differentiates between those issues that can be primarily resolved by stakeholders within a city (the first three categories) and those that involve stakeholders beyond the city's borders (the last two categories); (3) it distinguishes between the types of environmental issues faced by poorer cities (conceivably all five categories) and those of primary concern to more developed cities (primarily the latter two); and (4) it recognizes the interrelated importance of human health, natural capital, and economic well-being.

The major drawback of this approach is that it does not recommend a process or planning and managerial strategy that can be used to assess and address urban sustainability issues. Also, Satterthwaite does not recommend a set of measures or indicators to evaluate each of the five categories. However, these can be derived from other sources. The most problematic category in this regard is sustainable consumption, which probably requires further definition before it can be quantified for measurement.

Common Ground and Common Challenges

The previously described perspectives on urbanization and sustainable development may seem confusing, but there is some rich common ground. First, an entirely sustainable city (i.e., one that is self-sufficient) cannot exist, but cities do have important impacts on the sustainability of regional, national, and even international environments. Urban development itself will be more sustainable if stakeholders within and outside cities address the basic needs of city dwellers, such as health and quality living space; conserve and recycle materials and nutrients; use natural resources more efficiently; and invest in people through education and training. Finally, the "think globally, act locally" slogan should apply. As Haughton and Hunter's definition suggests, urban development should take place within the context of global sustainability.

BOX

The Land Plan Committee of Davidson, North Carolina, decided to pursue sustainable development as the growth option guiding preparation of its land use plan in 1994. However, they did not adopt any of the three definitions cited in this chapter, let alone others available in the literature. Rather, the committee voted to adopt neotraditional planning as their interpretation of urban sustainability, as opposed to business-as-usual and no-growth scenarios. The principles of sustainability thus became: "to retain Davidson's small-town character" and to "preserve the quality of life."

SCENARIO	MODEL AND ATTRIBUTES
Status quo	Suburban sprawl: low-density residential; auto-oriented design; rigid separation of uses; neglect of public space; population of 13,000 to 23,000 people
Sustainable	Traditional town: mix of densities; human-scaled design; integration of uses; emphasis on public space; connected streets; population of 15,000 to 23,000 people
No growth	Rural: low rural densities; rural character; emphasis on open space; population of 7500 to 10,000 people

This misinterpretation resulted in a focus on the nature and shape of growth; for example, maintaining a vibrant town center, preserving open space within and near the town, and limiting disruptive road development. The conflation of neotraditional planning and sustainable development caused the plan to avoid some of the key issues of urban sustainability: resource use, waste generation, human and ecosystem health, public awareness and participation, global environmental impacts, and indicators of sustainability.

Box 4-3 Urban sustainability open to misinterpretation.

SOURCE: Thomas and Furuseth 1997

This common ground should not be ignored. Settlements that seek to contribute to sustainable development may be seduced by the term but unconsciously or purposefully may imbue it with their own definition—which can have little to do with sustainability. An example of this is provided in Box 4-3. Misinterpretations of urban sustainability run the risk of ignoring key issues such as human and ecosystem health, resource use, waste management, global environmental impacts, public awareness and participation, and indicators of sustainability.

Applying Definitions of Urban Sustainability to Case Studies

Case studies are briefly presented here for Las Vegas, Nevada, and Mexico City, Mexico. Each case contains information from one source that has been reorganized according to the framework in Chapter 3: urban dynamics, special features of the urban environment, and key problems. Then, the three definitions of urban sustainability are applied to each case to assess whether the urban area is more or less sustainable environmentally. The results for these particular cases are negative. More positive urban examples are presented in later chapters, particularly in Chapter 9 on good managerial practice.

Las Vegas, Nevada*

URBAN DYNAMICS

Las Vegas is one of the fastest-growing metropolitan areas in the United States. Economically, the city has generated tens of thousands of new jobs in gambling, construction, and related services. Demographically, the city is located in Clark County, whose population surpassed one million in 1995 and is expected to grow by another million over the next generation. Nearly one thousand new residents arrive in the city each week. They consist mainly of three groups: (1) blue-collar families; (2) young Latinos; and (3) wealthy retirees. The first two groups seek to participate in the city's economic boom. The retirees are looking for a healthy climate and a tranquil suburban lifestyle.

Land use in Las Vegas is characterized by sprawl and "leap-frog" development. Population density is low; single-family housing predominates; large suburban developments are connected only by automobiles; and vacant urban space is not filled in but instead "leapt over" so that the next desirable plot of land further from the center is developed. Also, little space is devoted to parks and recreation. Las Vegas has 1.4 acres of park space per 1000 residents, compared to a recommended U.S. minimum of 10 acres. Finally, individual houses as well as hotel develop-

*SOURCE: Davis 1995.

ments usually have green lawns, swimming pools, and air conditioning, resulting in increased consumption of water and energy resources.

SPECIAL FEATURES OF THE URBAN ENVIRONMENT

The two most significant features of Las Vegas' environment are its surrounding ecosystem and its institutional setting. The city is located in a desert basin that receives just 10 centimeters of rain per year. In dramatic contrast to this meager supply is the city's daily water consumption of 360 gallons (1260 liters) per person, which requires the equivalent of another 50 to 75 centimeters for the irrigation of lawns and golf courses, and the creation of artificial lakes and lagoons. This consumption is profligate, even in comparison to other thirsty arid cities like Los Angeles (211 gallons or 740 liters per day per person) and Tucson (160 gallons or 560 liters per day per person). The city long ago outstripped its water resource base; it now augments its supply by overdrawing groundwater resources, purchasing water from Arizona farmers, obtaining water from ranchers in other Nevada counties, and diverting water from the Virgin River (a tributary of the Colorado).

Third definition of urban sustainability: *Cities that reduce health risks, minimize pollution, and maximize use of renewable resources contribute more to overall sustainable development.*

Institutionally, environmental management is hampered by jurisdictional problems. Local government is fragmented, with only one-third of the metropolitan population living within the Las Vegas city limits. Moreover, many of the city's potential sources of revenue—its casinos, convention center, university, and international airport—are located in an unincorporated area that does not contribute tax revenues to the management of Las Vegas' problems. Politically, the gambling industry provides contributions to elected officials who support the city's continued growth, with its implied resource consumption patterns. Finally, the lifestyle pursued by most key actors, espe-

QUOTES

RISING CO_2 LEVELS COULD HELP NEVADA RANCHING, GOLF AND LANDSCAPING INDUSTRIES

. . . But in the long run, the greenhouse effect would be bad for business by wiping out the environment.

—(Headline in the *Las Vegas Business Press*)

cially consumers, has a high environmental impact. Land use patterns and consumer preference result in the lowest vehicle occupancy rate in the country and the longest per person, per trip, per day ratio. As indicated previously, residential preferences result in dwellings that are water- and energy-intensive.

KEY ENVIRONMENTAL PROBLEMS

Las Vegas suffers from environmental problems linked to its patterns of water and energy resource consumption. Overextraction of groundwater has resulted in land subsidence that results in damage to public infrastructure and private property. The growing search for a water supply outside the Las Vegas desert basin has brought the metropolitan area into increasing conflict with farmers and ranchers over water resource use. Impermeabilization that comes with urban sprawl and road development has increased the problem of flash flooding.

Energy consumption patterns create local and regional environmental problems. Land use patterns and consumer preferences result in heavy automobile use, congestion, and subsequent air pollution. Las Vegas tied with New York City for fifth place in CO pollution. Regionally, its smog contributes to pollution of the Grand Canyon and is beginning to reduce visibility in California's East Mojave National Recreation Area. The city's waste heat, primarily from universal air conditioning and vehicular emissions, creates nighttime temperatures that are 5 to 10°F hotter than in the surrounding desert. Electricity consumption also contributes to regional pollution: Air pollution is generated from the Mojave Power Plant that is fed by a slurry of water and coal resources pumped from the Hopi mesas hundreds of miles to the east.

IS LAS VEGAS SUSTAINABLE?

According to our first definition, Las Vegas undoubtedly has a large ecological footprint that is growing even bigger. The nature and style of housing development continue to promote excessive energy and water resource use. There do not seem to be efforts to conserve these resources; in fact, water consumption has been subsidized. Moreover, despite its high water use, the Las Vegas area produces very little of the food that it consumes. As its population expands, this component of the ecological footprint will only increase. Thus, the city is pursuing an unsustainable development path because of factors that cause its footprint to grow.

Sustainability rating: Two thumbs down

Not enough information is available to yield a clear conclusion from applying the second definition. The produced assets component of wealth appears to be increasing on a per capita basis. However, consumption patterns in Las Vegas seem to be reducing the present value of the stock of natural capital, as the city's high demand for electricity is partially met by a nonrenewable resource (coal), and high levels of water consumption are resulting in degradation of renewable surface and groundwater resources. The status of human resource development is not known. Thus, more information is required to assess whether wealth in Las Vegas is nondeclining on a per capita basis.

Las Vegas has a mixed record in addressing the third definition's critical urban environmental problem areas. Like most U.S. cities, it has successfully reduced the incidence of infectious and parasitic diseases (though these are low to begin with in desert ecosystems), and has minimized chemical and physical hazards in homes, workplaces, and citywide, except for the problem of flash flooding. The low availability of public park and recreational space indicates a failure to improve quality of life. Rather than minimizing the transfer of environmental costs to surrounding ecosystems and people, it has accelerated this transfer (e.g., to ranchers and farmers, parks in Arizona and California, coal mines in the Hopi mesas, and watersheds outside of the desert basin). Finally, little progress has been made toward sustainable consumption, as renewable resources and clean technologies do not play a major role in the city's energy, water, and space-cooling regimes. By the third definition, then, Las Vegas is not a source of support for overall sustainable development.

Mexico City, Mexico*

URBAN DYNAMICS

Mexico City is one of the world's largest urban agglomerations, with a metropolitan population of 20 million projected for the year 2000. Demographically, the city grew rapidly between 1950 and 1980, with an overall annual population growth of 4.8 percent and a very high 13.6 percent in its chief industrial zone. Growth slowed to 1.8 percent annually between 1980 and 1990. Economically, the Mexico City basin holds 50 percent of Mexico's industries, and the 20 percent of the country's population that resides there accounts for one-third of the nation's oil and electricity consumption.

Land use has resulted in relatively high-density development (three times the density of Paris and four times that of London); only a handful of Asian cities have higher population densities. New, often illegal settlements are more dense, less planned, and have less open space than do the pre-1950 urban neighborhoods. Hillside settlements are particularly problematic, as they contribute to soil erosion, excess runoff, and flash flooding. Fertile agricultural and grazing land have steadily been converted to built-up areas.

SPECIAL FEATURES OF THE URBAN ENVIRONMENT

Mexico City's ecosystem features, institutional issues, aspects of local environmental policy, and status of the poor are all important characteristics of its urban environment. The city is located on a closed hydrological basin which was a lake bed that was drained in the 1600s. It is also a mountainous basin surrounded by volcanos; the city's average altitude is 2240 m above sea level. Mexico City can also be classified as a riverine ecosystem (wastewater from a hydropower dam drains into the city's river system) and a cold weather ecosystem (winter air pollution is intensified due to a thermal inversion).

Institutionally, the metropolitan area encompasses a federal district and 26 municipalities, and it cuts across four states. Sectorally, some environmental issues are fragmented; for example,

*Sources: Ezcurra and Mazari-Hiriart 1996; Pezzoli 1998.

authority for water management is divided between local, state, and federal water authorities and the Secretariat of Health. Other issues are more clear-cut; for instance, air pollution control is the responsibility of a Metropolitan Commission for the Protection of Air Quality that involves local, state, and federal agencies. Politically, Mexico City has long been the administrative and political center of the country, so its residents have enjoyed a privileged status regarding resource consumption.

This privileged status is reflected in one aspect of local environmental policy—subsidies. The government spends around $450 million to supply water to Mexico City, but receives only $42 million in annual revenues from the sale of water. The metro system, used by about four million passengers per day, costs about $2 million to operate each day but generates daily revenues of only $280,000. Electricity, gas, solid waste collection, and road maintenance are subsidized throughout the country, but because Mexico City receives these services in a higher proportion than the rest of the country, it gets a higher share of the subsidy. Privilege, though, does not necessarily mean greater awareness about environmental conditions: Water quality is regularly monitored but the results are not publicized and there is no evaluation of health risks from industrial wastes in the city.

Environmental quality can be disproportionately worse for lower-income groups in Mexico City. Exposure to certain air pollutants is worse in the poorer southwestern area (ozone) and the industrial areas of the north and northeast (sulfur dioxide and particulates). Access to urban infrastructure and services is lower and less reliable in newer and poorer settlements. In terms of open space, the working class eastern area of the city has experienced the greatest loss; wealthy areas enjoy more than 10 m^3 per capita of green space while the industrial area of Azcapotzalco (population 700,000) has only 0.9 m^3 per capita.

KEY ENVIRONMENTAL PROBLEMS

Mexico City's three critical urban environmental problems are water resource management, water quality and sanitation, and air pollution. Over two-thirds of the city's water supply comes from surface and groundwater in the basin. Overextraction of groundwater has caused land subsidence averaging 6 cm per year in the central area and 15 to 40 cm per year in peripheral areas. The remaining supply comes from interbasin water transfer that results in degradation of the supplying basins and high energy costs for water pumping. In 1990, daily water consumption was 320 liters per capita, which is greater than in many European cities. A quarter of the water supply is lost due to leaking pipes.

The city suffers from a number of water quality and sanitation problems. Overextraction of groundwater has accelerated aquifer pollution from traditional sources such as polluted lakes and leachates from waste dumps. Much of the basin's surface water is polluted or at risk of being degraded. The lowered water table, combined with pollution of water canals, has damaged traditional agricultural production. Inadequate sanitation has contributed to both groundwater and soil contamination. Only 7 percent of the city's domestic and industrial wastewater is treated. The remainder flows to reservoirs, where some is used for irrigation or to generate electricity. Ultimately, the wastewater ends up in the Gulf of Mexico via the Tula-Moctezuma-Panuco river system.

The health care costs and productivity losses associated with air pollution in Mexico City are estimated at $1.1 billion per year. Transportation is the main source of air pollution in Mexico City. In recent years, the vehicle fleet has grown at 5 percent annually, more than double the population growth rate. Efforts to solve one air pollution problem (lead in gasoline) ended up worsening another (the level of ozone). Between 1991 and 1994, ozone concentrations exceeded air quality standards more than 90 percent of the time. Acid rain from urban air pollution has damaged forests in the mountains surrounding the basin and accelerated the deterioration of water quantity and quality in the watershed.

IS MEXICO CITY SUSTAINABLE?

Mexico City's ecological footprint appears to be large and growing. This metropolitan area consumes more water per capita than more developed cities in Europe; a third of the water comes from outside the city's watershed; and consumption is subsidized. Agricultural land is being converted to built-up areas, so less food is being produced within the basin, requiring more land from outside the city's immediate hinterland. Increasing air pollution from the city's growing vehicle fleet and burgeoning industries requires more land for absorbing greenhouse gases. Thus, with a growing ecological footprint, Mexico City is on an unsustainable development path.

Applying the wealth-centered definition of sustainability yields inconclusive results. Produced assets per capita have been increasing in the metropolitan area. Mexico City has probably had a negative impact on the present value of natural capital. Overextraction of groundwater has degraded what was once a renewable resource. Accelerating consumption of electricity and fuel for transportation has contributed to reducing Mexico's stock of oil resources. Air pollution has had some limited impact on the stock of forest resources. The case study does not provide information on how the human resource component of wealth has fared, but air pollution has had a negative impact on human health and productivity.

The critical environmental problem approach to sustainability also yields mixed results. In terms of infections and parasitic diseases, the top three causes of death in Mexico City in the 1950s were gastroenteritis, influenza/pneumonia, and early childhood diseases. Thirty years later, the city had gone through a partial health transition, with heart disease and accidents occupying first and second place; influenza/pneumonia had fallen to third. It is unclear whether chemical and physical hazards have been minimized. For example, exposure to lead was reduced, but the hazard of ozone pollution increased. Quality of life has probably decreased if one considers declining park and recreational space per capita. Environmental costs have been transferred to surrounding people and ecosystems, rather than minimized: for example, degradation related to interbasin water transfers, wastewater pollution ending in the Gulf of Mexico, subsidies paid for by the rest of the country for the capital's resource consumption. These subsidies inhibit renewable resource consumption, but some progress has been made to introduce clean technologies in industries and the transportation system. On balance, these mixed results weigh more heavily toward an unsustainable pattern of urban development.

Sustainability rating: One and a half thumbs down

Are Cities Sustainable?

The relatively recent concern with urban sustainability can be traced to two roots: the notion that there are limits to urban growth, and the application of the carrying capacity concept. The former stems from concern in the 1960s and 1970s that rapid urban growth, particularly in the increasing number of Third World megacities, had natural limits. This, in turn, came from earlier thinking that each city has an optimal size. The latter comes from ecological science (see Chapter 2) and implies that cities can cross a threshold, exceed the capacity of their surrounding environment to supply critical resources and/or absorb wastes, and then become unsustainable.

What, indeed, are the environmental and other limits to growth that might render a city unsustainable or even condemn it to extinction? The environmental limits to urban development are geographical constraints, resource limits, and natural disasters. Other limits are political constraints and human-induced disasters. A brief run through history will suggest that these factors can limit urban growth, but only on rare occasions.

Figure 4-4 The ghost city of Fatipur Sikhri, India.

Figure 4-5 The lost city of Tikal, Guatemala.

Geographically, physical features may prevent a city from expanding outward. Typical constraints are valleys, mountain ranges, and bodies of water. From our case studies, Mexico City is located in a volcanic basin that delimits its ultimate physical size. Las Vegas, on the other hand, is surrounded by open desert. Singapore is located on an island, so its size is finite (see case study in Chapter 9). However, these physical limitations have not posed constraints on population size. When cities confront such limits, they usually build up instead of out, and population densities increase.

Water, air, food, energy, and minerals are natural resource constraints that can affect urban development. There are scattered examples of changes in water supply that have seriously disrupted cities. Ur, located on the Euphrates River in what is now Iraq, was dependent on its river-fed irrigation system. Some time after the Persian conquest, the Euphrates' main channel shifted 16 km east, and the city was abandoned (Trefil 1994). The city of Fatipur Sikhri was constructed near the Taj Mahal in India on a limited water supply. It had to be evacuated less than two decades after it was built when the water dried up. These are striking but rare examples. The ability of the air to absorb urban pollution can also be a limiting factor. The killer fogs of London in the 1950s resulted in many deaths and caused some people to abandon the city. Numerous cities have been decimated by famine or subject to energy shortages. However, in all but the most extreme of these cases, cities overcome resource challenges in a number of ways:

- *Water supply.* When local sources are depleted, cities find other, costlier sources of supply (e.g., from other water basins, from deeper aquifers, or by conserving and reusing water).
- *Water quality.* Similarly, when local waterways become polluted, cities seek cleaner but more expensive sources of supply and/or invest in cleaning up.
- *Air quality.* When air quality becomes intolerable, pollution control measures are introduced. Industries are relocated; a switch is made from more- to less-polluting fuels; and constraints are placed on polluting activities.

Figure 4-6 Antigua, Guatemala: Decimated and rebuilt.

- *Food.* Famine may be less likely to affect cities than the countryside. Urban areas, because of their wealth and political clout, can often (but not always) ensure a regular supply of food.
- *Energy.* As with water, cities may have to look farther afield and pay a higher price in times of energy scarcity. Availability is usually achieved through conservation, fuel substitution, technological change, development of new sources, and paying a higher price for existing energy sources.
- *Minerals.* When critical minerals are in short supply, users find ways to conserve, recycle, use alternative technologies, or employ substitute materials that are more available.

So, cities have coping mechanisms that prevent breaches of carrying capacity from sounding their death knell.

Natural disasters can also affect urban sustainability. In the extreme, the eruption of Mount Vesuvius in 79 A.D. rendered Pompeii uninhabitable. On the island of Martinique, the 1902 eruption of Mount Pelee killed 30,000 and left only 10 survivors in the town of Saint Pierre. Most recently, the Soufriere eruption in Montserrat led to the permanent evacuation of the town of Plymouth. These are dramatic examples, but relatively rare events. The reaction to earthquakes and floods is more typical: A devastating natural disaster occurs; part or all of a city is destroyed; and then rebuilding begins (rightly or wrongly), often by taking precautions against future disasters. Box 4-4 provides an example of how natural disasters and resource constraints affected an ancient predecessor of Mexico City.

BOX

Teotihuacan, a predecessor of Mexico City, had about 30,000 residents in 100 A.D. At about the same time, the neighboring city of Cuicuilco was devastated by the eruption of the Xitle volcano, which buried the region's best agricultural soil under a large lava flow. This disaster helped Teotihuacan flourish as an important commercial and trading center. By 650 A.D., its population had risen to 150,000, but less than a century later, it collapsed to under 10,000. Around 750 A.D., the city was looted and burned, leading to its demise. Some scholars say this decline was due to exhaustion of natural resources.

Teotihuacan was located in a fertile alluvial plain in a valley that was suitable for irrigated agriculture. However, as the city grew, food had to be imported from other growing areas and paid for with local resources such as obsidian. Obsidian's value came from its hard, sharp cutting edge. However, local deposits began to run out after 500 A.D. In addition, local hillsides were being deforested (ironically, using obsidian axes). This caused soil erosion, moisture loss, and declining agricultural productivity. Thus, a natural disaster contributed to Teotihuacan's growth, while mineral and food shortages eventually accelerated the city's collapse.

Box 4-4 Environmental factors in the rise and fall of Teotihuacan.

SOURCES: Ezcurra and Mazari-Hiriart 1996; Girardet 1996.

There are political factors and human-induced constraints on urban sustainability. Political boundaries may prevent a city from physically expanding, as was the case with Hong Kong until 1998. The colony's response was to build upward instead of to sprawl. Antiurban policies may lead to urban decline. In the 1970s, the Pol Pot regime forcibly depopulated Cambodia's capital of Phnom Penh. During the same decade, the government of Tanzania limited investment in urban infrastructure and services, leading to reduced economic and population growth in Dar es Salaam. Finally, there have been political limits on freedom of movement that have affected urban development. In China and in apartheid South Africa, migration to select urban areas was legally constrained. However, almost all of these policies have had finite lifetimes, and urbanization has proceeded.

Lastly, human-induced disasters can make cities unsustainable. The most extreme of such disasters is war. Carthage was razed by the Romans at the end of the Punic Wars in 146 B.C. and never rebuilt. Angkor Wat was sacked by the Siamese army in 1431 and never recovered. World War II saw the near-

Figure 4-7 War and the ruins of Carthage, Tunisia.

complete destruction of several cities: Hiroshima, Nagasaki, and Dresden. Fire has also been a major threat to urban sustainability: Cities from Chicago to Istanbul to Tokyo have seen their urban cores destroyed due to fires from human causes. Yet, more often than not, cities devastated by such disasters are gradually or quickly rebuilt; Carthage and Angkor Wat are among the exceptions.

The Case for Urban Environmental Planning and Management

The key question is not *whether* cities can be sustained, but *how are they* being sustained? Urbanization will proceed, and cities will increasingly be the predominant source of national wealth for most countries around the world. This does not mean that cities will necessarily make positive contributions to sustainable national and global development or that life will be good for urban dwellers. Active intervention is needed to reduce the environmental impact of urban areas, improve the health of residents, and increase economic productivity while lowering the incidence of poverty.

Our definitions of urban sustainability suggest that action is needed in several areas. The first definition implies that cities should reduce their ecological footprint if they are to be more successful partners in sustainable development. The second definition points to prudent management of scarce resources, investment in human capital, and increased economic productivity as keys to sustaining urban wealth. The third definition calls for action to improve environmental health, reduce pollution, and conserve resources. However, these will not be achieved automatically.

Evidence and projections indicate that well-planned and managed interventions can make an important different in the quality of urban life. The sanitation revolution in nineteenth-century Europe contributed greatly to both increased lifespans and improved quality of urban life. Chapter 3 noted that a significant amount of death and disease could be avoided by

BOX

Clean drinking water and adequate sanitation have always been critically linked to environmental health in cities. In addition, water supply has been important for combating urban fires. However, nineteenth-century North American cities were reluctant to supply water and sanitation until after disaster had struck.

Philadelphia decided to construct a public water supply system after an outbreak of yellow fever in 1801. While yellow fever is not a waterborne disease, the logic was that the disease was linked to heaps of garbage and sewage in the streets, which could best be cleaned by flushing them away with water.

In New York City, the disasters that spurred action were a cholera outbreak in 1832 that killed 3500 people and forced 100,000 to leave the city, and a fire that destroyed the core of the city three years later and bankrupted many insurance companies with the ensuing claims.

In both cases, the response was too late and rather modest. Early engineers calculated daily demand on the basis of 20 gallons (75 liters) per capita, or just a tenth of what is assumed in today's industrialized cities.

Box 4-5 The role of disasters in nineteenth-century cities.

SOURCE: White 1994, 121.

improving urban environmental quality. In Chapter 1, some of the economic costs of environmental problems in cities were listed; these could be turned into benefits if such problems were avoided or resolved. Projections show that with a moderate level of investment in planning and managerial interventions, Chinese cities could reduce the cost of air pollution as a percentage of urban income from 23 percent in 1995 to about 10 percent in 2020 (World Bank 1997).

Despite this evidence, more often than not cities do not experience a major incentive to act on urban environmental problems until *after* a disaster occurs (see Box 4-5). This reactive approach to the urban environment usually exacts a heavy toll in human lives, suffering, property damage, economic productivity, and ecosystem functioning. An alternative approach is called for that identifies and prioritizes critical environmental problems in cities; involves stakeholders to develop and rank solutions; and results in implementation of policies, programs, and projects to manage the urban environment. This alternative framework is further developed in the following chapter. Thus, urban environmental planning and management is a more humane route to sustainable development than the disastrous alternative.

Resources and Exercises for Further Thought

Resources

The references cited for the three different approaches to urban sustainability are the major resources for this chapter.

Exercises for Further Thought

1. Calculate the ecological footprint of a city or a region. Compare the results with similar cities or regions and draw conclusions about how the area is developing.
2. Estimate a city's annual production of wealth (produced assets, natural capital base, and human resources). Compare the results with similar cities, regions, or national wealth per capita and draw conclusions about how the area is developing.
3. Assess a city's contribution to sustainable development according to Satterthwaite's key environmental impacts. Compare the results with similar cities and draw conclusions about how the city is developing.
4. If Las Vegas and Mexico City receive such negative ratings according to the three definitions of urban sustainability, why do people keep moving to them?
5. Why do disasters provoke urban environmental interventions?

References

Costanza, Robert, and Herman Daly. 1992. Natural capital and sustainable development. *Conservation Biology* 1: 37–45.

Davis, Mike. 1995. House of cards. *Sierra*. November/December.

Ezcurra, Exequiel, and Marisa Mazari-Hiriart. 1996. Are megacities viable? A cautionary tale from Mexico City. *Environment*. January/February.

Girardet, Herbert. 1996. *The Gaia atlas of cities: New directions for sustainable urban living*. London: Gaia Books, Ltd.

Haughton, Graham, and Colin Hunter. 1994. *Sustainable cities*. London: Jessica Kingsley Publishers, Ltd.

Pezzoli, Keith. 1998. *Human settlements and planning for ecological sustainability: The case of Mexico City*. Cambridge: MIT Press.

Rees, William. 1997. Urban ecosystems: The human dimension. *Urban Ecosystems* 1: 63–75.

Rees, William, and Mathis Wackernagel. 1996. Urban ecological footprints: Why cities cannot be sustainable—and why they are a key to sustainability. *Environmental Impact Assessment Review* 16: 223–248.

Satterthwaite, David. 1997. Sustainable cities or cities that contribute to sustainable development? *Urban Studies* 34(10): 1667–1691.

Serageldin, Ismail. 1996. Sustainability and the wealth of nations: First steps in an ongoing journey. Environmentally Sustainable Development Studies and Monographs Series No. 5. Washington, D.C.: World Bank.

Thomas, Deborah, and Owen Furuseth. 1997. The realities of incorporating sustainable development into local-level planning: A case study of Davidson, North Carolina. *Cities* 14(4): 219–226.

Trefil, James. 1994. *A scientist in the city.* New York: Doubleday.

Wackernagel, Mathis. 1998. The ecological footprint of Santiago de Chile. *Local Environment* 3(1): 7–19.

Wackernagel, Mathis, and William Rees. 1995. *Our ecological footprint: Reducing human impact on the earth.* Gabriola Island, British Columbia, and Philadelphia: New Society Publishers.

Walker, L. 1995. The influence of dwelling type and residential density on the appropriated carrying capacity of Canadian households. Unpublished M.Sc. thesis. Vancouver: University of British Columbia School of Community and Regional Planning.

White, Rodney. 1994. *Urban environmental management: Environmental change and urban design.* Chichester: John Wiley & Sons.

World Bank. 1997a. *Can the environment wait? Priorities for East Asia.* Washington, D.C.: World Bank.

———. 1997b. Expanding the measure of wealth: Indicators of environmentally sustainable development. Environmentally Sustainable Development Studies and Monographs Series No. 17. Washington, D.C.: World Bank.

PART

II

PLANNING TO SUSTAIN CITIES

CHAPTER 5

The LEAP: A Framework for Urban Environmental Planning

Styles of Urban Environmental Planning

There are two main styles for integrating environmental concerns into the planning and management of cities: reactive and strategic. Reactive approaches include postdisaster planning and project-specific environmental impact assessments. The strategic approach is more proactive and involves developing and implementing a local environmental action plan (LEAP). This section reviews the main reactive approach for dealing with many urban environmental problems, environmental impact assessment, and argues in favor of a more comprehensive, issue-oriented process of urban environmental planning and management.

Reactive Approaches

Many cities have traditionally used two planning approaches to address their environmental problems. The first is the more unfortunate one—scrambling to catch up after a disaster strikes, as noted in Chapter 4. Though all too common, it is not a *bona fide* type of planning because it is *ex post;* after the situation exists, plans are made to correct what has already occurred or to avoid future reoccurrences. The second approach, environmental impact assessment, is perhaps the most commonly used planning system by both the public and private sectors in cities around the world.

Environmental impact assessment (EIA) is used to identify the potential environmental consequences of a proposed project, policy, or investment program in order to incorporate features with positive environmental effects as well as mitigating measures for negative effects early in the development process. The urban environmental consequences typically covered by EIAs are elaborated, and a generic environmental impact assessment process is described in the following paragraphs.

Developers of urban projects (e.g., land development, water supply, sewerage and other sanitation, drainage, solid waste management, electrification) must be alert to a number of adverse environmental impacts that generally occur when the investments are not properly planned, sited, designed, constructed, operated, and/or maintained. Site selection for *land development* usually involves a number of potential environmental effects, such as changes in soil and slope stability, risk of flooding in low-lying sites, damage to sensitive ecosystems such as wetlands, and conflict with culturally valued land uses. *Water supply* can result in groundwater depletion if the aquifer is tapped; surface water abstraction can affect aquatic and bird life; dam and reservoir construction generally have a range of potentially negative impacts; and increased water consumption will also increase the output of wastewater, which can have negative health effects if unchecked. Some of the potential negative impacts of *sanitation systems* include interference with other utilities, impacts from sludge disposal, subsurface leaching to groundwater, degradation of water quality from overflows or improperly treated sewage, and health and safety hazards associated with sewers (trench cave-in during construction, toxic gas buildup, exposure to pathogens in sewage and sludge). Many of the potentially adverse effects of *solid waste management* have to do with dump or sanitary landfill siting and management: aquifer contamination, improper disposal of hazardous wastes, air pollution from burning wastes, landfill gas migration, subsurface leaching, and landscape degradation. *Drainage* construction can result in displacement and involuntary resettlement of households and, if drains are not maintained and become contaminated with solid and liquid wastes, they can overflow and spread pathogens. *Electrification* at the community and household level poses health and safety risks from improper in-house wiring and collapse of overhead wiring during extreme weather conditions; there may also be upstream impacts, depending on how the power is generated.

Many guides have been written on environmental impact assessment. The process should identify the potential environmental impacts of an investment early in the design stage *and* ways of improving the intervention by preventing, minimizing, mitigating, or compensating for adverse environmental effects. According to World Bank guidelines, a project-specific environmental assessment should cover (1) baseline environmental conditions; (2) potential environmental impacts, both positive and negative, in the area of influence of a project; (3) a systematic environmental comparison of alternative investments, sites, technologies, and designs; (4) preventive, mitigating, and compensatory measures, generally in the form of an environmental mitigation or management plan; (5) recommended environmental management and training; and (6) a proposal for environmental monitoring (World Bank 1991b). Preparation of the assessment should involve representatives of potentially affected groups, and draft findings should be disseminated for public review and comment.

The advantages of this one-off type of EIA are that it allows for early identification of potential conflicts between an intervention, the environment, and society; it can integrate environmental concerns into the design of a project, policy, or program; and it can raise awareness among planners, decision-makers, and beneficiaries about environmental issues. The major drawbacks of relying on EIA as an approach to urban environmental planning are:

- *Reactive and ad hoc:* The EIA process is invoked only when interventions have been proposed for review. Thus, the agenda for study is set by developers of proposals; a particular EIA or set of EIAs do not necessarily address a city's priority environmental problems.
- *Cumulative and interactive effects:* Because the classic EIA deals with one project, policy, or program at a time, it cannot identify or mitigate environmental impacts that accumulate over time due to a series of interventions or that interact at the same time in the same place but originate from different actions.

Figure 5-1 Tunis, Tunisia: In need of an EIA?

- *Upstream and downstream:* The temporal and spatial boundaries of a classic EIA may be too limited to capture all of the environmental impacts of a proposed change. Cities are complex places where one intervention may have important consequences beyond administrative or project borders (upstream and downstream effects) or far into the future.

These limitations make classic EIA an unpromising planning framework for effectively addressing priority environmental concerns in a complex urban setting. Environmental planners have recognized these problems and have developed some alternative approaches to the classic EIA.

Moving Toward a Strategic Approach

Alternatives to the project-specific assessment include (1) a *regional environmental assessment,* where a number of similar and significant development activities with potentially cumulative impacts are planned for a localized area; (2) *sectoral assessments,* where the environmental impact of investments, policies, and numerous smaller investments in one sector can be reviewed together; and (3) application of *environmental guidance criteria* to projects (e.g., pollution standards, construction design criteria, siting guidelines, monitoring and inspection procedures). Environmental assessment, in whatever form, should help project designers and implementers to address environmental issues in a timely fashion, and help avoid costs and delays in implementation due to unanticipated environmental problems (World Bank 1991b).

In addition to these, *strategic environmental assessment* (SEA) has been developed to overcome some of the shortcomings of one-off impact assessments. SEA is applicable to policies, plans, and programs, or for a region, such as a city, that covers more than one sector (Goodland 1997). An example of a recent application of SEA at the city level is provided in Box 5-1. The SEA can also be used for preparation of an environmental action plan. For example, the Midlands Region of the UK Environment Agency follows up on their SEAs by preparing an action plan to ensure that

BOX

In 1990, Hong Kong began a review of its Territorial Development Strategy to formulate a land use/transport/environment framework for development to the year 2011, when population was expected to reach 8.1 million from the then-current 6.4 million. The review was completed in 1996 and included a strategic environmental assessment (SEA) for issues of sustainability.

The SEA involved the following steps:

1. **Prepare an environmental profile to identify key environmental attributes and constraints**
2. **Formulate environmental principles, criteria, and evaluation framework**
3. **Identify options to minimize the depletion of Hong Kong's natural capital**
4. **Hold public consultation and use results to identify key issues (1993)**
5. **Assess environmental carrying capacities and devise mitigation strategies**
6. **Evaluate sectoral issues and policies**
7. **Analyze cumulative impacts of development strategy and recommend alternatives**
8. **Prepare action plans and related monitoring system**
9. **Hold second public consultation to review draft SEA (1996)**
10. **Present findings to high-level decision-makers (1996–1997)**

The major results of the SEA for the review were: (1) agreement to protect key natural assets such as the Ramsar Site (wetland of international importance) in Mai Po against development; (2) dropping development components that had adverse impacts or would impair self-purification processes; and (3) incorporation of a transportation plan that maximized use of the railway. The process built consensus on the need for environmental action and resulted in a more concrete environmental agenda. Finally, a policy of off-site ecological compensation was promulgated in 1997. However, the process may not yet be institutionalized; an article by Hong Kong's director of environmental protection does not even refer to the experience in an environmental overview of the special administrative region (Law 1998).

Box 5-1 Using strategic environmental assessment in Hong Kong.

SOURCE: Au 1998.

the constraints and mitigation measures in the SEA are implemented (Hickie and Wade 1997). However, strategic assessment is not widely practiced in cities and does not yet constitute a means of integrating sustainability concerns into the urban management and development processes (Partidario 1996).

The Strategic Alternative of Local Environmental Action Planning

A planning process is needed that avoids the problems inherent in the classic EIA approach and that addresses the underlying causes of urban environmental degradation that were identified in Chapter 3. A framework for urban environmental planning can be used to formulate an integrated set of policies, programs, and projects that solve priority problems and support strategic objectives instead of (or in addition to) EIA. With differing urban problems and many tools for dealing with them, each city will need a process for determining the most appropriate mix of actions and investments that respond to its environmental priorities. When confronting environmental problems, cities exhibit different degrees of awareness, political commitment, and capacity to mobilize resources. A strategic approach to urban environmental planning and management is recommended based on enabling participation and building commitment. It has been tested in industrialized and developing-country cities (see the following sections on the Sustainable Cities Programme and the Local Agenda 21 Initiative) and is a viable approach for cities seeking to address priority problems of sustainable development.

Local environmental action planning involves several activities, each of which emphasizes strengthening local capacity:

- *Informed consultation,* wherein rapid assessments are conducted, environmental issues are clarified, key stakeholders are involved, political commitment is achieved, and priorities are set through an informed consultative process

- *An integrated local environmental action plan,* which embodies (1) long-term goals and phased targets for meeting the goals; (2) agreement on issues-oriented solutions that cut across the concerns of various stakeholders; and (3) stakeholder-specific action plans that cut across various issues for achieving the targets, including the identification of least-cost project options, policy reforms, and institutional improvements

- *Implementation,* in which agreed programs and projects are initiated, policy reforms and institutional arrangements are solidified, needed research is conducted, the overall process is made routine, and monitoring and evaluation procedures are put in place. Results can then be fed back to adjust priorities and solutions.

These elements of a strategic approach, and examples of their application, are more fully described in the text that follows. The process is diagrammed in Figure 5-2.

The advantages of this approach over disaster-driven environmental planning or classic EIA are that it:

- Addresses a city's priority problems and anticipates future needs
- Is equipped to deal with cumulative, interactive, and upstream/downstream effects
- Relies strongly on stakeholder participation and awareness
- Seeks to improve governance through an accountable, transparent, and participatory process

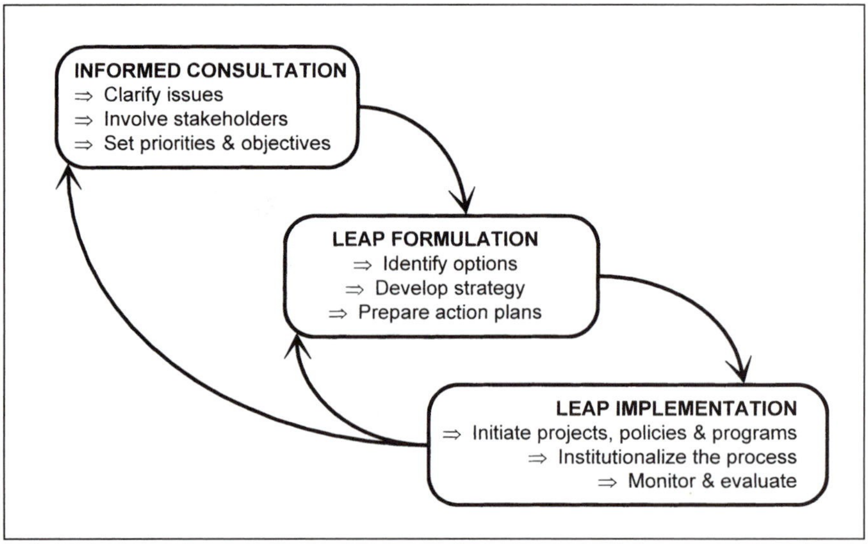

Figure 5-2 The LEAP process diagrammed.

- Focuses on the need to improve policies as well as institutions and investments
- Assembles existing knowledge and highlights information gaps

The manner by which this planning framework attains these advantages is detailed in the following descriptions of the three phases of the process.

Informed Consultation

From Chapters 1 and 3 we learned that the level, nature, and impact of urban environmental problems can be diverse. Also, there are a range of different stakeholders who affect, know about, or are affected by these problems. Thus, an initial phase is needed where (1) information is gathered and analyzed in order to clarify issues; (2) key stakeholders are identified and brought into the process; and (3) consensus is reached on priority problems as well as environmental quality objectives. This first phase ensures that the views of experts and concerned citizens can be heard, planning is focused on the most important problems, and ownership of the results is increased through participation and consensus. It can take three months to one year to complete, depending on the availability of information, the number and involvement of stakeholders, the complexity of issues, and the availability of resources (Leitmann 1993). Tools that can be used to support the process of informed consultation are presented in Chapter 6.

Clarifying Issues

Information about environmental issues in a city is often not available to the public, is rarely organized in a clear manner, and is usually scattered among different sources. Thus, there may be a need to collect existing data, assemble it in a coherent fashion, and present it for public review in order to obtain a complete panorama of the environmental problems faced by a city. Ideally, this process of clarifying issues should capture urban problems that (1) harm the health and quality of life of city residents;

(2) reduce the economic efficiency and productivity of the city; (3) risk permanent damage to local or regional ecosystems; (4) cut across conventional jurisdictions, sectors, and time frames; and (5) require coordinated responses (Bartone et al. 1994).

A three-step process, known as *rapid urban environmental assessment,* can be used to clarify urban environmental issues. First, researchers assemble and analyze existing information from readily available data and special studies on pollution sources, environmental infrastructure and services, environmental health, natural ecosystems, and environmental policies, regulations, and institutions. This is done using an urban environmental questionnaire that is more fully described in Chapter 6. Second, this and other information are used to prepare an environmental profile or "state-of-the-city environment" report that reviews the status of the urban environment (air, water, land, and hazards), key relationships between urban development and the environment, and the institutional setting for environmental management. Third, questionnaire data and the profile are publicly distributed and reviewed at a stakeholder workshop to ensure that the information is both known and accurate (Leitmann 1993). More information about rapid urban environmental assessment as a planning tool is given in Chapter 6. Variations of this approach are used by two of the programs described here which promote the urban environmental planning framework.

Involving Stakeholders

Generally, three sets of stakeholders need to be involved throughout the environmental planning process: (1) those who are affected by the problems; (2) decision-makers in the public and private sectors who have the power to solve problems; and (3) experts who have specialized knowledge about the problems. The list of stakeholders presented in Chapter 3 can be rearranged in these three groups as follows:

Affected. Concerned residents and community-based organizations; nongovernmental organizations

Decision-makers. Environmental protection agencies; politicians; sector agencies; private and informal-sector enterprises

Figure 5-3 Affected stakeholders in Chichicastenango, Guatemala.

Experts. Planning agencies; the professional news media; the scientific and academic community; external sources of support/expertise

These groups need to be involved in the process of informed consultation *and* in the latter phases of strategy formulation and implementation. Obtaining the endorsement and sponsorship of the planning process by key politicians and community leaders is usually a critical element for a successful outcome.

At least three different approaches exist for structuring participation throughout the phases of urban environmental planning: (1) the "priority problem" approach; (2) the sectoral or municipal services approach; and (3) the stakeholder or thematic approach. Each approach is described here, along with a flow chart, list of requirements, advantages and disadvantages, and an example of its application in a city.

PRIORITY PROBLEM APPROACH

The most commonly used means of structuring public involvement in local environmental planning is to involve stakeholders in determining priority urban environmental problems and then structure participation around key problem areas. The process is as follows: (1) background information on the city's urban environment is prepared (e.g., environmental data and a "state-of-the-environment" report); (2) a stakeholder workshop is held to discuss the background information and prioritize urban environmental problems; (3) stakeholder working groups are created around the highest-priority problems; (4) the working groups identify and prioritize options for solving the problems; and (5) a panel with representatives from each working group, along with experts, develops an integrated strategy and individual action plans for each priority problem.

The priority problem approach requires (1) consensus about which problems are the most important ones; (2) consensus within each problem area as to priority options; and (3) participation of relevant stakeholders, especially decision-makers. Its advantages are that it focuses the local environmental action planning process on addressing the most important issues and promotes an integrated approach to strategy development. Its

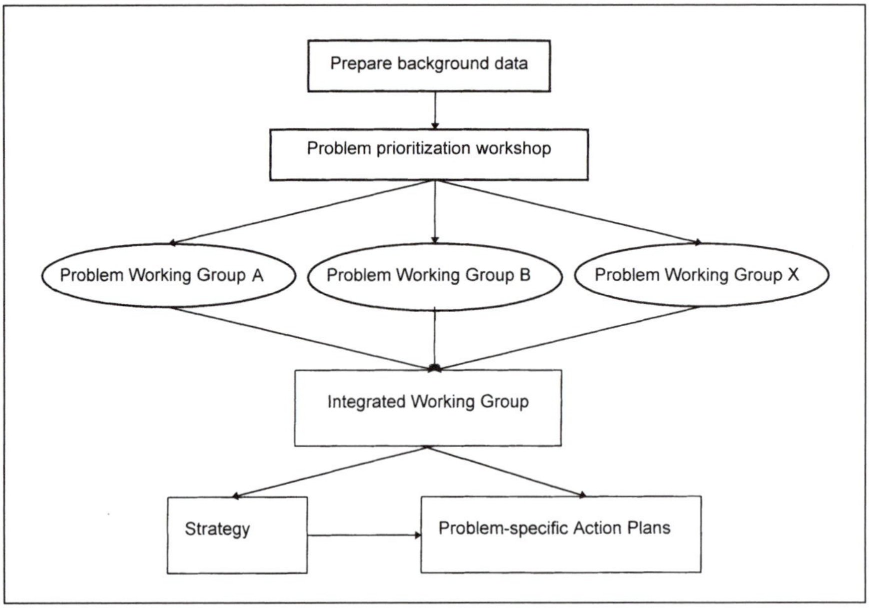

Figure 5-4 Priority problem flow chart.

disadvantages are that real-life problems may be different from identified priorities if the process takes too long, and it may be difficult to achieve consensus on priority problems and options. An example of the approach as used in an African city is presented in Box 5-2.

BOX

In 1993, a start-up workshop was held to discuss the LEAP process with 80 representatives of stakeholders and to seek their cooperation. This was followed in midyear by a rapid assessment of the urban environment by local consultants who assembled relevant data and prepared an environmental profile. Toward the end of the year, a consultative workshop was held to discuss the profile and identify priority issues. Working groups identified general problems (natural and industrial risks, air pollution, solid waste, sanitation, and environmental awareness) and geographically specific ones (pollution of the Hann Bay, coastal erosion). At the final plenary, a consensus was reached to proceed with action planning on the bay pollution and industrial risks.

Strategy development and action planning followed in 1994. Environmental profiles were prepared on the two priority problem areas. These profiles, prepared by local consultants, examined the nature of each problem, the relationship between the problem and urban development, and the institutional setting surrounding the problem. Toward the end of the year, a three-day consultation with over 100 stakeholders was held to discuss industrial risks, Hann Bay pollution, and next steps. The results of this work were used to develop action plans that covered needed investments, technical assistance, institutional measures, and policy reforms.

Box 5-2 Priority problem approach in Dakar, Senegal.

SOURCE: UNCHS and UNEP 1997.

SECTORAL OR MUNICIPAL SERVICE APPROACH

This approach is based on the environmental dimensions of a city's existing sectors or municipal services. The process is as follows: (1) an analysis is made of sector-by-sector or service-by-service issues, either by experts or by a stakeholder workshop; (2) stakeholder working groups are established for each key sector or municipal service; (3) working groups prioritize issues, identify options, and prioritize options for each sector or service; and (4) an integrated working group develops an intersectoral or cross-service strategy and sector- or service-specific action plans.

The sector- or service-specific approach requires:

- Active participation of key sectoral actors (e.g., industries and neighborhoods affected by industrial pollution)
- Key services (e.g., the water and sanitation company directors as well as representatives of their industrial, commercial, and residential customers)
- A willingness to evaluate real problems in each sector or service

The advantages of this approach are that it focuses on operational problems in each sector or service and that it results in practical,

Figure 5-5 Industrial risk site in Dakar, Senegal.

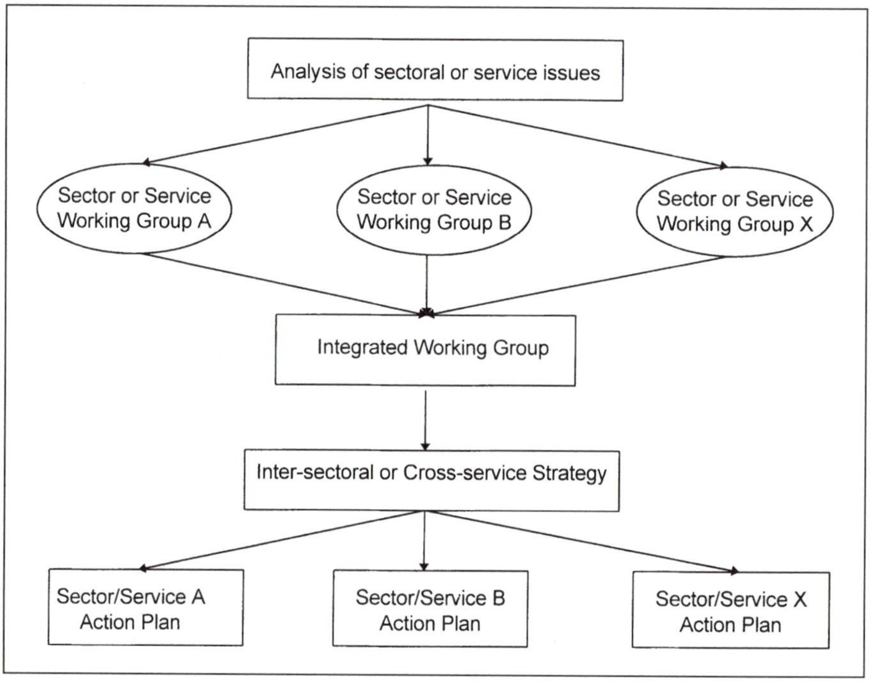

Figure 5-6 Sectoral or municipal service flow chart.

institution-specific recommendations. The disadvantages are that it may not identify and address the most important environmental issues in a city, and it tends to reinforce the existing sectoral structure or service delivery system. An example of the approach as used in a European city is presented in Box 5-3.

BOX

In 1990, the city of Tilburg formulated a Municipal Environmental Policy Plan (MEPP). After four years, an evaluation concluded that environmental problems had not been solved, and that an important policy document could not be drawn up in a top-down manner from behind a desk.

The second MEPP was developed in 1994. An overall strategy was prepared based on the need for placing environmental policy in a broader context of sustainable development; the importance of using measurable policy targets; and the view that implementation of environmental policy is the joint responsibility of all parties involved (the municipality, target groups, and interest groups). Action plans (called sustainability strategies) were developed with stakeholders for *municipal services* (urban planning, traffic control, and the management of wastes and water) and *high-priority sectors* (industry, households, construction, and energy). The action plan for urban planning serves as a framework for the MEPP, and the other plans are designed as inputs to it.

Implementation of the MEPP began in 1995. The municipality reports annually on implementation of the plan using source, effect, and performance indicators. Consultation has been built into the process: The construction sector, industries, and environmental groups are involved with the municipality in both implementing and reviewing the process along the way.

Box 5-3 Sectoral and municipal services approach in Tilburg, The Netherlands.

SOURCE: UNCHS and UNEP 1997.

STAKEHOLDER OR THEMATIC APPROACH

In this approach, public participation is organized around groups of key stakeholders or preidentified urban themes. The process involves:

1. Identification of relevant stakeholders or themes
2. Establishment of stakeholder or thematic working groups
3. Optional preparation of background environmental documents (e.g., environmental data and an urban environmental profile for use by the working groups)
4. Identification and prioritization of stakeholder- or theme-specific strategies and action plans
5. Integration of working group outputs into a citywide action program by a stakeholder workshop or a group of experts

Figure 5-7 presents a flow diagram of the process.

This approach requires the active involvement of all key stakeholders and/or consensus on central themes. The advantages are that it is easy to establish and understand, and that it can address cross-sectoral and interjurisdictional problems. The disadvantages are that (1) the resulting strategies and action plans may not

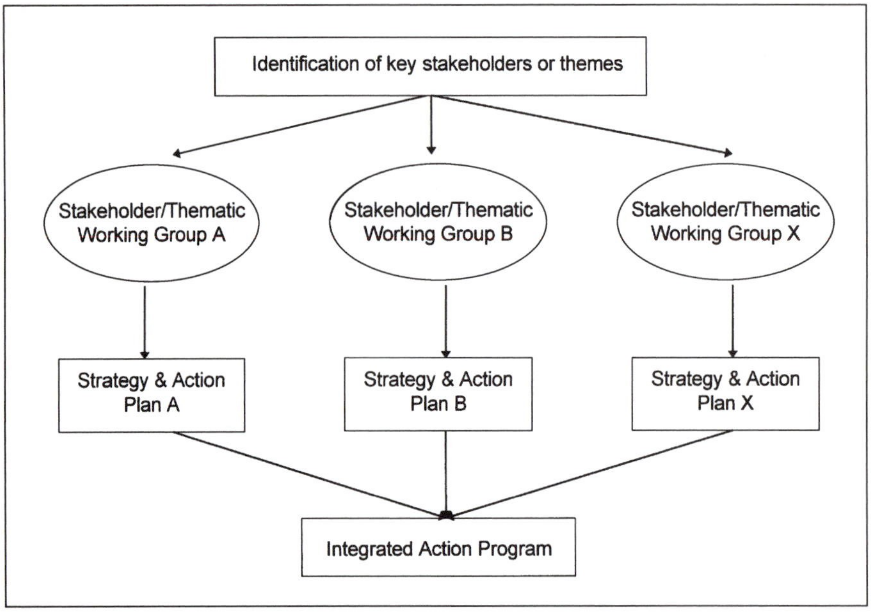

Figure 5-7 Stakeholder or thematic flow chart.

Figure 5-8 Women's Group, Local Agenda 21, Bursa, Turkey.

address a city's most important environmental problems; (2) recommendations may be too general to guide action at the level of individual institutions; and (3) separating stakeholders may create an "us against them" mentality that could lead to divisiveness. An example of the approach as used in an Asian city is presented in Box 5-4.

BOX

In late 1995, the city of Bursa established a Local Agenda 21 General Secretariat. Early in 1996, the Secretariat organized an Urban Forum to discuss sustainable development and urban environmental priorities. The Forum was attended by 800 citizens representing municipal government, NGOs, professional associations, the private sector, unions, and universities. Participants identified key themes and volunteered to work on these themes. As a result, 12 working groups were formed. This has now expanded to 21 groups involving 2200 volunteers on the following themes: Waste; Land Use; Urban Structure; Industry; Climate Change; Water; Socioeconomic Life; Historical and Cultural Heritage; Art and Culture; Education; Environmental Regulations; Public Awareness; Health; Sport; The Disabled; Children; Women; Young People; Scout Groups; Pensioners; and Combating Poverty.

Environmental data are being collected and a "State of the Environment" report is being prepared to assist the working groups. The working groups have come up with 33 crosscutting recommendations that are being integrated into a citywide action program.

Box 5-4 Thematic approach in Bursa, Turkey.

SOURCE: Bursa Metropolitan Municipality 1998.

Setting Priorities and Objectives

Most cities face more environmental problems than can be solved with the available resources and time. Thus, there is a need to set priorities so that scarce resources and time can be spent on the most important urban environmental challenges. But how do cities determine what is most important? The process of clarifying issues should identify the universe of problems, along with background data. The involvement of stakeholders brings together the group of citizens who can set priorities. This group then needs a set of criteria that can be used to rank urban environmental issues.

Criteria can include some or all of the following:

- Magnitude of human health effects associated with the problem
- Size of urban economic losses caused by the problem
- Degree that the problem disproportionately affects the urban poor
- Extent to which the problem results in or is caused by unsustainable consumption of resources
- Whether the problem leads to an irreversible ecological outcome

- Degree of political or social consensus on the need to address the problem
- Whether the problem can be significantly influenced by local action (Leitmann 1993; UNCHS and UNEP 1997)

Most cities do not have a full set of consistent and up-to-date quantitative data to assess problems according to these criteria. Thus, a mix of quantitative analysis and subjective judgment is typically used to evaluate the criteria in relation to a particular problem. The subjective judgment of participating stakeholders may also be used to assign greater weight to certain criteria than to others. The outcome of the ranking process should reflect a consensus to the greatest extent possible.

This first phase of informed consultation can also be an important opportunity to discuss and obtain consensus on broad objectives for a city's environmental quality. This requires selecting one or more time horizons (short, medium, or long-term) and then coming up with general answers to questions such as: What level of air and water quality do we want to enjoy? What quality and quantity of open space should we have in the future? To what extent should our consumption be based on renewable resources? How much of our waste should be recovered for reuse? The resulting set of objectives will be different for each city and should reflect priority problems, available resources, and a consensus among stakeholders. Cities with a high degree of consensus and information may also want to attach quantitative targets to some or all objectives at this point (e.g., X tons of CO_2 emissions per capita in 15 years' time, or Y square meters of green space per person in five years' time). Target-setting can also be done during the strategy formulation phase.

LEAP Development

A LEAP is usually based on an urban environmental strategy that identifies a coordinated set of investments, policies, and institutional reforms to help resolve the priority problems and environmental quality objectives identified during the previous phase of informed consultation. The development of the strategy should be based on the continued involvement of stakeholders. Stakeholders can be organized to focus on priority issues, sectors, or themes, as suggested in Figures 5-4, 5-6, and 5-7, respectively. However, the most strategic approach is for public participation to be organized around priority problems. The elements of this phase are (1) identifying the options available to address priority problems; (2) developing priority, issue-specific solutions that can be linked together in a citywide environmental strategy; and (3) formulating detailed recommendations in the form of actor-specific action plans. Experience indicates that this phase requires from nine months to two years, depending on a city's size, complexity, opportunity for consensus, and availability of resources to support the process (Leitmann 1993). Tools for evaluating strategic alternatives are presented in Chapter 6. Examples of urban environmental management strategies and action plans are presented in Chapter 7.

Identifying Options

Working groups can be organized for each priority problem, with representation from the three categories of stakeholders. Specialized expertise may be especially important to help the working groups devise a range of options for resolving problems. It is often useful to establish a steering committee which can facilitate the working groups by: ensuring that information is shared between groups; identifying potentially inconsistent recommendations at an early stage; serving as a focal point to inform the public and politicians about progress; mobilizing resources for the working groups; and formulating approaches that cut across issues. The steering committee can be set up during the period of informed consultation. Membership should include top local decision-makers; representatives of relevant regional and central government agencies; leaders of key businesses, community groups, and NGOs; and media people.

Options should include:

- Financial investments in projects and programs for improving access to services, preventing or reducing emissions and wastes, protecting resources, and reducing hazards

- Policy reforms involving economic instruments, regulations, property rights, and improved land management
- Institutional modifications such as revised or new jurisdictional arrangements, cross-sectoral coordination, and capacity building
- Research/information needs for increasing public awareness and filling knowledge gaps

Information should then be developed on the costs, sources of finance, likely benefits and beneficiaries, time frame, institutional requirements, and level of political support for each option.

Selecting and Integrating Solutions

Several options may be identified to solve each priority problem. The information generated for each option should be used to rank them and to select priority solutions. Criteria that might be used by each working group to rank options include (1) health and ecological benefits; (2) the results of cost-benefit analysis (see Table 5-1 for an example) or, when monetary information about benefits is lacking, cost-effectiveness analysis (see Figure 5-9 for an application); (3) the degree to which low-income people benefit; (4) political and institutional feasibility; and (5) household and citywide affordability. Tools for analyzing options are reviewed in the following chapter.

Table 5-1 Results of Cost-Benefit Analysis in Metropolitan Jakarta, Indonesia

Option	Net present value (billions of rupiah)*	Rank
Reduction of lead in petrol	712.1	1
Improved solid waste disposal	127.9	2
Environmental auditing for industries	50.7	3
Diesel vehicle exhaust control	38.7	4
Substitution of LPG for other fuels	32.9	5
Septic tank maintenance	17.8	6
Using CNG in large buses	12.1	7
Promoting 4-stroke motorcycles	3.6	8
Using LPG in small buses and taxis	1.8	9

* In 1994 rupiahs using a 15 percent discount rate.
SOURCE: SME and BAPEDAL 1994.

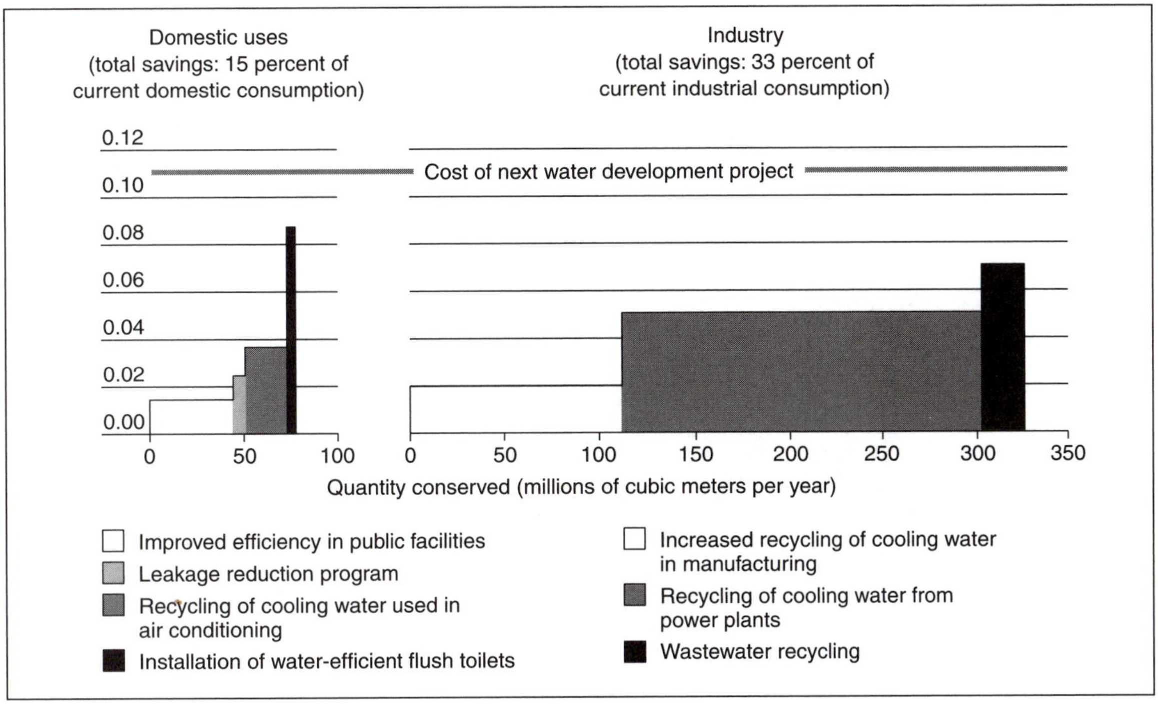

Figure 5-9 Cost-effectiveness of water conservation and supply options in Beijing, China.
SOURCE: World Bank 1992.

The selection of priority solutions is rarely a purely technical exercise. Stakeholders will differ as to which criteria should be used and what weight should be assigned to each criterion. For example, a particular option may yield the highest net present value; however, it may also provide little benefit to low-income groups and not be politically feasible. Thus, solutions and recommendations about their implementation will usually involve judgment and negotiation among stakeholders.

The priority solutions determined by each working group then need to be compared and coordinated into an overall strategy. This work can be spearheaded by the steering committee, with participation from representatives of the various problem-specific working groups. This important step in strategy formulation should seek to resolve inconsistencies between priority solutions; identify opportunities for solving more than one problem with the same solution; ensure that investments, policy reforms, and institutional modifications are mutually supportive; and maximize

Figure 5-10 Integrating solutions in Singapore.

other opportunities for complementarity (e.g., shared budget allocations, concentrated geographic impact, and coordinated implementation).

Results from the strategy formulation process should be summarized in a draft public report. This document can summarize the following:

- *Review of environment/development issues*—a description of the nature, causes, and impacts of each issue, ranking criteria and resulting priorities, the stakeholders who are affected, and those who should be involved in solutions

- *Goals and objectives*—the long-term goals for achieving improvements in urban environmental quality, medium-term quantitative targets for realizing each goal, and priority geographic areas and sectors

- *Solutions*—a summary of the responses to each priority issue, the criteria and procedures used to select priority solutions, and estimates of how solutions will help achieve specified targets

- *Strategic program*—an integrated set of recommended investments, policy reforms, institutional modifications, and research activities, along with supplemental information such as preliminary project profiles

This draft will not exist in a vacuum. It should be compared and, if sensible, be consistent with other strategic plans that the city has developed. The draft should then be disseminated for public review and discussion; resulting comments should then be integrated in a final strategy document. Ideally, this document should guide future exercises in urban, economic, infrastructure, natural resource, energy, and housing planning.

Action Planning

After the urban environmental strategy has been developed, it should be translated into a LEAP, which is an integrated set of action plans. Action planning can be done for priority problem areas, themes, or specific stakeholders. In practice, action plans are usually developed for specific actors. The strategy determines what should be done and why. Action plans answer the following questions: Who should be responsible for which priority solutions? How will they undertake needed work, pay for it, and cooperate with others? When and where should actions take place?

Preparation of action plans should be a continuation of the stakeholder participation process. Once the citywide strategy has been finalized, working groups can be re-formed according to the different stakeholders who are critical for implementation (e.g., municipal authorities, sector agencies, the private sector, NGOs, and community organizations). The steering committee can continue to function in an important way by reviewing action plans, resolving conflicts, and ensuring that strategic solutions and objectives are fully incorporated.

Each action plan should include a description, costing, and time schedule for key actions. Estimates of benefits and beneficiaries can also be included. Actions should be a mix of mutually reinforcing interventions, including new or revised capital improvements, regulatory instruments, economic incentives, institutional reform and capacity building, public education and awareness, and research.

Among the factors that will support successful LEAPs are:

- *Selecting appropriate and affordable technologies.* Technologies and standards for environmental infrastructure and services vary between cities and can differ within cities. They should be geared to a city or district's willingness and ability to pay for a service; the social acceptability of the technology; the city's ability to manage the system; and the technical suitability of the technology. The case study of strategic sanitation planning for Kumasi, Ghana (Chapter 9) is a good example of this principle.

- *Finding least-cost solutions.* The approaches that constitute an action plan should represent either the set of alternatives that yield the highest net present value of benefits (if benefits can be fully monetized so that cost-benefit analysis can be employed) or that achieve critical objectives at the least cost (using cost-effectiveness analysis). Examples of these approaches are provided in Table 5-1, Figure 5-9, and in Chapter 7.
- *Developing institutional innovations.* Chapters 3 and 4 made it clear that urban environmental problems rarely coincide with institutional jurisdictions or sectoral responsibilities. Thus, institutional innovations may be necessary, such as privatization, community management, intersectoral coordination, and new problem- or area-specific authorities (Bartone et al. 1994). These options are covered in Chapter 8.
- *Obtaining the stakeholder's agreement.* Each action plan should be an agreement with the concerned stakeholder on its commitment to achieve priority solutions. This includes allocation of human and financial resources, a clear timetable, institutional reforms, and sources of external support (financial, technical, informational, other), if needed (UNCHS and UNEP 1997).

Once stakeholder-specific action plans have been drafted, they can be disseminated for public review and formal agreement with the relevant stakeholders. Then, the set of action plans can be amalgamated into the citywide LEAP. In addition to summarizing the actor-specific action plans, this document should highlight crosscutting actions that require coordination between actors, citywide policy and institutional reforms, changes in citizen behavior, and a uniform monitoring and evaluation process to provide the public with information on progress toward achieving objectives.

LEAP Implementation

Implementation consists of at least three key elements: (1) ensuring the public, bureaucratic, and political support to initiate priority projects, policies, and programs; (2) institutionalizing the environmental planning process; and (3) using indicators to monitor progress toward solving central problems and achieving environmental quality objectives. The implementation phase will vary greatly between and within cities, so this section is necessarily generalized. Analytical tools that can be used in this phase are presented in the following chapter.

Initiating Projects, Policies, and Programs

Moving from LEAPs to actions will require the participation and support of the public, bureaucracies, and politicians. The process of stakeholder involvement in the first two phases should go a long way toward ensuring that this occurs. Public ownership of major decisions should be higher if concerned citizens have had their ideas and priorities reflected in final plans. Government agencies should be keen on implementation if they have had an active hand in developing their action plans and have formally agreed to carry them out. Political sponsorship, obtained at the beginning of the process, should link outcomes with politicians whose reputation will be partly evaluated on whether they follow up on the planning process. However, support can be undermined if (1) certain stakeholders were excluded from the planning process and then become opponents of its outcomes; (2) bureaucracies are not given the resources or incentives to implement their agreed action plans; or (3) the planning process spans a change in political leadership, and the new politicians have little awareness or ownership of the city's environmental strategy and action plan.

Figure 5-11 Young battery recyclers: Excluded stakeholders in Abidjan, Côte d'Ivoire?

Resource mobilization is usually a key to successful implementation. Some action plans can be implemented by improving the efficiency or allocation of existing resources. Some lessons from city experience (UNCHS and UNEP 1997) on mobilizing resources for implementing environmental action plans suggest:

- *Using special opportunities.* Unique events or crises may allow a city to reorient existing resources and obtain new ones to "kick start" implementation. Examples include: radical political and institutional changes as in the former Soviet Union, Eastern/Central Europe, and South Africa; high-profile international sporting and political events that require new urban investments; reconstruction after a major disaster; a change in the local political balance; or updating of an urban development or national environmental action plan.
- *Applying leveraging strategies.* Implementation of certain activities might begin with a pilot phase to demonstrate an innovation, attract resources, and replicate the approach at a larger scale. Local government might also play a facilitator role in stimulating the investment of private sector, community, and household resources to support aspects of the action plan.
- *Networking among cities.* Cities can share information and staff to support the spread of successful innovations. This can be done on a one-off basis or through formal twinning arrangements. Some innovations that have been recognized as worthy of sharing are listed in Chapter 9, while information about networks is provided in Annex A.
- *Strategically using external support.* Most cities rely to some extent on technical and financial resources that are beyond their borders, be they private banks, central governments, or development aid agencies. A city's environmental strategy and action plan can be used as tools to mobilize and channel the resources of external supporters. However, outside assistance should not substitute for locally available resources, nor should it exceed the absorptive capacity of local institutions. Summaries of some sources of external support are presented in Annex B.

Institutionalizing the Planning Process

Implementation should be an opportunity to institutionalize the environmental planning process in a given city. Most cities will want to avoid creating an "environmental czar" to implement action plans; creation of a new agency can require significant resources, generate turf battles, and generally be counterproductive. Rather, implementation should occur through partnerships between central and local government agencies, the public and private sectors, local governments and communities, and NGOs and communities. Only one small new institution or position may need to be created—an informational unit or municipal environmental officer (in smaller cities and towns) that helps negotiate partnerships, serves as a focal point for public and external interest in the strategy and action plan, monitors implementation, and disseminates results. One means of creating such a unit is to institutionalize the steering committee or its secretariat.

Capacity may need to be developed for the key stakeholders who are responsible for implementing action plans. Capacity building can take the form of improving rules and organizational structures, staff training, mobilizing additional funds for both capital and maintenance costs, providing appropriate equipment and facilities, networking, and improving cross-sectoral and inter-jurisdictional coordination. One measure of whether environmental planning has been institutionalized is if the feedback loops in Figure 5-2 are developed so that implementation experience is used to revise information about the urban environment and to update the strategy.

Another measure of success is whether stakeholder participation becomes institutionalized in the implementing agencies. Institutionalization of participation can be facilitated by:

- Presentation of key information using local, nontechnical language
- Regular and wide-scale dissemination of such information
- Capacity building for nongovernmental stakeholders
- Involvement of informal sector actors in implementation
- Developing gender awareness
- Sensitivity training for the public sector on the conditions and needs of stakeholders facing special environmental risks (UNCHS and UNEP 1997)

Monitoring and Indicators

Regular monitoring and evaluation are critical for two reasons: to identify emerging urban environmental issues so that they can be addressed before they become costly emergencies, and to assess implementation of action plans so that they can be adjusted and improved. It is usually necessary to monitor (1) the performance of environmental infrastructure and services; (2) the effectiveness of pollution prevention, mitigation, and rehabilitation measures; and (3) ambient environmental quality in relation to existing standards. Indicators are required for these types of monitoring; subsections are provided in the following text on developing and using urban environmental indicators.

Monitoring involves the regular collection of indicators. Evaluation entails the periodic analysis and assessment of indicators and other information to identify emerging problems and gauge the impacts of implementation. Both tasks initially should be undertaken by stakeholders responsible for implementation. This allows the results of monitoring and evaluation to be used for improving performance. A central entity, such as the information unit previously mentioned, might then consolidate and package the results of monitoring and evaluation for citywide consumption.

Public dissemination of the results of monitoring and evaluation can occur through:

- Regular publication and distribution of indicators
- Preparation of an annual "state of the city environment" report based on analysis of indicators, reports, feedback, and studies that become available during the year
- Creation of a Web site for public access to present and past indicators, "state of the environment" reports, and related documents
- Periodic stakeholder review of the indicators and monitoring process to assess their relevance and effectiveness

Information on specific types of environmental indicators is given in Chapter 6. The following subsections provide guidance on the process of developing indicators.

LOCAL AND PARTICIPATORY DEVELOPMENT OF INDICATORS

Situation-specific urban environmental indicators must be developed by someone, as there is no ideal "objective" set of indicators. Too often, these measures are formulated only by experts in a top-down fashion, and often at some distance from the people whose quality of life is to be assessed. Experience suggests that stakeholder participation improves the performance of development interventions (Isham, Narayan, and Pritchett 1994). More specifically, the joint evaluation of urban conditions by experts *and* decision-makers *and* stakeholders affected by problems within a city yields more comprehensive and more acceptable results than a purely expert-driven approach (Leitmann 1993; UNCHS 1997). Thus, urban environmental indicators should be developed at the level where they will be applied (e.g., neighborhood, district, city, metropolitan area, or region) and by representatives of the stakeholder groups that are both knowledgeable and concerned about environmental issues.

Merely designing and applying a local and participatory process does not guarantee that urban environmental indicators will be better and more relevant. Some of the problems that beset this phase of indicator development include:

- *Exclusion of stakeholders.* The full range of concerned stakeholders may not be invited to participate in the process of developing indicators. Typically, vulnerable groups such as women, low-income households, children, the elderly, and the disabled can be overlooked. This may result in failure to include key variables in the set of environmental measures.
- *Overweighted role of experts.* The data generated by "bottom-up" processes may need to be filtered and interpreted by experts. This process can lead to the imposition of the biases and disciplinary perspectives of the analysts, making the resulting indicators less representative and relevant.
- *Incompatibility for making comparisons.* The indicators that emerge from a stakeholder-driven development process may be so idiosyncratic that they cannot be used for comparative purposes with other communities. This makes it difficult for the locality to assess itself and learn from other cities.

Figure 5-12 Measuring resource flows in Jakarta, Indonesia.

There are remedies to overcome each of these constraints. A simple checklist of the vulnerable groups cited above can be used to ensure that no interest group is overlooked. Reviewing the range of participants involved in similar exercises in other cities can also help avoid the problem of exclusion. If experts need to be used to filter and evaluate the information generated by stakeholders, then their proposed set of indicators can be taken as a draft which should subsequently be reviewed by a representative range of stakeholders and modified if necessary. This should help minimize the bias that may enter into indicator development through filtration of stakeholder inputs. Incompatibility can be partially overcome by including a subset of nationally or internationally used urban environmental measures as part of the local indicators, such as from the UNCHS urban indicators or from a national process, as was the case in Australia (CSIRO and AHURI 1998).

LINKING URBAN INDICATORS TO THE DEVELOPMENT PROCESS

Relevant urban measures cannot be formulated without reference to the process of environmental planning, no matter how participatory the preparatory process. Indicators can be divided into two categories—purely physical indicators, and policy indicators (Young and Ryan 1995). Physical indicators are typically chosen from existing data sets that are readily accessible; they may or may not help evaluate whether a city is on a sustainable development path. Policy indicators can be either physical measures or process indicators; they are specifically selected to determine whether a city is achieving a policy objective.

Environmental indicators can be used throughout the process of urban policy development and implementation. Specifically, indicators can be used to (1) identify key environment/development problems that require new policies or modification of existing policy; (2) prioritize the range of identified problems; (3) facilitate the choice between competing policy options; (4) monitor progress toward policy objectives; and (5) provide feedback and inputs for developing new policies (Society for Development Studies 1996).

APPLYING GUIDELINES TO SELECT REALISTIC URBAN INDICATORS

Some of the technical problems that limit the relevance of urban measurements can be avoided or reduced by following a simple set of guidelines when developing indicators. Experience suggests that, in addition to being developed in a participatory manner and linked to the urban development process, a useful set of urban environmental indicators should have the following characteristics:

Measurable. Indicators should be quantifiable.

Based on existing data. When possible, indicators should be derived from reliable existing information to speed up their use and minimize costs.

Affordable. The financial cost and time required to assemble and analyze indicators should be prescribed by a predetermined budget.

Based on a time series. The same indicator should be collected over a regular interval so that change can be evaluated.

Quickly observable. Indicators that can be developed soon after data collection are more useful than those that require lengthy processing.

Change-sensitive. Indicators should change as conditions change so that they can accurately reflect reality.

Widely accepted. Indicators must be understood and accepted by users.

Easy to understand. Indicators should be reported in a simple fashion so that a wide range of people can understand them.

Balanced. Indicators should be politically neutral and allow for measurement of both positive and negative impacts (Young and Ryan 1995; Society for Development Studies 1996).

Some Procedural Considerations

There are three questions to consider before embarking on an environmental planning exercise in a city: Where should one begin in the process? What will it cost? What are the risks? Not every city will need to start at the beginning and go through all three phases of the environmental planning framework. Where to begin will largely depend on the degree of consensus and availability of feasible solutions in a particular urban area. Table 5-2 diagrams these conditions and how they affect where a city might want to enter the LEAP process. If there is consensus about goals and priorities, *and* effective solutions are known, then cities are in Box A, where they can proceed with implementation of solutions to address priority problems. If there is consensus, *but* solutions are unknown, then cities are in Box B and should start with the strategy development phase to identify appropriate solutions. If there is no consensus *but* solutions to a wide range of urban environmental problems are known, then cities are in Box C and should begin with informed consultation to forge agreement among stakeholders about goals and priority problems. With no consensus and no known solutions, then cities are in the hell of Box D and should begin with informed consultation to obtain consensus, followed by strategy development to identify solutions.

Funding the LEAP process will depend on several factors, including local budgetary flexibility, existing institutional capacity, and relative political priority attached to environmental issues.

Table 5-2 The LEAP Process: Consensus and Solutions

Solutions	Goals and priorities: Agreed	Goals and priorities: Not agreed
Known	**A** *Implementation* Example: Singapore case in Chapter 9	**C** *Informed consultation* Example: Jabotabek case in Chapter 7
Unknown	**B** *Strategy development* Example: Mexico City case in Chapter 7	**D** *Informed consultation* Example: Calcutta case in Chapter 7

SOURCE: Adapted from Christensen 1985, 69.

Costs can range from less than $20,000 for a rapid urban environmental assessment for the informed consultation phase to over $1 million for a complete strategy with detailed action plans. Local governments with a high level of in-house expertise and political commitment can undertake either exercise with their own resources. Municipalities with budgetary flexibility and political commitment can contract consultants, community expertise, and NGOs to assist them. If there is only political commitment, and little in the way of budget or expertise, then external resources must be mobilized. By comparison, financing of classic environmental impact assessment is usually built into the cost of the project or program and normally represents less than 1 percent of total project costs and no more than 5 percent (for smaller projects with significant impacts).

Some of the risks that have been discussed thus far in the chapter are:

- Public opposition to aspects of the planning process and products, often because certain stakeholders or their views may have been excluded or experts have dominated the process
- Political opposition, often because a new set of politicians comes to power during or after the planning process
- Bureaucratic opposition, because an agency fears that its interests have not been represented in the process or that it may lose power or resources

- Unfeasible or ineffective solutions included in the action plans

Means of minimizing these risks have also been suggested in this chapter. Stakeholder participation; review of stakeholders against a checklist of potentially excluded groups; regular dissemination of information; and public review of expert-generated documents can minimize public opposition. Political sponsorship for each stage of the process; involvement of opposition politicians; and the opportunity for a new political regime to claim credit for outputs of the process can overcome political opposition. However, excess involvement of elected or appointed municipal leaders and opposition members can create the risk of an overly politicized process. Participation of bureaucratic stakeholders; formal agreement of implementing agencies to undertake action plans; provision of adequate resources for implementation; and institutionalization of the planning process are ways to minimize bureaucratic opposition. The focus on priority problems and feasible, least-cost solutions should reduce the risk of irrelevant and ineffective action plans.

The greatest risk is that urban environmental planning will go the way that comprehensive planning went 30 years ago:

> *The incrementalists will argue that one cannot achieve a sustainable society in a single grand leap, for it requires too much social and ecological information and is too risky. The advocacy planners will argue that no common social interest in sustainable development exists, and that bureaucratic planners will invariably create a sustainable development scheme that neglects the interests both of the poor and of nature. . . . States will require communities to prepare "Sustainable Development Master Plans," which will prove to be glib wish lists of goals and suspiciously vague implementation steps. To achieve consensus for the plan, language will be reduced to the lowest common denominator, and the pleasing plans will gather dust (Campbell 1996, 304).*

This risk can be reduced, because the environmental planning framework has features that were less prevalent or even absent from urban master planning: a dynamic feedback loop whereby monitoring and evaluation allow for adjustments in the understanding of problems as well as the strategy and action plan; extensive stakeholder participation; a focus on priority problems and solutions; and an emphasis on institutionalizing the process.

Applying the Framework

Two international programs are actively supporting use of the LEAP framework in cities around the world. The Sustainable Cities Programme is a formal technical assistance program that aids cities in developing countries. The Local Agenda 21 Initiative is a blend of technical assistance and networking that is open to a wider group of cities. The approaches and activities of both efforts are briefly described below. Contacts for both programs can be found in Annex B. City-based experience with all stages of the framework is reviewed in Chapter 7.

Sustainable Cities Programme (SCP)

The SCP was launched in 1990 by UNCHS and was joined by UNEP in 1995. The program works with municipalities and other stakeholders at the local level to promote more efficient and equitable use of natural resources and control of environmental hazards through better urban governance. The SCP does this by helping cities improve their capacity for environmental planning and management. The process used is that of the environmental planning framework: involving stakeholders in consultation; strategy negotiation; and implementation of priority projects.

SCP operates at four levels. At the city level, issue-specific stakeholder working groups and a full-time project team are supported in each partner city. At the national level, the results of a city planning process are replicated and scaled up to other cities in the same country. At the regional level, partner cities exchange information, share know-how, and pool expertise and other technical resources. At the global level, the program compiles lessons of experience and good practice, develops tools and procedures, and operationally supports program activities at the other levels from its base in Nairobi, Kenya (UNCHS and UNEP 1996).

Local Agenda 21 Initiative (LA21)

LA21 was started in 1991 by the International Council for Local Environmental Initiatives (ICLEI) and was adopted in 1992 by the Earth Summit as the key mechanism for local authority implementation of Agenda 21. The initiative seeks to enhance the institutional and participatory capacities of local authorities to manage critical environmental problems. LA21's approach parallels that of the environmental planning framework: (1) Local governments and other stakeholders are mobilized in a partnership to determine a community's priority problems of sustainable development; (2) action goals and targets are set, and strategies are created to achieve them, all of which are formalized in an action plan; and (3) implementation proceeds with clear monitoring, evaluation, and feedback.

LA21 supports this approach through research collaboration between municipalities, training of municipal officials, and dissemination of information and research through the Web, a newsletter, case studies, and planning guides. ICLEI is an international association of local authorities, governed on a democratic basis by its members. It works with regional sections of the International Union of Local Authorities, national municipal associations, and national government departments to promote the framework. ICLEI is headquartered in Toronto, Canada, and has regional offices in Europe, Asia, Latin America, and Africa (ICLEI 1996; UNCHS and UNEP 1996).

Resources and Exercises for Further Thought

Resources

CLASSIC VERSUS STRATEGIC URBAN ENVIRONMENTAL PLANNING

Three texts provide good advice about local environmental action planning: Bartone et al. 1994, ICLEI 1996, and UNCHS and UNEP 1997.

INFORMED CONSULTATION

A number of good publications focus on the involvement of citizens in planning and decision-making processes. A user-friendly set of materials is *The participation toolkit,* available from the World Bank.

STRATEGY DEVELOPMENT

There is no one model for how cities should develop their local environmental action plans. Several different approaches are covered in Chapter 7.

IMPLEMENTATION

Updated information on urban indicators, including environmental ones, that have been developed at the global level can be found at http://www.undp.org/un/habitat/indicators. In the United States, there is a Community Indicators Network that maintains a Web site at http://www.rprogress.org.

THE FRAMEWORK IN ACTION

Updated information on the Sustainable Cities Programme can be obtained at http://www.unchs.unon.org/unon/unchs/scp/scphome.htm, and for the Local Agenda 21 Initiative at http://www.iclei.org.

Exercises for Further Thought

1. Why has environmental impact assessment become the default approach to handling environmental problems in many cities?
2. How is strategic environmental assessment different from the LEAP process? How might the two be used together?
3. The LEAP process can take several years. What should be done in the interim to address critical environmental problems?

4. How might a city's level of development and other characteristics influence the way it proceeds with urban environmental planning?
5. Design a LEAP process that would be most suited to your city.
6. Stakeholder participation is emphasized throughout the planning framework. What are the risks of continuous public involvement in environmental planning?
7. Develop a list of the key stakeholders who should be involved in urban environmental planning in your city.
8. How might the perspectives and priorities of affected stakeholders, decision-makers, and experts differ?
9. Why is the "priority problem" approach more strategic than organizing the LEAP process according to sectors or themes?
10. What problems might be encountered in collecting urban environmental data that are dispersed among several sources and levels of government?
11. Why will the prioritization of urban environmental issues and options be somewhat subjective?
12. Develop indicators for monitoring environmental conditions in your city.
13. Where should your city enter the LEAP process? What risks will it face in following the framework?

References

Au, Elvis W. K. 1998. Analysis of environmental sustainability of Hong Kong's territorial development strategy review—Lessons and experiences. *Environmental Assessment* March: 20–22.

Bartone, Carl, Janis Bernstein, Josef Leitmann, and Jochen Eigen. 1994. Toward environmental strategies for cities: Policy considerations for urban environmental management in developing countries. UMP Policy Paper No. 18. Washington, D.C.: World Bank.

Bursa Metropolitan Municipality. 1998. The city of Bursa: Towards a sustainable development—A new consensus. Report prepared for ICLEI Executive Committee meeting, 12–15 March, Bursa.

Campbell, Scott. 1996. Green cities, growing cities, just cities? Urban planning and the contradictions of sustainable development. *APA Journal* 62(3): 296–312.

Christensen, Karen. 1985. Coping with uncertainty in planning. *APA Journal* Winter: 69.

CSIRO (Commonwealth Scientific and Industrial Research Organization) and AHURI (Australian Housing and Urban Research Institute). 1998. Key environmental indicators for human settlements in Australia. Report to the State of the Environment Reporting Unit. Melbourne: CSIRO at AHURI.

Goodland, Robert. 1997. The strategic environmental assessment family. *Ea: The Magazine of the IEA & EARA* September: 17–19.

Hickie, David, and Max Wade. 1997. The development of environmental action plans: Turning statements into actions. *Journal of Environmental Planning and Management* 40(6): 789–801.

ICLEI (International Council for Local Environmental Initiatives). 1996. *The Local Agenda 21 planning guide.* Toronto: ICLEI, IDRC, and UNEP.

Isham, Jonathan, D. Narayan, and L. Pritchett. 1994. Does participation improve performance? Establishing causality with subjective data. Policy Research Working Paper No. 1357. Washington, D.C.: World Bank.

Law, Robert. 1998. Hong Kong: An environmental overview. *World Resource Review* 10(2): 264–272.

Leitmann, Josef. 1993. Rapid urban environmental assessment: Lessons from cities in the developing world. Volume I: Methodology and preliminary findings. UMP Discussion Paper No. 14. Washington, D.C.: World Bank.

Pan-American Health Organization. 1997. Healthy people—Healthy spaces. 1996 Annual Report. Washington, D.C.: PAHO.

Partidario, Maria Rosario. 1996. Strategic environmental assessment: Key issues emerging from recent practice. *Environmental Impact Assessment Review* 16: 31–55.

SME (Indonesian State Ministry of Environment) and BAPEDAL (Environmental Impact Control Agency). 1994. Environmental protection and pollution control strategy and action plan. Summary report. Prepared for Third Jabotabek Urban Development Project. Jakarta: SME/BAPEDAL.

Society for Development Studies. 1996. Housing and urban indicators: Management tools for human settlements—The case of India. New Delhi: Society for Development Studies.

———. 1997. Urban indicators programme phase two: 1997–2001. Program Document. Nairobi: UNCHS.

UNCHS and UNEP (UN Environmental Programme). 1997. Implementing the urban environment agenda. Environmental Planning and Management Source Book Vol. 1. Nairobi: UNCHS and UNEP.

———. 1996. Implementing the urban environment agenda. Meeting and background information for a global meeting of cities and international programs. Istanbul, June 1.

World Bank. 1991. Environmental assessment sourcebook. Volume II: Sectoral guidelines. Technical Paper No. 140. Washington, D.C.: World Bank.

———. 1992. *World development report 1992: Development and the environment.* New York: Oxford University Press.

Young, Mike, and S. Ryan. 1995. Using environmental indicators to promote environmentally, ecologically, and socially-sustainable resource use: A policy-oriented methodology. EPAT/MUCIA Manual No. 3. Washington, D.C.: USAID.

CHAPTER 6

Tools for Analysis and Planning

Once a city has decided to pursue a more environmentally sustainable development path, analytical and planning tools are essential in order to identify and prioritize urban environmental problems and options as well as to monitor implementation. This chapter briefly reviews nine data collection and analytical tools (urban environmental data questionnaire, collecting and ranking indicators, estimating ecological footprints, health risk assessment, economic valuation, three techniques for community and household assessment, and geographic information systems) and two processes (rapid urban environmental assessment and comparative risk assessment) that support planning by combining analytical tools with public consultation. The presentation of each tool and process is only a sketch that suggests where the approach might be most useful. Readers interested in applying a particular technique should consult the Resources and Exercises section in this chapter for more detailed guidance.

Analytical Tools

Techniques for urban environmental analysis can be used throughout the planning and management process. Figure 6-1 summarizes which analytical tools are most appropriate for the three stages of the planning and management framework described in Chapter 5. This section briefly describes each of the tools, reviews their strengths and weaknesses, and provides either technical information or an example of how the technique has been applied.

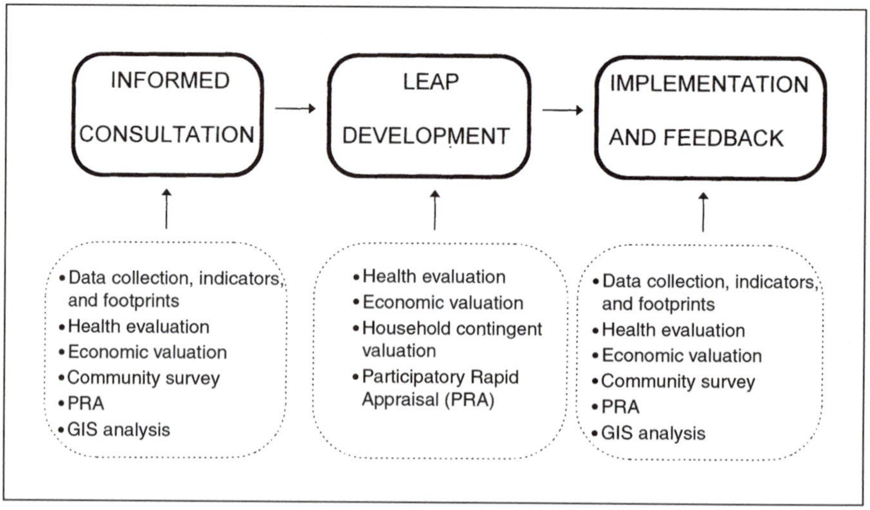

Figure 6-1 Analytical tools for local environmental action planning.

Data Collection, Citywide Indicators, and Ecological Footprints

Environmental data and resulting environmental indicators are essential to establish baseline information on urban environmental quality, problems, and trends. They also need to be assembled in order to monitor progress in implementing urban environmental action plans and policies. Typically, though, information about a city's environmental situation is scattered between different levels of government, in both public and private sources, and among different sectoral agencies within a municipality. Therefore, tools are needed to centralize, prioritize, and analyze such information.

DATA QUESTIONNAIRE

An urban environmental data questionnaire has been designed for use in developing country cities by the UNCHS/World Bank/UNDP Urban Management Program (Leitmann 1994a). The questionnaire is extensive (50 pages) and covers a comprehensive range of topics. An outline of these topics is presented in Box 6-1. The questionnaire is available on diskette, with a downloadable database and help screens. Translations are available in Spanish, French, Arabic, Russian, Turkish, and Hebrew. Data can be entered at the level of the city, the metropolitan area, and/or the urban agglomeration. It is intended to support preparation of an urban environmental profile and to inform a consultative process as part of a rapid urban environmental assessment (see the following section on planning tools).

URBAN INDICATORS

There have been a number of efforts to develop indicators of urban environmental quality at the international, national, and city levels. Indicators allow for a static assessment of conditions, monitoring of change over time, and/or ranking within or between cities. Guidance for developing and using indicators in the LEAP framework is provided in Chapter 5. Internationally, UNCHS, in cooperation with the World Bank, developed a set of urban indicators to help countries prepare for the 1996 Habitat II conference. The group of policy-linked environmental indica-

BOX

GENERAL INFORMATION

I. **Socioeconomic Background**
(Urban population, demographics, income and poverty, employment, municipal services, municipal expenditures)

II. **Housing Conditions**
(Ownership, facilities, size, marginal units)

III. **Health Conditions**
(Basic statistics, mortality rates)

IV. **Natural Environment**
(Location, ecosystem type, meteorological data, dispersion conditions, topography, environmental hazards)

V. **Land Use**
(Urban land use, newly incorporated urban land, land ownership, land registration, land use regulation, land market)

VI. **Urban Transport**
(Basic statistics, vehicle stocks, motorized travel by mode, emissions, injuries from accidents, passenger car restrictions)

VII. **Energy Use**
(Annual gross energy consumption, emissions from combustion, interconnected electricity grid, in-city electricity utility, urban electricity self-generation, household energy consumption, other indicators, energy pricing)

VIII. **Air Pollution**
(Emissions intensity, emissions control, policy implementation, ambient concentrations, monitoring, environmental health)

IX. **Noise Pollution**
(Noise levels, noise pollution control)

X. **Water and Sanitation**
(Water resources, groundwater abstraction problems, future resources, water supply, water delivery, household sanitation installations, drainage network coverage, sewage flow rates, sewage treatment plants, sewage disposal, industrial effluents, water pollution policy instruments, water quality monitoring, monitoring)

XI. **Solid and Hazardous Wastes**
(Total solid wastes generated, municipal solid wastes, disposal of municipal solid wastes, municipal expenditures for solid waste management, dumpsites, hazardous waste facilities, hazardous waste policies being implemented)

Box 6-1 Outline of urban environmental data questionnaire.

tors, summarized in Table 6-1, is one of five sets that make up the urban indicators. They are currently being revised to support a Global Urban Observatory program.

At the national level, China uses its own set of urban environmental indicators to monitor progress in individual cities over time, to make comparisons between cities, to prepare compara-

Table 6-1 UNCHS Urban Indicators for Environmental Management

Policy goals and subgoals	Indicators*
Improve urban air quality	
• Achieve targeted standards	A43: Air pollution concentrations
• Limit emissions	A44: Emissions per capita
• Reduce respiratory disease	A45: Acute respiratory deaths
Improve urban water quality	15: Percent of wastewater treated
• Improve wastewater treatment	A46: Percent of BOD removed
• Reduce costs and promote efficiency	A47: Wastewater treatment cost
• Improve recycling of "gray" water	A48: Lowering of water table
• Improve sustainability of supply	A49: Wastewater recycled
	A50: Level of treatment
Improve solid waste collection and disposal	16: Solid waste generated
• Improve access to collection	17: Disposal methods for waste
• Improve affordability of service	18: Regularity of waste collection
• Improve convenience and reliability	A51: Biodegradable waste
• Improve recycling of waste	A52: Recycling rate
• Ensure sustainability of collection	A53: Cost of waste disposal
	A54: Cost recovery
	A55: Industrial waste generation
Ensure sustainability of resource usage	A56: Energy use per person
• Sustainability of natural resource use	A57: Fuelwood use
• Reduce use of nonrenewables	A58: Renewable energy use
• Encourage sustainable food use	A59: Food consumption
Reduce effects of natural and man-made disaster	19: Housing destroyed
• Ensure housing is safely located	A60: Disaster mortality
• Reduce deaths and property damage	A61: Housing on fragile land
• Improve industrial safety	A62: Fatal industrial accidents
Improve urban natural and built environment	
• Provide adequate green space	A63: Green space per capita
• Minimize destruction of historic sites	A64: Monument list

* Primary indicators are numbered; secondary indicators begin with "A."

Source: UNCHS 1997.

Table 6-2 Urban Environmental Indicators for Tianjin, China, 1990

Indicator	Unit	Level	Score	Max. score
Daily average of TSP	mg/m^3	0.29	6.0	7.0
Daily average of SO_2	mg/m^3	0.10	0.1	3.0
Coverage of dust control area	%	100	5.0	5.0
Coverage of urban gasification	%	80.4	3.0	3.0
Coverage of urban district heating	%	10.9	0.6	3.0
Coal-using households	%	51.5	2.5	5.0
Industries meeting air quality standards	%	67.1	2.0	5.0
Vehicles meeting exhaust standards	%	75.6	2.5	4.0
Drinking water meeting standards	%	96.4	6.0	7.0
Average COD in urban surface water	mg/l	6.4	4.5	5.0
Wastewater per value of output	t/Y10,000	69.5	5.0	5.0
Municipal wastewater treated	%	22.0	3.5	5.0
Industrial wastewater meeting standards	%	77.7	3.0	4.0
Industrial wastewater treated	%	59.6	2.0	4.0
Average ambient noise	dB(A)	59.0	6.0	10.0
Average traffic noise on main roads	dB(A)	71.0	4.5	5.0
Industrial solid waste recovered	%	62.3	4.5	5.0
Industrial solid waste treated	%	31.0	2.5	5.0
Municipal solid waste disposed	%	100	5.0	5.0
Green area per capita	m^2	2.32	1.0	5.0
TOTAL			69.2	100.0

Source: Chinese NEPA 1991.

tive rankings, and to financially reward performance (Leitmann 1994b). An example of urban environmental indicator results for one city is provided in Table 6-2. In a developed country, the World Resources Institute at one time collected environmental data for the 75 largest U.S. metropolitan areas and conducted an unweighted "green metro" ranking based on nine indicators (moderate air pollution days, unhealthy air pollution days, drinking water quality, toxic releases and transfers, number of toxic waste sites, solid waste collected per capita, heating- and cooling-degree days, vehicle miles traveled per capita, and mass transit passenger miles traveled per capita). In addition, indicators are collected on population density, percentage of urban area devoted to parkland, percentage of waste recycled, water use per capita, percentage of groundwater dependence, and miles of bike paths (WRI 1994).

At the local level, many cities have developed their own urban indicators according to local conditions and needs. The environment often features prominently as a key set of indicators. In the United States, the Community Indicators Network monitors nearly 150 communities around the country that are developing and applying "report cards" of their long-term health and sustainability. Jacksonville, Florida, has the oldest indicators in the United States; they were initially developed by a nonprofit organization. Citywide environmental indicators in Jacksonville include days with good air quality, potable water consumption per household, number of septic tank permits issued (undesirable), and compliance with dissolved oxygen standards. An "equity index" is also issued for the city's 17 neighborhoods to compare and improve fairness in the delivery of urban services (Andrews 1996; Jacksonville 1997).

ECOLOGICAL FOOTPRINT ANALYSIS

The ecological footprint tool has been described in Chapter 4. It requires the following steps:

1. Collecting data on a city's population, physical size, annual resource use, and annual waste generation
2. Identifying and applying conversion factors to translate resource consumption into the land and sea area needed each year to produce the resources, and the surface area needed to absorb wastes
3. Summing up the land and sea area requirements and determining per capita ecological footprints
4. Comparing these figures with city size, national land area, the city's previous footprint, average global land availability, etc.

An example of a partial ecological footprint analysis for London is presented in Box 6-2.

Systematic collection of data, indicators, and footprints of the urban environment is useful for two stages of the environmental planning and management framework: They generate baseline information that can be used in informed consultation, and they provide for evaluation and comparison that can aid implementa-

BOX

Greater London, with a population of 7 million, has the following resource use and waste profile:

RESOURCES USED	TONNES PER YEAR
Fuel (oil equivalent)	20,000,000
Oxygen	40,000,000
Water	1,002,000,000
Food	2,400,000
Timber	1,200,000
Paper	2,200,000
Plastics	2,100,000
Glass	360,000
Cement	1,940,000
Bricks, blocks, sand, and tarmac	6,000,000
Metals (total)	1,200,000

WASTES	TONNES PER YEAR
Industrial and construction wastes	11,400,000
Household, civic, and commercial wastes	3,900,000
Wet, digested sewage sludge	7,500,000
CO_2	60,000,000
SO_2	400,000
NO_x	280,000

Based on these figures, a partial ecological footprint was calculated for Greater London, consisting of the land area required to supply the city with food, fiber, and wood products, and the area of vegetation needed to absorb its carbon dioxide output.

	ACRES
London's surface area:	390,000
Farmland used (average 3 acres/person):	21,000,000
Forest area for wood products (average 0.27 acres/person):	1,900,000
Land for carbon absorption (average 3.7 acres/person):	26,000,000
Total ecological footprint:	48,900,000
= 125 times Greater London's surface area	
Britain's productive land area:	52,000,000
Britain's total surface area:	60,000,000

Box 6-2 Calculating London's ecological footprint.

SOURCE: Girardet cited in Sustainable London Trust 1997.

tion. The strengths of using these informational tools are that they (1) centralize information that is normally dispersed among a wide range of sources; (2) identify gaps where critical information may be missing; and (3) are useful for analysis when comparisons are made between baseline and future data or indicators, or between cities when a common data or indicators framework is applied. The weaknesses of the tools are (1) that they are purely descriptive, and (2) there can be problems because environmental data (and subsequent indicators) typically come from varied sources and may apply to dissimilar time periods or areas (e.g., a watershed versus the city versus the metropolitan area), or may have differing degrees of reliability.

Health Evaluation

Urban environmental problems and solutions can be assessed according to their effects on human health. The most common analytical tool for this type of evaluation is health risk assessment; in addition, there are techniques for studying intraurban health differences, assessing the health dimensions of urban crowding and using urban health indicators. Finally, there is an integrated methodology for rating environmental health problems that has been developed for cities and is called environmental health assessment.

Health risk assessment consists of four steps: (1) hazard identification; (2) exposure assessment; (3) dose-response assessment; and (4) risk characterization (National Research Council 1983). The process is diagrammed in Figure 6-2. *Hazard identification* is a qualitative determination of whether human exposure to an agent might result in adverse health effects. *Exposure assessment* involves a quantitative or qualitative estimation of the level and duration of a population's exposure to a toxic agent. The *dose-response assessment* uses a mathematical model to estimate the probability of occurrence of a health effect based on human exposure to a hazardous substance. *Characterizing risk* means estimating the incidence of an adverse effect on a population (WASH 1993a). This technique has been used in several developing country cities to rank environmental problems according to their

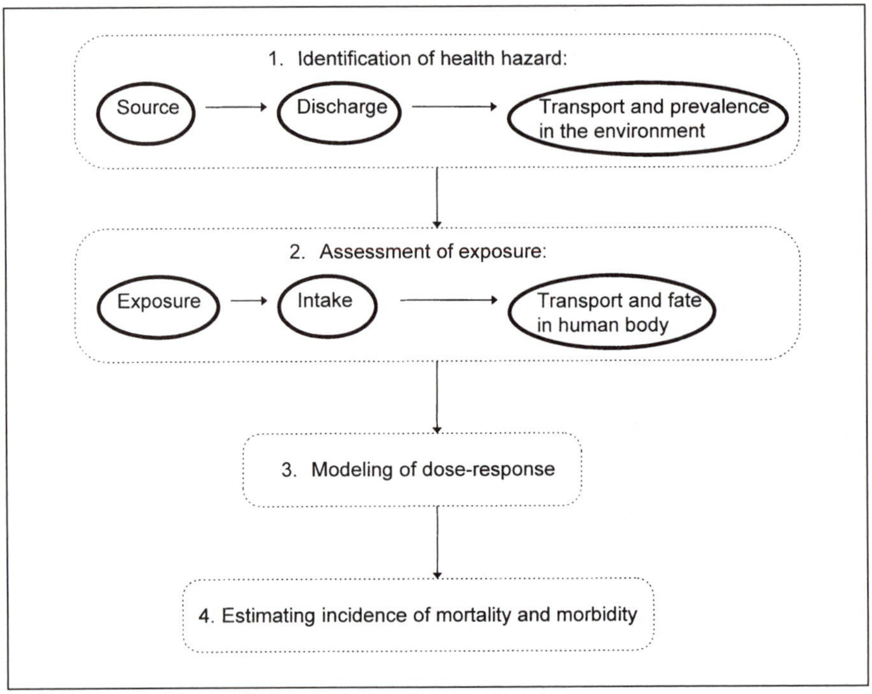

Figure 6-2 Health risk assessment diagram.

effects on human health. It can also be used to estimate the health benefits of addressing one particular environmental problem. For example, if particulate matter in Jakarta were to be reduced to the WHO standard, the range of benefits has been estimated to include 900 to 1900 fewer premature deaths; 6100 to 18,400 avoided cases of chronic bronchitis; 26,600 to 71,000 avoided emergency room visits; and 5.4 to 11.9 million fewer restricted-activity days (Ostro 1994). The results of some recent health risk assessments are summarized in Table 6-3 and suggest that different cities have distinctively different risk profiles.

Intraurban health differential analysis involves disaggregating existing data on health and the environment for a city. This can be based on locally available health statistics as well as urban data from demographic and health survey results in certain countries. Health disparities between groups are analyzed in relation to a composite index of both social and physical environmental conditions. Results of such studies have provided support for the idea

Table 6-3 Top Environmental Health Risks in Five Cities

Risk/City	Bangkok, Thailand (1990)	Quito, Ecuador (1993)	Cairo, Egypt (1994)	Ahmedabad, India (1995)	Lima, Peru (1997)
Sanitation and microbial disease	✓	✓	✓		✓
Ambient particulates	✓	✓	✓	✓	
Lead	✓		✓		
Indoor air pollution		✓*		✓	
Water supply					✓
Solid waste					✓
Transport air pollution				✓	

* Priority risk primarily in slum areas
SOURCE: Brantly 1998.

that the urban poor bear a double burden from infectious and noncommunicable diseases, and that children's health is affected by both the household and neighborhood physical environment (Stephens 1995).

The analysis of crowding is a specialized technique that focuses on a health issue most prevalent in poor communities—

Figure 6-3 Contemplating health risks in Bangkok, Thailand.

the overcrowding of residential space and basic services. The health effects of overcrowding can be evaluated using short-term cross-sectional studies, longer-term epidemiological studies, participatory methods, or crowding indicators. These studies indicate that urban overcrowding increases the risk of disease transmission, multiple infections, severe disease, and the long-term negative effects of infection. UNCHS has concluded that the most cost-effective approach can be the preparation and analysis of crowding indicators, and a set of model indicators has been developed for this purpose (UNCHS 1995).

Broader indicators of urban environmental health are also used to evaluate the impact of environmental conditions on the health of a city's population. In one such effort (WASH 1993b), indicators were developed in order to assess relative health risks across sectors and cities in Central America. Lack of available data prevented achievement of this objective, but the initiative did identify important knowledge gaps. Aggregate indicators can also be used to assess intraurban as well as interurban health differences. A relatively recent aggregate health indicator is the disability-adjusted life year (DALY), which is a measure that combines healthy life years lost because of premature mortality with those lost as a result of disability (World Bank 1993).

Some or all of these techniques can be combined using the urban environmental health assessment approach. The assessment method integrates three approaches to investigate environmental health problems (health risk assessment; health outcomes assessment, such as the intraurban differentials or crowding indicators tools; and ethnographic studies of health-related behavior). A multidisciplinary team uses these tools to examine environment/health relations in eight categories: potable water supply, sanitation and wastewater, solid waste, food hygiene, occupational health, air pollution (indoor and ambient), toxic and hazardous materials, and traffic and household injuries. Original data may also be collected using focus group discussions, in-depth interviews, and structured observations. The outcomes are ratings of environmental health risks and their causes (WASH 1993a). In one application of the health assessment approach in Quito, gastrointestinal problems were rated as a key risk, and food contamination from microorganisms was discovered to be the main cause, leading to a focus on food hygiene and street vendors (Arcia et al. 1993).

Figure 6-4 Valuing the environment in Singapore: A plastic tree at the Ministry of Environment.

Health evaluation techniques can be applied at all stages in the LEAP framework. During informed consultations, the assessment can help to prioritize problems according to the severity of health outcomes (as in Bangkok). Options that yield the most significant health benefits can be selected during the strategy development phase. During implementation, health risk assessment can evaluate impacts by estimating changes in a city's health profile due to environmental improvements. The tool's strengths are that it is useful for ranking both problems and options; it can be used to predict outcomes; it is an input for economic valuation analysis (see following section); and it can help identify the causes of certain problems (as was the case in Quito). The disadvantages of these evaluation tools (especially health risk assessment) are that (1) some of the assumptions, especially the transferability of dose-response functions, are subject to question, and (2) the tools focus exclusively on human health effects, leaving out potentially important ecosystem problems.

Economic Valuation

Urban environmental problems have real economic costs that are usually linked to lowered productivity, congestion, and increased health care needs. The most commonly used economic valuation techniques for the urban environment are:

- *Loss in earnings.* Earnings loss is defined as the present value of estimated future earnings lost, plus increased medical expenditures. This technique is commonly used to assess the productivity losses associated with air and water pollution as well as natural and man-made disasters.

- *Actual defensive or preventive expenditures.* These are the costs incurred to avoid negative environmental outcomes. For example, additional costs must be paid by a water utility to treat water that is polluted upstream by industries or another settlement.
- *Replacement cost.* How much would it cost to repair or replace an environmental asset once it has been damaged? For example, energy and water utilities often calculate the cost of electricity from the next power plant or water from the next source of supply to compare with demand management alternatives.
- *Hedonic pricing.* Econometrics is used to determine how environmental (and other) factors affect property values. For example, calculations are made about the effect of proximity to an environmental bad (an airport or waste dump) or good (a park or area with low air pollution) on property values.
- *Travel cost.* A demand curve is developed for an environmentally valued site depending on how much people spend in time and transportation costs to visit the site. For example, the value of an urban park or historical site can be assessed based on the costs incurred by the number of visitors.
- *Contingent valuation.* Survey questions are used to determine what people are willing to pay for an environmental service or to avoid the negative effects of an environmental problem, or what they are willing to accept as payment to tolerate an environmental cost. This technique is used by utilities to determine how much potential consumers will pay for a level or quality of service, and by city agencies facing a not-in-my-backyard situation to determine compensation for siting an environmental facility that is seen by a community as a "bad" such as a sanitary landfill, sewage treatment plant, or waste incinerator. (See the following section for more details on this option.)

These analyses can also include an equity dimension to determine the burden of costs that are borne by the poor. The results from these valuation techniques can then be used to rank problems according to their economic impact, assess options by the economic benefits that might be generated, and evaluate overall strategies using cost-benefit or cost-effectiveness analysis. Examples of economic valuation of urban environmental issues are presented in Table 6-4.

Economic valuation can play a role in all stages of the planning and management process. During informed consultation, problems can be prioritized according to the magnitude of their economic costs. During strategy development, options can be selected by their economic impact, using cost-benefit or cost-effectiveness analysis. During implementation, the net economic benefits of different interventions can be evaluated. Economic valuation has the following advantages as an analytical tool: (1) It facilitates a quantitative ranking of problems and options; (2) cost and/or benefit estimates are critical inputs for calculating the net present value or effectiveness of different strategies; and (3) it yields essential information for investment planning. On the negative side, ethical problems arise when valuation techniques are used to calculate the worth of a human life; data may not be avail-

Table 6-4 Economic Valuation of Urban Environmental Problems

Technique	Application	Source
Loss of earnings	Mexico City: Health and productivity costs of air pollution estimated at over $1 billion per year	Margulis 1992
Defensive and preventive costs	Istanbul: Water treatment costs are 10 to 100 times higher in one district due to slums with poor drainage and sanitation	Leitmann and Baharoglu 1997
Replacement cost	Beijing: Water from next supply project would cost $0.11 per m^3, which is higher than conservation costs	World Bank 1992
Hedonic pricing	Boston: Housing values would increase $3.6 to $17.4 million if 3 hazardous-waste sites were cleaned up	Harrison and Stock 1984
Travel cost	Bangkok: Consumer's surplus of 2 million annual visitors to Lumpinee Park estimated at $520,000 per year	Dixon and Sherman 1990
Contingent valuation	Ouagadougou: Consumers would be willing to cover payback costs of on-site sanitation over 4 to 5 years	Altaf and Hughes 1994

able for the proper use of a valuation technique; and not all environmental costs and benefits can be valued in monetary terms.

Household and Community Techniques

Households and neighborhoods are often at the locus of urban environmental problems *and* solutions. Several techniques can be used to better understand the types of environmental problems faced by urban dwellers, and what households and communities view as their priority environmental problems. These include: (1) classic random-sample household surveys; (2) participatory rapid appraisal; and (3) contingent valuation to assess a household or a community's willingness to pay for a service or an amenity.

RANDOM-SAMPLE SURVEYS

This technique involves collecting and analyzing a broad spectrum of data on household and neighborhood environments and related health conditions. Experts prepare a questionnaire and select a sample of households that is representative of a neighborhood, district, city, or even metropolitan area. The questionnaire is administered by enumerators who usually have limited environmental and health expertise. Responses are then tabulated, and the resulting data are analyzed. The survey may be repeated over time to assess changes in environmental quality and health status. The Stockholm Environment Institute, for example, has used local researchers and international expertise to design and conduct household environmental surveys in four cities (Accra, Jakarta, Port Elizabeth, and Sao Paulo).

Conducting a random-sample survey can generate baseline data for the informed consultation phase and, by comparing baseline data with information from a follow-up survey, it can be used as a monitoring tool during the implementation phase. The strength of this community assessment tool is that it produces representative, geographically specific information where none may have existed previously. The disadvantages of random-sample surveys are that they produce time-limited "snapshots" (unless the survey is repeated); they are not prescriptive; and questionnaire development by experts holds the top-down risk of missing key environmental issues that may be valued by the community being surveyed.

PARTICIPATORY RAPID APPRAISAL (PRA)

Rapid appraisal techniques seek to elicit residents' perspectives on environmental conditions through systematic analysis and a structured presentation of information. PRA can involve one or more of the following approaches: problem mapping; issue and option ranking in focus groups; well-being analysis; seasonal calendars of key community events; life histories; role playing; action research; and small surveys. For example, USAID's Water and Sanitation for Health program has used household interviews and focus groups to investigate comparative health risks in Quito and Pedro Moncayo, Ecuador.

PRA is a technique that can be used throughout the environmental planning and management process. During informed consultation, it can be used to identify and rank problems. Similarly, during strategy development, the PRA approach can help identify and prioritize options. Participatory rapid appraisal is also useful for mobilizing support and community involvement during the implementation of an environmental action plan. On the positive side, PRA helps to build awareness about environmental issues and to develop a consensus about needed actions. Its disadvantages are that PRA may not be genuinely representative of a community's will, partly because the process can be subject to political manipulation, and partly because a comprehensive and representative group of stakeholders may not be involved in the appraisal.

CONTINGENT VALUATION

Contingent valuation can be categorized as both an economic tool and one for community analysis. The approach is based on interviews with a representative sample of an area. The interview consists of (1) a detailed description of the good(s) to be valued as well as the hypothetical situation whereby they are to be made available; (2) questions about the respondent's willingness to pay for the good(s); and (3) data about the respondents, their preferences concerning the good(s), and their use of the good(s) (Mitchell and Carson 1989). The UNDP/World Bank Water and Sanitation Program has undertaken household-level research in, for example, Ghana and Indonesia, to assess consumer willingness to pay for urban water. The technique can also be used for other urban environmental services and facilities such as sanitation, waste collection, drainage, and parks.

In the planning and management framework, contingent valuation is most useful during the strategy development phase, where it can be used to guide pricing policy for an environmental good (such as a park) or service (such as piped water), or for matching technologies with customers' willingness to pay for them. The strength of contingent valuation is that it links planning options to their affordability, thus allowing for more realistic choices. Its weaknesses are that it yields individual rather than social valuations about the importance of different options, and it can only be used for environmental goods and services that can be charged for.

A COMPARISON OF NEIGHBORHOOD-LEVEL TECHNIQUES

Atma Jaya University in Jakarta, supported by the Urban Management Program and the Stockholm Environment Institute, has tested and compared all three techniques to assess their utility for

Table 6-5 Relative Strengths of Household and Community Techniques

	Sample survey	**PRA**	**Contingent valuation**
Monitoring changing conditions	*Very useful*	Less useful	NA
Providing data for central planning	*Very useful*	Less useful	Less useful
Identifying obstacles to environmental improvement	Useful	*Very useful*	Useful
Establishing basis for participation	Less useful	*Very useful*	Less useful
Evaluating economic benefit of an environmental improvement	Less useful	Useful	*Very useful*
Pricing environmental services	Less useful	Less useful	*Very useful*

SOURCE: McGranahan, Leitmann, and Surjadi 1997.

different purposes. The results, summarized in Table 6-5, are that: (1) random-sample surveys are most effective for monitoring changing environmental and health conditions across an urban area or several areas; (2) participatory appraisal is best for establishing a basis for local participation in environmental management; and (3) contingent valuation is most helpful for generating data for an economic evaluation of a particular environmental improvement (McGranahan, Leitmann, and Surjadi 1997). Each technique does not have to be used exclusively; they can be applied in parallel or sequentially. For example, PRA might be used to identify key issues. This information could then be used to design a random-sample survey. Based on survey results, a subsample might form part of a contingent valuation analysis.

Geographic Information Systems

Geographic information system (GIS) analysis, often combined with remotely sensed data, is a powerful tool for urban environmental analysis that is now fairly common in industrialized countries and is increasingly being used in the developing world. Environmental applications of GIS in cities have included: land suitability analysis, hazard and environmental "hot spot" identification, land-use and land cover mapping, watershed analysis, and siting of environmental services and infrastructure. Some real-world examples include:

- Conducting long-term ecological research in Baltimore, Maryland, and Phoenix, Arizona (Parlange 1998)
- Assessing environmental risks from peri-urban soil contamination in The Netherlands (Stein et al. 1995)
- Modeling urban non-point-source pollution in the city of Beaver Dam, Wisconsin (Ventura and Kim 1993)
- Mapping priority urban environmental problems in Ahmedabad, Bombay, Delhi, and Vadodara (India) (National Institute of Urban Affairs 1993)
- Combining satellite remote sensing and GIS analysis to detect conflicts between actual land use and zoning requirements in Cebu City and Lipa City, the Philippines (Rabley 1995)

Other urban applications of GIS include preparation of base maps, change analysis, management of infrastructure networks, housing typologies, and demographic analysis (Paulsson 1992).

GIS analysis is best applied during the informed consultation phase to generate physical and social information, including key correlations, and for monitoring the implementation of environmental action plans in a city. GIS positives are its usefulness as a powerful visual tool for communicating information and creating awareness, and its value as an analytical technique. However, certain features of GIS create limitations: (1) it takes time to train the users of its software and hardware so that they are operational; (2) useful GIS analysis at the city level has high data and maintenance requirements; and (3) it can become a tool of the elite if GIS data and systems are not made publicly available or presented in a way that the public can understand.

Planning Tools That Use Analysis and Public Consultation

The analytical tools just described are useful for assembling information, analyzing data, portraying problems, ranking issues, prioritizing options, and monitoring implementation. Most require specialized expertise, however, and do not provide much of a role for stakeholder input. Also, a particular approach is often chosen as the sole tool for analysis. Two processes for urban environmental planning do allow for interaction between stakeholders and experts, and can make use of a range of analytical tools: These are rapid urban environmental assessment and comparative risk assessment. Finally, analytical tools and a planning tool may be used in a particular city over time to understand and respond to urban environmental challenges, as in the West African city of Accra (see Box 6-4 in the following section).

Figure 6-5 Rapid assessment in Abidjan, Côte d'Ivoire included informal waste management.

Rapid Urban Environmental Assessment

Rapid urban environmental assessment is a process that builds on data and analysis to clarify issues, involve stakeholders, set priorities, and achieve political consensus for action. The assessment consists of three steps: (1) assembly of existing data; (2) analysis of environmental conditions and causal relationships; and (3) public consultation. Data are collected from a range of sources, including the urban questionnaire described previously, routine monitoring, information on existing infrastructure and services, epidemiological and other health statistics, and information on natural resources and systems. These data and the results of existing studies, including environmental health risk assessments, indicators, and GIS analysis, can be used to prepare an environmental profile that reviews environmental quality in an urban area, development-environment interactions, and the institutional setting for environmental management. A generic outline of a profile, also called a "state of the urban environment" report, is presented in Box 6-3. The profile and background data are then shared with a range of stakeholders who are brought together to discuss problems, constraints, priorities, and ways forward. The process is a useful first step toward tackling urban environmental problems because it can address issues that cut across conventional lines of authority, geographical boundaries, and time horizons (Leitmann 1994a).

Comparative Risk Assessment

Each urban environmental problem poses some degree of damage that may be done to human health, the ecology, the economic system, and/or quality of life. According to the U.S. Environmental Protection Agency, comparative risk assessment is "the process by which the form, dimension, and characteristics of that risk are estimated" (USEPA 1990, 2). In 1987, the USEPA issued a national comparative risk report, *Unfinished Business,* that assessed 35 environmental problems and concluded that there were discrepancies between the importance of some problems and the allocation of resources to solve them. This helped popularize the process, and

BOX

I. INTRODUCTION
   Background
   Geophysical and land use
   Socioeconomic setting (demographics, economic structure, urban poverty)
   Environment-development linkages

II. STATUS OF THE ENVIRONMENT IN THE URBAN REGION
   Natural resources
      Air quality
      Water quality (surface, ground, coastal, fisheries)
      Land (forests and natural vegetation; agricultural land; parks, recreation, and open space; historical sites and cultural property)
   Environmental hazards
      Natural risks
      Human-induced risks

III. DEVELOPMENT-ENVIRONMENT INTERACTIONS
   Water supply
   Sewerage and sanitation
   Flood control
   Solid waste management
   Industrial pollution control/hazardous waste management
   Transportation and telecommunications
   Energy and power generation
   Housing
   Health care
   Other

IV. THE SETTING FOR ENVIRONMENTAL MANAGEMENT
   Key actors
      Government (central, regional, local)
      Private sector
      Popular sector (community groups and NGOs, media)
   Management functions
      Instruments of intervention (legislative and regulatory; economic and fiscal; direct investment; planning and policy development; community organizations; education, training, and research; promotion and protest)
      Environmental coordination and decision making (mechanisms for public participation; intersectoral coordination; across levels of government; between public and private sector; intertemporal; information and technical expertise)
   Constraints on effective management
   Ongoing initiatives for institutional strengthening

Box 6-3 Generic outline for urban environmental profile.

SOURCE: Leitmann 1994a.

Figure 6-6 Sustaining Seattle, Washington.

the approach has been applied at the local level in U.S. cities as well as communities in Bulgaria, Hungary, and Russia.

In its urban form, comparative risk assessment involves the following steps:

1. Creating a group of technical experts who identify the major urban environmental problems to be assessed
2. Assembling information on the risks each problem poses for human health, ecosystems, the economy, and urban quality of life
3. Creating a broad group of stakeholders to evaluate the technical risk information, consider the city's ability to manage different risks, and come up with a preliminary ranking of problems
4. Presenting the preliminary rankings at one or more public workshops
5. Incorporating public comment to derive a final ranking of urban environmental risks (Nicholas 1997)

Table 6-6 Comparative Risk Assessment for Seattle, Washington

Environmental problem area	Highest risks
Air quality	Transportation sources of air pollution Wood burning Tobacco smoke
Water quality	Contaminated sediments Combined sewer overflows Storm water discharges
Land use	Loss and degradation of greenbelts Loss and degradation of riparian corridors
Cross-media	Environmental lead Toxins in house dust Hazardous materials use by business/industry

SOURCE: Nicholas 1997.

Comparative risk assessment can draw upon almost all of the analytical tools mentioned here to identify problems, quantify risks, and involve stakeholders. An example of the output from such an assessment for the city of Seattle, Washington, is summarized in Table 6-6.

The head of the Seattle city council assessed the strengths and weaknesses of the risk assessment experience as follows. The planning tool was successful because of capable staff supervision, strong support from the mayor, availability of good data, and good collaboration with citizens. The outputs were useful because they focused on what was feasible for the municipality to do, results helped raise environmental awareness and improve interdepartmental communication, and themes could be incorporated in the city's comprehensive plan. Weaknesses were mainly related to implementation: Staff resources for implementation were limited; some departments resisted internal reforms; and the city's administrative, budgetary, and political organizations did not lend themselves to institutionalizing the action agenda (Street 1998).

Using Several Tools Over Time

Cities may have the resources, interest, or political will to apply only one analytical or planning tool at a time. In lower-income cities, it may be necessary to fill in knowledge gaps about the existence, extent, and impact of various urban environmental problems. Once a critical mass of information and awareness has been achieved, a city can then proceed with completing and implementing environmental action plans. An example of this situation, for Accra, Ghana, is given in Box 6-4.

Tools and Processes: A Suitability Summary

Selection of analytical and planning tools will depend on a number of factors that can differ by city and over time. These include:

BOX

Accra, the capital of the West African country of Ghana, is a low-income city with a population of 1.7 million. Per capita income in Ghana is $350, and nearly half of Accra's population lives in relative poverty. Priority environmental problems include poor sanitation, contaminated surface and groundwater, inadequate solid waste management, and coastal degradation.

Since 1990, there have been a number of initiatives to focus on Accra's environmental problems and to shed light on potential solutions. These have included:

YEAR	INITIATIVE	TOOL OR OUTPUT
1990	UNCHS Structure Plan Project	Consultant report on environmental conditions
1991	National Environmental Action Plan	Economic valuation of environmental costs
1991	UMP tool development project	Rapid urban environmental assessment
1992	Stockholm Environment Institute	Random sample household survey
1993	London School of Hygiene and Tropical Medicine research program	Intraurban health differentials analysis
1995	UNCHS Habitat II preparation	Indicators

The information and awareness generated by these different initiatives have helped the Accra Metropolitan Authority to prepare an urban environmental strategy through the UNCHS/UNEP Sustainable Cities Programme and to implement action plan recommendations with World Bank financing and technical support from the EU/World Bank program for Managing the Environment Locally in Sub-Saharan Africa (MELISSA).

Box 6-4 Applying analytical and planning tools over time in Accra, Ghana.

(1) the availability and quality of existing information about urban environmental issues; (2) the nature of the problem(s) to be analyzed; (3) that stage in the planning framework where analysis is needed; (4) the availability of resources (financial, human, and technical) for analysis; and (5) the urgency with which results are needed. Table 6-7 summarizes information that may be useful to determine their suitability.

Resources and Exercises for Further Thought

Resources

The sketches and examples of different analytical and planning tools may be insufficient for readers who are interested in more details or who would like to actually use a technique for urban environmental analysis and planning. Thus, this section recommends references that provide in-depth guidance.

DATA COLLECTION AND INDICATORS

For a paper copy of the urban environmental questionnaire, as well as information about how it has been applied, see: Leitmann, Josef. 1994a. Rapid urban environmental assessment: Tools and outputs. Volume 2. UNCHS/World Bank/UNDP Urban Management Program Discussion Paper No. 15. Washington, D.C.: World Bank. A database diskette (English only) and translations of the questionnaire (in French, Spanish, Arabic, Russian, Turkish, and Hebrew) can be obtained from the author.

For a complete copy and explanation of the UNCHS urban indicators, see: UNCHS. 1995. Indicators programme—Monitoring the city: Urban indicators review—The survey instrument. Volume 2. Nairobi: UNCHS. Ongoing information about the UNCHS Urban Indicators Programme can be obtained from its Web site at http://www.undp.org/un/habitat/indicators.

A review of experience with indicators in industrialized countries, as well as a sample set of selected indicators for the urban environment, can be found in: OECD (Organization for Economic Cooperation and Development). 1997. *Better understanding our cities: The role of urban indicators*. Paris: OECD.

EcoCal is an on-line tool for calculating urban ecological

Table 6-7 Considerations for Selecting Tools

Tool	Applications	Limitations	Cost	Time
Data questionnaire	1. Assemble secondary data 2. Identification of data gaps 3. Comparative analysis	1. Not prescriptive 2. Data often not comparable over time, areas, populations 3. Variable reliability	$*	As little as one staff-month
Indicators and footprints	1. Development of baseline information 2. Monitoring and evaluation 3. Comparative analysis	1. Not prescriptive 2. Garbage in, garbage out (GIGO): reliability of indicator is only as good as input data	$	Depends on frequency and level of detail
Health risk assessment	1. Ranking problems and options 2. Prediction of outcomes 3. Input for economic valuation 4. Identification of causal factors	1. Variable validity depending on source of assumptions 2. Identifies problems but not solutions	$–$$$	Months (d/r model) to years (epidem.)
Economic valuation	1. Ranking problems and options 2. Input to cost-benefit or cost-effectiveness analysis 3. Investment planning	1. "Valuation of human life" controversy 2. GIGO 3. All costs cannot be captured in economic terms	$–$$	Months
Random-sample surveys	1. Development of baseline data 2. Monitoring changing conditions over time 3. Problem identification	1. Only provides snapshot 2. Not prescriptive 3. Issues are often predetermined by survey designers	$	Depends on experience and sample size
Participatory rapid appraisal	1. Problem identification 2. Consensus building 3. Community awareness	1. Not necessarily representative (nonrandom) 2. Subject to political manipulation	$	Days to months
Contingent valuation	1. Determination of pricing policy for service utility 2. Choice of technology 3. Valuation of amenity	1. Provides individual perspective, not societal value 2. Useful only for issues that can be monetarily valued 3. Limited application	$	Months
GIS	1. Physical information 2. Correlation analysis 3. Monitoring 4. Problem investigation	1. Takes time to understand hardware and software 2. Potential for limited transparency 3. Data requirements high	$–$$$	Variable, depending on data required
Rapid urban environmental assessment	1. Identification and prioritization of issues and options 2. Data and methodology for decision-making 3. Input to strategic process	1. Requires political commitment for follow-up 2. Can be subject to political manipulation	$$	Months
Comparative risk assessment	1. Identification and prioritization of issues 2. Generates data for decision-making 3. Input to strategic process	1. Requires political commitment for follow-up 2. Can be subject to political manipulation	$–$$	Months to years

* $ = under US$10,000; $$ = $10,000 to $50,000; $$$ = over $50,000.

footprints, based on U.K. data. It can be accessed at www.bestfootforward.com.

HEALTH EVALUATION

For a summary of approaches and results of different techniques for understanding urban environmental health, see:

Atkinson, Sarah, Jacob Songsore, and Edmundo Werna (eds.). 1996. *Urban health research in developing countries: Implications for policy.* Oxon (UK): CAB International.

Bradley, David, Carolyn Stephens, Trudy Harpham, and Sandy Cairncross. 1992. A review of environmental health impacts in developing country cities. Urban Management Programme Paper No. 6. Washington, D.C.: World Bank.

ECONOMIC VALUATION

A recent overview of economic valuation methods, their application in urban areas of Asia, and their suitability for different types of problems is: Shin, Euisoon et al. 1997. Valuating the economic impacts of urban environmental problems: Asian cities. UMP Working Paper No. 13. Washington, D.C.: World Bank.

HOUSEHOLD AND COMMUNITY TECHNIQUES

Many references are available for preparation of random-sample surveys. A good manual that includes examples of household environmental issues is: Nichols, P. 1991. *Social survey methods: A fieldguide for development workers.* Oxford: Oxfam.

Several different handbooks are available on techniques that support PRA. The following, for example, provides an overview of participatory philosophy and 101 activities to support PRA: Pretty, J. N., I. Gujit, I. Scoones, and J. Thompson. 1995. *A trainer's guide for participatory learning and action.* London: International Institute for Environment and Development.

The application of PRA in urban areas as well as the technique's limits are reviewed in: Mitlin, Diana, and J. Thompson. 1995. Participatory approaches in urban areas: Strengthening civil society or reinforcing the status quo? *Environment and Urbanization* 7(1):231–250.

While it is somewhat dated, the closest thing to a textbook on contingent valuation is: Mitchell, R. C., and R. T. Carson. 1989. *Using surveys to value public goods: The contingent valuation method*. Washington, D.C.: Resources for the Future.

For a presentation, application, and comparison of all three neighborhood-level techniques, see: McGranahan, Gordon, Josef Leitmann, and Charles Surjadi. 1997. Understanding environmental problems in disadvantaged neighborhoods: Broad spectrum surveys, participatory appraisal and contingent valuation. UMP Working Paper No. 16. Washington, D.C.: World Bank.

GEOGRAPHIC INFORMATION SYSTEMS

For a useful review of urban applications of GIS analysis, often in combination with satellite remote sensing, see: Paulsson, Bengt. 1992. Urban applications of satellite remote sensing and GIS analysis. UMP Discussion Paper No. 9. Washington, D.C.: World Bank.

PLANNING PROCESSES

A description of rapid urban environmental assessment, a set of tools, examples of their application, and an assessment of results in seven cities around the world can be found in: Leitmann, Josef. 1994. Rapid urban environmental assessment. Volumes 1 and 2. UNCHS/World Bank/UNDP Urban Management Program Discussion Papers Nos. 14 and 15. Washington, D.C.: World Bank.

A good handbook on using comparative or environmental risk assessment is: Asian Development Bank. 1990. Environmental risk assessment: Dealing with uncertainty in environmental impact assessment. Environment Paper No. 7. Manila: Asian Development Bank. Recent experience with using several planning tools over time for urban management can be found in the urban chapters of the 1999/2000 *World Development Report* (World Bank 1999).

Exercises for Further Thought

Students and practitioners can "get their feet wet" by trying out one or more of the following exercises:

1. Collect baseline environmental data on a city or region using the "Urban Environmental Questionnaire."
2. Select a set of environmental indicators, collect the necessary data, and calculate the indicators for a city or region.
3. Calculate the ecological footprint of a city or region.
4. Prepare an "Urban Environmental Profile" of a city or region.
5. Organize an "Urban Environmental Consultation" of stakeholders in a neighborhood or city to identify and prioritize environmental problems and identify options.
6. Conduct a health risk assessment for a city or region to either (a) identify the major health effects of a single environmental problem or (b) rank a range of environmental problems according to their health effects.
7. Calculate the economic cost of an environmental problem in a city or region.
8. Estimate the annual wealth (produced assets + natural capital + human resources) of a city or region.
9. Conduct a random-sample survey on household environmental problems in a neighborhood.
10. Prepare a participatory rapid appraisal of a neighborhood's environmental issues.
11. Undertake a contingent valuation survey to assess a neighborhood's willingness to pay for an environmental service.
12. Use geographic information system (GIS) analysis to prepare an environmental constraint map of a city or region.
13. Assemble available information on environmental risks to prepare a preliminary comparative risk assessment of a city's environmental problems.

References

Altaf, Mir, and Jeffrey Hughes. 1994. Measuring the demand for improved urban sanitation services: Results of a contingent valuation study in Ouagadougou, Burkina Faso. *Urban Studies* 31(10): 1763–1776.

Andrews, James H. 1996. Going by the numbers: Using indicators to know where you've been—and where you're going. *Planning*. September.

Arcia, Gustavo, et al. 1993. Environmental health assessment: A case study conducted in the City of Quito and the County of Pedro Moncayo, Pichincha Province, Ecuador. WASH Field Report No. 401. Washington, D.C.: USAID.

Bartone, Carl, Janis Bernstein, Josef Leitmann, and Jochen Eigen. 1994. Toward environmental strategies for cities. UNCHS/World Bank/UNDP Urban Management Program Policy Paper No. 18. Washington, D.C.: World Bank.

Brantly, Gene. 1998. Comparative risk assessment: Setting priorities for urban environmental management in developing countries. Overhead presentation to training session on "Urban environment: Management strategies, action plans and metropolitan challenges." Washington, D.C., World Bank, March 2–4.

Chinese NEPA (National Environmental Protection Agency). 1991. Report on the State of the Environment in China, 1990. Beijing: NEPA.

Davidson, Forbes, et al. 1993. Relocation and resettlement manual. Rotterdam: Institute for Housing and Development Studies.

Dixon, John, and Paul Sherman. 1990. *Economics of protected areas: A new look at benefits and costs*. Washington, D.C.: Island Press.

GTZ (Gesellschaft fur Technische Zusammenarbeit). 1994. Manual for urban environmental management. Eschborn (Germany): GTZ.

Harrison, David, and James Stock. 1984. Hedonic housing values, local public goods and the benefits of hazardous waste clean-up. Discussion Paper E-84-09. Cambridge, Mass.: Energy and Environmental Policy Center, John F. Kennedy School of Government, Harvard University.

Jacksonville Chamber of Commerce and City of Jacksonville. 1997. Quality of life in Jacksonville: Indicators for progress. Executive Summary. Jacksonville: Jacksonville Community Council Inc.

Leitmann, Josef. 1994a. Rapid urban environmental assessment. Volumes 1 and 2. UNCHS/World Bank/UNDP Urban Management Program Discussion Papers Nos. 14 and 15. Washington, D.C.: World Bank.

——— 1994b. Urban environmental profile of Tianjin. *Cities* 11(5).

Leitmann, Josef, and Deniz Baharoglu. 1997. Reaching Turkey's spontaneous settlements: The institutional dimension of infrastructure provision. World Bank Research Report. Washington, D.C.: World Bank.

Margulis, Sergio. 1992. Back-of-the-envelope estimates of environmental damage costs in Mexico. Working Paper Series No. 824. Washington, D.C.: World Bank.

McGranahan, Gordon, Josef Leitmann, and Charles Surjadi. 1997. Understanding environmental problems in disadvantaged neighborhoods: Broad spectrum surveys, participatory appraisal and contingent valuation. UMP Working Paper No. 16. Washington, D.C.: World Bank.

METAP (Mediterranean Environmental Technical Assistance Program). 1993. Tangiers environmental audit. Washington, D.C.: World Bank.

Mitchell, R. C., and R. T. Carson. 1989. *Using surveys to value public goods: The contingent valuation method.* Washington, D.C.: Resources for the Future.

National Research Council. 1983. *Risk assessment in the Federal Government: Managing the process.* Washington, D.C.: National Academy Press.

National Institute of Urban Affairs. 1993. Urban environmental maps for Bombay, Delhi, Ahmedabad, Vadodara. New Delhi: National Institute of Urban Affairs.

Nicholas, Steven. 1997. Risk-based urban environmental planning: The Seattle experience. In Donald Miller and Gert de Roo (eds.). *Urban environmental planning,* 87–106. Aldershot (UK): Avebury.

OECD (Organization for Economic Cooperation and Development). 1997. *Better understanding our cities: The role of urban indicators*. Paris: OECD.

Ostro, Bart. 1994. Estimating the health effects of air pollutants: A method with an application to Jakarta. Policy Research Working Paper No. 1301. Washington, D.C.: World Bank.

Parlange, Mary. 1998. The city as an ecosystem. *Bioscience* 48(8): 581–585.

Paulsson, Bengt. 1992. Urban applications of satellite remote sensing and GIS analysis. UMP Discussion Paper No. 9. Washington, D.C.: World Bank.

Rabley, Peter. 1995. Developing a framework for planning support systems in Philippine cities: A case study from Cebu City, Visayas and Lipa City, Luzon. *Regional Development Dialogue* 16(1): 36–52.

Shin, Euisoon, et al. 1997. Valuating the economic impacts of urban environmental problems: Asian cities. UMP Working Paper No. 13. Washington, D.C.: World Bank.

Stein, Alfred, Igor Staritsky, Johan Bouma, and Jan Willem van Groenigen. 1995. Interactive GIS for environmental risk assessment. *International Journal of Geographical Information Systems* 9(5): 509–525.

Stephens, Carolyn. 1995. The urban environment, poverty and health in developing countries. *Health Policy and Planning* 10(2): 109–121.

Street, Jim. 1998. Environmental stewardship in Seattle: Setting an environmental action agenda and the realities of implementation. Presentation to World Bank course, "Urban environment: Management strategies, action plans and metropolitan challenges." Washington, D.C., March 3.

Sustainable London Trust. 1997. *Creating a sustainable London*. London: Sustainable London Trust.

UNCHS. 1995. Human settlement interventions addressing crowding and health issues. Nairobi: UNCHS.

———. 1997. Indicators programme 1994–96: Programme activities—Analysis of data collection. Nairobi: UNCHS.

USEPA (Environmental Protection Agency). 1990. Reducing risk:

Setting priorities and strategies for environmental protection. Report SAB-EC-90-201. Washington, D.C.: USEPA.

Ventura, Stephen, and Kyehyun Kim. 1993. Modeling urban nonpoint source pollution with a geographic information system. *Water Resources Bulletin* 29(2): 189–198.

WASH (Water and Sanitation for Health Project). 1993a. Environmental health assessment: An integrated methodology for rating environmental health problems. WASH Field Report No. 436. Washington, D.C.: USAID.

———. 1993b. Planning for urban environmental health programs in Central America: The development of water and sanitation-related environmental health indicators and the survey of existing data in three cities. WASH Field Report No. 420. Washington, D.C.: USAID.

World Bank. 1992. *World development report 1992: Development and the environment*. New York: Oxford University Press.

——— 1993. *World development report 1993: Investing in health*. New York: Oxford University Press.

———. 1999. *World development report 1999/2000: Entering the 21st century—development imperatives*. New York: Oxford University Press.

WRI (World Resources Institute). 1994. *The 1994 Information Please environmental almanac*. Boston: Houghton Mifflin Company.

CHAPTER 7

The LEAP Process in Action

Chapter Outline

- Informed consultation
  - Examples
  - Lessons
- LEAP formulation
  - Examples
  - Lessons
- LEAP implementation
  - Examples
  - Lessons
- Resources and exercises for further thought
- References

Local environmental action planning is an ideal approach for anticipating, mitigating, and resolving priority environmental problems in cities. In reality, bits and pieces of the LEAP process are usually pursued and implemented. LEAP planning and implementation are not easy, inexpensive, or irreversible. This chapter offers real-world experience and lessons learned about informed consultation, LEAP formulation, and LEAP implementation.

Informed Consultation

Examples

One of the first systematic attempts to develop informed consultation for urban environmental planning was the formulation and testing of rapid urban environmental assessment. The rapid assessment approach to informed consultation consists of three steps: (1) collecting existing urban environmental data using a standard questionnaire; (2) assessing the state of the urban environment and management by preparing a profile; and (3) organizing a stakeholder consultation to review information and set priorities. This planning tool is more fully described in the previous chapter.

The case study approach was selected to test the methodology because it is a valid research tool in the absence of theoretical guidance in this field. The following criteria were used to select the cases: (1) Cities were chosen from different continents, cultures, and political systems; (2) they reflected different levels of per capita income, with varying degrees of poverty; (3) they were characterized by different stages and types of industrialization; (4) both large and smaller cities were included in the sample; and (5) baseline data were available from ongoing activities so that primary research can be minimized. These criteria were combined with a resource constraint to select six cities and one urbanizing area: Accra (Ghana), Jakarta (Indonesia), Katowice (Poland), Sao Paulo (Brazil), Tianjin (China), Tunis (Tunisia), and the Singrauli region (India).

Results from the data collection and profile activities in the seven case studies yielded three sets of preliminary findings. In the area of urban poverty and economic structure, it appears that:

- *Urban environmental degradation has a disproportionate negative impact on the poor.* The poor suffer disproportionately from urban environmental insults; environmentally sensitive and hazardous urban areas are often inhabited by the poor; the poor pay more for basic environmental services and infrastructure; income is not always the best measure of poor quality of life; and targeted interventions can improve the environmental conditions of low-income groups.

- *Economic structure shapes environmental problems.* The structure and location of economic activities in and around cities affect the prevalence and severity of particular environmental problems. The important economic variables that appear to influence environmental problems are: spatial patterns of industrial location and impacts on health; the effectiveness of industrial pollution control; energy use and industrial structure; and the size and nature of the informal sector.
- *Level of urban wealth is linked to certain environmental problems.* Basic sanitation is a problem of low-income cities. Hazardous wastes, ambient air pollution, and lack of green space are priority problems of higher-income cities. Surface water pollution and inadequate solid waste management are problems that plague developing urban areas, regardless of their level of wealth.

In the area of urban institutions and management, information resulting from the process of collecting data and preparing profiles indicated:

- *Coherent environmental management is complicated.* Managing urban environmental problems is complex because it involves a large number of actors per problem area; cross-jurisdictional conflicts; central-local conflicts; and tension between forces for centralization and devolution of authority.
- *Institutions, policies, and problems are not synchronized.* Part of the managerial complexity stems from the fact that often there is little relationship between the spatial scale or nature of urban environmental problems, which are often cross-sectoral, and the design of sectoral institutions and policies.
- *Municipal capacity affects environmental quality.* If solutions to particular environmental problems are within the purview of municipal institutions, then they must have appropriate financial and human resources. When resources are inadequate, the maintenance and/or expansion of environmental services and infrastructure will be constrained.

Stakeholder consultations were conducted in four of the seven areas (Accra, Jakarta, Katowice, and Sao Paulo). The priority problems identified during these discussions are summarized in Table 7-1. This phase of informed consultation yielded two interesting results. First, public opinion and professional/scientific priorities may differ: Neither public opinion nor scientific analysis provides the optimal means of ranking urban environmental problems; both public and analytic processes have their biases; and a combined approach offers the potential for improving each process. Second, cities have significant extraurban environmental impacts; urban demand for resources and the disposal of city wastes that result from resource transformation can harm environmental systems outside the city proper.

These findings offer potentially important advice for those seeking to improve environmental management, especially in Third World cities. The following general conclusions flowed from this experience: (1) Urban environmental strategies should have an explicit focus on the problems of the poor; (2) city-specific

Table 7-1 Environmental Priorities from Four Informed Consultations

Problem priority	City			
	Accra	**Jakarta**	**Katowice**	**Sao Paulo**
High	Ineffective land use controls	Poor solid waste management	Inadequate public awareness	Substandard housing
	Poor solid waste management	Groundwater pollution	Industrial pollution and structure	Lack of urban infrastructure for poor
	Inadequate sanitation	Surface/bay water pollution	Solid and hazardous waste pollution	Settlement of risk-prone areas
	Poor drainage	Air pollution	Air pollution	Limited green space
Medium	Insufficient housing and green space	Substandard housing	Water pollution and inadequate supply	Inadequate sewage treatment
	Poor transport management	Poor transport management	Inadequate sanitation	Water supply not protected
	Low public awareness	Deteriorating public utilities	Lack of green space/ clean soil	Flooding
Low	Industrial pollution	Inadequate social infrastructure	Poor transport management	Vehicular air pollution
	Environment not part of planning	Lack of green and open spaces	Energy-related pollution	Poor transport management

Figure 7-1 Poor solid waste management: Stakeholder priority in Jakarta, Indonesia.

strategies should be guided by the configuration of key economic variables; (3) solutions that are not heavily dependent on institutional performance may be necessary in the short run because of the organizational problems of complexity and synchronization; (4) enhanced public awareness, consultation, and participation can improve environmental management; and (5) when designing interventions, careful attention should be paid to the selection of problem areas, their scale, and institutional capacity.

Lessons

Early experiences with rapid urban environmental assessment (Leitmann 1994) yielded lessons about using this process as an approach to informed consultation. The benefits and disadvantages of the overall methodology will be reviewed first, followed by comments on each of the three components (questionnaire, profile, and consultations). Briefly, the advantages of the general approach are that it (1) is rapid; (2) costs relatively little; (3) centralizes diverse information; and (4) benefits from local access to information. On average, the three-step rapid assessment required six person-months of effort over an elapsed period of five to nine months. The local costs for research, writing, and organizing the consultations ranged between $16,000 (Accra) and $27,000 (Jakarta) per city. The research and public discussions led to the centralization of a wide range of environmental information in one place for the first time in each city. Involving local researchers and institutions facilitated access to information and decision-makers for a variety of reasons (knowledge of the local language(s) and cultural practices; past experience with the subject matter, relevant organizations, and individuals; and established reputation in the field).

The general methodology also suffered from three main disadvantages. The first limitation is intrinsically part of the process: The methodology generates purely descriptive information. It provides some guidance as to what might be a priority problem, but little to no indication as to what might constitute the range of possible solutions. This can be overcome if rapid assessment is part of a LEAP process where options are identified as part of the LEAP formulation phase. Second, the approach relies on existing sources of information. By using secondary data, results (numbers, analyses, and discussions) are confined by the range and quality of work that has already been done. The reverse side of this coin is that the methodology identifies gaps in knowledge. Third, results cannot always be used for comparison between cities because the respective data may apply to different time periods, could have been derived in different ways, or are based on different samples.

Narrowing the critique to examine each step of the process, the benefits of the *questionnaire* are that it (1) is a straightforward guide to gathering a comprehensive set of data on a particular city or metropolitan area; (2) brings together data from many different sources and allows for intra- and intersectoral comparisons that are often not possible from a single source of information; and (3) can serve several useful purposes (e.g., by generating information for preparing the profile, the consultations, and intercity comparisons). On the negative side, some of the questions were subject to misinterpretation. A good deal of effort went into correcting these errors and/or explaining the meaning and means of answering particular questions. This may be an unavoidable learning curve phenomenon that does have educational benefits. Also, in each city, certain data were simply not available from secondary sources. This meant that the question or table was left blank, conversion factors from other cities were used to calculate values (with uncertain degrees of error), or primary data should have been collected. (Unfortunately, funds were not available for this option.)

For practitioners, the following lessons were learned about collecting data on the urban environment:

- *Needed skills:* The individual, firm, institution, or study team that prepares the questionnaire should have a professional background in urban and environmental issues, an understanding of the range of information sources, and access to those sources.
- *Preparation process:* Mailing or distributing all or parts of the questionnaire to officials for them to fill in is usually less productive and more time-consuming than directly requesting, compiling, and summarizing data.
- *Access to information:* Gathering information to prepare the questionnaire will require access to a range of governmental and other organizations at the local, regional, and national levels. This takes knowledge of information sources, appropriate contacts within the agencies where the data are located, and patience. A letter of introduction from a respected official or group can be helpful.

The benefits of preparing the *profile* were that (1) it summarized information on causal relationships between environmental quality and development activities, and the institutional dimension of urban environmental issues that were not collected in the questionnaire; (2) it brought together conclusions from reports developed in different sectors or over time that referred to a common problem; and (3) it served as a useful background document for, among other things, the consultations, government agencies, NGOs, and donors. The principal drawback of the profile is that it is a static document. Each profile has a relatively short lifespan as no provisions were made to institutionalize the updating of the profile. There were also a set of practical problems, similar to those for the questionnaire, concerning preparation of the document: Information was missing; key reports were not available in the city or were not used by the local researcher(s); significant amounts of time and effort were required to explain particular sections and review the draft information; and the quality of the writing itself was often poor. In most cases, the revised version of the profile, which benefited from a literature review process, bore little resemblance to the initial locally prepared research.

For practitioners, the following advice was culled from experience with profile preparation:

- *Preparation process*. The same entity that assembled the questionnaire is usually capable of preparing the profile. Data from the questionnaire, along with existing studies, annual reports, and interviews, are useful sources of information.
- *Flexibility in content*. At a minimum, the structure of the standard profile outline should be respected so that results can be compared and contrasted with other cities. The contents of each section should be covered, assuming that they are relevant to the city in question. Additional points that add insight to the state of a city's environment should be added.
- *Common errors*. Questionnaire data and other relevant information are not used, analyzed, or referenced; key points in the outline are not covered, especially concerning the institutional setting; maps are not used to graphically illustrate issues; and/or recommendations are included. The profile should be a descriptive, not prescriptive, document that informs the consultative process in a nonjudgmental way.

The *consultations* and town meetings had the advantage of being flexible instruments for involving a broad spectrum of concerned publics. Because they were organized locally and according to local traditions, they generated meaningful discussion for the participants and allowed them to reach a consensus in each case. However, since the method for arriving at a consensus differed in each case (from subtle negotiation and polite acquiescence in Jakarta to a formal parliamentary-style session in Sao Paulo), the ability to compare results is limited. More important, the consultation process on which this case study research is based formally ended with the final forum. The consensus was not initially linked to any formal planning or decision-making process (though the mayor's or governor's office was centrally involved in each of the town meetings). However, the results of the rapid assessment, culminating in the consultations, were used in different ways in each city. Accra, Jakarta, and Katowice are part of the UNCHS Sustainable Cities Programme, largely on the basis of their involvement in this process; the results of the Jakarta data and consultations were incorporated in the Jabotabek project supported by the World Bank and the UNDP/World Bank Metropolitan Environmental Improvement Program; and the priorities selected by the Sao Paulo town meeting gave political support to the then-mayor to have the Guarapiranga Reservoir included in a World Bank urban watershed project for Brazil. In the future, it would be more effective to associate the consultations more directly with these sorts of opportunities for follow-up.

Figure 7-2 Consultations identified contamination of water supply by agricultural runoff as a priority in Abengorou, Côte d'Ivoire.

For practitioners, the following lessons were learned about consultations:

- *Involving stakeholders.* Sometimes it can be useful to secure the endorsement of the top local political official (e.g., mayor, governor, or metropolitan chairperson). In politically complicated situations, it may be more useful to have a neutral sponsor.
- *Organizing consultations.* There is no set recipe for preparing consultations. Meetings with individuals and stakeholder groups and a final forum can be organized differently in each city, according to local customs and practices. However, there should be a common set of issues and questions that are discussed throughout.
- *Common errors.* One or more key stakeholders are overlooked in the process; key concerns of particular stakeholders are misinterpreted or not included in final discussions; the consultation process becomes overly politicized; the profile and questionnaire data are not fully used as background material; and/or premature assumptions about consensus may be made. While it may not be possible to achieve consensus about priorities, the process can be useful by allowing stakeholders to clarify their positions and inform others about them.

Additional guidance from experience with preparing face-to-face discussions for informed consultation was gained during the European Union's Local Environmental Charter project and is summarized in Table 7-2.

LEAP Formulation

Experience

Experiences with environmental planning and management in three of the world's megacities (metropolitan Jakarta, Mexico City, and Calcutta) are described in the following sections. The Jakarta case covers strategy development; the Mexico City example focuses on preparation of a problem- and sector-specific

Table 7-2 Do's and Don'ts of Organizing Successful Consultations

Do	Avoid
Invite all groups	Politicians that try to direct meetings
Include all contributions in a short report	Individuals who seek to dominate proceedings
Create a friendly atmosphere	Age, racial, ethnic, gender, and other imbalances
Adapt the process by learning from mistakes	Domination of discussion by extreme viewpoints
Use a standard approach (e.g., this textbook) and adapt it to local circumstances	Bureaucratic or excessively formal approach
Inform participants about the next steps in the process	Inaccessible venue
Specify a contact point for further information	Environmentally unfriendly practices (e.g., wasting paper and energy)
Be sure to formulate a list of decisions and priority actions	Preparation at the last minute
Use facilitators who are well informed and skilled in involving everyone	Discussion of topics that are not of general interest

SOURCE: IIUE 1995, 69.

action plan; and the Calcutta experience covers an integrated, citywide strategy and action plan. Each is graded according to the framework developed in Chapter 5. A box is paired with each case study to illustrate similar experience in a smaller or more developed city (see Boxes 7-1, 7-2, and 7-3 in this chapter).

ENVIRONMENTAL PROTECTION AND POLLUTION CONTROL STRATEGY IN JABOTABEK*

Jabotabek is the acronym for metropolitan Jakarta, a megacity approaching 20 million inhabitants. An environmental protection and pollution control strategy was initiated in 1992 as part of the World Bank–supported Jabotabek Urban Development Project III and financed by the World Bank/UNDP Metropolitan Environmental Improvement Program (MEIP). The objectives of the strategy were to:

- Define current and future priority problems of environmental management
- Describe the cost of environmental degradation

* SOURCE: SME and BAPEDAL 1994.

- Assist the government in selecting pollution control targets for water, air, and land
- Formulate a least-cost strategy for achieving a beneficial reduction in pollution and an appropriate degree of protection against future degradation
- Develop an action plan to carry out the strategy
- Define institutional arrangements for action plan implementation
- Estimate the benefits and costs of plan implementation
- Define any additional studies needed

An action plan, as defined in this text, was not fully developed, so this case focuses on the strategy.

A team of local and international consultants was hired to achieve these objectives. Its members were supervised by the government of Indonesia, with support from World Bank and MEIP experts. The strategy was completed in 1994 at a cost of several hundred thousand dollars.

Jabotabek's priority environmental problems were determined to be (1) BOD and fecal contamination of water resulting from the lack of sewerage in most of the urban area; (2) BOD and toxic waste contamination of water from industry due to the lack of wastewater treatment and use of processes that do not minimize waste generation; (3) particulate lead in the atmosphere resulting from the use of lead in gasoline; and (4) other air pollutants emitted by uncontrolled vehicle exhausts, the use of solid and liquid fuels for domestic purposes, open burning of solid waste, and the lack of industrial air pollution controls.

A series of 21 options were then identified or developed by the consultants to address these priority problems. These fell into four categories:

1. *Existing programs.* Programs that had already been proposed or were under implementation included: urban sewerage; hazardous waste management; mass transit; urban greening; and river cleanup.
2. *Water pollution control.* New options were developed to protect water quality and consisted of: local drain water treat-

ment; septic tank maintenance; community septic tanks; and sewerage in new estates.

3. *Air pollution control.* New programs were formulated to improve air quality and consisted of: control of smoke from diesel vehicles; use of compressed natural gas in large buses; use of liquefied petroleum gas (LPG) in small buses and taxis; promotion of four-stroke motorcycles; motor vehicle design rules; removal of lead in gasoline; and substitution of LPG for more polluting household fuels.

4. *Control of multimedia pollution.* The options that addressed problems of more than one environmental medium were: improved solid waste management; minimizing environmental impacts of existing practices; minimizing environmental effects of future developments; and creation of an environmental protection and pollution control inspection and advisory service for small- and medium-scale industries.

To assess the effectiveness of these options, the consultants developed predictive models for particulate air pollution and for BOD and fecal coliform contamination in Jabotabek rivers.

Of the 21 options, 13 were subjected to economic cost-benefit analysis and 11 were ranked. The results have been summarized earlier in Table 5-1. The top five options that yielded the highest net present value were: removal of lead from gasoline; improved solid waste manage-

BOX

The Royal Borough of Kensington and Chelsea (London) has prepared its fourth Environmental Policy Statement, which covers the period 1996 to 1999. The document sets out the Borough Council's strategy on environmental issues until the end of the century. It is implemented through action plans that are prepared on an annual basis.

Strategy development began in February 1995 when the Council's Environmental Services Committee approved a public consultation process to involve residents, businesses, and voluntary organizations in preparation of a new environmental policy. A launch meeting was held in March that recruited stakeholders into consultation panels that were organized according to each chapter of the policy statement. The panels then met to discuss issues and identify options. A draft policy statement and action plan were drawn up and endorsed by all executive committees of the Council in September. Drafts were then released for formal public consultation. Public concerns were then incorporated in final documents.

The resulting policy goals for the Council are to:

- **Improve the quality of local life by making the Borough cleaner, safer, healthier, and more attractive**
- **Reduce consumption of natural resources and reduce any waste and pollution caused by its own activities**
- **Encourage and enable residents, visitors, and people working in the Borough to improve the environment for themselves and reduce the waste and pollution they generate**
- **Work in partnership with residents, local business organizations and the voluntary sector, other local authorities, and central government agencies to develop environmental policies and implement action plans**

These goals were then translated into specific policies for the Council's own good housekeeping, transport, pollution, wastes and recycling, green space and conservation, the built environment, energy, environmental health, environmental education, visitors and tourists, economic development, and managing and monitoring performance.

Box 7-1 Environmental strategizing in London, UK.

SOURCE: Royal Borough of Kensington and Chelsea 1996.

ment; the inspection and advisory service; control of smoke from diesel vehicles; and substitution of LPG as a household fuel.

Implementation of the ranked options would cost about $4.1 billion (at constant 1992 prices). The consultants proposed that 61 percent of costs be borne by the private sector, 27 percent by government, 10 percent from loans, and 2 percent from grants. They also recommended a range of cost recovery measures based on the "polluter pays" principle.

An integrated action plan was not completed. The consultants recommended that the government follow up on the strategy by: selecting a final list of options for implementation; determining the most desirable method of cost recovery for each; assigning responsibility for each option to a specific organization; implementing recommended institutional reforms; developing public awareness campaigns; and beginning to mobilize donor support.

The Jabotabek strategy did not generate widespread discussion, support, or action after it was issued. Aspects of the report did support a growing demand to phase lead out of gasoline. In 1997, results of the strategy were resurrected and used as part of informed consultation in the preparation of a World Bank environmental management project for the cities of West Java and Jakarta.

The strengths of this experience were: good use of economic analysis as a tool for prioritizing problems and options; detailed development of options; recognition and incorporation of existing action plans; and consideration of cost recovery alternatives. The weaknesses were: the strategy was developed almost entirely by experts, with little stakeholder consultation outside of the government; there was little analysis of implementation requirements beyond financing needs; the study excluded key problems that were not suited to cost-benefit analysis, such as flooding; and it failed to consider the institutional and political feasibility of implementing options.

Scorecard: *Jabotabek*

Process	
Clarification of issues	A–
Involvement of stakeholders	D
Prioritization of issues and objectives	B
Substance	
Identification of options	A–
Development of strategy	B
Preparation of action plan	D
Overall Grade:	**C+**

TRANSPORT AIR QUALITY MANAGEMENT ACTION PLAN FOR MEXICO CITY*

The Mexico City Metropolitan Area (MCMA) is one of the world's largest cities and has the worst air quality of any city in the Western Hemisphere (see case study in Chapter 4). In 1990, the MCMA had a population of 15 million—which is expected to reach 20 million by 2010. Key air pollutants are lead, ozone, CO, and fine particulates. For example, peak ozone emissions were the highest of any city in the world, averaging four times accepted national and international norms. Vehicle-related emissions account for 84 percent of the total on a mass basis and 56 percent on a toxicity-weighted basis.

The Mexican government and the World Bank undertook a sector study, drafted in 1991, that would constitute an action plan for a World Bank loan on transport air quality management in the MCMA. The study was prepared by the bank staff and consultants, and draws heavily on work conducted by the Mexican government for its *Programa integral contra la contaminacion atmosferica de la Zona Metropolitana de la Ciudad de Mexico* (integrated air pollution program) as well as work carried out by a joint team of Mexican and foreign consultants for the Federal District of Mexico City.

Development of the action plan involved (1) estimating health and economic impacts of air pollutants, based on sources, total emissions, toxicity, and exposure patterns; (2) evaluating the government's existing air quality strategy for the MCMA; (3) assessing transport policy options, based on their cost-effectiveness; and (4) designing an action plan that includes institutional improvements.

The objectives of the action plan were to:

- Limit vehicle emissions per vehicle-kilometer (such as by the use of catalytic converters)
- Make better use of existing road space (e.g., by increasing vehicle occupancy)
- Shift the relative use of public over private transportation

* SOURCES: World Bank 1992; Bartone et al. 1994.

BOX

In 1994, the town of Pittsford, New York (population 25,000) began to update its comprehensive plan. The revision, adopted in 1996, highlighted the importance of preserving farmland and natural resources but did not provide mechanisms to do so; by then only 3600 acres of undeveloped land remained.

The town then commissioned a detailed resource inventory of the 94 undeveloped parcels larger than 5 acres each. A committee of farmers, builders, engineers, residents, preservationists, local board members, and resource agency personnel worked together with the planning team. They developed a method for ranking the resources on each property according to agricultural, ecological, greenway, historic, and scenic value. Over 100 community meetings were held to discuss options. This work resulted in *Greenprint for the Future,* a plan that identified 2000 acres for environmental preservation.

The Greenprint called for the town to finance purchase of development rights on 7 farms totaling 1200 acres. The remaining 800 acres would be protected by a newly adopted zoning law. A fiscal impact analysis concluded that implementation would cost the average taxpayer $1400 more in property and school taxes over the next 20 years; however, existing policies would cost $5000 more.

Preliminary implementation is promising: The 1998 tax increase on a $175,000 house will be only $46 a year, rather than the estimated $67; two external grants have been received to assist implementation; and negotiations for trails, easements, and development rights are proceeding. In recognition, the American Planning Association gave the Greenprint initiative its 1998 Current Topic Award for planning and conservation of places.

Box 7-2 An issue-specific action plan in Pittsford, New York.

SOURCE: Andrews 1998.

- Reduce vehicle-kilometers by limiting the use of private vehicles or shortening travel distances
- Reduce total passenger-kilometers
- Minimize motorized travel

The following options to reduce transport emissions were identified: fuel pricing; emissions standards for new vehicles; reformulation of fuels; gasoline vapor recovery; segregated transit; improved bus service; upgrading of road infrastructure; freight redistribution; and a range of demand-management measures.

Cost-benefit analysis was not used to evaluate and rank these options, because data linking emission reductions with human health and economic impacts were not yet available. Thus, the options were assessed in terms of their cost-effectiveness (i.e., the cost per kilogram of emissions eliminated). Figure 7-3 summarizes the results of the cost-effectiveness analysis. The most effective options—such as retrofitting cars to use liquefied petroleum gas, and making service stations recover vapors—yield net savings. Some options, such as strengthening emissions standards, are low-cost; others, such as programs for vehicle inspections and maintenance, are in the midrange. Beyond $1200 to $1500 a ton, emission reduction options get very expensive.

The action plan also includes recommendations for strengthening key institutions. Financial resources would be strengthened to fund the action plan by applying the "polluter pays" principle for an Environmental Trust Fund. The capacity of existing institutions would

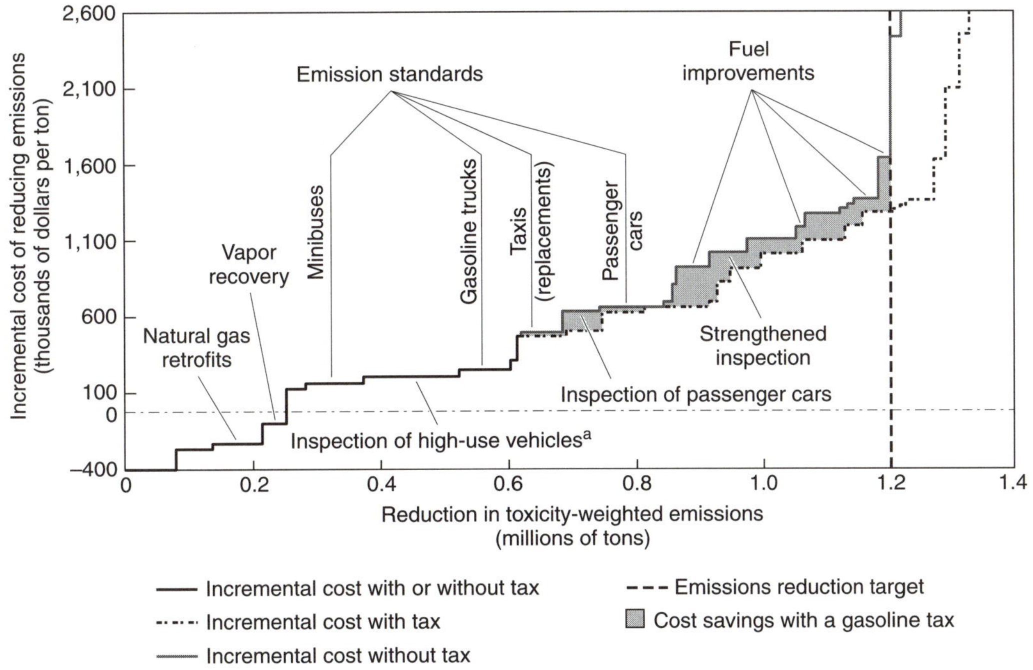

a. Including taxis, light-duty trucks, and minibuses.
Source: Eskeland 1992.

Figure 7-3 Cost-effectiveness of options for controlling transport-related air pollution in Mexico City.

be built through improved staffing and technical assistance. Performance would be assessed through independent air quality audits each year. Longer-term capacity for air pollution control would be developed through research, university, and midcareer training programs. Public awareness campaigns would be carried out to develop support for the action plan.

In 1992, the action plan was used to develop a $220 million project; the World Bank approved a $179 million loan, with the remainder being financed by the Mexican government. The majority of the project is a $103 million vehicles component that consists of (1) development and enforcement of emissions standards for new vehicles; (2) inspection and maintenance programs for high-use vehicles and private cars; (3) lines of credit to finance conversion of high-use vehicles to LPG or compressed natural gas; and (4) improvements in the vehicle registration system. $34 million is being used to fund installation of vapor recovery systems at service stations and a pilot program to speed conversion to LPG or CNG. Additional funds are being used for scientific research, institutional strengthening, and development of transport and management policies.

After the first year of these and other measures, Mexico City experienced a 23 percent reduction in total pollutant emissions, or over 2000 tons per day. Air quality indices for CO, sulfur oxides, hydrocarbons, and lead had improved by 10 to 15 percent. Winter ozone levels decreased by more than 40 percent (ICLEI 1997). After four years, ambient lead levels had been reduced by 98 percent compared to 1988 concentrations. Sulfur dioxide pollution has been reduced to healthy levels, and there are very few violations of CO air quality standards. On the other hand, concentrations of ozone are high on most days, often exceeding standards by a factor of two or more. High levels of particulate matter persist, particularly in areas with concentrations of industry, traffic, and/or erosion problems. There are slight downward trends in the highest concentrations of ozone and for the number of days with high particulate air pollution, despite growth in the number of people and vehicles in the city. Much of this progress is directly related to the introduction of cleaner gasoline, diesel, and fuel oil in the MCMA (World Bank 1997).

The strengths of the transport air quality action plan were: detailed analysis of a high-priority health problem; extensive and detailed development of policy, program, and project options; careful consideration of the institutional dimension of the problem and feasibility of options; evaluation of existing efforts; and integration with existing programs. The weak-

Scorecard: Mexico City

Process	
Clarification of issues	B
Involvement of stakeholders	D
Prioritization of issues and objectives	B
Substance	
Identification of options	B
Development of strategy	C
Preparation of action plan	B
Overall Grade:	**C+**

nesses were: an expert-driven process that was based on the result of one study and visit with little time for stakeholder consultation; failure to consider options that involved mass transportation (other than raising the cost of using private cars); and exclusion of nontransport sources of air pollution, which are responsible for 44 percent of toxicity-weighted air contamination.

ENVIRONMENTAL MANAGEMENT STRATEGY AND ACTION PLAN FOR CALCUTTA*

The government of West Bengal, India, commissioned the Calcutta Environmental Management Strategy and Action Plan (CEMSAP) in 1995, with assistance from the UK Overseas Development Administration, to promote sustainable urban development.

The CEMSAP was developed through a series of stakeholder consultations and partnerships. The consultation process involved 16 months of public workshops and discussion groups at each key stage of strategy and action plan preparation. These were supported by hundreds of meetings on various aspects of environmental management and three "area focus studies" of low-income settlements to determine the priority needs of the urban poor. Suppliers and users of environmental services were brought together in partnerships to assess service provision, cost recovery, and management issues.

During a period of informed consultation, key environmental problems, pressures, and underlying causes were identified. Priority problems included water supply, sanitation, flooding, solid waste disposal, housing quality, air pollution, noise pollution, and lack of open space, although these vary according to socioeconomic status (see Table 7-3). The major environmental pressures in Calcutta were population growth, poor housing, economic stagnation, and poverty. Priority problems were attributed to two sets of underlying causes: (1) policy, planning, and market failures (inefficient pricing, insufficient resource mobilization to provide services, low capacity to enforce regulations, weak planning, and polluters not paying the cost of pollution); and (2) institutional

* SOURCE: Department of Environment 1996.

Table 7-3 Priority Environmental Problems by Socioeconomic Group, Calcutta, India

Problem	Vulnerable group	Low-income group	Mid-income group
Housing	1	4	—
Water supply	2	2	4
Sanitation	2	1	—
Drainage/flooding	2	3	3
Solid waste collection	3	3	2
Open space	4	6	5
Air pollution	—	5	1
Noise pollution	—	5	1

1 = most important; 6 = least important

failures (lack of transparency and accountability, and low public confidence in government due to poor past performance).

From this assessment and the results of consultations, an overall vision was developed: Calcutta should be a better place to live, work, and invest in. The following strategic principles were developed to guide strategy preparation:

Figure 7-4 Sustaining the San Francisco Bay Area, California.

- Build ownership and partnerships through consultation and negotiation among stakeholders, awareness, and transparency.
- Create environmental management capacity through flexible institutions, learning by doing, responsible financial management, and cost-effectiveness.
- Get resource prices right using the principles of cost recovery and "polluter pays."
- Use a phased approach to match actions with capacities.
- Build on current initiatives.

These principles were subsumed under two major emphases: the need to strengthen urban environmental governance, and a focus on the needs of the urban poor and vulnerable groups.

Six strategies were then prepared in consultation with primary and secondary stakeholders. Three strategies were designed to create an enabling institutional framework by (1) strengthening institutions and resources; (2) improving access to and provision of municipal environment-related services; and (3) supporting community-based environmental management. Three sector strategies were then developed for industrial pollution control, the planning and regulatory framework for urban environmental management, and environmentally friendly transportation. Sector strategies included an overview of issues, the major causes of environmental

BOX

During the same month that Calcutta issued its CEMSAP, another metropolitan area on the other side of the world (the San Francisco Bay Area) issued a similar strategy and action plan, known as the *Blueprint for a Sustainable Bay Area*. The document was developed by a local NGO, Urban Ecology, using a stakeholder participation process.

Urban Ecology first convened a management team that reviewed existing literature, interviewed experts, and identified seven principles for the Blueprint: choice, conservation, context, community, accessibility, nature, and justice. The next phase, called the Vision Forum process, was designed to encourage community participation and discussion of Blueprint topics. Forums were held on Saturdays during the summer of 1995 on the home; the neighborhood; transportation, land use, and who pays; the greenbelt and estuary; jobs and industry; energy, materials, and water; and tools and actions. Each forum began with a panel discussion of issues; participants then broke into working groups to discuss problems, causes, and solutions. At the end of each day-long forum, the groups came together to present results which were then incorporated in the outline and text of the Blueprint. A focus group representing a range of stakeholders also met periodically to review work by the management team.

The result of this process is a document with strategies and action plans at the household, neighborhood, city, and regional levels, complete with local, national, and international examples of good practice. Urban Ecology has now convened a working group of developers, municipal officials, and builders to determine how development decisions can be made more sustainable within the Blueprint framework. The American Planning Association also recognized this effort, giving it the 1998 award for public education.

Box 7-3 Blueprint for a sustainable Bay Area.

SOURCES: Urban Ecology 1996; Turner 1996.

risks, goals and priorities for environmental improvement in the sector, and options to guide future sector investment.

Action plans were then developed to institutionalize the guiding principles and decision-making framework of the environmental management strategies. Plans were developed for institutional strengthening, municipal environmental services, industrial pollution control, transportation, environmental health, and cultural heritage. They consist of incremental improvements in management practices that move from an immediate to short-, medium-, and long-term time frames. Each plan identifies responsible implementing agencies, investments, costs, and funding mechanisms. A set of projects for immediate action was then distilled from the plans, as was a guide to major investment requirements.

Available information on implementation of the CEMSAP is as follows: (1) The Calcutta Municipal Corporation announced in mid-1996 that it will introduce water charges on all consumers with house connections (industrial and commercial users already pay); (2) USAID is supporting a disaster management program in the Calcutta metropolitan area that is complementary to the CEMSAP; (3) the World Bank, UNDP, WHO, and UK ODA have expressed interest in supporting various components; and (4) the state government has requested that a West Bengal Urban Environmental Program be developed using the CEMSAP approach and focusing on seven secondary growth centers.

The strengths of the CEMSAP were: use of informed consultation; a focus on poor and vulnerable groups; use of trend analysis to assess the effects of doing nothing; identification and response to underlying causes; costing investments; and preparation of action plans that were both issue- and sector-specific. Weaknesses of the approach were that it did not involve an impact analysis to discern the benefits of the action plans; criteria for selecting actions were not explicitly applied; no monitoring and evaluation process was

Scorecard: Calcutta

Process	
Clarification of issues	A
Involvement of stakeholders	A
Prioritization of issues and objectives	B+
Substance	
Identification of options	B+
Development of strategy	A
Preparation of action plan	A–
Overall Grade:	A–

developed; and the exercise was driven by outside forces ($1 million in aid and a large involvement of foreign consultants). Overall, implementation is being coordinated with other proactive, holistic initiatives of both the city and the government of West Bengal (Hasan and Khan 1998).

Lessons

The case studies in the previous section suggest several lessons for developing more effective urban environmental strategies and action plans:

- *Increased use of informed consultation.* The Jabotabek strategy and Mexico City action plan were drawn up earlier in the 1990s, primarily using inputs from experts. The CEMSAP, as well as experiences from London, Pittsford, and the San Francisco Bay Area, prepared later in the decade, consciously sought to involve a wider set of stakeholders. Presumably, a lesson was learned about how participation can improve ownership and implementation.
- *Integrated development of strategies and action plans.* The Jabotabek case is an example of a strategy without an action plan—which partially explains why it did not go anywhere. Consensus was achieved in Mexico City about the strategic importance of air pollution (see Figure 5-13) and in Pittsford about the value of open space, so issue-specific action planning could proceed. Calcutta, London, and the Bay Area represent instances where it was deemed wise to move from a strategy to an action plan in a single process.
- *Increasing concern for the poor and vulnerable.* The earlier efforts in Jabotabek and Mexico City do not evidence concern for the problems of low-income groups. In later efforts, this becomes an explicit focus of action planning (e.g., in Calcutta, voiced directly as a focus on the urban poor and vulnerable groups, and in the Bay Area, expressed as the concept of environmental justice).
- *Importance of identifying and costing actions.* Identification of financeable alternatives that have been carefully costed

BOX

Environmental strategy as guidance for other plans: The Leeds (UK) city council's *Green Strategy* was developed not only to correct past environmental abuse but also to guide existing and future strategic plans for transport, nature conservation, economic development, and overall urban development. Integration is being monitored through production of a "State of the local environment" report (Leeds City Council 1991).

The importance of setting objectives and targets: Kanagawa Prefecture, located south of Tokyo and home to 8 million people, launched a Local Agenda 21 planning process in 1992. One of the key features of the resulting agenda for action is the use of clear, measurable targets for each proposal (e.g., "reduce electricity use by 10 percent"). Targets are also expressed in understandable terms such as "equivalent to four days' energy output from all the power stations in Kanagawa would be saved" (ICLEI 1995).

Obtaining the agreement of implementing authorities: The Local Environmental Charters Project, involving 20 European municipalities, successfully used a charter to indicate how action plans will be implemented. The charter serves as a type of contract between various partners and is a framework for their individual behavior and cooperation during the implementation period (IIUE 1994). For example, the city of Strasbourg (France) adopted its environmental charter in 1993, obtained financing of 1 billion French francs, and by 1996 had been able to start or complete 85 percent of charter-specified actions (*Communaute urbaine de Strasbourg* 1996).

Matching options with capacities: In the process of developing its action plans, the city of Concepcion (Chile) conducted inventories by each of its six working groups to identify financial resources, technical capabilities, and institutional responsibilities. A realistic division of labor, budgets, and schedules could then be set as part of the action plans (UNCHS and UNEP 1997).

Box 7-4 Additional lessons for LEAP preparation.

can aid implementation, as was the case in Mexico City, Calcutta, and Pittsford, where clear financial analysis made it easier to attract donor support. In Pittsford, this policy also helped garner public support when it became evident that the Greenprint was affordable to the community.

Some additional lessons that have been learned from other experiences with local environmental action planning are summarized in Box 7-4.

LEAP Implementation

Implementing local environmental action plans requires attention to three key areas as identified in Chapter 5: (1) mobilization of support and resources; (2) institutionalization of the environmental planning process; and (3) use of monitoring and indicators. Experience with these aspects of implementation is reviewed in the section that follows, and lessons are extracted for practitioners.

Experience

MOBILIZING SUPPORT AND RESOURCES

Support for implementation needs to be mobilized at the political level and also with a range of other stakeholders. Success will often depend upon (1) the existence of political will, to see that the approach is enforced, and (2) political continuity, so that implementation is carried out over time until it becomes routine. When will and continuity are missing, implementa-

Figure 7-5 Bridging continents but not political administrations in Istanbul, Turkey.

tion can be erratic, costly, and incomplete, as was the case in Istanbul, Turkey, described in Box 7-5. Interestingly, politicians in other Turkish cities are very keen to join the country's Local Agenda 21 program, partly because they perceive political benefits from improving and broadening the delivery of environmental services. In Ibadan, Nigeria, the Sustainable Ibadan Project involved politicians from the beginning: It was designed with the participation of state and local government leaders. In addition, the project developed bureaucratic support by holding one-day workshops with local government officials to discuss objectives, processes, and outputs (UNCHS and UNEP 1997).

Resources can be mobilized to implement LEAPs by taking advantage of special opportunities, using leveraging strategies, benefiting from a network of cities, and strategically using external support. Special opportunities can come in many forms, for example:

- *Information.* In many cities of Eastern Europe and the former Soviet Union, the fall of Communism provided citizens with access to previously classified environmental information. Public awareness and reaction to data on health and other environmental risks were used to catalyze action.
- *Disasters.* Unfortunately, as we have noted earlier, it often takes an emergency to mobilize both the support and resources for implementation. For example, floods, epidemics,

BOX

The Ilkitelli Small Industry Zone was proposed by Istanbul's mayor in 1982 to relocate small industries from a historic part of the city, reduce traffic congestion, minimize negative health and environmental impacts, and improve export capacity. After plans were drawn up and business cooperatives were formed, construction began in 1985 on a site intended to employ 300,000 people at 33,000 workplaces.

This promising beginning was followed by nearly a decade of inaction due to lack of political continuity. New metropolitan and district governments did not share the previous mayor's enthusiasm for the project. New construction did not receive licenses and was considered illegal. Detailed plans by the cooperatives were not approved, and the stores of merchants who had moved to the area were sealed. In 1989, the district government canceled the Zone's original plans and did not come up with new plans. Cooperatives protested cancellation of their plans; the resulting court cases were inconclusive and went on to appeal. Finally, an agreement was reached in late 1994 and a protocol was signed that provided the basis for a new Zone plan.

New construction contracts were then awarded in 1994 for roads, drainage, wastewater treatment, rehabilitation of streams, drinking water, telecommunications, and energy. Sixteen years after its conception, 35 percent of infrastructure and 90 percent of the superstructure in Ilkitelli had been completed. The Zone is now partially operational, with over one-third of the anticipated employees in 33 cooperatives and 30,000 workplaces.

Box 7-5 Industrial policy and the lack of political commitment in Istanbul, Turkey.

SOURCE: Ozturk 1998.

and industrial accidents have accelerated the implementation of LEAPs in cities as diverse as Sao Paulo (Brazil), Surat (India), and Dakar (Senegal).

- *Political change.* A shift from one politician or party to another, increasing democratization, or revision of municipal boundaries has presented opportunities to push for LEAP implementation in African, East European, and Latin American cities. However, this can cut both ways, with political change leading to a reaction against the LEAP.

There are also a range of special events that can be used for implementing environmental improvements in a city. Barcelona's use of the 1992 Olympic Games to transform itself environmentally and in other ways is summarized in Box 7-6. On a more limited scale, Sydney is using the 2000 Olympics to develop the Olympic Village as a model for sustainable urban living (Caswell 1995).

Leveraging resources is another way that implementation can be broadened and deepened. Experience with LEAP implementation in African cities provides some good examples:

- *Durban, South Africa.* The action plan for Durban's Metropolitan Open Space System was largely self-financed by leveraging internal resources. Ecologically desirable land for the system was purchased by selling less desirable surplus municipal properties.
- *Ibadan, Nigeria.* A pilot project demonstrated that small amounts of locally generated funds, combined with public participation, could improve urban water supply. This helped convince local philanthropists to establish a "Project

Development Trust Fund" to implement similar initiatives.

- *Windhoek, Namibia.* In 1990, the city health officer supported a pilot initiative for private collection of household solid waste. Its success helped implement a plan that now involves 96 private waste collection contractors (UNCHS and UNEP 1997).

Learning from the experiences, both good and bad, of other cities can help guide and improve LEAP implementation. A wide variety of networks exist at the international, regional, and national levels that can facilitate this sharing and learning; information about them is provided in Annex B. Cities can also conduct their own research, tailored to their specific circumstances and needs. For example, stakeholders from Cape Town, South Africa, visited Los Angeles in the United States and Curitiba and Sao Paulo in Brazil to help develop and implement environmental aspects of their new spatial plan. In other instances, cities may wish to forge more long-lasting alliances such as twinning arrangements or specialized networks. Thailand provides an example of the latter, where seven cities formed a network under the auspices of an urban environmental management project supported by German technical cooperation (GTZ). They successfully used their experiences and contacts to obtain resources for implementing LEAP projects from the central government (e.g., its Environment Fund) and donors (e.g., the UNDP Local Initia-

BOX

Barcelona was selected in 1986 as the site for the 1992 Olympic Games. The metropolitan area, with a population of 3.3 million covering an area of 650 km^2, was in a period of economic decline, having lost 300,000 jobs between 1978 and 1983. The city decided to use the Olympics as a strategic opportunity to engage in a process of urban renovation, broadly known as *Programa '92.*

In addition to the normal construction associated with the Olympic Games, Barcelona used a consultative process to plan and implement a series of urban, economic, and social transformations. A total of 754 billion pesetas were invested in a range of projects between 1987 and 1992. Major environmental investments were made in enhanced circulation (e.g., improving the rail network, decongesting roadways), stormwater drainage, sanitation, neighborhood upgrading, park development, and industrial relocation. Specific environmental programs were initiated for coastal management, energy conservation, groundwater protection, air pollution control, nonmotorized transportation, urban greening, and public awareness.

In one typical effort, the city initiated a campaign to improve the urban landscape, known as *Barcelona, posa't guapa* (Barcelona, make yourself beautiful). The goal of the campaign was to give the city a face-lift by restoring its architectural heritage, developing parks, and improving the quality of public spaces. Tax rebates, exemptions, grants, and other incentives were used at a public cost of 1.5 billion pesetas; this mobilized another 18 billion pesetas of private investment in restoration. In the 10 years of the campaign (1986–1996), 2 million square meters of facades were restored through 8000 specific interventions.

The overall effect of the program has been to transform Barcelona into a European economic hub and a world-class city. Economic growth, stimulated by investment for the Olympics, has continued after 1992. Quality of life, measured by citizen satisfaction, is also high: More than 80 percent of the metropolitan residents have a positive view of their environment, and 90 percent would not want to live anywhere else.

Box 7-6 Using the Olympics as a special opportunity in Barcelona, Spain.

SOURCES: Borja 1995; Ajuntament de Barcelona 1996.

BOX

Troyan is a town of 46,000 people located 150 kilometers east of Sofia, Bulgaria's capital, in the foothills of the Balkan Mountains at the edge of a biosphere reserve and national park. The city suffers from water quality problems and shortages, inadequate wastewater treatment, poor solid waste disposal, and air pollution from combustion of low-quality fuels. The Troyan Environmental Action Project was initiated in 1992 to improve the environmental management capacity of the municipality. Support and resources were mobilized by:

- *Using special opportunities.* The fall of communism, increased availability of information, and interest of the United States in assisting all created a window of opportunity for planning and implementation.
- *Leveraging resources.* Wastewater audits for five industries revealed enormous opportunities for water conservation and wastewater reduction. This pilot experience led to creation of an industrial water audit and control program, a training program, and an ordinance requiring industries to file reports and plans on their water practices.
- *Learning and networking.* Information and expertise from U.S. communities were used to develop a water-leak-detection program that involved mapping the water network using a geographic information system, purchasing detection equipment, and making repairs. Measures have so far saved more than 10 percent of the system's total flow.
- *Using external support.* The project was managed by the U.S.-based Institute for Sustainable Communities; a U.S. Peace Corps volunteer provided logistical support for stakeholder participation; and the U.S. Water Resources Authority helped with the leak-detection program.

Box 7-7 Mobilizing support for LEAP implementation in Troyan, Bulgaria.

SOURCE: ICLEI 1995b.

tives Facility for the Urban Environment) (Atkinson and Vorratnchaiphan 1996; Vorratnchaiphan and Hollister 1998).

Cities with limited resources, low-income cities, and urban areas in highly centralized political systems often need to look beyond their borders for resources to implement LEAPs. For example, Accra, Ghana, was able to use the information, recommendations, and consensus that came from a number of urban environmental activities (see Box 6-4) to obtain financing from the World Bank for LEAP implementation. Conversely, where the possibility of negative impact exists, cities may want to resist the temptation of using external resources. For example, the military government of Brazil during the 1970s was providing money to cities to build motorways. The city of Curitiba resisted this offer and followed its own path that stressed public and nonmotorized transportation over the private car (see Box 9-5). An example of how the different elements of mobilizing resources and support were brought together is presented in Box 7-7.

INSTITUTIONALIZING THE PROCESS

Cities have taken a range of political, bureaucratic, procedural, and partnership approaches to institutionalizing the LEAP process. Some examples include:

- *Political approach.* The British city of Sheffield has an Environmental Working Party that is part of the city council's policy committee, to oversee municipal implementation of its LEAP, known as "The Living City" (Patton and Worthington 1996).

- *Light bureaucratic approach.* Many cities appoint a focus group which monitors and coordinates LEAP implementation. For example, the Directorate of Health, Housing and Urbanisation in metropolitan Johannesburg, South Africa, has an environment and development branch that coordinates development and execution of its LEAP (UNCHS and UNEP 1997).
- *Heavy bureaucratic approach.* Some cities create large and specialized bureaucracies for managing urban environmental problems. China is perhaps the best example; most of its major cities have environmental protection bureaus employing hundreds of people in environmental research, planning, management, implementation, and monitoring.
- *Procedural approach.* Other cities institutionalize an emphasis on the environment by modifying standard operating procedures. For example, Leeds, UK, requires each municipal department to develop an environmental action plan that is linked to its Green Strategy Steering Group, which coordinates plans and considers issues with a citywide dimension (Patton and Worthington 1996).
- *Partnership approach.* Forming coalitions that include but reach beyond municipal government can be one of the most effective means of institutionalization. After preparing their Industrial Environmental Plan, stakeholders in Dunkirk, France, formalized their relationship by forming a steering committee of elected officials, industry associations, the port authority, environmental NGOs, and central government representatives to address ongoing environmental issues (UNCHS and UNEP 1997).

The process of institutionalization can be more successful if it is anticipated within the LEAP itself. In the Canadian city of Guelph's *Green Plan,* there is an entire chapter on the implementation process. It recommends creation of a Green Strategy Steering Committee, with membership from environmental interest groups, the private sector, city officialdom, and the citizenry at large, all to be appointed by the city council. The committee's responsibilities include reporting on implementation of the plan,

BOX

Leicester is a medium-sized city of about 300,000 located in the middle of Britain with rich and diverse communities. In response to the challenge of the Earth Summit, the city conducted an in-depth consultation to find what was important to its citizens' long-term quality of life. The process involved three steps:

1. ***Short questionnaire:*** **This survey was sent to all residents, asking their views on what was good and not so good about Leicester and which issues most affected their quality of life (QOL).**
2. ***In-depth questionnaire:*** **A representative sample of about 800 citizens were interviewed in their homes with a detailed survey that again focused on key QOL issues.**
3. ***Stakeholder consultations:*** **Specific groups of stakeholders were asked to respond to material envisaging future urban QOL. These included young people, the disabled, businesses, women's groups, ethnic minorities, trade unions, and faith groups.**

This information was then combined with expert judgment to select 14 core QOL indicators to indicate trends toward or away from sustainability. The indicators were: homelessness; satisfaction with neighborhood; perceived improvement in the city center; levels of earned income; unemployment rate; energy use; loss of good-quality wildlife habitat; air quality; river and canal pollution; asthma levels; violent crime; educational attainment; mode of transport to work; and rate of domestic refuse collected.

Box 7-8 Participatory development of indicators in Leicester, UK.

SOURCE: UNCHS 1996.

environmental coordination within city hall, gathering information on natural systems, and formulating future goals and policies (City of Guelph 1994).

MONITORING AND INDICATORS

Monitoring LEAP implementation is critical in order to assess effectiveness, identify emerging problems, and make modifications in the LEAP. As suggested in Chapter 5, monitoring should be an inherent part of the LEAP, results should be publicly disseminated, stakeholders should be involved in the development of indicators, and indicators should be linked to policy objectives. Examples of stakeholder involvement and policy-linked indicators are presented in Boxes 7-8 and 7-9, respectively. An example of how a city incorporated monitoring in its LEAP and how it disseminates the results is given in the following paragraph.

In Tilburg, The Netherlands, the city's municipal environmental policy plan is based on concrete targets that are being measured by source, effect, and performance indicators. Source indicators point to the origin or cause of environmental problems. Effect indicators measure the impact of actions on environmental quality. Performance indicators are used to assess institutional implementation of the policy plan. The municipality then reports annually on implementation of the plan using these indicators. Implementation can then be adjusted on the basis of monitoring results (UNCHS and UNEP 1997). Evidence from the private sector suggests that such reporting improves transparency, accountability, awareness, and decision-making; the same evidence recommends broadening dissemination by use of the World Wide Web (Walton et al. 1997).

Lessons

In preparation for the 1997 United Nations "Rio+5" meeting in New York City, an assessment was made of local government implementation of Agenda 21 (ICLEI 1997). The general lessons learned from LEAP implementation were that:

- Participatory local action planning is a valuable way to promote the principles of sustainable development in cities and towns.

BOX

The World Bank recommends that its urban projects contain a set of indicators that can be used for evaluation of performance and impact. All indicators, including environmental ones, are linked to policy objectives.

POLICY OBJECTIVE	EXAMPLE OF INDICATOR
Improve access to basic environmental infrastructure and services	Percent of population with regular solid waste collection
	Percent of households with access to safe drinking water
Reduce or prevent urban pollution	Percent of BOD removed from urban wastewater produced
Encourage sustainable resource use	Percent of housing stock located on fragile lands
Encourage sustainable environmental practices	Percent of urban trips made by public and nonmotorized modes
	Percent of waste that is recycled, recovered, or reused
Minimize vulnerability to environmental hazards	Mortality and morbidity rates attributable to man-made and natural disasters

Box 7-9 Urban environmental indicators linked to policy objectives.

SOURCE: World Bank 1995.

- Public regulation of private and municipal activities is fundamental to improvements in local environmental conditions.
- Decentralization and reorganization of municipal jurisdictions is often a prerequisite to addressing the pollution problems of rapidly growing cities.
- Implementation of international environmental accords usually requires action at the local level that can be facilitated by involving local governments in such accords.
- The protection of biodiversity is a local management challenge of global importance that is increasingly being reflected in municipal plans and procedures.

The assessment also identified a number of obstacles to LEAP implementation: (1) In many countries, existing policies and fiscal arrangements at all levels of government act as barriers to efficient resource use and development control at the local level; (2) transfer of environmental responsibility to local government without parallel establishment of new sources of local revenues weakens public sector capacity for LEAP implementation; (3) environmental deregulation to the local level can backfire by legalizing environmentally damaging practices and increasing the complexity of holding actors responsible for the environmental damage that they cause; (4) globalization is opening cities to investment and development by external actors who may not be accountable and committed to LEAP objectives; and (5) local governments do not always have direct control over the source of their problems (e.g., design and packaging of consumer products that account for a large portion of the local solid waste stream).

The implications of these findings and constraints are that:

- To resolve local and global environmental problems, LEAP initiatives should be strengthened and supported.
- Partnerships between local, regional, and national stakeholders are necessary to evaluate policies, laws, and fiscal frameworks that work against sustainable development.

Figure 7-6 Involving the private sector in Jakarta, Indonesia.

- The financial capacity of local governments must be enhanced, especially when environmental responsibilities are decentralized.
- Private sector accountability to LEAP objectives should be increased through cooperative agreements between local stakeholders and especially international businesses.
- Local governments should band together nationally and internationally to use their purchasing and legal powers to influence problems that are beyond their immediate control, such as product design and packaging.

More specific lessons for LEAP implementation can be extracted from the cases referenced in this chapter. Lessons for mobilizing support and resources include: (1) Develop support for implementation among politicians *and* other stakeholders, such as city administrators and community leaders; (2) be alert for special opportunities to accelerate implementation, but do not slow down to wait for them to appear; (3) identify creative leveraging approaches, such as replicating successful demonstration projects; (4) use networks and experience in other cities to obtain some of the human, financial, and technical resources needed for implementation; and (5) pursue external assistance with caution, because cities face the risks that the agenda of the supporting entity might dominate or distort what the city wants to accomplish, that anticipation of or dependence on aid can preclude the possibility of addressing problems using local resources, and that less developed cities may not have the capacity to manage large and rapid inflows of external assistance.

For institutionalizing and monitoring the process of LEAP implementation, the following lessons can be learned:

- Assess the political, bureaucratic, procedural, and partnership approaches to institutionalizing local environmental action planning to determine which is most appropriate.
- Incorporate an institutionalization plan with the LEAP.
- Involve stakeholders in developing and carrying out monitoring.
- Link indicators to policy objectives.
- Disseminate the results of monitoring broadly and regularly.
- Use findings to modify LEAP implementation.

Resources and Exercises for Further Thought

Resources

The publication on implementing the urban environmental agenda (UNCHS and UNEP 1997) synthesizes experience with LEAPs in over 50 cities around the world. More complete case studies can be obtained from the UNCHS Sustainable Cities Programme at http://www.unchs.unon.org/unon/unchs/scp/.

Experience with informed consultation can be found in the two-volume set on rapid urban environmental assessment (Leitmann 1993). The survey on local implementation of Agenda 21 (ICLEI 1997) includes both general findings and case studies. Country-specific assessments of LEAP implementation also exist, e.g., for the U.K. (Selman 1998). Chapter 9 of this volume provides examples of good practice from around the world, with an emphasis on implementation. Information on networks and sources of external support for LEAPs is presented in Annex A; Annex B offers resources for training and research.

Exercises for Further Thought

1. To what extent do cities learn from each other about local environmental action planning, and how do they learn?
2. What factors may cause experts and the broader public to have different environmental priorities?
3. How can some of the limitations of rapid urban environmental assessment be avoided or overcome?
4. What are some of the risks of relying on secondary data about the urban environment?
5. How might cultural differences affect the organization of informed consultation?
6. Are the experiences with LEAP formulation in megacities representative or transferable to smaller human settlements?
7. Compare and contrast the use of external expertise in the Jabotabek, Mexico City, and Calcutta cases.
8. Compare and contrast these cases from lower-income cities with the developed country examples in Boxes 7-1, 7-2, and 7-3.
9. To what extent does LEAP implementation depend on factors beyond local control (e.g., special opportunities and external resources)?
10. What are the implications of economic globalization for local environmental action planning and implementation?
11. How can the financial capacity of local authorities be enhanced to improve LEAP implementation?

References

Ajuntament de Barcelona. 1996. *Barcelona, posa't guapa: Ten years of campaign*. Barcelona: Ajuntament de Barcelona.

Andrews, James. 1998. Pittsford's Greenprint initiative. *Planning* 64(4): 6–7.

Atkinson, Adrian, and Chamniern Vorratnchaiphan. 1996. A systematic approach to urban environmental planning and management: Project report from Thailand. *Environment and Urbanization* 8(1): 235–248.

Bartone, Carl, Janis Bernstein, Josef Leitmann, and Jochen Eigen. 1994. Toward environmental strategies for cities: Policy considerations for urban environmental management in developing countries. UMP Policy Paper No. 18. Washington, D.C.: World Bank.

Borja, Jordi (ed.). 1995. *Barcelona: Un modelo de transformacion urbana 1980–1995*. Urban Management Series Vol. 4. Quito: Programa de Gestion Urbana.

Caswell, Patricia. 1995. Ecologically sustainable cities in Australia: The Australian Conservation Foundation's perspective. In OECD. *Urban policies for an environmentally sustainable world*. Paris: OECD.

City of Guelph. 1994. Guelph's green plan. Guelph: Cleartech Documentation.

Communaute urbaine de Strasbourg. 1996. Urban environment charter. *Naturopa* 80: 28.

Department of Environment. 1996. Calcutta environmental management strategy and action plan (CEMSAP). Draft Report. Calcutta: Government of West Bengal.

Eskeland, Gunnar. 1992. The objective: Reduce pollution at low cost. *Outreach* No. 2. Washington, D.C.: World Bank.

Hasan, Samiul, and M. Khan. 1998. Management of Calcutta megacity: A transition from a reactive to a proactive strategy. *Sustainable Development* 6: 59–67.

ICLEI (International Council for Local Environmental Initiatives). 1995a. Action planning: Kanagawa Prefecture, Japan. Case Study No. 28. Toronto: ICLEI.

———. 1995b. Participatory priority setting: Troyan, Bulgaria. Case Study No. 29. Toronto: ICLEI.

———. 1997. Local government implementation of Agenda 21. Toronto: ICLEI.

IIUE (International Institute for the Urban Environment). 1994. The local environmental charters project: Guide for participating towns. Delft: IIUE.

———. 1995. The local environmental charters report. Delft: IIUE.

Leeds City Council. 1991. Leeds green strategy. Leeds: The Digital Printing Company, Ltd.

Leitmann, Josef. 1993. Rapid urban environmental assessment: Lessons from cities in the developing world. Volume 1: Methodology and preliminary findings. UMP Discussion Paper No. 14. Washington, D.C.: World Bank.

———. 1993. Rapid urban environmental assessment: Lessons from cities in the developing world. Volume 2: Tools and outputs. UMP Tool Paper No. 15. Washington, D.C.: World Bank.

Ozturk, Neslihan. 1998. 'Ilkitelli' the industrial center of the future. *Turkish Daily News,* 18 April, A8.

Patton, D., and I. Worthington. 1996. Developing Local Agenda 21: A case study of five local authorities in the UK. *Sustainable Development* 4:36–41.

Royal Borough of Kensington and Chelsea. 1996. Environmental policy statement 1996–99. London: Royal Borough.

Selman, Paul. 1998. Local Agenda 21: Substance or spin? *Journal of Environmental Planning and Management* 41(5): 533–553.

SME (Indonesian State Ministry of Environment) and BAPEDAL (Environmental Impact Control Agency). 1994. Environmental protection and pollution control strategy and action plan. Summary Report. Prepared for Third Jabotabek Urban Development Project. Jakarta: SME/BAPEDAL.

Turner, Wood. 1996. Creating the blueprint: A participatory process. *The Urban Ecologist* 4:3.

UNCHS (United Nations Centre for Human Settlements). 1996. Leicester environment city. Best practices database. New York: Together Foundation and UNCHS.

PART

III

MANAGING TO SUSTAIN CITIES

CHAPTER 8

Choosing Appropriate Management Options

Chapter Outline

Some cities will find it useful to engage in and institutionalize the planning framework for environmental management that is presented in Part 2. Other cities may not want or need to incorporate the framework in their approach to urban development. In either case, it is likely that a given city will have day-to-day environmental challenges that need to be addressed. Thus, cities will need to identify and select management options for their particular set of priority environmental problems.

Part 3 presents a menu of such options (Chapter 8) and examples of good practice for managing environmental problems that occur at different spatial levels from cities around the world (Chapter 9). This chapter begins with a set of management objectives, a general description of management instruments, and principles that can be used to choose among options. Then, two broad categories of management options are presented—options for involving stakeholders, and options that build capacity for urban environmental management. Within these categories, options are organized according to the principles of good governance: transparency, participation of civil society, a professional public service, and accountability. Finally, a promising set of options for achieving management objectives is summarized in a compendium.

Management Instruments and Selection Criteria

Management needs to be focused on a set of objectives in order to environmentally sustain cities. These objectives should address the key problem areas described in Chapter 3; options can then be selected that confront underlying causes of urban environmental degradation while achieving the objectives. A recommended set of management objectives includes:

- Improving access to environmental infrastructure and services
- Controlling, reducing, or preventing pollution
- Using resources sustainably
- Developing environmental planning and institutional capacity
- Reducing risk and preserving natural/cultural heritage

These objectives also draw on the definitions of sustainable urban development in Chapter 4 as well as the lessons learned from planning in Chapter 7.

Instruments for managing the urban environment can be roughly categorized as: regulatory; economic incentives; direct investment; property rights; land use controls; and information, education, and research. Each is briefly described in the following paragraphs, with select examples of their application in cities.

Instruments for environmental regulation consist of discharge standards, permits and licenses, land and water use controls, and public health codes. They are essential for avoiding or reducing the degradation of air, water, and land resources. Regulation requires both rules and an effective system of monitoring and enforcement. By themselves, regulatory instruments can be inefficient and costly to enforce. On the positive side, they yield predictable results and are necessary to establish a baseline of acceptable behavior. Santiago, Chile, uses environmental regulation to cope with air pollution emergencies: In a state of emergency, 80 percent of vehicles that run on leaded gas are banned from circulating, and factories that are major emitters of air pollutants can be closed down. In addition, all new vehicles must use lead-free gasoline (Inter Press Service 1998).

Economic incentives for managing the urban environment include user charges, resource pricing, pollution taxes, congestion charges, grants and subsidies, tax credits, rebates, and fines. These instruments often involve applying direct costs on polluters (the "polluter pays" principle) such as industrial effluent charges for air or water pollution, based on the amount and toxicity of discharges. However, they can also involve indirect charges; for example, the taxation of fuel use can be a powerful indirect instrument for controlling air pollution because of the relationship between fuel use and emissions (Eskeland and Devarajan 1996). In comparison with regulations, economic instruments are more efficient and flexible. They can also increase equity, generate revenue, and continuously exert pressure on polluters. Economic instruments are rarely used alone; they typically rely on and reinforce regulations (Bernstein 1991). For example, the city of Brisbane, Australia, has a set of regulations to protect the rich biodiversity of its bushlands. These are supplemented with two economic instruments: A ratepayer fee is levied that raises over $5 million a year for bushland acquisition and maintenance, and landowners who agree to protect private bushland from development can receive up to a 50 percent reduction in their general ratepayer levy (ICLEI 1996a).

Direct investment is one of the most powerful tools that a city can use to protect, improve, or rehabilitate the environment. Revenues can be raised for municipal investment in a range of environmental infrastructure and services such as water purification and distribution, wastewater treatment, drainage, sanitary landfilling, and public transportation. Cities can also acquire land to increase recreational opportunities and protect sensitive ecosystems. Additionally, municipalities can encourage other stakeholders to make investments that improve environmental management. For example, the environmental and other investments in upgrading slums can unleash private resources for environmental improvement (see Box 8-1 later in the chapter for a representative case). Investment along with policy options for achieving management objectives is summarized at the end of the chapter in Table 8-2.

Clarifying *property rights* can greatly improve management of air, water, and land resources. Better definition of water rights can be used to promote water conservation; defining and allocating discharge rights can help control air and water pollution; and providing secure land tenure can increase both public and private investment in housing and infrastructure improvements. For example, the opportunity to own land gave slum residents in Solo, Indonesia, the incentive to upgrade their plots and neighborhoods, resulting in key improvements to water supply, drainage, sanitation, solid waste management, and urban greening (USAID 1992).

A range of *land use controls* can be used to manage the urban environment, including environmental zoning, acquisition, expropriation, easements, land exchanges, purchase or transfer of development rights, land readjustment, and guided land development. Land use controls can be effectively combined with infrastructure provision to guide development away from environmentally sensitive areas; this was done in metropolitan Jakarta to protect the city's key watershed (Hadiwinoto and Leitmann 1994). Land use controls can also be blended with investment in public transportation and roads to reduce congestion and air pollution, as was done in Curitiba, Brazil (Rabinovitch and Leitmann 1996). Specific options for land use are presented in a subsection that follows, on improving municipal operations.

The final set of tools—information, education, and research—is essential for developing awareness and knowledge about the urban environment. Information about a city's environmental situation can be acquired using some of the techniques described in earlier chapters, such as rapid assessment, geographic and land information systems, and environmental assessment. Access to this and other information, via educational initiatives, underpins public consciousness about the urban environment. Options for environmental education are reviewed in the following subsection on transparency and awareness. Research is essential to close knowledge gaps about the urban environment. Good research should yield information on the characteristics of media-specific environmental problems, the dynamics of environmental degradation, and the magnitude and distribution of impacts (Bartone et al. 1994).

Management instruments are more effective when they are used in mutually supportive packages. The way that various instruments are selected and used to reinforce each other will depend on a number of factors that were highlighted in Chapter 5:

- Urgency of the problem that needs to be addressed
- Political, social, and institutional acceptability of the solution
- Cost and anticipated benefits
- Degree to which low-income and vulnerable groups benefit
- Compatibility with existing bureaucratic, legal, political, and fiscal regimes
- Ease of monitoring and enforcement
- Harmony with the city's overall environmental strategy

An example of the set of instruments that might be used to address a problem, depending on level of commitment, is presented in Table 8-1. Cities with a medium level of commitment may combine options 3 through 5, while cities that have a high level of commitment can use options 3 through 8.

Another way of considering which management options are most appropriate is to link them to management objectives, which can differ according to a city's level of development. For example,

Table 8-1 Management Options for Local Responses to Global Warming

Level of local commitment	Management options
LOW:	
1. Ignore the law	1. Tolerate polluting vehicles and industries
2. Obey the letter of the law	2. Do neither more nor less than is required
MEDIUM:	
3. Set a good municipal example	3. Recycling at city hall; use clean fuels in city fleet
4. Advocate within jurisdiction	4. Promote recycling, public transit, and energy efficiency
5. Legislate within jurisdiction	5. Local restrictions on automobiles and energy
HIGH:	
6. Advocate outside jurisdiction	6. Lobby for stricter air pollution standards; promote regional transportation system
7. Seek new legislative power	7. Ban sale of items made with CFCs; levy carbon and vehicle taxes
8. Legislate outside jurisdiction	8. Advocate for CFC ban; carbon and vehicle taxes to be applied beyond city limits

Source: Adapted from Roseland 1998, 186.

a low-income city may place greater priority on the management objective of improving citizen access to environmental services and infrastructure. Thus, it would pursue management options such as regulation (enforcing the legalization of connections to networks), direct investment (obtaining funds to expand networks), and land use controls (regularizing spontaneous settlements to lower the costs of infrastructure and service provision). This perspective on the selection of management options is graphically presented in Figure 8-1.

Beyond these factors, several principles can be applied to assist urban managers in selecting instruments for managing the environment. These principles are:

- Look for win-win solutions, where two or more problems are solved or where both the environment and the economy benefit.
- Choose the options that address the environmental problems of the poor and vulnerable groups in a city.
- Seek cost-effective approaches that pay their way.

These principles are elaborated with the examples that follow.

	Low-income	Medium-income	High-income
Priority management objectives	Improving access to infrastructure Building capacity for planning and management	Improving access to infrastructure Controlling pollution Reducing risks	Sustainable resource use Preserving natural and cultural heritage
Related management options	Regulate access Direct investment Cost recovery Cross-subsidies Public education Information-gathering Research	Regulate access Direct investment Cost recovery Cross-subsidies Pollution charges Emissions standards Land use controls	Full resource pricing Efficiency incentives Public transit investment Land use controls Public education Research
Level of development	Low-income	Medium-income	High-income

Figure 8-1 Level of urban development, management objectives, and options.

SOURCE: Adapted from Haughton and Hunter 1994, 237.

Win-win situations occur when a management option or package solves more than one problem or meets both environmental and economic objectives. Curitiba, Brazil, is famous for its win-win approach to problems. For example, the problems of flooding, housing exposed to environmental hazards, and lack of green space were solved by a program to resettle riverbank dwellers, create artificial lakes, and turn these spaces into parks. Floods are now a thing of the past, and green space has risen from 0.5 to 50 m^2 per citizen, despite a 20-year period of rapid population growth (see Box 9-5). Win-win options that can yield both environmental and economic returns include incentives to support low-polluting or environment-related industries; investment in energy efficiency and water conservation measures; modernization of industrial equipment and pro-

Figure 8-2 The KIP experience in Bandung, Indonesia.

BOX

Slum upgrading in Indonesia, known as the Kampung Improvement Program (KIP), was first introduced during the colonial government. Kampungs are densely populated, primarily low-income urban neighborhoods. While city governments began to upgrade slums as early as 1924, it was during the late 1960s that KIP began to expand and take off. The upgrading program gradually came to include a standardized upgrading package for poor neighborhoods that included improved vehicular roads and drains; paved footpaths; improved kampung-wide drainage; garbage bins and collection vehicles; provision of safe drinking water through public taps; public washing and toilet facilities; neighborhood health clinics; and primary school buildings.

The World Bank became a strong partner in the KIP effort through urban development lending that began in 1974. In an analysis of its first four investments in KIP, the World Bank concluded that slum upgrading could be a powerful force for environmental improvement. To begin, relatively modest investments in upgrading (ranging from an average of $118 per person in Jakarta to $23 in smaller cities, in 1993 U.S.$) encouraged households to invest in home improvements. A 1983 study found that households in KIP neighborhoods invested about $220 more in home improvement than those in non-KIP areas. The evaluation also showed that residents associated KIP with wider access to drinking water, improved sanitation, less flooding around homes, a cleaner living space, lower housing density, and reduced fire risk through improved access and use of better building materials.

Because KIP operated primarily at the neighborhood level, it was not able to solve a number of citywide environmental problems that include irregular solid waste collection and unsanitary disposal; flooding due to lack of primary drainage infrastructure; poor drinking water quality; and air pollution.

Box 8-1 Upgrading slums and the environment: The KIP experience.

SOURCE: World Bank 1995, 21–42.

cesses, and recycling/reuse of wastes. Overall, an OECD study on the ecological city concluded that "the most successful innovations, represented in case studies and elsewhere, combine environmental achievements and economic benefits while favoring social reconciliation and local democracy" (OECD 1996, 53).

Chapter 3 stressed that many urban environmental problems disproportionately affect the poor and vulnerable, who are least able to cope with or escape from risks. Thus, it is logical that environmental solutions should, at a minimum, benefit this segment of society. In fact, a triple-win approach is advocated in the urban policies of international aid agencies: Urban development should help to alleviate poverty, be environmentally sustainable, and contribute to economic productivity (UNDP 1991; World Bank 1991). One way of ensuring that low-income groups benefit is to target a package of management options on the environmental problems of low-income neighborhoods. An example of this approach is presented in Box 8-1.

The benefits and costs of management options under consideration should be as explicit as possible. In the case of win-win solutions, both environmental and economic benefits should be calculated. Distributional consequences (who benefits) should also be estimated in order to apply the previous principle. On the cost side, interventions that match cost to users' ability and willingness to pay should be favored. An example of this principle in action is the case of strategic sanitation planning in Kumasi, Ghana, in Chapter 9.

Management options that pay their own way by recovering costs are inherently more financially sustainable than those that must be subsidized. However, cost recovery can conflict with an emphasis on serving the poor, so targeted subsidies or cross-subsidization may be warranted in particular cases. Overall, the identification of options requires creativity so that the full range of costs and benefits is considered. Box 8-2 gives an example of how thinking creatively can result in a more beneficial package of options.

Failure to apply these principles can lead to the selection of management options that are limited in scope, do not yield economic benefits, fail to benefit the poor and vulnerable (or actually harm their interests), and/or are neither cost-effective nor financially sustainable. This does not mean that they will not be selected and even implemented. Box 8-3 provides an example of how a management option (rationing) backfired and actually worked against the achievement of a management objective (reducing pollution).

BOX

Option A: **$20 million is spent on building two-bedroom low-cost housing units for the poor. Each unit costs $10,000, which includes land purchase, site preparation, construction costs, infrastructure, and allocation of units. Thus, 2000 households and 12,000 people receive a good-quality living environment, assuming 6 people per household. Cost recovery would be difficult if the units were allocated to truly poor people.**

Option B: **$20 million is spent on a serviced-site project: $12 million is used to buy a relatively central undeveloped site, and $8 million goes for site preparation, infrastructure, and plot allocation. Assuming a cost of $2000 per plot, 10,000 households and 60,000 people would benefit from a higher-quality living environment. Some costs could be recovered, but most poor households would not be able to afford the combined cost of the plot plus construction of a dwelling.**

Option C: **$15 million is used to create a fund for community upgrading; $5 million is spent on improving priority citywide infrastructure and services. The fund makes $100,000 grants to community organizations that combine the money with local inputs such as labor to upgrade drainage, water supply and sanitation, roads, and green spaces. Assuming 500 households per community, the program could reach 450,000 people. The citywide portion of the investment would add to the number of beneficiaries. Cost recovery would be higher than Options A and B since most households could repay the relatively low cost of $200 per household over time.**

Box 8-2 Options for investing $20 million in improved living environment.

SOURCE: Summarized from Hardoy and Satterthwaite 1989, 142–143.

Options for Involving Stakeholders

The urban environment cannot be successfully managed without the involvement of constituencies that demand a better quality of life. Understanding of the environmental risks faced by different stakeholders is the foundation of participation. Once awareness has generated concern, then constituencies can articulate their demands and apply political pressure to achieve improvements in the urban environment. Based on this logic, options for increasing transparency and awareness, and for

Figure 8-3 An unaffordable serviced site project in Cape Town, South Africa.

BOX

In order to reduce air pollution and congestion, in 1989 Mexico City imposed a regulation banning each car from driving on a specific day of the week. The *Hoy no circula* (Day without a car) regulation prevents cars with license plate numbers ending in "0" or "1" from driving on Mondays, "2" and "3" on Tuesdays, etc.; restrictions do not apply on weekends. The regulation applies to all cars except emergency vehicles.

Analysis of the driving ban indicates that it backfired and actually contributed to increased car use in Mexico City. It appears that many households acquired an additional car (with a different restricted day) to get around the regulation. This is an expensive option, so household preference was for a less-expensive, used car with lower technical standards. Travel may have shifted toward these less fuel-efficient and more polluting vehicles, thus working against both goals of the management option that was chosen.

Box 8-3 The road to hell in Mexico City, Mexico.

SOURCE: Eskeland and Feyzioglu 1997.

enhancing civil society participation in environmental management, are summarized.

Transparency and Awareness

Building environmental consciousness requires two steps. First, there must be public access to information about urban environmental conditions, underlying causes, and possible solutions (transparency). Second, this information must be disseminated in a manner that it can be understood by different stakeholders.

Some options for improving transparency have already been presented in previous chapters: assembling environmental data using a questionnaire; preparing an environmental profile or "state of the environment" report; preparing a regular set of urban environmental indicators; and public review of draft environmental documents. As an example of these approaches, the city of Hamilton-Wentworth, Ontario, involves the public in setting and revising environmental goals and objectives of its sustainability plan, called Vision 2020. It then monitors the implementation of the plan using community-developed indicators. These are analyzed and submitted for public review as a report card each year on Sustainable Community Day (ICLEI 1996b). Other measures for increasing transparency include regular and fast access to municipal and other environmental regulations, decisions, data bases, and reports. For example, citizens in Curitiba, Brazil, can use computers at city hall to obtain environmental, legal, and other information about any plot of land in the city within a matter of minutes; this both spreads awareness about environmental conditions and improves the functioning of the land market. Higher levels of government can improve the transparency of environmental information in the private sector by green or eco-label programs that assess the environmental impact of products or by ratings of industries according to their environmental performance.

Figure 8-4 Raising environmental awareness in Soweto, South Africa.

Dissemination of environmental information to raise awareness can be done through many different mechanisms. Management options that have been used in cities include:

- *Formal community education.* Courses are taught by community organizers in neighborhoods where awareness is low and/or environmental problems are severe. These typically focus on public health, urban sanitation, or disaster preparedness.
- *School curriculum.* Material about the dynamics of the urban environment is included in primary and secondary school science and social science courses.
- *Targeted environmental campaigns.* The media and other mechanisms are used to raise awareness about a specific program such as river cleanup—as was done with the Tiete River in Sao Paulo, Chao Phraya in Bangkok, and Singapore River in Singapore. Such campaigns have also been undertaken in cities to promote energy and water conservation, recycling, and fuel-switching (e.g., to unleaded gas).
- *Specialized training.* Focused courses have been used to raise the environmental consciousness of politicians, municipal officials, business people, the media, and community leaders.
- *Regular evaluations and awards.* Publicized competitions for improvements in environmental quality can both inform citizens about relative environmental conditions and serve as an incentive for municipalities to improve. The Environmental Responsibility System in Chinese cities and the ADIPURA (Clean city) competitions in Indonesia are examples of formal urban evaluations.
- *Monitoring data.* Many cities use electronic billboards to instantaneously report air quality data. The media are also used to disseminate this and other information such as reports on water quality and food hygiene (Bartone et al. 1994).

Participation of Civil Society

In most cities of the world, a powerful constituency for the urban environment already exists—the wealthy. The upper class is most often concerned about preservation of low-density residential neighborhoods; development of parks and recreational areas; protection of biodiversity and other green issues; and continued access to high-quality, often subsidized environmental infrastructure and services. The challenge is to build constituencies of poor and vulnerable groups.

Constituencies can be built from either the bottom up or the top down. Starting from the bottom, groups of concerned citizens organize to demand improvements in environmental quality or services from decision-makers in government, the private sector, or both. In many squatter areas of developing cities, for example, residents organize to lobby politicians for provision of services, infrastructure, and land tenure. In the top-down approach, a politician or government agency may promise to address environmental problems in exchange for votes at the next election or public support from a constituency. In reality, both approaches to constituency-building may be used over time. For example, in the Cubatao case in Box 8-4, a nongovernmental organization was formed at the bottom and was later supported from the top by a state bureaucracy as a means of pressuring industries to clean up.

Once constituencies have been organized, they need effective avenues for participating in urban environmental governance. Participation can occur at one or more stages: (1) gathering information on community conditions, needs, and coping strategies; (2) articulation and advocacy of local positions and priorities; (3) involvement in the selection and design of interventions; (4) participation in the implementation of policies, programs, and projects; (5) information dissemination and education; and (6) monitoring and evaluation. Regardless of the stage, two general approaches can be taken to improve the involvement of stakeholders in environmental management: formal avenues, and direct action.

Formal approaches are officially recognized mechanisms for stakeholders to become involved in environmental planning and management. Examples include the informed consultation phase of the planning framework advocated in this text; community involvement in the development of urban indicators; public review of environmental impact assessments and land use decisions; environmental hot lines (see Box 8-5); and environmental forums organized by municipalities or NGOs on critical issues. In

BOX

Cubatao is a highly industrialized city that was once known as the "Valley of Death." Industries were first drawn to Cubatao in the 1950s because of its location between Sao Paulo (Brazil's largest market) and Santos (Brazil's main port). Eventually, 23 large industries (with 230 individual pollution sources) settled in the Cubatao valley, making it Brazil's most important petrochemical and metallurgical complex, currently generating 2.6 percent of the country's GNP. Through 1980, however, little attention was paid to pollution control and environmental impacts.

Development of Cubatao led to destruction of wetlands, accumulation of polluted air between the city and the adjacent mountains, destruction of adjacent forests due to acid rain, and resulting landslides from erosion. The city had one of the highest per capita incomes in Brazil in 1980, but 35 percent of its 90,000 people lived in slums. Only 25 percent of residences had clean water, and only 20 percent were sewered. In 1982, almost 30 percent of newborns died before their first year.

In 1980, a grassroots movement called the Association of the Victims of Pollution and Bad Living Conditions (AVPM) emerged. Formed by parents of children with birth defects and residents of a slum who were resisting relocation, AVPM successfully called attention to the social dimensions of environmental degradation. In 1983, Sao Paulo state elected its first governor after a long period of military rule; he made solving the pollution problem in Cubatao a high priority. The state environment agency, CETESB, was commissioned to design and implement a comprehensive air, water, and soil pollution control program for Cubatao. Public participation and transparency were to be cornerstones of the program.

In practical terms, these cornerstones were gradually achieved through: (1) meetings between CETESB staff and neighborhood associations; (2) creation of a toll-free complaint line about Cubatao pollution problems; (3) quarterly public information meetings at Cubatao's city hall; (4) public meetings, with industry participation, to evaluate problems in implementing pollution controls; (5) scientific seminars on the effects of pollution for the public; and (6) meetings with labor unions on workplace hazards. These approaches helped give CETESB the political clout it needed to overcome resistance by Cubatao's industries, which had stymied earlier efforts.

The Cubatao cleanup was largely successful. Nine years after initiation of the program, emissions of major pollutants had been reduced by up to 80 percent, and Cubatao was heralded as an urban success story at the 1992 Earth Summit. Vulnerable neighborhoods have been relocated to less risky areas. Basic sanitation and toxic waste management have improved. Fish stocks are returning to Cubatao rivers, and new vegetation has returned to deforested areas. Community participation and transparency were critical in helping achieve these results by giving CETESB the political clout to pressure polluting industries to comply with controls.

Box 8-4 People's power in Cubatao, Brazil.

SOURCE: Lemos 1998.

addition, regular NGO or community lobbying of decision-makers can become a formalized process. Another form of stakeholder involvement is to use the court system to achieve environmental objectives. Citizen groups often seek legal action to close down polluting industries and power plants, or to get polluters to clean up degraded sites.

When formal mechanisms have not been developed or are actively avoided, then participation in environmental management is stimulated by *direct action.* This can include public protest and community environmental management. When environmental conditions are bad and visible, or when frustration mounts over inaction, then protests ranging from peaceful to violent can occur. For example, citizens in the town of Bergama, Turkey, initiated a series of public actions to successfully pressure the government to deny a license to a multinational gold mining company that was going to use arsenic processing. Another response to poor conditions or inaction is for communities to take matters into their own hands. Examples of community environmental management include: (1) local monitoring and reporting on polluters in Sao Paulo and Singapore; (2) provision of environmental services in the San Juan and Valenzuela municipalities of Metro Manila, Philippines; (3) improvements to streets and sidewalks in the barrios of Buenos Aires, Argentina (Bartone et al. 1994); and (4) construction of low-cost sewers in Karachi, Pakistan (see Box 9-6).

The challenge of involving excluded stakeholders is an overall consideration for these options to improve the participation in environmental management. This problem was identified in

BOX

The Green Phone is an option for formal stakeholder involvement in environmental management in Croatia initiated by an NGO, *Zelena Akcija* (Green Action). Since its inception in 1992, the Green Phone has become an important communication link between citizens and city government on environmental issues. The Green Phone provides a forum for citizen complaints and requests for information about how to solve environmental problems, and to network with environmental groups to promote ecological protection. In this way, the public has become a more effective pressure group that acts both upon city government and private businesses.

Since 1992, the Green Phone has received more than 4000 calls from throughout Croatia. The three most common questions are related to (1) solid waste management, (2) maintenance of green areas within urban centers, and (3) disposal of old, abandoned cars. The Green Phone has also stimulated a number of environmental activities such as:

- **An Earth Day exhibit on "The dark side of the metropolis" to raise awareness about environmental degradation in suburbs**
- **Media campaigns to draw attention to oil spills in the Zutica oak forest and an illegal auto rally on Medvednica mountain**
- **A protest action to prevent the municipality from cutting down trees around a square in the heart of Zagreb.**

Box 8-5 The green phone in Zagreb, Croatia.
SOURCE: Council of Europe 1996, 19.

Figure 8-5 Community action in Fortaleza, Brazil.

Chapters 3 and 7, where it was noted that low-income neighborhoods, NGOs, women's associations, groups representing children, the elderly, and the disabled, and representatives of the informal sector are typically left out of environmental planning and management in cities. This can be particularly detrimental because these groups are often the most harmed by urban environmental degradation. Exclusion is also bad management because these stakeholders are often a critical part of the problem and/or solution. For example, small-scale and cottage industries in many developing cities account for up to half of all hazardous waste generated (Bartone and Benavides 1993); urban agriculturalists produce an average of a third of food consumed by cities around the world (UNDP 1996); and a large percentage of the waste stream in Asian cities is managed by the informal sector (World Bank 1999). An example of how the informal sector can be brought into the process of environmental management, benefiting both themselves and the city, is the case of the Zabbaleen in Cairo, Egypt, that is presented in Chapter 9.

Options for Building Environmental Management Capacity

Three sets of management options can be used to improve the ability of cities to plan for and manage environmental problems. First, specific measures—such as the development of public-private partnerships—can be pursued to build institutional capacity. Second, the performance of urban infrastructure and services can be enhanced; this alone can go a long way toward solving many environmental woes in urban areas. The most relevant of such municipal operations are water, sanitation, and drainage; solid waste management; land use (including transportation); energy; and natural and cultural heritage. Third, new institutions and systems can be introduced to improve accountability and effectiveness.

General Measures for Capacity-Building

General management options for building financial, human resource, and technical capacity include:

- *Financial resources.* Environmental institutions need to develop stable and adequate sources of finance if they are to carry out their managerial responsibilities. Options to achieve this will vary in the public, private, and voluntary sectors.
- *Training.* Professional and managerial staff can be trained in a range of areas, for example, identification and analysis of problems, the use of specialized equipment and software, project preparation, selection and implementation of management options, monitoring and evaluation, and stakeholder participation. Training can be in-service or outside of the municipality.
- *Staff exchanges.* "Learning by doing" is a useful form of capacity building whereby technical or managerial staff from one institution spend time working in a similar setting in another city that has a record of good performance.
- *Technical assistance.* Institutions may need specialized expertise for identifying and solving a particular problem, or in

managing new systems and institutions. Assistance that draws on examples of successful practice elsewhere is especially useful.

- *Equipment.* Institutions may have adequately trained staff but are missing key pieces of equipment that can make them more effective in monitoring and reducing pollution or otherwise protecting the environment.

These measures can be used to build environmental capacity both inside and out of government.

Options for building public sector capacity should be pursued at both the national and local levels. At the national level, capacity can be developed to assist the resolution of local-level environmental problems by: (1) establishing environmental standards and effective systems for monitoring and enforcement; (2) establishing and administering programs of technical and financial assistance to support environmental agencies at lower levels of government; (3) empowering local governments to carry out environmental management by establishing standards for local performance and adopting measures to ensure accountability; and (4) enabling private and community participation in environmental management. At the local level, officials usually need to upgrade their skills in environmental monitoring and enforcement, municipal finance, development of laws and regulations, feasibility analysis, environmental impact assessment, environmental policy making, and public education (Bartone et al. 1994).

Capacity also needs to be developed outside of government, including the private and voluntary sectors. In the private sector, for example, industries need to strengthen pollution control technology and resource conservation. Real estate developers need improved skills in environmentally safe, resource-conserving land development and construction techniques. One internationally accepted option, known as ISO14001, involves training and certifying businesses in the use of environmental management systems; this is described with an example in Box 8-6. In the voluntary sector, nongovernmental and community-based organizations can benefit from development of stable financial resources, technical assistance, improved negotiation and consensus-building skills, strengthened linkages with government, networking with other voluntary organizations, and increased professionalization of their operations (Lee 1994, 1998).

Capacity-building does not just have to occur within the pub-

BOX

The International Standards Organization (ISO) has a standard (ISO14001) for voluntary adoption of an environmental management system by an organization. The standard does not specify pollution control targets, but establishes the required elements of an effective system as:

- **An environmental policy, defined by top management and communicated throughout the organization, specifying commitment to complying with environmental legislation, pollution prevention, and continual improvement**
- **Planning, including objectives and targets incorporated into a management program consistent with the environmental policy, defining responsibilities, resources, and a time-frame**
- **Mechanisms for implementing the environmental management program**
- **Procedures for checking and corrective action**
- **Periodic management review of the system to ensure effectiveness**

This standard has attracted a good deal of interest in the private sector because of the importance of ISO standards in the global economy.

As interest in ISO14001 was growing among Mexican manufacturers, a survey of environmental management practices in Mexican industry drew a correlation between higher levels of environmental performance and the adoption of the listed elements. The survey also indicated that environmental management systems were particularly underdeveloped among small and medium-sized enterprises.

These events led to the development of the Guadalajara Environmental Management Pilot (GEMP). The GEMP is an agreement with 11 major companies that are ISO14001-certified to work with selected small and medium-sized industries in Guadalajara to develop and improve their environmental management systems. Technical assistance is being financed by the World Bank. Preliminary results indicate the importance of initial encouragement from large client or supplier companies; the availability of expert and local technical assistance; and the use of simple analytical tools to achieve scheduled milestones.

Box 8-6 Building private sector environmental capacity in Guadalajara, Mexico.

SOURCE: World Bank 1997.

Figure 8-6 Public-private partnership in Jakarta, Indonesia.

lic, private, or voluntary sectors. In fact, one of the most powerful forms of institutional capacity-building for environmental management is the development of partnerships between key stakeholders. Perhaps the most widely touted arrangement of this nature is public–private partnerships for environmental management; there is even a UNDP technical assistance program that goes by this name. This brand of partnership can be used to improve the availability and quality of urban environmental infrastructure and services; conserve resources; provide technical assistance, research, and managerial skills; and conduct training. Some examples are given in Box 8-7. However, partnerships are often much richer and diverse than this. For example, the city of Ahmedabad in India has a wealth of partnerships between local and central government units, professional associations, corporations, community organizations, NGOs, local financial institutions, and international donors for slum upgrading, water and sanitation, solid waste management, and urban forestry (Ahmedabad Municipal Corporation 1998).

Improving Municipal Operations

In many cities, a large part of the urban environmental challenge can be met by good management of existing municipal operations. Key among these are water, sanitation, and drainage; solid waste collection and disposal; land use management; energy; and preservation of natural and cultural heritage. Each municipal agency responsible for these areas should focus on improving the efficiency, effectiveness, coverage, and environmental impact of its operations. In addition, operations will need to work together; for example, drainage and parks can cooperate to control flooding and increase green space. Promising management options for each set of operations are summarized in the paragraphs that follow.

BOX

- ***Ilo, Peru:*** **A partnership between the municipality and the city's largest industrial concern, Southern Peru Ltd., resulted in a commitment by the company to invest $100 million in environmental improvements such as wastewater treatment, a landfill, and reforestation (OECD 1998, 110).**
- ***Abidjan, Côte d'Ivoire:*** **A private company, SODECI, began operating the city's water supply system in the 1960s and now manages 300 systems that reach 70 percent of the country's 4.5 million urban residents. With a high percentage of poor customers, SODECI forgoes hook-up charges on three out of four connections; however, it has a 98 percent collection rate and a profitable track record (World Bank 1997, 37).**
- ***Various cities, Senegal:*** **AGETIP is a private, nonprofit enterprise that contracts with the government to execute urban infrastructure and service projects with labor-intensive methods. It has handled hundreds of projects involving millions of dollars and thousands of new jobs in over 78 municipalities (UNCHS 1996, 311).**
- ***Phoenix, Arizona:*** **The city council reduced expenses on solid waste services by privatizing a portion of the collection service, but allowed the public works department to participate in the bidding process. Competitive privatization has improved productivity, accelerated use of cutting-edge waste technology, and saved money (World Bank 1997, 38).**
- ***San Jose, California:*** **Industries participated in a citywide water conservation effort during a drought in the 1980s. A detailed analysis of 15 companies showed water savings of 27 to 90 percent after conservation measures and a payback period that was usually less than 12 months (Postel 1992, 140).**

Box 8-7 Public/private partnerships for urban environmental management.

WATER, SANITATION, AND DRAINAGE

These operations are grouped together because of their water-based nature and their collective impact on urban health. The introduction of piped water to communities usually requires parallel investments in sanitation and drainage. As cities develop and extend sewer systems, they must determine their connection with stormwater drainage.

An estimated 280 million urban dwellers in the Third World do not have access to a safe and reliable water source (UNCHS 1996). Options for improved urban water supply management include:

- *Watershed management.* Water utilities are increasingly seeking to protect and manage the watersheds that are criti-

Figure 8-7 Water purification plant in Bandung, Indonesia.

cal sources of supply. An example of how France has successfully approached this task is presented in Box 8-8.

- *Cost recovery.* The 1998 UN conference on managing the world's limited fresh water supplies agreed that water should be paid for as a commodity rather than be supplied free of cost. Revenues should be used to extend service to those without access.

- *Water conservation.* As was previously noted in Chapter 5 (Figure 5-9), it can be much less costly to promote conservation of domestic and industrial water use than to increase supply. Conservation can be promoted through water pricing, technical auditing and assistance, and consumer education. The case of Singapore in Chapter 9 contains a good example of an integrated water conservation program.

- *Operations and maintenance.* Poorly maintained water systems in many cities lead to leakage and contamination, with associated financial and health costs. In many developing cities, half or more of the municipal water supply is unaccounted for.

- *Appropriate standards.* Often, water supply standards are set too high, making water supply systems expensive, inflexible, and unaffordable to many.

BOX

France has created the equivalent of "water parliaments" to handle urban water supply. The country is divided into six administrative water agencies that were established in 1964 according to natural watershed boundaries.

Each water basin is governed by a committee that consists of elected officials, water consumers, and those with a special interest in water to collectively manage its use, distribution, and pricing. The committees work on the principles that water is a commodity with a cost, the polluter should pay for pollution, and those who purify or improve water quality deserve assistance. Income generated by water distribution is used to finance improvements in the supply system.

Box 8-8 Watershed management in France.

SOURCE: *The Earth Times* 1998, 15.

A quarter of the world's urban population in developing countries does not have access to sanitation services (WRI 1996). One of the key management options for sanitation is the selection of appropriate technologies. Cities can use strategic sanitation planning to gear the levels of service and related technologies used within a city to technical, economic, and social considerations. An example of this approach is provided for the city of Kumasi, Ghana, in Chapter 9. In poor areas, there is scope for community involvement in the provision and maintenance of low-cost sanitation technologies; this is illustrated by the case of the Orangi district in Karachi (see Box 9-6). Untreated sewage is a major source of water pollution for both rich and poor cities. Conventional sewage treatment is costly, so alternative methods need to be considered—such as biological treatment using ponds, wetlands, and lagoons; wastewater reuse; and groundwater recharge.

Well-planned stormwater drainage is essential to reduce the negative health and economic costs of flooding, to protect sensitive ecosystems, and to improve water supply. At the citywide level, investment in systems that work with nature by using existing water channels should be pursued. These areas can be protected, expanded, and developed as green and recreational spaces. At the same time, vulnerable populations living in flood plains should be encouraged to resettle. At the local level, there is scope for community involvement in the development, expansion, and maintenance of tertiary drains which should connect to the citywide network. All levels of drainage works need to be coordinated with road construction and land use planning to prevent new developments from blocking natural drainage routes. Improvements in drains also need to go hand-in-hand with better solid waste management so that uncollected garbage does not end up blocking drains (Bartone et al. 1994).

SOLID-WASTE MANAGEMENT

Half to two-thirds of garbage is not picked up in poorer cities, while in the same cities solid-waste collection and disposal eat up a significant portion of municipal budgets (UNCHS 1996). As with sanitation, solid-waste services should be planned in a strategic fashion that accounts for technical factors, consumers' ability to pay, waste composition, and alternative technologies. Often, the quality and cost of both collection and disposal can be improved by involving the private and informal sectors; the Zabbaleen of Cairo, Egypt, described in Chapter 9, provide an example of the benefits of recognizing and supporting the role of the

(a)

(b)

Figure 8-8 Waste recycling in Tunis, Tunisia, and Singapore.

informal sector in waste management. One of the most cost-effective management options for improving solid-waste management is to promote measures for reducing waste at the source by recovering, recycling, and reuse, so that it does not require collection and disposal. Pricing can provide an incentive for source reduction by charging households and industries on the basis of the weight or volume of waste produced. On the disposal side, municipalities should consider options for obtaining value from wastes by recovering resources, composting, biogas digestion, and electric power production from incineration, provided that the risk of air pollution is controlled. Institutionally, in metropolitan areas solid-waste collection is usually best handled at the municipal or lower level, while disposal is more efficiently managed at the metropolitan level. An example of how many of these options can be brought together is provided for the case of Lille, France, in Box 8-9.

BOX

Lille is a major industrial and service center; the Lille Metropolitan Area Authority (CUDL) consists of 86 municipalities with over one million people. Conventional waste disposal was handled through landfilling and incineration. Beginning in 1991, the CUDL embarked on a program to manage its solid waste in a more cost-effective and environmentally sound manner.

The CUDL's new system, being implemented at a cost of $400 million over a decade, has the following features:

- ***Source separation.* Households are using containers that partition waste between clean and dry refuse (paper, glass, metal, and plastics) and organic wastes that can be composted.**
- ***Recycling.* Dry wastes are separated at an intermediate processing center to remove the maximum amount of recyclables.**
- ***Composting.* Biodegradable organic wastes are taken to a composting plant that can handle 130,000 tons per year.**
- ***Waste to energy.* An incineration plant is being constructed to produce electricity from wastes that cannot be recycled.**
- ***Public awareness.* The public was involved and informed at all stages of project development.**

The CUDL has been able to recover half of its wastes with this new system: about 25 percent of the total waste stream is composted, and another 25 percent is recycled.

Box 8-9 A softer path for waste management in Lille, France.

SOURCE: Gilbert et al. 1996, 46–47.

LAND USE

Options for improving land use in cities can reduce the negative effects of urbanization on environmentally sensitive land, lower the exposure of vulnerable groups to natural and human-induced hazards, and improve energy efficiency and lessen transport-related air pollution. These can be partially achieved by removing distortions and enabling land markets to function; increased supply of affordable land will reduce pressure on sensitive areas. A second key approach is to develop land use rules, roads, and public transportation in an integrated manner so that high-density development coincides with affordable public tran-

(a)

sit, as in the case of Curitiba (see Box 9-5). Management options that specifically focus on the transportation dimension of land use are summarized in Box 8-10.

Other management options include:

- *Providing infrastructure.* The placement of environmental infrastructure and roads (including pedestrian and bicycle paths) is a powerful force for guiding land development away from fragile areas and for increasing densities where appropriate.

- *Compact land use.* Rules, taxes, and incentives can be used to increase densities, encourage mixed land use, and limit sprawl in order to increase energy efficiency, reduce the cost of providing urban services, and lower air pollution.

(b)

Figure 8-9 Compact land use: Low-density slum (*a*) and redeveloped mid-rises (*b*) in Tianjin, China.

BOX

Cities around the world have developed a number of innovative options for controlling the environmental impact of motorized vehicles. In addition to the examples from Singapore and Curitiba presented in Chapter 9, one can cite:

- *Proof of parking space.* In order to buy a car in Tokyo and other Japanese cities, drivers must present a certificate issued by their local police station showing that they have a parking space within 2 km of their home.
- *Road pricing.* Oslo, Bergen, and Trondheim, Norway, use an electronic toll system similar to Singapore's (see Chapter 9) that reads a smart card on the car's dashboard and charges drivers for entering the city center.
- *Parking limits.* Zurich, Switzerland, has progressively lowered the parking time for nonresidents to a maximum of 90 minutes, encouraging commuters to park on the edge of town and take public transportation. Bologna and 41 other Italian cities limit parking to local residents only.
- *Calming traffic.* In London, England, the central city has closed many small streets to traffic and restricted entry to a few main points, sharply reducing traffic volume. A large part of the city center in Athens, Greece, is now closed to traffic; only odd- and even-numbered cars are allowed into the center on alternate days; and in the future access may be limited to low-pollution vehicles only. This latter option, clean-car zones, is the basis of a campaign being promoted throughout the European Union.
- *Public transit.* Portland, Oregon, restricts new suburban development, and encourages higher densities in town that make public transportation more viable. Car use has also been decreased by creating pedestrian zones and opening a light-rail system.
- *Nonmotorized transport.* Groningen, The Netherlands, promotes bicycle use by subdividing the city into zones, making direct crosstown car trips impossible, and concentrating new developments on public transportation routes. Bikes now account for 50 percent of all trips.

Box 8-10 Management options for controlling traffic.

SOURCE: McNulty and Parker 1998.

- *Protecting sensitive areas.* Zoning, development standards, building codes, permits, and economic incentives can be used to restrict development in environmentally fragile areas and encourage appropriate use of sensitive lands.
- *Encouraging preservation.* Incentives such as transferable development rights should be used to preserve existing and historic urban areas, encouraging redevelopment instead of new development.

Figure 8-10 Nonmotorized transport in Bandung, Indonesia.

ENERGY

Cities are major fuel consumers, and the extraction, transformation, and combustion of energy is an important cause of environmental degradation. As with water supply, demand management is one of the most important options for reducing the environmental impact of energy use; in the case of electricity, it can also be less expensive than developing new power plants. Options for energy conservation include: (1) the integration of land use controls, public transit, and road development to promote a more compact, energy-efficient urban form; (2) regulations and incentives for the construction of energy-efficient buildings; (3) energy audits and conservation measures for industries and existing buildings; and (4) public awareness campaigns about conservation measures, along with product labeling for energy efficiency. On the production side, the environmental impact of urban energy supply can be mitigated through the increased use of renewable energy, cogeneration, and natural gas, and by developing district heating and cooling systems in colder climates. Examples of innovations in urban energy management from U.S. cities are provided in Box 8-11.

Figure 8-11 Preserving architectural heritage in Kuala Lumpur, Malaysia.

NATURAL AND CULTURAL HERITAGE

Cities can protect their surrounding natural areas through a variety of management options. Parks and other green spaces can be expanded through the use of land and conservation trusts; municipal purchase of environmentally sensitive areas, financed by the sale of surplus, less desirable land (see the case of Durban in Chapter 7); development of flood-control areas as parks; restoration of urban watercourses and natural corridors; and inventories and restrictions on the development

BOX

- *Clean power.* In late 1997 Electric Lite, a subsidiary of Portland General Electric, began offering electricity produced by cleaner methods to residential and business customers in four Oregon cities. At least half of the electricity produced in the company's cleaner program, Electric Lite Green, comes from renewable sources such as wind, solar, and geothermal, and from low-impact sources like landfill gas. An additional 35 percent is generated by clean sources such as hydropower and natural gas. About 15 percent of the power provided comes from sources with a greater negative environmental impact, like coal and nuclear. This compares favorably with the regional power mix, which is 54 percent hydro, 32 percent coal, 8 percent natural gas, and 6 percent nuclear and other sources. Customers who choose Electric Lite Green pay $0.01 more per kilowatt-hour, which amounts to an average of $7 per month more than a bill for the standard, higher-polluting service. For more information: www.electriclite.com (Business Wire 1998).
- *Solar technologies.* The Million Solar Roofs Initiative, announced in 1997, will use federal resources to promote solar energy sales and will work with local governments and other groups to find ways to rapidly expand the use of solar technology. The Utility Photovoltaic Group, a nonprofit association of 89 electric utilities and energy service companies, is cooperating to develop photovoltaic power as a commercial energy option for its utilities and their customers. It is hoped that the initiative will help achieve the necessary economies of scale to make solar technologies everyday commodities (Tucker 1997).
- *Better buildings.* Buildings for the 21st Century is a partnership between the U.S. Department of Energy; the building design, construction, and finance industries; and local communities to create a new generation of high-quality, energy-efficient, affordable, and environmentally sustainable buildings and communities. The partnership advocates using a whole-buildings approach to new construction and renovation (Tucker 1997).
- *Incentives for renewables.* Twenty states now allow net metering, whereby households and industries that produce electricity from renewable sources can sell to the grid, with electricity meters running backward during production. In California, residents who install solar panels between 1998 and 2002 can be reimbursed three cents per watt of generating capacity or up to 50 percent of their investment, whichever is less (Slater 1998).

Box 8-11 Cleaner energy in U.S. cities.

of environmentally valued areas. Urban greening can be promoted through tree-planting campaigns, rules concerning landscaping, community awareness and participation measures, distribution of seedlings, and support for urban agriculture.

Cultural and historical landmarks in cities can be protected by

Figure 8-12 Preserving culture in the face of globalization in Bangkok, Thailand.

a variety of measures. Transferable development rights allow historic buildings and sites in attractive locations to be preserved by allowing owners to market the unbuilt portion for use in another part of the city. In Denver, Colorado, this approach has been used as collateral for loans to cover the cost of restoring landmark buildings. A revolving fund can be used to acquire, renovate, and resell valued sites. In the United States, the National Trust for Historic Preservation and a variety of local funds use this approach to preservation; Savannah, Georgia, was especially successful in using its revolving fund to preserve its historic areas and benefit from subsequent tourism revenues. Property tax relief for rehabilitation of buildings can save historic structures from decay and demolition. New York exempts residential buildings from any increase in real estate taxes due to rehabilitation and abates a large portion of the taxes that would otherwise have had to be paid, resulting in the preservation of thousands of historic structures. Similarly, income tax benefits can encourage preservation by allowing for accelerated depreciation of rehabilitated structures or providing tax credits for renovation. In the United States, the 1981 Economic Recovery Tax Act provided a credit equal to 25 percent of the cost of rehabilitation and permitted full depreciation of the tax credit; this resulted in more than 10,000 restoration projects worth $7.8 billion between 1982 and 1985 (all examples from Garvin 1995).

Introducing New Institutions and Systems

Cities can tackle major environmental problems via two general management options—by realigning power arrangements through new institutions, and by introducing new systems. Subsidiarity is an important principle in this regard: The management of environmental services should be decentralized to the lowest effective level. Note that this is not a blanket call for every neighborhood to become an environmental manager. The example was given earlier in this chapter where it may be appropriate to decentralize solid waste collection to the municipal or district level, but disposal is more effectively handled at the metropolitan or regional level. An example of how this approach can dramatically improve the urban environment is provided in Box 8-12.

Two broad management options have been pursued to create new institutions that can address urban environmental problems. The first is to develop an institution that has an ecological jurisdiction such as a watershed (as in France), a watercourse, or an airshed. This approach can take the form of an informal policy body, a formal commission, or a powerful new institution. In an example of an informal approach, a planning and advisory

BOX

Surat is an industrial boomtown with a population of 2.2 million that is also the second-fastest-growing city in India. The city gained worldwide notoriety in 1994 with the outbreak of the plague. Poorly functioning municipal services were partly to blame: Only 45 percent of citizens received water supply and sewerage services; only half of solid waste was collected; only 40 percent of the city benefited from street cleaning; and maintenance of most municipal infrastructure was erratic.

In May 1995, a new Municipal Commissioner took action. He decentralized all of his administrative and financial powers (except for policy issues and high-cost projects) to chiefs of six territorial zones and four functional heads of projects (for water supply, sewerage, town planning, and finance). This allowed for more intersectoral coordination. These 10 commissioners and the Municipal Commissioner were then obligated to spend a minimum of four hours each day out of their offices and in the field. They then worked with the city's new mayor to develop solutions.

Among the priority approaches they pursued were: improving the morale and dignity of sanitation workers; standardizing work methods across all six zones; reducing littering by citizens; getting street vendors to switch from plastic to natural packaging material; expanding basic services in slums; creating a citizen grievance system; developing an early warning system for the outbreak of environmental health problems; and expanding capital investment in sanitation. These changes were largely self-financed through more efficient tax recovery, transparency in tax assessments, and plugging tax loopholes.

Just 18 months after action was initiated, Surat was judged to be the second-cleanest city in India. Ninety-two percent of slums had gained access to basic services; the city's share of public health morbidity in the State of Gujarat dropped from 50 to 5 percent; solid waste collection more than doubled, from 400 to 850 tons per day; hundreds of kilometers of new roads and water and sewage lines had been built; and the tax recovery rate jumped from 32 to 83 percent.

Box 8-12 Decentralization with accountability in Surat, India.
SOURCE: Surat Municipal Corporation 1998.

body of citizens, government, and industry was created to prepare a remedial action plan for the Cuyahoga River, which has been historically polluted by urban runoff, industrial waste, and sewage overflow from Akron and Cleveland, Ohio. Although the advisory body has no enforcement powers, it has overseen investigations, prepared status reports, set up a charitable organization for river cleanup, analyzed pollution sources, and contributed to a policy consensus that has helped improve river water quality (Loucks 1994). In another case, in 1983 six municipalities, local industries, the Sao Paulo state water company, and local community groups joined together to design and implement a strategy for cleaning the polluted Jundiai River and its catchment basin in Brazil. Resulting actions included construction of a regional sewage treatment facility, building of a retention dam for stormwater runoff, reforestation of the watershed, protection of a forest reserve, and updating of local land use plans. By 1992, direct pollution loading into the river had been reduced by 70 percent in the city of Jundiai alone (ICLEI 1996b). As an example of a more formal approach, the California legislature created the South Coast Air Quality Management District in 1976 to address air pollution in the Los Angeles airshed. The management district has responsibility for stationary sources and consumer products; it has implemented a variety of innovative strategies to address air pollution (WRI 1996).

The second institutional option is to create an organization that has integrated responsibility for urban environmental management. This is the favored approach in China, where every major city has an environmental protection bureau. For example, the Beijing bureau's responsibilities include drafting environmental policies, regulations, and standards for the city; formulating measures to implement these rules; monitoring execution of environmental regulations by economic enterprises; reviewing and approving construction project EIAs and environmental protection facilities; collecting pollution discharge fees and penalties; and organizing citywide monitoring, scientific studies, and public awareness campaigns. This is done through a significant bureaucracy that employs over 800 people in 19 sections (MEIP 1994). Similarly, the city-state of Singapore centralizes many of its management functions within the Ministry of the Environment (see case study in Chapter 9).

Another set of management options is to introduce new systems that improve accountability and environmental performance. Examples of these, ranging from simple to comprehensive, include:

- *Checklists.* These help cities evaluate their environmental performance and identify areas for improvement on topics such as partnerships for environmental protection, housing and land use, greening, energy policy and climate protection, transport, water, waste, municipal purchasing, and tourism (for an example, see BAUM 1995).
- *Guidelines.* These provide local governments with a set of key issues, options, approaches, and resources for urban environmental management. (For an example of guidelines that were developed for municipalities in Thailand, see GTZ 1994.)
- *Impact assessment.* Cities can screen their own operations and subject those with the potential for environmental harm to impact assessments, with all the strengths and drawbacks identified in Chapter 5. This is done, for example in Ottawa, Ontario, through the city's Municipal Environmental Evaluation Process (ICLEI 1996b).
- *Ecomanagement and audit scheme.* The EMAS is a voluntary regulation of the European Union that can be applied to city services. Each city unit is asked to develop an environmental policy, conduct a review of its operational units, develop an environmental program with quantified objectives for each unit, regularly audit its performance, issue an annual environmental statement based on the audit, and seek independent verification of compliance with the EMAS (Hillary 1995). See Box 8-13 for an application of the system.
- *LEAPs.* The framework for informed consultation, formulation of a local environmental action plan, and implementation with feedback that is advocated in this text is perhaps the most comprehensive new system that can be introduced for urban environmental management.

BOX

Kirklees has a sizeable municipal authority, with a staff of 19,500. The city developed an Environmental Action Programme that placed priority on raising environmental awareness, transport, energy conservation, and health. Over 400 recommendations were translated into specific actions for the city's 37 departments.

In 1994, an EMAS approach was introduced to implement the program. Progress is assessed against targets that are audited during a three-year rolling program. Targets include:

- Use of recycled paper
- Energy-saving measures in municipal buildings
- Environmental clauses in standard service contracts
- A "green" purchasing policy
- Involvement of the voluntary and private sectors
- Pollution monitoring and public information

The city publishes an annual "Vision" statement that provides information on achievement of the various targets and implementation of the Programme.

Box 8-13 EMAS applied in Kirklees, UK.

SOURCE: Webber 1995.

Compendium of Management Options

This chapter does not seek to provide a comprehensive and thorough review of options for urban environmental management. Hundreds of books and articles have been written to provide guidance on the various facets of managing environmental problems in cities, and innovations are constantly being developed. Rather, some of the promising approaches to environmental management have been summarized in Table 8-2 according to the management objectives developed at the beginning of the chapter, in order to stimulate thinking, discussion, and further inquiry.

Resources and Exercises for Further Thought

Resources

MANAGEMENT INSTRUMENTS AND SELECTION CRITERIA

A broad overview of regulatory and economic instruments for environmental management is well presented in Bernstein (1991). ICLEI (1996a) is a good guide for local governments on using economic instruments to improve environmental performance, with examples from many cities. Miller and De Roo (1997) contains a set of articles that provide experience and insight into the use of urban environmental zoning as a land-use option.

OPTIONS FOR INVOLVING STAKEHOLDERS

More information on the direct-action option of community environmental management can be found in the proceedings of an associated event to the 1994 World Bank Conference on Environ-

Table 8-2 Compendium of Promising Management Options

Management objective	Management options*
IMPROVED ACCESS TO ENVIRONMENTAL INFRASTRUCTURE AND SERVICES	
• Serviced land and shelter	P: Clarify property rights; reduce unneeded regulations, government involvement, and subsidies for land market
	I: Upgrade slums; develop sites and services projects
• Water supply, sanitation, drainage, solid waste collection, energy	P: Incentives for demand management; reduce subsidies, and recover costs; target subsidies for the poor; strategic planning; introduce affordable standards; coordinate between sectors; use new infrastructure to guide land use; design with nature
	I: Use appropriate technologies; expand access to basic services; increase use of private and community resources; improve operations and maintenance
CONTROLLING, REDUCING, OR PREVENTING POLLUTION	
• Water pollution	P: Introduce water pricing and effluent charges; subsidize sewage treatment; plan and manage watersheds
	I: Improve monitoring and enforcement; develop facilities for reusing wastewater; introduce clean technologies
• Air pollution and energy use	P: Remove energy and vehicle subsidies; introduce road and emissions charges; integrate transport, land use, and road planning; least-cost energy planning; improve traffic management
	I: Develop clean technologies, renewable energy, district heating, energy-efficient buildings, substitution to cleaner fuels, nonmotorized transport, vehicle maintenance, and related public awareness campaigns; improve performance of public transit
• Solid and hazardous wastes	P: Incentives for waste minimization; develop regulations, licensing, and charges; enable informal sector operators
	I: Involve private sector in treatment and disposal operations; develop sanitary landfills, recycling, and composting facilities; technical assistance for small and medium-scale industries
SUSTAINABLY USING RESOURCES	
• Groundwater depletion	P: Reform property rights; introduce extraction charges
	I: Control leakage from sewers and leaching from solid waste; increase recharge of good-quality water
• Land and ecosystem degradation	P: Remove artificial shortages of land and subsidies on natural resources; identify critical areas for protection; incentives for sustainable use of sensitive areas; ecolabeling; resource-efficient building standards; promote compact land use
	I: Improve monitoring and enforcement of land-use controls; purchase sensitive and valued lands; resources for urban greening and agriculture
DEVELOPING ENVIRONMENTAL PLANNING AND INSTITUTIONAL CAPACITY	
	P: Introduce new institutions and systems where appropriate; enhance public participation; improve municipal financing; initiate LEAP process; institute capacity-building measures; decentralize to appropriate level; network with other cities and initiatives such as ICLEI and WHO Healthy Cities Program
	I: Research to fill knowledge gaps for all objectives
REDUCING RISK AND PRESERVING NATURAL/CULTURAL HERITAGE	
• Natural hazards	P: Enable land markets; disincentives for occupation of high-risk areas; disaster mitigation and preparedness planning; incentives for disaster-resistant construction techniques
	I: Public awareness campaigns about risks and mitigation
• Human-induced hazards	P: Environmental zoning
	I: Improve emergency response capacity; public awareness
• Natural heritage	P: See land options
	I: See land options
• Cultural/historic heritage	P: Transferable development rights; tax incentives; clarify property rights; introduce heritage zoning and building codes
	I: Create revolving fund for conservation

* P = policy and institutional options; I = investment options

SOURCE: Adapted from: Leitmann 1994, 74–76; Bartone et al. 1994, 39–40.

mentally Sustainable Development, entitled *Enabling Sustainable Community Development* (Serageldin, Cohen, and Leitmann 1995).

OPTIONS FOR BUILDING ENVIRONMENTAL MANAGEMENT CAPACITY

An elaborated set of recommendations for improving municipal operations geared to the industrialized world can be found in Roseland (1998) and OECD (1996). UNCHS (1996) and WRI (1996) have chapters on management options that are more weighted toward cities in the developing world. Options and case studies for managing air pollution from transport-related sources can be found in Walsh (1997). The strategic approach to solid waste management is fully presented in World Bank (1998). Approaches for managing groundwater are available in Foster, Lawrence, and Morris (1998). A good resource for management options to improve the supply and demand of energy, based on experience in industrialized cities, is OECD (1995).

For introducing new institutions and systems, ICLEI (1996) contains a good set of checklists for developing and implementing LEAPs. Operational details about how the EMAS is being applied in British cities can be found in various publications from the Local Government Management Board, such as *A Guide to the Eco-management and Audit Scheme for UK Local Government*. The board maintains an EMAS Help Desk that can be reached by phone at 44-1582-451166 or by fax at 44-1582-412525.

Exercises for Further Thought

1. Under what circumstances might a city not need or want to adopt the environmental planning framework?
2. Compare and contrast regulatory and economic instruments for urban environmental management.
3. Why do direct investment and clarification of property rights in squatter areas unleash private resources for environmental management?
4. Why do some cities fail to develop, analyze, and disseminate information about environmental quality?

5. Why can management objectives differ according to a city's level of development?
6. Prepare a list of win-win solutions to environmental problems in your city.
7. What are the environmental issues facing low-income communities and vulnerable groups in your city?
8. How can the objective of cost recovery for urban services be reconciled with a focus on increasing access by the poor?
9. Which environmental-awareness-raising techniques would be most effective in your community?
10. How might the environmental concerns of the wealthy differ from those of other socioeconomic groups?
11. What are the advantages and disadvantages of using the court system as an option for stakeholder involvement?
12. List examples as well as strengths and weaknesses of community environmental management.
13. What are some of the risks involved in public-private and other forms of partnership for environmental management?
14. Determine appropriate levels of decentralization for responding to different environmental problems in your city.
15. What are some constraints on establishing new institutions with ecological jurisdictions?

References

Ahmedabad Municipal Corporation. 1998. Innovations in urban partnership in Ahmedabad. Submission to UNCHS Best Practices Competition.

Bartone, Carl, and Livia Benavides. 1993. Local management of hazardous wastes from small-scale and cottage industries. Paper prepared for 5th Pacific Basin Conference on Hazardous Waste, November 8–12, Honolulu, Hawaii.

Bartone, Carl, Janis Bernstein, Josef Leitmann, and Jochen Eigen. 1994. Toward environmental strategies for cities: Policy considerations for urban environmental management in developing countries. UMP Policy Paper No. 18. Washington, D.C.: World Bank.

BAUM Consult Munchen. 1995. Environmental quick check for municipalities. Munich: Bavarian Ministry for Development and Environmental Questions.

Bernstein, Janis. 1991. Alternative approaches to pollution control and waste management: Regulatory and economic instruments. UMP Discussion Paper No. 3. Washington, D.C.: World Bank.

Business Wire. 1998. Electric Lite becomes Oregon's first "green" power company. *Los Angeles Times,* 11 February.

Council of Europe. 1996. Croatia: A green phone. *Naturopa* 81: 19–20.

Earth Times. 1998. Water parliaments: A French solution. April 16–30: 15.

Eskeland, Gunnar, and Shantayanan Devarajan. 1996. Taxing bads by taxing goods: Pollution control with presumptive charges. Directions in Development Series. Washington, D.C.: World Bank.

Eskeland, Gunnar, and Tarhan Feyzioglu. 1997. Rationing can backfire: The "day without a car" in Mexico City. *The World Bank Economic Review* 11(3): 383–408.

Foster, Stephen, Adrian Lawrence, and Brian Morris. 1998. Groundwater in urban development: Assessing management needs and formulating policy strategies. Technical Paper No. 390. Washington, D.C.: World Bank.

Garvin, Alexander. 1995. *The American city: What works, what doesn't*. New York: McGraw-Hill.

Gilbert, Richard, Don Stevenson, Herbert Girardet, and Richard Stren. 1996. *Making cities work: The role of local authorities in the urban environment*. London: Earthscan Publications Ltd.

GTZ (German Technical Cooperation). 1994. Urban environmental management guidelines for Thailand. Summary prepared in collaboration with Thai Office of Urban Development. Eschborn: GTZ.

Hadiwinoto, Suhadi, and Josef Leitmann. 1994. Environmental profile of Jakarta, Indonesia. *Cities* 11(3).

Hardoy, Jorge, and David Satterthwaite. 1989. *Squatter citizen: Life in the urban Third World.* London: Earthscan Publications, Inc.

Haughton, Graham, and Colin Hunter. 1994. *Sustainable cities.* London: Jessica Kingsley Publishers, Ltd.

Hillary, Ruth. 1995. Environmental reporting requirements under the EU: Ecomanagement and audit scheme (EMAS). *The Environmentalist* 15: 293–299.

ICLEI (International Council for Local Environmental Initiatives). 1996a. Economic instruments to improve environmental performance: A guide for local governments. Toronto: ICLEI.

———. 1996b. The Local Agenda 21 planning guide: An introduction to sustainable development planning. Toronto: ICLEI.

Inter Press Service. 1998. First smog emergency in Santiago since 1992. May 21.

Lee, Yok Shiu. 1994. Community-based urban environmental management: Local NGOs as catalysts. *Regional Development Dialogue* 15(2).

Lee, Yok Shiu. 1998. Intermediary institutions, community organizations and urban environmental management: The case of three Bangkok slums. *World Development* 26(6): 993–1011.

Leitmann, Josef. 1994. Rapid urban environmental assessment. Volumes 1 and 2, UNCHS/World Bank/UNDP Urban Management Program Discussion Papers Nos. 14 and 15. Washington, D.C.: World Bank.

Lemos, Maria Carmen de Mello. 1998. The Cubatao pollution control project: Popular participation and public accountability. *Journal of Environment and Development* 7(1): 60–76.

Loucks, Orie. 1994. Sustainability in urban ecosystems: Beyond an object of study. In Rutherford Platt, Rowan Rowntree, and Pamela Muick (eds.). *The ecological city.* Amherst: University of Massachusetts Press.

McNulty, Sheila, and John Parker. 1998. Measures to keep the world's motorists off the streets. *Financial Times,* May 9–10, 7.

MEIP (Metropolitan Environmental Improvement Program). 1994. Environmental management institutions and organizations in Beijing. Washington, D.C.: World Bank.

Miller, Donald, and Gert De Roo (eds.). 1997. *Urban environmental planning: Policies, instruments and methods in an international perspective*. Aldershot, UK: Avebury.

OECD (Organization for Economic Cooperation and Development). 1996. Innovative policies for sustainable urban development: The ecological city. Paris: OECD.

———. 1998. Globalisation and the environment: Perspectives from OECD and dynamic non-member countries. *OECD Proceedings*. Paris: OECD.

———. 1995. Urban energy handbook: Good local practice. Paris: OECD.

Postel, Sandra. 1992. *Last oasis: Facing water scarcity*. Worldwatch Environmental Alert Series. New York: W. W. Norton & Company.

Rabinovitch, Jonas, and Josef Leitmann. 1996. Improving the quality of urban life: Curitiba challenges conventional wisdom. *Scientific American* 274(3).

Roseland, Mark. 1998. *Toward sustainable communities: Resources for citizens and their governments*. Gabriola Island and Stony Creek: New Society Publishers.

Serageldin, Ismail, Michael Cohen, and Josef Leitmann. 1995. Enabling sustainable community development. Environmentally Sustainable Development Proceedings Series No. 8. Washington, D.C.: World Bank.

Slater, Dashka. 1998. Sunny prospects: The U.S. warms up to solar energy again. *Sierra* May/June.

Surat Municipal Corporation. 1998. Urban governance in environment and public health management: Surat's experience. Submission to UNCHS Best Practices Competition. Surat: The Municipal Commission.

Tucker, Mary. 1997. Why renewables and local governments? Washington, D.C.: Public Technologies Incorporated.

UNCHS (UN Centre for Human Settlements). 1996. *An urbanizing world: Global report on human settlements 1996*. London: Oxford University Press.

UNDP (United Nations Development Programme). 1991. Cities, people & poverty: Urban development cooperation for the 1990s. UNDP Strategy Paper. New York: UNDP.

———. 1996. Urban agriculture: Food, jobs and sustainable cities. New York: UNDP.

USAID (US Agency for International Development). 1992. Success stories of urban environmental management. Case Studies Prepared by RHUDO/Asia (Regional Housing and Urban Development Office/Asia). Bangkok: RHUDO/Asia.

Walsh, Michael. 1997. *Managing urban motor vehicle air pollution*. Washington, D.C.: World Bank and World Health Organization.

Webber, Philip. 1995. Case study: Kirklees. In OECD. Urban policies for an environmentally sustainable world. Paris: OECD.

World Bank. 1991. Urban policy and economic development: An agenda for the 1990s. Washington, D.C.: World Bank.

———. 1995. Enhancing the quality of life in urban Indonesia: The legacy of Kampung Improvement Program. Impact Evaluation Report No. 14747-IND. Washington, D.C.: World Bank.

———. 1997. Five years after Rio: Innovations in environmental policy. Environmentally Sustainable Development Studies and Monographs Series No. 18. Washington, D.C.: World Bank.

———. 1997b. The Guadalajara environmental management pilot. Information Brief. Washington, D.C.: World Bank.

———. 1998. Strategic municipal solid waste planning in municipal areas. Planning Guidelines Prepared with Swiss Development Cooperation. Washington, D.C.: World Bank.

———. 1999 (forthcoming). What a waste: Solid waste management in Asia. Washington, D.C.: World Bank.

WRI (World Resources Institute). 1996. *World resources 1996–97: The urban environment*. New York: Oxford University Press.

CHAPTER 9

Good Practice for Managing the Urban Environment

Chapter Outline

- Defining good practice
- International level: Global campaign to reduce greenhouse gas emissions
- National level: Phasing out leaded gasoline in Thailand
- City level: Integrating the environment in Singapore's development
- Sectoral level: Matching sanitation and socioeconomic status in Kumasi, Ghana
- Neighborhood level: Preserving an informal community's role in waste management in Cairo, Egypt
- Compendium: 200+ examples of good practice
- Resources and exercises for further thought
- References

What Is Good Practice?

There is a great deal of enthusiasm for identifying, documenting, and disseminating examples of "best" practice in urban planning and management. There is even a "Best Practice Awards" program sponsored by Dubai and administered by UNCHS in partnership with a number of leading urban research and capacity-building institutions. However, there is no standard definition of *best practice*—which makes it difficult to categorically state that one particular example of urban planning or management is at the pinnacle. Thus, a working definition of good practice is developed in this chapter and used to select examples of good urban environmental planning and management at the international, national, city, sectoral, and neighborhood levels.

In order to define *good practice,* it is useful to look at how *best practice* has been described. The Best Practice Awards, while never specifically defining the term, initially developed the following criteria for evaluation to select the 1996 awards:

- *Partnership.* The practice should involve a partnership between at least two of the following actors: national government, local authorities, NGOs and CBOs, the private sector, international agencies, academic/research institutes, professional associations, the media, civic leaders, and/or volunteers.
- *Impact.* The practice should have resulted in tangible improvements in people's living conditions.
- *Sustainability.* The practice should have led to lasting changes in legislation, the regulatory framework, bylaws, or standards; social or sectoral policies; harmonization of social, economic, and environmental strategies; or institutions and decision-making processes.

The Dubai International Conference on Best Practices (November 19–22, 1995) elaborated several additional considerations:

- *Leadership.* The practice should inspire innovative action, foster change, and promote transparent, accountable, and inclusive decision-making.

- *Community empowerment.* The practice should enhance the capacities of women and men to improve in their own lives, access resources and assistance, participate effectively in decision-making and partnerships, and hold organizations and leaders to account.
- *Gender and social inclusion.* The practice should accept and respond to social and cultural diversity, promote social equality and equity (e.g., on the basis of income, gender, and age), and recognize and value different abilities.

This combined set of criteria was used to select the 1998 Best Practice award winners (You 1998).

Good practice for urban environmental planning and management should exhibit all or most of these criteria (partnership, impact, sustainability, leadership, community empowerment, gender, and social inclusion). In addition, it should achieve at least one of the goals of urban environmental management. These can be summarized as:

- Improving the access of low-income and other excluded groups to urban infrastructure and services
- Promoting sustainable use of environmental resources and services
- Controlling, reducing, and/or preventing environmental pollution
- Building urban planning capacity or encouraging a city-level process that supports sustainable development
- Reducing natural or man-made risks and protecting natural/cultural heritage

This definition is not precise. Rather, like the term "sustainable development," it is a useful concept that can guide learning.

The preceding definition of *good practice* has been applied to identify several interesting cases of urban environmental planning and management. The criteria used for selecting each case are listed; the case is presented; and lessons for replication are extracted. Finally, more than 200 additional examples of good practice are summarized in tabular form according to the five management goals just listed.

International Level: Global Campaign to Reduce Greenhouse Gas Emissions

The practice: Cities for climate protection campaign
Criteria fulfilled: Partnership, impact, sustainability, leadership
Management goal: Reducing risks and protecting natural/ cultural heritage
Documentation: ICLEI 1997a,b; ICLEI 1998

Background

Cities for Climate Protection (CCP) is a global campaign whose goals are to slow down global warming, improve local air quality, and enhance urban livability. It seeks to achieve these goals by motivating and empowering local governments to reduce urban greenhouse gas emissions. CCP seeks, by the year 2000, to recruit a diverse set of municipalities that account for 10 percent of 1990 CO_2 emissions. The campaign is sponsored by an international association of local governments called the International Council for Local Environmental Initiatives (ICLEI).

ICLEI initiated an urban CO_2 reduction project in mid-1991, with support from the U.S. Environmental Protection Agency, the city and metropolitan governments of Toronto, and several private foundations. Fourteen municipalities in the United States, Canada, and Europe were recruited to participate in a two-year effort to develop comprehensive local strategies to reduce greenhouse gas emissions and quantification methods to support the strategies. At the conclusion of the project, the participating local governments made political commitments to reduce their CO_2 emissions.

ICLEI and the UN Environmental Program then sponsored the First Municipal Leaders' Summit on Climate Change and the Urban Environment in early 1993. The participants adopted a Municipal Leaders' Declaration on Climate Change. Signatories pledged to develop local action plans to reduce greenhouse gas emissions, undertake energy conservation measures for municipal operations and facilities, and support activities to increase public awareness about climate change. In addition, the Declaration requested that ICLEI create a CCP campaign.

The Approach

The primary purpose of the campaign is to motivate and support local governments to reduce greenhouse gas emissions. These emissions include: (1) CO_2, which in urban areas is emitted through combustion of fossil fuels by households, institutional and commercial buildings, vehicles, and industries; (2) conventional air pollutants such as nitrogen oxides (NO_x), carbon monoxide (CO), and nonmethane volatile organic compounds (VOC), which are also by-products of fossil fuel combustion; and (3) methane (CH_4), which is emitted in cities during waste disposal, especially via landfills and waste water treatment.

To accomplish this aim, the broad activities of the CCP were set in late 1995 as:

- Recruitment and coordination of cities from a variety of regions, population sizes, and developmental conditions. The initial focus was on cities from the industrialized world, because they are responsible for much of the rise in atmospheric CO_2. After an initial period, recruitment was expanded to attract participation from cities in lower-income countries.
- Development of municipal capacity through coordination, technical assistance, and provision of educational materials to help local governments develop Local Action Plans (see below) to reduce greenhouse gases.
- Promotion of accountability by encouraging campaign participants to monitor, quantify, and report their performance to their national governments and to ICLEI.
- Representation of CCP participants at the Conference of Parties and its Subsidiary Bodies as part of the Framework Convention on Climate Change.

These continue to be the main activities of the CCP campaign.

In order for a city to join the campaign, its elected council or an appropriate bureaucratic authority must adopt a local government resolution that endorses the aims of the CCP campaign as well as its approach. Once it has become a CCP participant, the local government then undertakes to complete five key tasks, known as *milestones*. These are:

1. Creating a profile of energy use and CO_2 emissions for a base year (1990 or 1995)
2. Forecasting energy use and greenhouse gas emissions in a "business as usual" scenario to the year 2010 or 2015
3. Establishing an emissions reduction target to be achieved by the year 2005 or 2010
4. Developing and obtaining approval for a Local Action Plan to reduce emissions and promote public awareness
5. Starting to implement measures as part of the plan

Endorsement of the resolution and the plan usually requires political will, expert analysis, and public discussion.

Results

As of 1998, 255 local governments with a combined population of well over 100 million had joined the campaign. Emissions that occur in these jurisdictions account for over 5 percent of worldwide CO_2 output. Over a third of these cities had adopted a target and timetable for CO_2 reductions. Over 15 percent had completed all five milestones required to implement their Local Action Plan.

Most of the cities that established reduction targets pledged to lower emissions from their 1990 levels by 20 percent or more by 2005 or 2020. If these commitments are met, their cumulative CO_2 emissions would represent a 90-million-ton reduction from the 1990 base year. This would represent almost 0.5 percent of 1990 global CO_2 emissions. Sixty-two cities had actually implemented 135 measures that resulted in CO_2 reductions of 42 million tons between 1990 and 1996. Average annual expenditures for these measures were $22 per capita; these investments yielded annual rates of return ranging from 10 to 20 percent, mostly from energy efficiency gains. Key measures include improving efficiency in power plants and district heating systems, retrofitting buildings to improve energy conservation, converting boilers from coal or oil to natural gas, improving public transportation, and reducing methane emissions from waste.

Lessons

Some of the programmatic lessons that have been learned are:

- CCP participants take an average of two to three years to complete all five milestones.
- Targets and timetables are set after careful analysis and deliberation, including identification of local energy conservation measures.
- Many cities begin to implement measures as a first step in order to gain experience with energy efficiency measures and to build public support before pursuing more comprehensive options.

Finally, there has been a positive response from cities in developing countries to join the campaign and initiate actions to reduce greenhouse gas emissions. CCP reports that there is an understanding that addressing local problems of air pollution, water quality, and waste management can also benefit the global climate. However, financial constraints are hindering efforts to implement local initiatives.

Three of the cities that made substantial progress toward achieving their targets (refer to Box 9-1) produced a number of lessons at the local level:

- Partnerships between local government, other levels of government, and private financial institutions have helped cities raise significant capital for energy retrofits.
- Energy pricing is an effective tool for demand-side management, especially if it can be controlled or influenced by the municipality.
- The most effective long-term measure to reduce transportation energy use is land use changes that promote more compact cities, integrated with public transit.
- Methane, a relatively small component of urban greenhouse gas emissions, can be significantly reduced through initiatives to reuse, recycle, and reduce solid waste.

BOX

Portland, Oregon: In 1993, Portland became the first U.S. city to adopt a strategy to reduce CO_2 emissions. Its goal is to reduce emissions throughout the metropolitan area to 20 percent below 1988 levels by 2010. Energy efficiency measures have included reducing energy consumption in municipal buildings by 15 percent since 1990, providing technical assistance for businesses and residences to conserve energy, and reducing electricity demand by 80 megawatts. Transportation measures have included expanding the light rail system, encouraging denser land use and limiting sprawl, providing incentives for using public transit and car pools, and encouraging employees to telecommute. Portland's population grew 10 percent between 1990 and 1995, while CO_2 emissions increased by only 8 percent and per capita emissions actually dropped by 3 percent.

Saarbrucken, Germany: In 1993, Saarbrucken adopted a Local Action Plan to reduce CO_2 emissions by 25 percent from 1990 levels by the year 2005. The most successful elements of the plan were a local energy management plan and expansion of the district heating system. Highlights of the energy management plan include a 50 percent reduction of energy use in municipal buildings and facilities, a loan program to finance energy conservation measures, and elimination of declining block pricing for electricity (the more you use, the less you pay) in favor of a more linear structure. District heating, produced by cogeneration, has been expanded to cover more than a third of the city's space heating needs, and district cooling is now being introduced. Additional investments are being made for solar energy, a new tram system, and construction of bicycle lanes. Between 1990 and 1996, overall emissions dropped by 15 percent and per capita emissions by 16 percent.

Toronto, Ontario: In 1990, Toronto adopted a strategy to reduce CO_2 emissions to 20 percent below 1988 levels by 2005. The two most successful elements of its strategy were establishment of the Toronto Atmospheric Fund and creation of the Better Buildings Partnership. The Fund was established in 1992 with $25 million in proceeds from the sale of surplus city property. It has financed household energy audits, a street lighting conversion program, energy retrofitting of municipal and commercial buildings, and other related projects. The partnership is with private financial institutions and energy service companies in order to retrofit 1 percent of the city's building stock with energy efficiency measures. Between 1990 and 1995, overall emissions dropped by 7 percent, and emissions per capita went down by 10 percent.

Box 9-1 Greenhouse gas reduction strategies in three cities.

- About $50 per capita has been invested by public and private sources for energy efficiency retrofits, renewable energy, and related measures. However, officials from these cities believe that the global and local benefits are substantially greater than the costs of reducing CO_2 emissions.

Some additional benefits of participating in the CCP program, beyond greenhouse gas reductions and energy savings, include reducing municipal budget deficits; creating thousands of new jobs (e.g., in construction and engineering); retaining existing jobs as local firms reposition themselves to work with municipal initiatives; improving air quality and public health; and enhancing urban livability.

National Level: Phasing Out Leaded Gasoline

The practice: Thailand unleaded gas program
Criteria fulfilled: Partnership, impact, sustainability, leadership
Management goal: Controlling, reducing, or preventing pollution
Documentation: USAID 1992, Sayeg 1998

Background

With rapid economic growth, Bangkok developed a reputation as a congested, polluted city. In 1980, the city had 600,000 cars and trucks; in 1991, there were 2.3 million vehicles on Bangkok's streets and little growth in road space. The environmental toll was predictable: By the mid-1980s, WHO standards for particulate matter were exceeded 97 days on average during each year. In 1991, 1.5 million tons of CO, 22 million tons of CO_2, and almost 1 million tons of lead were discharged by vehicles into Bangkok's air. Air samples taken along major bus routes in Bangkok found levels of CO nearly 20 times higher than those set by the national health standard.

Evidence about the health risks and economic costs of this air pollution began to mount in 1990. A health risk assessment was conducted that year in the city, supported by the Thai Development Research Institute (TDRI), the U.S. Agency for International Development, and the U.S. Environmental Protection Agency. It identified exposure to lead as the single greatest environmental health risk in Bangkok (see Box 9-2). The annual cost of lead exposure in the city was estimated to range between $40 and $50 million. The largest single source of lead was identified as leaded gasoline. The total cost of all pollution-related respiratory ailments was estimated at about $400 million per year.

Two other studies that year generated more information about

BOX

USAID, USEPA, and TDRI conducted a study in 1990 to evaluate human health risks associated with urban environmental problems in Bangkok. The technique used was developed by USEPA and had previously only been applied in the United States. The study's objectives were to establish a priority ranking of urban environmental health risks in Bangkok and to determine whether the USEPA methodology could be adapted for application in developing countries.

The study team collected data and estimated health risks. Each environmental problem was categorized as being high, medium, or low risk. The higher-risk environmental problems were: lead, airborne particulate matter, and infectious and parasitic organisms that cause microbiological disease. The medium risks were airborne CO and metals other than lead. The lower-risk group consisted of toxic air pollutants, airborne SO_2, nitrogen dioxide and ozone, surface and groundwater contamination, food contamination with pesticides and metals, and solid and hazardous waste disposal.

The additional health effects each year attributed to exposure to lead in Bangkok were estimated to be:

- **400,000 to 700,000 IQ points lost in children**
- **200,000 to 500,000 cases of hypertension in adults**
- **300 to 800 cases of heart attack and stroke in adults**
- **200 to 400 additional adult deaths**
- **500 to 60,000 children requiring medical attention**

Box 9-2 Health risk assessment in Bangkok, Thailand.
SOURCE: USAID 1990.

air pollution in Bangkok. An analysis by Dr. Pickhit Rattakul, former minister of science, technology, and energy, concluded that 15 percent of city residents suffered from respiratory illnesses that were caused or worsened by the level of air pollution. And 1990 statistics indicated that 60 percent of traffic police suffered from respiratory ailments during the year.

TDRI used these and other studies to focus on the lead problem during its 1990 conference on the environment. Lead pollution was of particular concern because of its adverse effects on the circulatory, reproductive, nervous, and kidney systems, and its relationship with irreversible learning defects in children. As a consequence, the conference strongly recommended a rapid phaseout of lead in gasoline.

Citizens also acted on this information to pressure the government for action on air pollution. An NGO, People Against Toxic Air Pollution, concentrated on the harmful effects of air pollution on young children. It encouraged children and adults to cover their faces with wet handkerchiefs while on the streets of Bangkok and distributed gas masks to the city's police force. A successful media campaign focused on the fate of people who worked outdoors (street vendors, drivers, traffic police, café operators) and had a higher exposure to air pollution. One result was a petition with 25,000 signatures that urged the prime minister to take urgent action on the problem.

The Royal Thai Government had been considering introduction of unleaded gasoline for some time, but felt that the cost would be prohibitive and did not want to raise the price of leaded fuel to pay for the additional cost. Efforts were initiated in 1989 to reduce lead in gasoline from 0.4 to 0.15 grams per liter. However, gasoline would not be available from Thai refineries until 1992 because of the time required for conversion of refining equipment. In early 1991, the Kuwait crisis and resulting Gulf War caused oil supply to tighten and prices nearly doubled. After the war ended, supply increased and prices fell.

Strategies and Results

After the Gulf War, the Thai Government through its National Energy Policy Office seized on a market opportunity to accelerate introduction of unleaded fuel. In May 1991, economic incentives were used to market and promote the use of premium unleaded fuel. The first incentive enabled multinational petroleum companies to import the costlier unleaded fuel at no extra cost; the price difference was subsidized by the government at a cost of 0.7 baht (U.S. $0.03) per liter. Importation was facilitated by the existence of spare refinery capacity in Singapore. The second incentive was a cross-subsidy for motorists that allowed unleaded fuel to be priced lower than regular leaded gasoline. Using the postwar drop in fuel prices, the government restructured the gasoline tax and, in effect, subsidized the purchase of unleaded by 0.3 baht (U.S. $0.01) per liter. Thus, with lower oil prices, a 1 baht (U.S. $0.04) per liter price reduction was split between oil companies and consumers, and unleaded was introduced on the market at a lower price than regular fuel.

In addition to creating a favorable tax structure, the National Energy Policy Office, the Ministry of Finance, and the Ministry of Commerce worked together to develop fuel specifications, agree on regulations, set a timetable for the complete phaseout of lead in gasoline, and provide guidance to the oil industry on establishing a distribution system for unleaded fuel throughout the country. Specifications were rapidly developed using outside experts. Regular meetings were held with industry leaders to keep them informed about the timetable and upcoming events.

Oil companies were spurred by competitive forces not to miss out on the opportunity to market a new fuel that could be attractively priced for consumers. They embarked on a range of major investments: Existing gas stations had to be altered so that each type of fuel could be stored and sold separately; refineries required modification; and storage, handling, and transportation systems had to be separated and streamlined to handle both fuels.

Simultaneously, oil companies launched major advertising campaigns to convince motorists that it was beneficial to switch fuels. Public opinion research indicated that environmental benefits alone would not be enough to sell unleaded, so the campaigns focused on the fact that unleaded could deliver power and performance similar to leaded fuel. Shell Oil alone allocated 20 million baht ($800,000) for an initial campaign, followed by 40 million baht ($1.6 million) for television ads, billboards, leaflets, and direct mail.

As a result of government policies, coordinated planning, market competition, and public awareness, unleaded gasoline captured 25 percent of the market share in Bangkok within five months of its introduction. Six months after introduction, the government agreed to cut tariffs on equipment such as catalytic converters for cars that exclusively use unleaded. At the beginning of 1992, there was a mandatory reduction in lead content for all gasoline, from 0.45 grams per liter to 0.15 grams per liter. Two environmental benefits resulted: (1) the amount of airborne lead pollution was reduced, and (2) the use of catalytic converters in new cars reduced their emissions of hydrocarbons. The first benefit was achieved immediately from all vehicles that switched to unleaded, and the second is being phased in over time as new cars replace older ones.

After four years, the use of leaded gasoline had been effectively ended in Thailand, and ambient lead had been reduced by a factor of 10. This was achieved at a cost of less than U.S. $0.02 per liter. Health benefits for just a 20 percent reduction in lead have been estimated at $0.12 per liter; the fuel switch also resulted in reduced maintenance costs. Thus, as the program caused a 93 percent reduction in ambient lead levels, its benefits far outweighed its costs.

Building on its success with the introduction of unleaded fuel, the Thai government developed a comprehensive clean air program to reduce vehicular air pollution by: (1) improving the quality of diesel fuel; (2) implementing a vehicle inspection program; (3) encouraging diesel buses to switch to compressed natural gas; (4) requiring catalytic converters for all new vehicles; and (5) introducing low-smoke motor oil to reduce pollution from motorcycles. Another type of impact is that pollution inventories, environmental impact assessment, environmental audits, and energy efficiency programs are more widely used than ever before.

Lessons

Factors that resulted in a successful program included:

- Good analysis (health risk assessment, economic valuation, other studies) combined with public pressure to focus the government's attention on the problem of lead.
- Favorable international petroleum prices and spare refinery capacity provided a window of opportunity for the government to restructure fuel prices.
- Integration of management tools (economic incentives, public awareness, regulation) was effectively used to support the program.
- The government/private sector partnership was successful because the government provided the private sector with clear objectives and adhered to an agreed-upon timetable.
- Competitive market forces were an important spur for oil companies to make necessary investments in a timely fashion.

A final lesson is that environmental problems in a primate city like Bangkok can be so important that they require the attention of the national government and can drive national policy. City policies can also influence national environmental policy, as is illustrated by the case of Japan in Box 9-3.

City Level: Integrating the Environment in Urban Development

The practice: Environmental planning and management in Singapore

BOX

With rapid urbanization, industrialization, and economic growth in the 1950s and 1960s, Japan experienced a range of local environmental problems. Public reaction to mercury and cadmium contamination of lakes and the sea and increased asthma due to air pollution led to environmental activism. Pressure was focused on municipal governments because most problems were local in nature and the central government did not yet have responsibility for addressing pollution problems. Opposition groups that had pollution as an important part of their platform won several mayoral and gubernatorial elections.

In this context, local governments were able to play a pioneering role in environmental management. They enacted pollution prevention ordinances such as those introduced by the Tokyo Metropolitan Government in 1949, the Osaka Prefecture in 1950, and the Kanagawa Prefecture in 1951. Cities also established pollution control departments. Pollution control agreements were drawn up that for the worst polluters had stricter standards than the national law. Early regulations were not too effective, because they lacked emission standards and effective enforcement measures. However, they developed into more powerful instruments over time.

National legislation followed local developments in the late 1960s and early 1970s. The first attempt by the central government to address local pollution would have weakened overall regulations and was rejected by local authorities. In 1970, with the "Environmental Pollution Diet," national pollution policy was approved, and laws were passed that gave local governments the power to impose stricter regulations than those specified at the national level.

This enabled local governments to continue to take the lead in applying environmental policy. In 1976, the central government dragged its feet on a bill that would have required EIAs for large projects. Kawasaki City enacted its own EIA program in 1977; Hokkaido Prefecture followed suit in 1978; and by 1980, two more prefectures and one city also required EIAs through extralegal guidelines.

Box 9-3 Cities shaped national environmental policy in Japan.

SOURCE: Lovei and Weiss 1998.

Criteria fulfilled: Partnership, impact, sustainability, leadership

Management goal: Encouraging a practice or process that supports sustainable development

Documentation: Various sources cited in case study

Background

Singapore is a highly industrialized and urbanized city-state of 3 million people, located in Southeast Asia. The city-state is located on an island of 647 km^2, nearly half of which is built-up; road infrastructure covers another 11 percent of the island's land mass. Singapore's economy developed rapidly, growing from a GNP per capita of $1972 in 1971 to $32,940 in 1997. During the past 30 years the population has doubled; the urbanized area of the island has doubled; housing units have trebled; and industrial land has grown sixfold (Tan 1995).

This rapid growth is largely attributed to Singapore's interventionist development strategy and replacement of corrupt with meritocratic governance (Quah 1998). With the loss of the Malaysian domestic market, stagnation of the entrepot trade, and withdrawal of the British military at independence in 1965, the government focused on labor-intensive manufacturing for export. Multinationals were drawn in with investment incentives since the local private sector had little industrial experience. By the early 1970s, the city had become the regional service and refining center for the petroleum industry and a regional finance center. Gradually, capital-intensive production such as the electronics industry began to replace labor-intensive manufacturing (Murray and Perera 1996).

Part of Singapore's environmental profile can be attributed to changes in its economic structure. In 1961, the natural resource-intensive and polluting sectors of food, printing and publishing, and wood products accounted for 40 percent of industrial employment. By 1991, these sectors had dropped to only 8 percent, while electronics and electrical appliances had risen to 40 percent (Chiu, Ho, and Liu 1997). However, much of Singapore's environmental success is due to its activist approaches to environmental planning and management.

Current Approaches to Environmental Management

Singapore currently uses four sets of instruments to manage environmental problems: (1) regulatory measures; (2) planning controls; (3) economic incentives; and (4) encouragement of public awareness and participation. Each set is briefly described below along with examples of application. These stem from a postindependence philosophy of active government involvement in many sectors of the economy and society. As former prime minister Lee Kuan Yew put it, "I am accused often enough of interfering in the private lives of citizens. If I did not, had I not done that, we wouldn't be here today" (Murray and Perera 1996, 20).

REGULATORY MEASURES

Singapore employs a range of regulatory instruments to protect and manage the city's environment. There are approximately 40 environmental laws covering the following subjects: cattle, clean air, destruction of disease-bearing insects, environmental public health, food, hydrogen cyanide, infectious diseases, poison, smoking, and water pollution control and drainage. Emissions standards have been set for 17 types of air pollutants covering a wide range of stationary sources. Allowable limits have also been set for liquid effluent discharge to sewers and waterways; these include limits on temperature, BOD, COD, total suspended solids, total dissolved solids, pH value, and 28 different chemicals. Maximum limits have been set for transport of hazardous materials, beyond which authorization must be obtained. And 26 categories of toxic industrial wastes are also subject to specific legislated controls (ENV 1997a).

Singapore is known as a "fine" city—partly because of its rigorous application of monetary fines to enforce regulatory measures. Examples of fines that are applied to enforce environmental regulations include:

- *Air pollution.* Violators of the Clean Air Act are subject to a maximum fine of S$10,000 (U.S. $6666) plus S$500 (U.S. $333) per day for continued noncompliance. Vehicles emitting smoke or visible vapor can be fined up to S$500 as well.
- *Water pollution.* The maximum fine for violating the acceptable effluent limits is S$5000 (U.S. $3333) per violation. Discharging oil into Singaporean coastal waters is subject to a maximum penalty of S$500,000 (U.S. $333,333) or two years' imprisonment.
- *Solid waste.* Littering is punishable by fines up to S$1000 (U.S. $666) per incidence. Serious and repeat offenders may also have to carry out public cleaning activities for up to three hours.
- *Noise pollution.* A range of fines has been set for vehicles, construction, and other activities that exceed acceptable limits.

This fine structure has yielded revenues that range from S$3.3 million (U.S. $2 million) to S$4.5 million (U.S. $2.8 million) annually during the 1990s (Foo 1996).

The ability to enforce regulations also depends on the existence of an effective monitoring system. Air pollution is measured through 12 monitoring stations, and mobile sources must pass an emissions inspection before they can be registered. Water quality is measured on a monthly basis in 47 streams within watersheds and in 17 rivers in non-water-catchment areas. Coastal water quality is measured regularly at 9 sample points in the Straits of Johor and 10 points in the Straits of Singapore. The Pollution Control Department of the Ministry of the Environment (ENV) monitors individual sites by conducting over 50,000 inspections per year. Finally, the ENV responds to citizen monitoring by investigating several hundred complaints about air and water pollution each year (ENV 1997c; Foo 1996).

PLANNING CONTROLS

Singapore's long-term development and land-use strategies are embodied in a Concept Plan. The most recent version was prepared in 1991 and is based on a time frame to the year X (beyond 2020) when the population will stabilize at 4 million. Spatially, the plan seeks to deconcentrate the existing central business district to four new regional centers. Environmentally, the plan seeks to:

- Identify development constraints and land uses that affect the environment
- Project land needs for environmental infrastructure
- Identify areas for siting pollution-prone services and infrastructure
- Locate areas for nature conservation
- Continue protection of water catchment areas

Overall, the plan states that "Singapore will be cloaked in greenery, both manicured by man and by protected tracts of natural growth, with water bodies woven into the landscape" (Foo 1996, 13).

Administratively, the Concept Plan is implemented by an Urban Redevelopment Authority (URA). The URA has subdivided the island into 55 planning areas, each with a local plan called a Development Guide Plan (DGP) to manage the development potential of each area (Hin et al. 1997). Some of the environmental outcomes of the URA's enforcement of the plan and DGPs are: (1) industries are located primarily in proper industrial parks; (2) a minimum of 0.8 hectare of parks and gardens is required per 1000 people; and (3) tree cutting is controlled in designated areas. All land development proposals need to be submitted to the URA for approval before implementation. For construction, the Public Works Department approves building permits and considers technical requirements for environmental health, drainage, sewerage, and pollution control; postconstruction inspections are carried out to ensure compliance. Several thousand planning consultations are held each year on land use and factory siting that include a review of environmental impacts. Finally, while environmental impact assessment is not legislated, it is a mandatory administrative requirement for developers seeking to undertake large projects that are likely to have a major environmental effect (Foo 1996).

ECONOMIC INCENTIVES

The key economic instruments used for environmental management in Singapore are user fees, licensing, fiscal measures, and auctions. User charges are levied for: (1) wastewater collection and treatment (households pay S$0.15 and other users pay S$0.32 per m^3 of potable water consumed, plus S$3 annually per sanitary fitting); (2) solid waste (businesses are charged according to the volume of refuse they generate, while households and street vendors pay a flat monthly rate); and (3) street vendors, restaurants, and port facilities pay fees to cover inspection costs. Revenue from these fees collected by the ENV can amount to between a third and nearly half of the ministry's total annual expenditure (ENV 1998). Licensing is used especially to limit traffic congestion in the central area of the city (see section that follows on transportation). Tax differentiation is used between leaded and unleaded fuel so that unleaded is sold at a lower price in order to encourage its use. There are also tax incentives to encourage the use of cleaner technologies. Finally, a Vehicle Quota System was introduced in 1990 that capped annual vehicle population growth at 3 percent. Vehicle purchasers must bid for Certificates of Entitlement (COE) that are issued in limited numbers for different categories of vehicles. The COE component of a car's final price can range from 30 to 40 percent for medium-sized cars and 15 to 25 percent for larger vehicles (Foo 1997b).

PUBLIC AWARENESS AND PARTICIPATION

Public awareness about environmental matters is developed in Singapore through three major avenues: specialized campaigns, the education system, and the "Clean and Green Week." The first campaign, "Keep Singapore Clean," was initiated in 1968. Since then, there have been focused campaigns to build public awareness about pollution, food hygiene, infectious diseases, waste management, sanitation, antispitting, antilittering, river cleanup, and global environmental issues. Often, a campaign will preclude introduction of an environmental or public health law; public education is then followed up with strict enforcement. Schools are important conveyors of environmental information: They participate in the national campaigns; environmental material is included in the curriculum; and students are encouraged to participate in environmental clubs and projects such as beach cleanups. Since 1990, Singapore has held a Clean and Green Week with a different theme each year. Activities include giving environmental awards to youth, other individuals, and organizations; cleanup of specific areas; special seminars; school competitions; public exhibits; and dissemination of new publications. NGOs and the private sector are increasingly involved as sponsors of activities during the week (ENV 1997a). The private sector is also promoting awareness about clean production technologies, waste minimization, environmentally friendly products, energy and water conservation, and implementation of ISO14000 standards (ENV 1997d).

Increased environmental awareness led to the development of environmental NGOs in Singapore in the 1980s and growing pressure for public participation in environmental decision-making. The oldest and most capable environmental NGO, the Nature Society, was established in 1954 (Mekani and Stengel 1995). By 1990, an umbrella National Council on the Environment (now called the Singapore Environment Council) was established by the private sector to promote environmental awareness. The Council facilitates networking of environmental NGOs, encourages public environmental responsibility, and develops environmental protection and management measures for both public and private implementation. As a nonprofit organization, it can receive tax-exempt donations from the public (ENV 1997d). However, neither the council nor other environmental NGOs are regularly consulted on environmental policy. Public participation in developing the Green Plan and action programs was also relatively limited.

The DGP planning process is perhaps the most structured opportunity for the public to take environmental factors into account, though the process is not set up for the sole purpose of incorporating environmental comments. An initial Outline Plan that covers broad strategies must be made available for public comment before the DGP is further developed and adopted. The draft DGP itself must also be available for public review over a period of two weeks before it can be finalized. During this exhibition period, the public can give their feedback and suggestions on the plans, including environmental issues. These are seen as wedges that may eventually open up the governmental process to more institutionalized stakeholder involvement (Mallone-Lee et al. 1998). A form of unstructured public participation has been the involvement of citizens and local environmental organizations who complain about particular incidents of air, water, and land pollution; these have been important sources of information for the ENV.

Innovative Activities

During its experience with environmental planning and management, Singapore has developed a number of examples of "good practice" in the fields of land use, transportation, water resource management, waste management, environmental health, air pollution control, urban greening and nature conservation, noise control, and support for environmental businesses and regional cooperation.

LAND USE

Land use controls, already generally described, are a major means of environmental management in Singapore. The URA is Singapore's land use planning authority. The ENV advises the URA on specific environmental measures that are needed in land use planning to protect watersheds; manage facilities for waste collection, treatment, and disposal; and ensure that new developments are both properly sited and compatible with surrounding land uses. One way that this is done is by providing advice in the development of DGPs so that these local plans use environmental factors to guide development activities. The URA also takes many other factors in addition to the environment into consideration in the planning of DGPs. Other public and private sector land developers also consult the ENV on needed environmental controls.

At the planning and building phases of new developments, the ENV checks development proposals and building plans to ensure the sufficiency of waste management, to make sure that pollution control requirements are incorporated into designs, and verify that measures are undertaken to mitigate negative environmental impacts. New developments must obtain occupation permits and completion certificates that are cleared by ENV's Sewerage, Drainage, Environmental Health, and Pollution Control Departments (ENV 1997c). This is done through the Central Building Plan Unit of ENV's Pollution Control Department. The unit is a "one-stop" service that is regularly consulted by private and public sector agencies with development proposals such as new housing estates and industrial facilities as well as alterations and additions to existing sites (Foo in Briffett and Lee 1993).

Particular attention is paid to developments in water catchment areas and to industrial siting. Industries are classified as clean, light, general, and special (high pollution potential), and separate land use rules are applied to each category. This integration of environmental features into land use planning has resulted in: proper siting of industries (separation of residential and industrial areas); rational provision of environmental infrastructure; encouragement of industries to use cleaner technologies; and effective protection of watersheds (ENV 1997b).

One of the largest developers in Singapore has been the government's Housing and Development Board. It has constructed over 600,000 units, which house an impressive 86 percent of the city-state's population. The HDB, guided by an earlier Concept Plan, helped to build 20 new or satellite towns around the central city to channel new development to areas that were both economically and environmentally appropriate, to improve infrastructure planning, and to reduce congestion. The center of each new town is also the terminal point for public transportation, and most residents are within five minutes' walking distance from their neighborhood center. Finally, the industrial development in each new town, accounting for about 20 percent of the land area, was restricted to light, nonpolluting facilities (Field 1992).

TRANSPORTATION

The goal of transportation planning in Singapore is to provide an efficient and reliable system for the mobility of people and goods. According to Singapore's Land Transport Authority, this should be achieved through the following strategies:

- Integrated and coordinated land use and transportation planning
- Increasing the capacity of Singapore's roads
- Improving the public transport system
- Effective travel demand management
- Improving traffic management (Foo 1997a)

To implement these strategies, the Land Transport Authority employs three innovative approaches that help minimize the environmental side-effects of traffic congestion: (1) the Area Licensing Scheme; (2) the Park-and-Ride System; and (3) demand management through the Vehicle Quota System. These innovations are reinforced by the existence of an affordable, efficient, and integrated public transportation system consisting of mass rapid transit, local and transisland buses, and taxis.

The Area Licensing Scheme (ALS) is a system of road pricing to manage demand for road space that is highly congested during peak hours. In 1975, the government designated an area of 725 hectares comprising the central business district plus the most important commercial and shopping corridor (Orchard Road) for intensified traffic management. Currently, there are 33 entry points into the area; these are marked with signs and lights and are policed during restricted periods. Motorists must purchase a special license and display it on their windshields if they want to enter the restricted area during peak periods. Peak times are 07:30 to 19:00 on Mondays through Fridays and 07:30 to 14:00 on Saturdays. Fees are progressively higher for motorcycles, private cars, and company vehicles, and licenses can be purchased for month, day, or part-day use. At present, charges range from S$1 to $6 for a one-day license and S$14 to $120 for a one-month license. Ambulances, fire engines, police vehicles, and public buses are exempted from licensing (Foo 1997a). In 1998,

Figure 9-1 Area Licensing Scheme gantry, Singapore.

an Electronic Road Pricing system was introduced using in-vehicle smart cards and road sensors to automatically charge users entering the restricted area. Electronic surveillance cameras photograph the license plates of vehicles without cards or with insufficient funds, and violators are fined by mail (McNulty and Parker 1998). Road pricing has also been extended to three expressways during peak morning commute hours (ENV 1997d).

The ALS has played an important role in reducing central-city congestion during peak hours. For example, the number of vehicles entering during the morning peak period (07:30 to 10:15) averaged 46,000 in May 1991, compared to 74,000 in March 1975 (before the scheme was implemented). This is even more remarkable considering that Singapore's vehicle population doubled during the same period. There was also an important shift in modal split after implementation of the ALS. In the pre-ALS period, 56 percent of trips to the CBD were by car and 33 percent by bus; by 1983 this had reversed, and 69 percent of trips were by bus and only 23 percent by car. Environmentally, accidents in the restricted area dropped from 4405 in 1978 to 3382 in 1982, while there were decreases in total acidity (−11 percent), smoke (–32 percent), and NO_x (–8 percent) in the same period (Foo 1997a). Most recently, the Land Transport Authority estimates that traffic volume has dropped a further 17 percent in the CBD since introduction of the electronic road pricing system. The average speed during peak hours has increased from 50 to 61 kph; this compares favorably with London, where the average speed is 16 kph, or slightly slower than horse-drawn vehicles at the turn of the century (McNulty and Parker 1998).

As with the ALS, the goal of the Park-and-Ride Scheme (PRS) is to alleviate congestion in the CBD during peak hours. Since it was first introduced in 1975, the PRS has gone through several incarnations. It began as a series of peripheral parking lots where drivers could leave their vehicles and board buses into the CBD. Following completion of Singapore's Mass Rapid Transit network in 1987, it evolved into a system where the lots were linked to rapid transit stations. In the current enhanced PRS system, there are 19 parking lots: 8 are located near both MRT stations and bus stops, another 8 are only near MRT stations, and 3 are only near bus stops. Drivers purchase monthly tickets for S$72 that enable them to park at a specified lot and use mass transit or a bus to commute to the CBD (Foo 1997b).

Average sales of monthly tickets have risen from 15 in 1991 to 572 in 1996. However, there are over 2900 spaces available in the 19 parking lots—indicating that only about a fifth of capacity is being used. In 1996, just over 1 percent of motorists who regularly drive into the CBD were diverted into the PRS system. User surveys indicate the following problems: Parking hours are too restrictive; parking lots are not available at all MRT stations; lots are too far from the stations; monthly tickets are restricted to only one lot; and monthly tickets are too expensive (Foo 1997b). Thus, the PRS is an innovative approach to traffic-demand management that has not yet achieved its potential due to a number of operational constraints.

The cost of vehicle ownership in Singapore is intentionally high in order to reduce growth of the vehicle population and to raise revenues to cover the social costs of motorization. Under the Vehicle Quota System (VQS), long-term growth in the vehicle fleet is set at 3 percent per year through issuance of Certificates of

Entitle (COE). Vehicle owners must bid to purchase a COE through the government before the vehicle can be used on the road. The final price of a private car in Singapore consists of the manufacturer's price, insurance, and freight costs (known as OMV); an additional registration fee, currently set at 140 percent of the OMV; import duty (currently 41 percent of the OMV); a S$140 registration fee; an annual road tax (ranging from S$0.70 to $1.75 per cc of engine capacity); and other costs (e.g., retailer's costs and profits). With COE costs typically ranging from 10 to 30 percent of total vehicle cost (Foo 1997a), a 2000-cc vehicle with an OMV of U.S.$20,000 might end up costing a Singaporean over U.S.$75,000. This and other measures to discourage car use have resulted in a relatively low level of car ownership in Singapore (85 cars per 1000 people) (ICLEI 1995) and have reduced vehicle population growth from 6 percent to 3 percent annually.

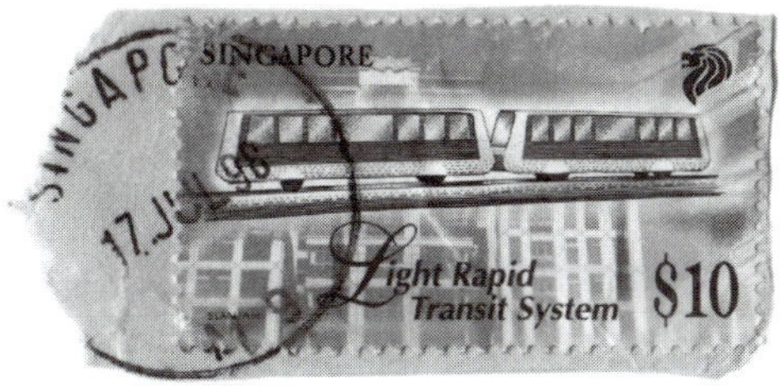

Figure 9-2 Singapore stamp of rapid transit system.

All of these transport innovations are bolstered by the existence of one of the world's cleanest and most efficient public transportation systems. Singapore has an integrated system consisting of city buses, suburban/city-center express buses, and the Mass Rapid Transit railway. The MRT is a 67-kilometer system that carries more than 560,000 passengers a day. TransitLink, a public corporation, was established in 1987 to operate and integrate all modes of public transport. Commuters can travel between trains, subways, and buses using one pass. Buses carry half of all road passenger traffic, and 65 percent of commuter trips are by public transit (ICLEI 1995).

WATER RESOURCE MANAGEMENT

Because Singapore is an island, water management there is critical. The city-state has been an innovator in drinking water resource management, wastewater and water pollution control, river cleanup, and flood control. Each of these areas is more fully described in the paragraphs that follow.

Singapore's water catchment areas meet less than half of residential, commercial, and industrial demands for clean water. The remainder must be imported from Malaysia. Thus, drinking water management has been not only an economic and environmental issue for Singapore but has also been perceived as a national security issue. Some of the innovative measures to conserve and manage drinking water include:

- Protection of water catchment areas through the land use planning measures described previously, as well as nature conservation activities
- Collection and treatment of urban stormwater as a source of raw water
- Water audits and technical assistance for industries and commercial users to help them conserve on water use, reuse wastewater, and substitute nonpotable for potable water where feasible
- Mandatory installation of water-saving devices in private commercial establishments and new public apartment buildings
- Metering of all water consumption and setting of water charges to recover costs and discourage excessive levels of consumption
- Use of a sophisticated monitoring system to measure and model water distribution, pressure, and leakage
- An apprentice plumber program whereby people seeking to become plumbers must apprentice in an apartment building, conduct regular inspections, and seek to minimize leaks and water wastage within the building
- Imposition of high standards for waterworks as well as residential and commercial plumbing in order to ensure efficient functioning of the water delivery system and reduce maintenance costs

These measures are primarily administered by the Water Department of the Public Utilities Board. In many low-income Asian cities, half of the water in the municipal system is unaccounted for. In Singapore, largely because of these measures, the city has increasingly achieved a level of unaccounted-for water approaching the theoretical minimum loss of 5 percent (PUB 1996).

Water pollution is controlled through several different measures. Polluting industries are generally sited in industrial estates that are located outside of water catchment areas and are served by public sewers. Industries must install pretreatment facilities to handle their liquid effluents that exceed discharge limits. Pretreatment plants must be installed prior to commissioning new factories (ENV 1997c). For household effluents, most of the island is sewered. There are now 2500 kilometers of sewer pipeline, 6 large sewage treatment plants serving an equal number of catchment areas, and 130 pumping stations. A deep-tunnel sewerage system is planned that will require only two centralized treatment facilities, less land as buffer zones, and, eventually, no pumping stations (ENV 1997e).

Figure 9-3 Utility metering in Singapore.

In 1977, the Singapore River and the Kallang Basin catchments, the latter covering a fifth of the island, were heavily polluted by organic and inorganic discharges. Stench pervaded the watercourses, and the rivers supported little or no marine life. Prime Minister Lee Kuan Yew challenged ENV to improve the watercourses, and ENV responded with a report the same year outlining priority problems and options. Over the next ten years, an action plan was implemented that involved: development of housing, industrial workshops, sewerage, and food centers; massive resettlement of squatters, cottage and other industries, and farmers out of sensitive areas; resiting of street vendors into food centers; phasing out of polluting activities; and turfing and landscaping of riverbanks. Work was implemented by various departments and agencies under five government ministries, all of which were coordinated by ENV. Financing came from central government revenues at a cost of S$200 million (U.S.$125 million), not including the costs of public housing, food centers, industrial workshops, and sewerage. These measures resulted in cleaner water, a return of aquatic life to the river and basin, and a more aesthetically pleasing waterfront (ENV 1987).

Singapore is a small island with one of the highest rainfall rates in the world, yet flooding is a thing of the past. Innovation in the field of drainage for water management has included: (1) using precast box culverts to cut drains on busy roads overnight in order to minimize construction time and traffic disruption; (2) using computer modeling to optimize canal design; (3) incorporating special engineering and landscaping features to retain a river's natural features as well as its flood-control role; and (4) using jet grouting to stabilize riverbanks while limiting disturbance to surrounding areas. These innovations have reduced the size of flood-prone areas in Singapore from 3000 hectares in the 1970s to 300 at present (ENV 1997e).

WASTE MANAGEMENT

Limited land area combined with rapid economic growth and industrialization have led Singapore to adopt several novel approaches to solid and hazardous waste management. These include: (1) adopting incineration as the main method for disposing of combustible wastes; (2) preparing an offshore landfill for disposal of nonburnable wastes and incineration ash residues; (3) increasing efforts to minimize waste generation; and (4) strict management of hazardous wastes.

As existing dump sites began to fill up in the 1970s, Singapore decided to opt for incineration as a means of reducing the volume of final waste that required disposal. Three incineration plants have been constructed since 1978, located in the central, northern, and western part of the island. Much of the city's solid waste is generated in the east, centralized at a transfer station, compacted into containers, and then hauled to incineration plants in the north and west. Of the 7600 tons of solid waste generated per day, 70 percent is incinerated. The remainder of the waste is disposed at a landfill site. Incinerators have pollution-control equipment, and emissions are monitored on a regular basis (ENV 1997e). A fourth plant is scheduled for completion in 2000; being built at a cost of S$1 billion (U.S. $666 million), it will be one of the world's largest, with a capacity of 3000 tons per day (ENV 1998).

The present landfill site is expected to be full by 1999, and no additional sites are available on the main island. Thus, an offshore landfill is being constructed adjacent to the island of Pulau Semakau. This will be a 350-hectare site that is anticipated to meet landfill needs beyond the year 2030. A marine transfer station is also being built that will receive and process noncombustible waste and incineration ash before it is barged to the offshore landfill. Works will cost an estimated S$840 million (U.S. $525 million) and should be completed by 1999 (ENV 1998).

The magnitude of investments for new landfill and incineration facilities has convinced the Singapore government of the need to minimize the generation of waste before it requires disposal. ENV undertakes the following waste reduction activities:

- Sets aside land for the private sector to operate recycling activities
- Creates in-house recycling centers in hotels, apartment buildings, factories, and other large establishments (1255 centers set up by 1995)
- Establishes public recycling centers in partnership with a private sector sponsor (58 created by 1995)
- Encourages government agencies to use recycled products, and issues a "green label" to inform consumers about products that are less damaging to the environment
- Provides free waste audits for promote better waste management (Foo 1997c)

In 1997, 1.79 million tons, or 39 percent of the 4.59 million tons of solid waste generated in the country, were recovered for reuse. The highest recovery rates are for ferrous metals (92 percent), nonferrous metals (84 percent), and construction debris (60 percent); the lowest rates are for food waste (2 percent), wood/timber (12 percent), glass (14 percent), and plastic (18 percent) (ENV 1998).

ENV controls the collection, treatment, and disposal of hazardous wastes in Singapore. Private companies are licensed to establish treatment and disposal facilities in industrial estates. By the end of 1997, 116 such companies were licensed. That year, they collected 65,820 m^3 of toxic industrial wastes such as used oil, waste solvents, spent etchants, and chemical wastes. Eighty percent of this was recovered for reuse, and the remainder was treated and rendered safe for landfill disposal. Hospital and clinic waste is separated into color-coded plastic bags and placed in special containers. Two licensed companies then collect the biohazardous material for disposal in special high-temperature incinerators (ENV 1998).

ENVIRONMENTAL HEALTH

There has been a focus on improving environmental health in Singapore for over a century. Beyond proper solid waste management, the main innovative features of the city's approach to environmental health include:

- *Food hygiene.* Over a period of 15 years (1972–1986), street vendors were relocated to over 150 markets and food centers in order to improve sanitary conditions as well as to facilitate inspection. All food handlers are registered with ENV; inoculated against typhoid; given X-ray exams if they are older than 45; and must pass a basic food hygiene course. Finally, all food establishments are regularly inspected, and hygiene standards are strictly enforced.
- *Vector control.* Mosquitoes, rats, and other disease-bearing pests are kept in check through public education campaigns, vector control programs, and engineering measures like an antimalarial drainage system.

- *Infectious disease control.* ENV integrates services like Quarantine and Environmental Epidemiology in order to both control entry of infectious diseases into the island and effectively trace outbreaks if they occur.

Results are that despite its tropical climate Singapore has one of the lowest food-poisoning rates in the world, and the island was declared malaria-free by the World Health Organization in 1982 (ENV 1997a,e).

AIR POLLUTION CONTROL

The key principles of air pollution control in Singapore are to minimize emissions at their source and to reduce emissions exposure through careful siting of industries. Efforts to minimize the emission of air pollutants include:

- Control of fuels used by industries and commercial enterprises
- Requirements that industries install air pollution control equipment to comply with emissions standards
- Regular inspection of stationary sources to ensure that control equipment is properly maintained and operated (nearly 50,000 in 1996)
- Source emission tests required by over 100 industries to regularly monitor pollution (initiated in 1997)
- Promotion of unleaded fuel for vehicles
- Gradual tightening of emissions standards for vehicles
- Regular mandatory emissions inspections for vehicles
- Prohibitions on the open burning of wastes
- Ban on the importation of CFCs
- Use of auctionable permits for the consumption of ozone-depleting substances
- Regular monitoring of air pollutants throughout the island
- Rapid response to citizen complaints about stationary and mobile sources of air pollution

Overall results are that measured levels of pollutants are almost always within the WHO long-term goals and USEPA standards, and unleaded fuel now accounts for 70 percent of gasoline sales since its introduction in 1991 (ENV 1997a,c). Standards may not be met at all times; for example, in 1997 and 1998 a regional haze affected the area from fires in Kalimantan and Borneo in Indonesia.

URBAN GREENING AND NATURE CONSERVATION

In 1963, Prime Minister Lee Kuan Yew launched a tree-planting campaign for all roads, vacant plots, reclaimed land, and other new development sites. This evolved into the Garden City campaign in 1967 to promote greening throughout the island. The campaign began by accelerating the tree planting; by the late 1970s, lush greenery was prominent across the island. During the 1980s, the campaign sought to add dashes of color by planting free-flowering trees and shrubs. At the same time, park development was emphasized. Existing parks were improved and many new ones were developed. Singapore currently has 337 parks and open spaces covering 1934 hectares (PRD 1992); development is guided by a standard of 0.8 hectare of parklands per 1000 population (Lee 1995).

Proposals for the protection of the natural environment initially stemmed from an NGO. The Nature Society of Singapore, in its 1990 Master Plan for the Conservation of Nature in Singapore, identified 28 sites that had sufficient nature conservation to warrant permanent protection. These included the Bukit Timah primary forest and the Central Catchment mature secondary forest. Tidal mudflats and mangroves, freshwater marshes and wetlands, and some undeveloped offshore islands were also listed (Briffett 1990; Wee in Briffett and Lee 1993).

Singapore's nature conservation policy has a goal of setting aside 5 percent of its land mass for preservation. Currently, 19 areas, comprising 3130 hectares, have been designated as natural sites and are managed by a Natural Parks Board. They include a wide range of habitats such as primary and secondary forests, marshlands, and mangrove swamps. Sites were selected because of their ecological value; for watershed protection; or because of their potential for recreation, education, and scientific research. The DGPs are being drawn up for these sites and they will serve as management tools for the future. A 360-kilometer Park Connectors Network is being implemented so that flora and fauna corridors will link many of the sites (ENV 1997d). Urban greening has also been actively promoted: Over 1 million trees have been planted since independence, and all public areas as well as new private developments must meet high standards for landscaping (Hin et al. 1997).

NOISE CONTROL

Singapore is tackling noise problems through government actions. An Environmental Noise Management Unit was established in 1994. The unit is supported by an Environmental Noise Advisory Committee consisting of industry, professional, academic, and government representatives. Together, they have developed noise action programs for: monitoring; control of road traffic and MRT train noise; indoor noise for future residential buildings; control of noise from indoor and outdoor entertainment; boundary noise limits for factories; promotion of good management practices for noise reduction at construction sites; and planning guidelines for noise control. An environmental noise monitoring system has been set up which conducts twice-yearly, week-long measurements at 21 representative sites around the island (ENV 1997a, 1998).

ENVIRONMENTAL BUSINESS AND REGIONAL COOPERATION

Singapore is actively seeking to use its experience and comparative advantages to both attract environmental businesses and to develop itself as a regional center for environmental cooperation. Over 100 environmental technology companies are currently located on the island. New local, foreign, and joint-venture environmental enterprises are being encouraged through tax incentives and by touting Singapore's role in the regional market; its existing stock of human resources, research, and development facilities; manufacturing support; and the island's quality of life (ENV 1997f).

Singapore is seeking to become a regional center through project activities, institutional development, and agreements. Environmental firms provide technical assistance and equipment for investments in other countries in the region. For example, consortia involving Singaporean firms have helped develop four industrial parks, including environmental controls, in Indonesia and China. Institutionally, the government and the EU have established a Regional Institute of Environmental Technology to facilitate the transfer of technical expertise from the EU to the region; ENV has a Center for Environmental Training which serves as a regional training agency for environmental engineering and public health; and the ENV's Institute of Environmental Epidemiology provides regional assistance (ENV 1997f). Finally, Singapore has concluded a regional environmental cooperation agreement with ASEAN and bilateral agreements with Indonesia, Malaysia, and Vietnam (ENV 1997c).

Challenges and Lessons for the Future

Singapore has enjoyed many successes in urban environmental planning and management. All the same, there are several areas for improvement. Critics have noted the following:

- Environmental impact assessment of projects is not required in Singapore, and it would be advantageous to do so (Briffett 1992).
- Public participation in planning decisions is nascent, and greater involvement would improve the quality and outcome of planning decisions (Mallone-Lee et al. 1998).
- The recycling rate is well below that of a similarly land-constrained, densely populated country (Japan's rate is over 50 percent), and a number of additional approaches are warranted (Foo 1997c).

In addition, the predominant style of environmental planning and management has been top-down and more reliant on regulatory instruments. Environmental protection could be more efficient and effective through participation, some decentralization, and greater use of economic incentives in combination with command-and-control approaches. Finally, ENV may not always have sufficient knowledge, commitment, or clout to fully protect the environment in planning and investment decisions.

In the eyes of the government, Singapore faces the following environmental challenges:

- Meeting rising expectations about air and water quality, cleaner surroundings, and public health that come with economic development
- Continuing to reconcile environmental needs with the demands of economic growth and competitiveness
- Ensuring the cooperation of an environmentally conscious population
- Accelerating the introduction of clean technologies
- Fulfilling international and regional environmental commitments (ENV 1997e)

These and other challenges have been successfully faced by another city that exemplifies good practice—Curitiba, Brazil—which is presented in Box 9-4.

In conclusion, several lessons can be drawn from Singapore's impressive experience with addressing and resolving environmental issues. Lessons for urban environmental planning include:

1. *Start with the basics.* Singapore pursued a phased approach to tackling problems, beginning with environmental health issues (sanitation, vector control, food hygiene) and highly visible problems such as river and basin pollution.
2. *Coordinate planning in key sectors.* The integration of land use, public transportation, and motorization plans and policies has allowed Singapore to reduce the environmental impact of the private automobile.
3. *Integrate environmental considerations in standard procedures.* Environmental protection is an integral part of land-use planning, industrial siting, and building controls, largely negating the need for an environmental impact assessment process.
4. *Get the politicians on board.* Political will has been an essential force behind successful planning and implementation of

BOX

Curitiba, capital of Parana state, is also known as the ecological capital of Brazil. By the late 1960s, metropolitan Curitiba with a population of 800,000 (now 2.2 million) was on its way to becoming another automobile-dominated city plagued by traffic congestion, air pollution, urban sprawl, and inadequate infrastructure. Instead, the city took a different course by giving preference to public transportation over the private car, working with nature instead of against it, using appropriate rather than high-technology solutions, and innovating with citizen participation instead of master planning.

A number of measures, sustained and improved over the last 25 years, have produced impressive results:

- ***Integration of transport and land-use policies:*** **Land-use legislation enforces higher densities around major transportation corridors. Curitiba has one of the lowest rates of ambient air pollution in Brazil; gasoline use per vehicle is 25 percent less than in other Brazilian cities.**
- ***Emphasis on efficient public transportation:*** **Main corridors have express bus lanes; each line is integrated for rapid transfers; the system is faster and cheaper than those in other Brazilian cities. The bus system serves 1.3 million passengers per day (75 percent of all commuters) despite the fact that the city has the second highest car ownership in Brazil. People spend about 10 percent of their income on transport, which is low for Brazil.**
- ***Controlling flooding:*** **Measures include protection of natural drainage systems, conversion of riverbanks to parks, and construction of artificial lakes to contain floodwaters. Damage from flooding is a thing of the past, and green space has been increased from 0.5 to 50 m^3 per capita during a period of rapid population growth.**
- ***Managing solid waste:*** **Measures include curbside collection of recyclables and central separation facility; use of informal sector; purchase of garbage from poor neighborhoods. The city has a 70 percent participation rate in recycling program; waste collection has been extended to marginal areas; life of landfill has been extended; and resources have been conserved.**
- ***Developing institutional capacity:*** **The city has its own urban planning institute, offers incentives for private sector involvement in management, and enjoys public participation and transparency. Ninety-nine percent of citizens polled would not want to live anywhere else, and Curitiba's most innovative mayor averaged a 70 percent approval rating.**

Box 9-4 Challenging conventional wisdom in Curitiba, Brazil.

SOURCES: Rabinovitch with Leitmann 1993, Rabinovitch and Leitmann 1996.

environmental measures; for example, the prime minister's support for tree planting, the Garden City campaign and river cleanup, and the Cabinet's endorsement of the Green Plan.

Singapore teaches the following lessons about urban environmental management:

1. *Educate, monitor, and enforce.* Environmental regulation has been so successful in Singapore because public awareness of new environmental measures is followed by monitoring and inspection, with strict and consistent enforcement of serious penalties.
2. *Manage through institutions with clout.* The ENV provides strong environmental management because it integrates important functions like infrastructure and environmental health, and because it has real enforcement powers.
3. *Try and try again.* A willingness to experiment, learn, and evolve has benefited institutions such as the ENV, and programs such as the various incarnations of the Park-and-Ride program.
4. *Combine economic instruments with regulatory measures.* Traffic management, one of Singapore's biggest successes, is a good example of how rules can be complemented by economic incentives such as road pricing, the high cost of vehicle ownership, and, of course, fines.
5. *Involve the private sector.* Singapore has made effective use of the private sector for implementing environmental policies such as partnerships to sponsor recycling centers and licensing for hazardous-waste collection and treatment.

Overall, Singapore has had a strong government that exercised power in a pragmatic and forceful way. Its small size, concentrated economic development, and compact state government have assisted in achieving tight controls. The compliant population has generally learned to accept government leadership because it is responsible, largely uncorrupt, and sincere in attempting to meet the needs of the community. A committed top-down approach has combined flexible responses with rapid action for environmental management. The main challenge now, with increasing education, higher aspirations for environmental quality, and a desire for more public involvement, is that new strategies for planning and management are in order.

Sectoral Level: Matching Sanitation Services and Socioeconomic Status

The practice: Strategic sanitation planning in Kumasi, Ghana
Criteria fulfilled: Impact, sustainability, leadership, gender, and social inclusion
Management goal: Improving the access of low-income and other excluded groups to urban infrastructure and services
Documentation: Roche 1995

Background

Kumasi is Ghana's second largest city with a 1990 population of 575,000, that is expected to reach 1 million by 2010. The metropolitan area covers 150 km^2 and is made up of four districts. Kumasi is a growing industrial center, a major commercial center, and the hub of much of Ghana's agricultural economy.

In the sanitation sector, Kumasi can be divided into four housing types:

1. *Tenement areas* (high-density and low income) with 10 to 20 families (40 to 100 people) living in a 2 or 3 story building. Population densities are 300 to 600 people per hectare.
2. *Indigenous areas* (low-density and medium-income) where homes are single-story buildings with 5 to 10 rooms shared by 4 to 10 families. Densities are 80 to 250 people per hectare.
3. *New government areas* (medium-density and medium-income) with single-story bungalows built in rows. One or two households occupy a residence, and the density is about 50 people per hectare.
4. *High-cost areas* (low-density and high-income) where residences are detached, single-household structures on large plots. Densities range between 10 and 15 people per hectare.

On average, 95 percent of households have electricity, and 65 percent have water connections.

There are four major types of sanitation facilities in Kumasi:

1. *Public facilities.* Forty percent of the population (230,000 people) rely on 250 sanitary sites around the city. These consists of aqua privies (60 percent), bucket latrines (25 percent) and Kumasi ventilated improved pit latrines (KVIP) (15 percent), with each charging a small user fee and exhibiting varying standards of hygiene.
2. *Bucket latrines.* Twenty-five percent of the population (150,000 people) use their own bucket or pan latrines. These are collected 3 to 5 times a week by sanitation workers, most of whom are freelance contractors operating with very little supervision.
3. *WC/septic tanks.* Another 25 percent of Kumasi's citizens use water closets linked to septic tanks. These can be found in all high-cost areas, in 65 percent of new government housing, and in 15 percent of tenement and indigenous residences.
4. *Sewerage.* Two small-scale conventional sewerage systems exist that serve 6000 people, but neither has a working treatment plant.

Only 40 percent of Kumasi's 600 primary, junior, and senior secondary schools have sanitation facilities. The city's main industries generate about 1500 m^3 of wastewater per day, all of which is dumped into city drains without treatment.

Institutionally, the Kumasi Metropolitan Assembly is responsible for overall urban management, and there are four submetropolitan councils. Sanitation management is divided, with the Metropolitan Engineer's Department, the Mechanical Engineer's Department, and the Medical Officer of Health sharing responsibility for planning, development, and operation and maintenance of on-site systems.

Environmentally, 90 percent of all excreta generated by the city is retained in the urban environment. This occurs through (1) indiscriminate dumping of waste by sanitation workers; (2) overflowing septic tanks and public latrines, caused in part by lack of disposal trucks, and (3) open defecation by people in the city who do not have access to sanitary facilities. Much of this waste enters the local storm and natural drains, turning them into open sewers. These, in turn, drain into the Oda River, which is used for municipal and agricultural water supply, wildlife habitat, and water-related recreation. Thus, the sanitation situation in Kumasi decreases local quality of life and increases public health risks.

Strategic Planning

In the early 1990s, Kumasi decided to tackle this situation by preparing a strategic sanitation plan (SSP) that would link the choice of sanitation technology to relevant technical, financial, and social factors. Technological choices included three options for sewerage (standard, simplified, and small-bore) and three on-site options (ventilated improved pit latrines, pour-flush toilets, and WC/septic tank systems). Technical considerations comprised the housing type, water supply facilities, geological conditions, and operations and maintenance requirements. Financial factors included construction cost, operations and maintenance costs, and the consumer's willingness to pay for each system. Social considerations are based on the user's preference.

Technically, it was concluded that sewerage was the only viable option in tenement areas; on-site options were most appropriate in indigenous areas; and all technologies were viable in the new government and high-cost areas. Financially, simplified sewers were the least-cost option in tenement areas, while VIP latrines were the least-cost solution in all other areas. Combining technical viability and cost, sewers were deemed the best option in the tenement area; VIP latrines in the indigenous area; and septic tanks in the new government and high-cost areas.

These outcomes were then checked against user preference and willingness to pay. This was done because the government did not want to invest scarce resources in technologies that people would not use or pay for. The contingent valuation survey concluded that willingness to pay in the indigenous and tenement areas would cover the full cost of on-site systems if amortized over a long time at a low interest rate. However, local interest rates are high, and even VIP latrines would be unaffordable if full-cost recovery was required. A household survey on social preference indicated that most people with private sanitation were satisfied with their system; people who relied on public latrines were dissatisfied by the level of privacy and convenience.

A sanitation plan was then drawn up based on the outcomes of this matching between sanitation options and technical, financial, and social factors. The plan proposes that sewers be installed in the tenement area; latrines (VIP or pour-flush) or WC/septic tanks in the indigenous area; and septic tanks in the new government and high-cost areas. The city would subsidize sewers in the tenement area and latrines in the indigenous area. The city would finance rehabilitation and/or construction of public facilities in key residential and commercial areas to supplement private sanitation.

Institutionally, the plan called for creation of a Waste Management Department that centralizes responsibility for human, industrial, and solid waste collection, treatment, and disposal. The department was created in 1993 and is responsible for implementation of the plan. It is gradually moving away from direct provision of sanitation services toward promoting and managing community and private-sector involvement in service delivery.

Some of the innovative features of the sanitation plan, which is now being implemented, include:

- Construction of simplified sewers and waste stabilization ponds for treatment
- Contracting operation and maintenance of the sewers and ponds to a private operator
- Relying on one or more local firms to manage the city's household latrine program, including training and hiring local artisans and small contractors
- Operation and maintenance of public facilities would be contracted to private franchise operators on a competitive basis
- Installation of latrines at schools, combined with hygiene education, with mostly grant financing

- Privatization of the septage hauling business, with disposal required at a ponding system within the city's landfill site

These and other features of the plan are being financed by central government grants to a Sanitation Fund managed by the metropolitan authority. The fund finances construction of household, school, and public latrines. Fees from private contractors go into a separate account to finance the Waste Management Department's operations and additional facilities.

Lessons

Kumasi's SSP demonstrates how a low-income city can begin to tackle a fundamental urban environmental problem in a climate of limited resources. Some of the specific lessons it offers include:

- *Wide range of options.* The Kumasi SSP did not immediately latch onto a standard technology but rather considered the full range of options, from simple to sophisticated.
- *Spatial information.* The collection and analysis of geographic information about housing types, geology, slopes, and densities was essential for conducting a technical analysis of sanitation options.
- *Cost data.* Capital as well as operating and maintenance costs were carefully prepared so that each option could be evaluated in each housing area on a life-cycle basis.
- *Consumer preference.* An understanding of what users want and what they are willing to pay helped guide the SSP in both the choice of technology and financing options.
- *Realistic choice of options.* Assessing options according to their technical soundness, cost, affordability, and social acceptability by housing area resulted in a plan made up of the most realistic options.
- *Involving the private sector.* Contracting with the private sector allowed the city to expand its sanitation operations and improve performance while keeping costs down.
- *Subsidizing the poor.* Full cost recovery was not possible in low-income areas, so the city justified subsidies on equity and public health grounds.

Box 9-5 provides another enlightening experience using appropriate technology for sanitation; in this case, the focus is on a community-based initiative.

Neighborhood Level: Preserving an Informal Community's Role in Waste Management

The practice: Zabbaleen environmental and development program in Cairo, Egypt

Criteria fulfilled: Partnership, impact, sustainability, leadership, community empowerment

Management goal: Promoting sustainable use of environmental resources and services

Documentation: Mega-Cities 1994, Mega-Cities 1996

Background

Greater Cairo, one of the world's mega-cities, generates about 6000 tons of solid waste per year. In the past, two groups have worked together to collect and transport the city's waste. The Wahis, a group that migrated to Cairo from oases a century ago, were Cairo's garbage collectors for fifty years; they now control the transportation routes and manage contracts with individual households. The Zabbaleen, a marginalized and landless Coptic Christian community who came to Cairo from Upper Egypt over 50 years ago, collect the waste and transport it to their neighborhood, where it is sorted, recycled, or used for animal fodder.

BOX

The Orangi Pilot Project (OPP) was initiated in 1980 to provide affordable sewerage through community participation in one of Karachi's largest squatter settlements, where open drains, lack of stormwater drainage, and flooding harmed residents' health and property values. The process begins with formation of a lane committee (the slum is divided into small lanes, each of which has 20 to 40 households). The lane committee, with technical support from the OPP, mobilizes funds for purchasing sewer piping, household connectors, and related materials, and organizes community labor inputs for digging trenches. The lane committees also elect representatives to a neighborhood committee (around 600 households) that is responsible for building and managing secondary sewers.

OPP staff began the project by explaining the health benefits of improved sanitation to residents, identifying technical options, and conducting research. It took three years to convince the first lane to establish its committee. The project gained momentum after initial success in the first lanes. Its role then shifted more toward technical assistance and applying political pressure on the city government to use municipal funds for construction of primary and secondary sewers in the slum. The OPP later evolved into the OPP Research and Training Institute, developing model programs for low-cost housing, basic health, family planning, job training for women, credit for microenterprises, and upgrading private schools.

Sewerage has now been provided to 600,000 poor people in Karachi, largely through the OPP's initiative. By eliminating corruption and using community labor, the costs of sewerage (in-house sanitary latrine, house sewer on the plot, and underground sewers in the lane and nearest street) average less than $90 per household. The OPP is also able to provide sewer lines at one-fifth the cost of the municipality. Property values also increased in neighborhoods where sewers had been installed, further propelling the appeal of the project.

Box 9-5 Implementing community-based sanitation in Orangi, Pakistan.

SOURCE: Khan 1992, Badshah 1996.

As Cairo and its waste output grew, the Zabbaleen could no longer provide adequate services. They were economically impoverished and politically weak. The government began to look elsewhere for more "modern" alternatives such as mechanization to meet the growing demand for waste collection. This posed a major threat to the Zabbaleen's traditional source of income.

A number of NGOs, community organizations, technical assistance groups, and international donors recognized that the Zabbaleen were a threatened minority group that provided a valuable service to Greater Cairo which should be preserved. An umbrella Zabbaleen Environmental and Development Program started in 1981 to improve the living conditions and develop the capacity of the Zabbaleen community in the Moqattam area, where more than half of Cairo's waste collectors lived in degraded conditions.

At the beginning of the program, living conditions in Moqattam were terrible. The settlement had no water supply, sewerage system, or telephone connections, and few homes had electricity. There was no government school, health clinic, or pharmacy. The streets were literally lined with garbage, recyclable waste, piles of animal manure mixed with organic residues, and animal carcasses. Millions of flies swarmed about, and the air was usually polluted with smoke from fires that were set to burn unwanted paper or that resulted from spontaneous combustion. Although located only two kilometers from one of Cairo's most densely populated areas, Moqattam was effectively invisible to the rest of the city.

Programmatic Innovations

Environmental Quality International (EQI), a local consulting firm, received a grant from the Ford Foundation to help upgrade Moqattam. The Zabbaleen Gameya, the main leadership group in the community, was already involved in helping provide services to the neighborhood. EQI began by helping the Gameya become the representative of waste collectors. Together, they then developed a number of projects that were initiated over a five-year period. An experimental approach was used, where project ideas and designs came from EQI's field experience with the community.

Looking backward, the program's main components can be categorized as: slum upgrading; an internal cleanup project; a small-industries project; a female-headed households project; a veterinary center; a waste collection route extension project; a mechanization project; a composting plant; and health-care projects. Although individual projects met with varying degrees of success, from an overall standpoint the program helped to bring about positive changes in Moqattam.

Slum upgrading consisted of a project to construct basic infrastructure and facilities that was financed by the government of Egypt and the World Bank. Piped water, electricity, and sewerage systems were installed. The streets were leveled, paved, named, and mapped. A primary school and a health center were built. These investments were designed to serve an estimated 700 to 800 buildings; since then, this number has doubled and there is tremendous pressure on the infrastructure. Informal settlers were also invited to buy the land that they were squatting on; however, regularization has not been fully achieved due to conflicts over land prices and property rights.

The Internal Cleanup Project sought to improve hygiene in the settlement and was supported by the Ford Foundation, Oxfam, and the Soeur Emmanuelle Fund. Under the supervision of the Gameya, Zabbaleen residents removed tons of waste and manure from Moqattam using four trucks. This project worked well until 1987, when the installments on the trucks were paid for and the owners were no longer as committed to collecting the settlement's waste. This attitude was reinforced when the nearby municipal dump closed and the truck drivers were ordered to haul the waste to a site 50 kilometers away. The service became erratic, and people began throwing their waste into illegal local dumps or on the streets.

Figure 9-4 Plastic recycling in Cairo, Egypt.

The Small Industries Project, funded by Oxfam, was designed to develop new business opportunities for the Zabbaleen. It supported community-based recycling by providing credit for families to purchase plastic-granulating machines to recycle plastic and rag-pulling machines to recycle rags. The project successfully created a number of new businesses within Moqattam and created awareness about the economic potential of recycling. It did not create as many economic opportunities for Zabbaleen outside of Moqattam, who did not have access to electricity to run the machines; also, some of the machines have become a new source of localized air pollution.

The Female-Headed Households Project, supported by the Ford Foundation, aimed to provide income-generating opportunities for women who head their households. The Gameya were provided with funds to manage a microcredit loan program that was supported by community extension workers. Women formed credit groups and supported each other with small enterprise development. It is one of the most successful components in the program. However, even after six years of operation, the revolving fund is not sustainable as it does not cover administrative expenses.

A veterinary center was originally funded by Catholic Relief Services to improve animal-husbandry practices and reduce health hazards for both humans and animals. These goals were achieved during its first four years of operation. However, in 1990, funding was discontinued, and membership plus service fees did not cover operating costs of the center. It is subsidized by the Gameya and has a hard time keeping up with demand. Also, the Zabbaleen were not involved in planning or implementing the project, so they continue as recipients rather than participants.

The Route Extension Project, funded by Oxfam, sought to extend the Zabbaleen's waste-collection routes to low-income areas that were inadequately served. Initially, the Zabbaleen were not interested in these areas because little value could be recovered from the waste stream. To overcome this, the Gameya started collecting fees from households in the newly serviced areas and paying the waste collectors a fixed sum for their services. The low-income communities have been willing to pay for the service, which continues to be provided on a regular basis.

The Mechanization Project was started by EQI and the Gameya when a decree was issued in 1987 by the Governorate of Cairo prohibiting the use of donkey carts for waste collection. As a result, the Zabbaleen had to mechanize or lose their livelihood. An Environmental Protection Company was set up by EQI and the Gameya, with support from the Soeur Emmanuelle Fund and shareholders, to purchase vehicles for the settlements. The Wahis and Zabbaleen then organized themselves into more than 50 small companies, which then rented or bought trucks to collect waste along their traditional routes. Mechanization speeded up collection times and reduced the reliance on child labor. On the negative side, it has imposed a heavy financial burden on the community and perpetuated the Wahis' dominance over the Zabbaleen.

A composting plant, supported by the European Community, the Ford Foundation, and the Soeur Emmanuelle Fund, sought to develop a composting system that was easy to maintain and operate. The plant composts organic waste, sells fertilizer, and uses the income to fund other development activities. It is run by an NGO, the Association for the Protection of the Environment. The Association has used revenues to initiate a school for carpet weaving, literacy classes, a paper recycling project, and a health-awareness program for pregnant women. Technically, the plant suffers from inadequate maintenance, frequent breakdowns, and low-quality inputs (because the Zabbaleen are not paid for the manure they provide).

Many residents have benefited from a variety of health-care projects that are part of the program. A maternal health-care program trains girls from the community to promote health awareness for pregnant mothers. A midwives project works with these trainees to match local midwives with mothers near their term. A health and immunization program also works with the trainees to educate families about the importance of vaccination; doctors then provide the immunization at an integrated government health-care center.

The Zabbaleen Environmental and Development Program has generated a number of important benefits for the Moqattam community:

- *Environmental benefits*. The settlement has been upgraded, waste collection has been extended to poor communities, and recycling and composting have decreased the volume of neighborhood waste while generating income.
- *Economic benefits*. The Zabbaleen's main source of livelihood has been protected, household income has increased by a factor of 20 during the first 10 years of the Program, and thousands of new jobs have been created from the increase in cottage industries and the expansion of waste-collection services.
- *Social benefits*. Child labor has been significantly reduced, social services are now available in the community, and health indicators have greatly improved.
- *Capacity building*. Through participation in program planning and management, the Zabbaleen have developed useful new administrative, business, and technical skills.
- *Enhanced self-image*. The Zabbaleen, once a hidden, primitive community, are now a recognized and appreciated service provider meeting the requirements of modern urban life.

On the negative side, the Program encountered a number of obstacles that included (1) a lack of coordination between community organizations; (2) uneven participation and development of human resources in the Zabbaleen community; (3) a dependency on donor-driven initiatives; (4) inequitable distribution of program benefits to the more powerful people in Moqattam; (5) an infrastructure that cannot fully cope with growing community needs; and (6) uncertain sustainability of some projects.

Lessons

Several clear lessons can be drawn from this complicated program to upgrade a neighborhood consisting of an underprivileged minority:

- *Formalizing the informal sector*. An overall lesson of the program is that informal sector activities need not be neglected or destroyed in favor of high-technology solutions. Rather, the important contributions of informal groups can be recognized, improved, and formalized to the benefit of all.

- *Linking environmental improvement to enterprise development.* Environmental upgrading can be paid for by the community if economic development is promoted simultaneously with the improvements. This requires improving access to capital as well as training for business development.
- *Selecting appropriate technologies.* Economic development was facilitated by program support for technologies that were low-cost, geared to the capacity of users, easy to operate and maintain, environmentally friendly, and use little energy.
- *Community participation improves chance of successful outcome.* Projects that involved the community in assessing their needs and making decisions, and which sustained this participation over the life of the project, had a higher degree of success.
- *Partnership pays off.* The program was more successful because a partnership was gradually forged between external donors, local experts, the Cairo Governorate, and community groups like the Gameya.
- *Addressing environmental health issues.* In addition to the health-care projects, the projects on animal health, internal cleanup, and composting all helped to minimize the negative health effects of people, animals, and garbage being in close proximity.

Box 9-6 provides another example of good practice, also involving solid-waste management in a low-income neighborhood.

Compendium: 200+ Examples of Good Practice

The tables on the following pages summarize more than 200 examples of good environmental practice from cities around the world. Each table represents a different goal of urban environmental management: improving access to infrastructure; controlling, reducing or preventing pollution; sustainably using resources; developing planning and institutional capacity; reducing risk; and preserving

BOX

The Ants' Villa was a community of 50 households located on reclaimed land along the waterfront of Tokyo Bay; the economic activity of the community consisted of recovering and recycling metal, glass, paper, rags, rubber, straw, wood, and other wastes. By 1960, their work process was highly rationalized: Waste was collected in large quantities from businesses in central Tokyo, trucked to community workshops, sorted by teams of worker-residents, packed by machines, and delivered to commercial recyclers. The organization of the work compared favorably with any efficient small-scale firm in Tokyo. The community's compound was spacious, with four residential structures, a child-care center, a community restaurant, workshops, a store for basic needs, and a chapel.

However, ten years earlier, the Ants' Villa was a far cry from its 1960 level of prosperity, cleanliness, and tranquility. It was located on marginal land along the banks of the Sumida River and was substandard in every sense. The original Villa housed many vagrants and people engaged in marginally criminal activities. They were not officially recognized or served, as the Villa was squatting on public parkland.

The intervention of a few key individuals led to community as well as professional development. The Ants' Villa was organized as a ragpickers' cooperative by Motomu Ozawa when he took charge of 15 unemployed ragpickers dismissed by a retiring ragpicker in 1950. Ozawa received legal and organizational assistance from Toru Matsui, a retired impresario and junk dealer. Ozawa's leadership and Matsui's intellectual advice helped to develop an efficient scavengers' cooperative. Community development, though, began only in 1951 with the arrival of Ms. Satoko Kitahara. Between 1951 and her death in 1958, she worked at various jobs in the Villa—matron of the Villa's 150 children, ragpicker, and community recreation organizer. Her efforts fostered essential elements of community life, such as solidarity, identity, and a desire to collectively plan for the future.

Through the efforts of Ozawa, Matsui, and Kitahara, the Villa began negotiations with the Tokyo Metropolitan Government for acquisition of a legal plot of land where the community could move en masse. They successfully argued that it would be poor social policy to destroy a community that had demonstrated its social integrity and economic viability. In 1958, the Villa reached an agreement with the Metropolitan Government for purchasing a plot of land in installments over five years. The Villa worked for two years to save money and develop facilities on the new land, finally moving in mid-1960.

Box 9-6 Community environmental management in Tokyo, Japan, 1960.

SOURCE: Taira in McQuade 1971.

the natural environment. These examples are drawn from three international sources: the UNCHS database on best practice (1996), the UNCHS "Award, Best and Good Submissions" list (1998), and ICLEI's case-study series. More information on each example can be obtained from the UNCHS and ICLEI Web sites (http://www.unhabitat.org/blp/ and http://www.iclei.org).

Table 9-1 200+ Examples of Good Urban Environmental Practice: Improving Access to Infrastructure

City or Country	Program	Source
	AFRICA	
Abidjan, Côte d'Ivoire	Institutionalizing community-based development	UNCHS
Botswana	Housing the low-income populace	UNCHS
Minago, Burundi	Integrated development project	UNCHS
Cape Town, S Africa	Serviced land project	UNCHS
Cape Town, S Africa	Strategic management plans for former black local authorities	ICLEI
Dakar, Senegal	Community participation in urban environmental management	UNCHS
Dakar, Senegal	New management system for household solid waste	ICLEI
Dalifort, Senegal	Settlement upgrading project	UNCHS
Darfur, Sudan	Upgrading water supply system in Nyala and El Geneina	UNCHS
E London, S Africa	Provision of sustainable electrical reticulation	UNCHS
Egypt	Aqueduct area project by GOPP	UNCHS
Lesotho	Urban upgrading project	UNCHS
Mafikeng, S Africa	Integrated development project	UNCHS
Malawi	Low-cost housing project	UNCHS
Maputo, Mozambique	Promotion of latrine construction by low-income households	UNCHS
Nairobi, Kenya	Undugu slum upgrading and sanitation program	UNCHS
Sambizanga, Angola	Peri-urban upgrading program	UNCHS
Senegal	Improved-lot project	UNCHS
Tanzania	Community infrastructure upgrading project	UNCHS
Tanzania	Health through sanitation and water program	UNCHS
Voi, Kenya	Tanzania-Bondeni community land trust project	UNCHS
	EAST ASIA/PACIFIC	
Beijing, China	Xin Xing housing cooperative	UNCHS
Foshan City, China	Comprehensive development of urban infrastructure	UNCHS
Hong Kong, China	Public housing program	UNCHS
Shanghai, China	Housing settlement project	UNCHS
Surabaya, Indonesia	Kampung improvement program	ICLEI
	EUROPE/MIDEAST	
Asbraten, Norway	Housing area program	UNCHS
East Wehdat, Jordan	Upgrading project	UNCHS
Manningham, UK	Housing association	UNCHS
Saudi Arabia	Improving living environments for low-income households	UNCHS
Timisoara, Romania	Single-family housing project	UNCHS
Turkey	Housing on Housing Development Administration lands	UNCHS
Turkey	Urban basic services for mothers and children	UNCHS

Table 9-1 200+ Examples of Good Urban Environmental Practice: Improving Access to Infrastructure (*Continued*)

City or country	Program	Source
	LATIN AMERICA	
Alijuela, Costa Rica	Ecologically sustainable low-income housing	UNCHS
Buenos Aires, Argentina	Sites and services for low-income family groups	UNCHS
Cali, Colombia	Low-income community drinking water provision	UNCHS
Costa Rica	Bamboo housing national project	UNCHS
Costa Rica	Popular urban habitat program	UNCHS
Cuba	Sustainable nationwide and low-cost housing program	UNCHS
Diadema, Brazil	Municipal transportation policy	UNCHS
La Paz, Bolivia	Managed privatization of solid-waste services	ICLEI
Fortaleza, Brazil	Mutirao 50 self-help housing program	UNCHS
Maracaibo, Venezuela	Mobile clinics program	ICLEI
Matamoros, Mexico	Urban-regional integral planning	UNCHS
Rio de Janeiro, Brazil	Rio-Cidade (Urbanism back-to-the-streets program)	UNCHS
Sao Paulo, Brazil	Cingapura project: Urbanization and verticalization of slums	UNCHS
Sao Paulo, Brazil	Municipalization of public transportation	ICLEI
Tegucigalpa, Honduras	Empowering poor communities for water supply management	UNCHS
NORTH AMERICA:	None	
	SOUTH ASIA	
Sindh, Pakistan	Innovation and success in sheltering the poor	UNCHS
Karachi, Pakistan	Orangi pilot project	UNCHS

Table 9-2 200+ Examples of Good Urban Environmental Practice: Pollution Control/Reduction/Prevention

City or country	Program	Source
	AFRICA	
Dar es Salaam, Tanzania	Manual pit latrine emptying technology	UNCHS
Karyan El Ou, Morocco	Integrated community sanitation program in shantytown	UNCHS
Mathare, Kenya	Youth self-help and environmental cleanup project	UNCHS
	EAST ASIA/PACIFIC	
Manila, Philippines	Paco environmental enhancement project	ICLEI
Singapore	Phasing out industries in Bukit Timah and Bukit Batok	UNCHS
Western Australia	Sewerage and wastewater quality program	UNCHS
	EUROPE/MIDEAST	
Cordoba, Spain	Control of waste experience	UNCHS
Gothenburg, Sweden	The chemical sweep and clean lubricants program	ICLEI
Graz, Austria	ECOPROFIT Graz	ICLEI
Hampshire, UK	Changing travel behavior and public attitudes to transport	UNCHS
Kirovo-Chepetsk, Russian Federation	Air protection	UNCHS
Navarra, Spain	Water and waste management	UNCHS
Poznan, Poland	Environmental conditions for qualitative development	UNCHS
San Sebastian, Spain	Pedestrian-friendly network	UNCHS
Slobozia, Romania	New technologies for water-treatment plant	UNCHS
Stockholm, Sweden	Measures at the source	ICLEI
Vienna, Austria	Air monitoring network	UNCHS
	LATIN AMERICA	
Costa Rica	School farms free from chemicals program	UNCHS
Ecuador	Salud para el pueblo—Health and sanitation Rotary project	UNCHS
Santos, Brazil	Santos beaches recovery program	ICLEI
Sao Paulo, Brazil	Guarapiranga waterbasin environmental sanitation	UNCHS
	NORTH AMERICA	
Chicago, Illinois	Urban greening initiative	ICLEI
Chula Vista, California	Telecommuting promotion program	ICLEI
Dayton, Ohio	Police bicycle patrol	ICLEI
Denver, Colorado	The green fleets policy	ICLEI
Los Angeles, California	Clean water program	ICLEI
Los Angeles, California	Commuter services program	ICLEI
Muncie, Indiana	Bureau of water quality	ICLEI
Portland, Oregon	Regional transportation plan in Region 2040 Growth Concept	ICLEI
Public Technology Inc., USA	Alternatively fueled vehicles (Web) conference	ICLEI
United States	Carbon dioxide reduction plan	UNCHS
United States	ZPG children's environmental index	UNCHS
Ventura County, California	Ventura Country hazardous waste volume reduction and alternative technology program	ICLEI
	SOUTH ASIA	
Calcutta, India	Integrated wetland system for low-cost treatment	UNCHS
India	Sulabh International cost-effective and appropriate sanitation	UNCHS
India	Urban sanitation in low-income area	UNCHS
Nepal	Urban hygiene and environment programs	UNCHS

Table 9-3 200+ Examples of Good Urban Environmental Practice: Sustainable Resource Use

City or country	Program	Source
	AFRICA	
Cairo, Egypt	Household solid-waste management (Zabbaleen)	UNCHS
Dar es Salaam, Tanzania	Traditional energy and environment conservation	UNCHS
Egypt	National public scheme for conserving drinking water	UNCHS
Nairobi, Kenya	House rehabilitation program	UNCHS
Senegal	Management and community use of domestic waste by women	UNCHS
	EAST ASIA/PACIFIC	
Bandung, Indonesia	The integrated resource recovery system	ICLEI
Beijing, China	Ju'er Hutong housing rehabilitation project	ICLEI
Crystal Waters, Australia	Permaculture village	UNCHS
Kavieng, PNG	Building water tanks and houses using indigenous materials	UNCHS
Southwell Park, Australia	Wastewater recycling pilot scheme	UNCHS
Sumida City, Japan	Rainwater storage and utilization	ICLEI
Victoria, Australia	Greenhouse neighborhood project: The low-energy suburb	ICLEI
	EUROPE/MIDEAST	
Barcelona, Spain	Restoring the old center	UNCHS
Barnamil, Spain	Solar hot water heating	UNCHS
Beirut, Lebanon	Development and reconstruction of the city center	UNCHS
Berlin, Germany	Careful urban renewal in Prenzlauer Berg	UNCHS
Copenhagen, Denmark	Refuse plan: Comprehensive urban waste regulatory system	ICLEI
Damascus, Syria	Solid-waste management	UNCHS
Glasgow, Scotland	Action for warm houses	UNCHS
Gotland, Sweden	Converting wind to energy	UNCHS
Linz, Austria	Solar city Pichling: Sustainable urban development	UNCHS
Madrid, Spain	Participation in urban renewal	UNCHS
Manchester, UK	Regeneration of Hulme inner-city area	UNCHS
Poland	Tested and organic food for industrialized urban areas	UNCHS
Saarbrucken, Germany	Solar energy initiative	ICLEI
Saarbrucken, Germany	Participation program for energy conservation	ICLEI
Spittelau, Austria	Waste incineration plant	UNCHS
Vienna, Austria	Biowaste management and organic farming	UNCHS
Zaragoza, Spain	Water-saving city	UNCHS
	LATIN AMERICA	
Belo Horizonte, Brazil	Integrated waste management system	UNCHS
Brazil	ReciproCity Program of selective collection and recycling	UNCHS
Brazil	Return to nature program	UNCHS
Peru	Integrated solid-waste management system	UNCHS
Quito, Ecuador	Neighborhood recycling program	ICLEI
Recife, Brazil	Solid-waste collection and recycling project	UNCHS
Tome, Chile	Grassroots development, food security, and recycling	UNCHS

Table 9-3 200+ Examples of Good Urban Environmental Practice: Sustainable Resource Use (*Continued*)

City or country	Program	Source
	NORTH AMERICA	
Austin, Texas	Energy Star and Green Builder programs	ICLEI
Canada	Auto-recycling best practices	UNCHS
Canada	Zero Waste 2005	UNCHS
Edmonton, Canada	Driver education fuel savings incentive program	ICLEI
Chattanooga, Tennessee	Recycling and job creation	UNCHS
Minneapolis, Minnesota	Neighborhood revitalization project	UNCHS
Newark, New Jersey	Planet Newark recycling business development program	ICLEI
Santa Monica, California	Baysaver plumbing fixture rebate program	ICLEI
Tucson, Arizona	Beat the peak and related water conservation programs	ICLEI
	SOUTH ASIA	
Ahmedabad, India	Energy management initiative	UNCHS
India	Environmentally sound and productive use of city garbage	UNCHS
Tamil Nadu, India	Wind energy development program	ICLEI

Table 9-4 200+ Examples of Good Urban Environmental Practice: Supporting Sustainable Development

City or country	Practice or process	Source
	AFRICA	
Dar es Salaam, Tanzania	Sustainable Dar es Salaam program	UNCHS
Jinga, Uganda	Local level capacity strengthening with Guelph, Canada	UNCHS
Kenya	Green towns environment and urban development training	UNCHS
Kenya	Slums information development and resource center	UNCHS
Maseru (Lesotho)	Mabote project: Coping with rapid urbanization	UNCHS
Soweto, S Africa	Mobilizing the community	UNCHS
	EAST ASIA/PACIFIC	
Cebu City, Philippines	Partnerships for poverty alleviation	UNCHS
Foshan City, China	Deepening reform to gain sustainable development	UNCHS
Halifax, Australia	Wirranendi—The Halifax ecocity project	UNCHS
Kanagawa, Japan	Agenda 21 Kanagawa	ICLEI
Naga City, Philippines	Participatory planning initiatives	UNCHS
Philippines	Urban poor elderly health workers	UNCHS
Puerto Princesa, Philippines	Bantay Puerto program	UNCHS
SE Queensland, Australia	Development plan	UNCHS
Singapore	Evolving a world-class transport system	UNCHS
Weihai, China	Ecologically balanced coastal city program	UNCHS
Zhuhai, China	Comprehensive improvement of the urban environment	UNCHS
	EUROPE/MIDEAST	
Barcelona, Spain	Indicators for sustainability	UNCHS
Berlin, Germany	Hellersdorf forum for environment	UNCHS
Berlin, Germany	1994 land use plan	UNCHS
Blackburn, UK	Groundwork Blackburn	ICLEI
Denmark	Triangle region program	UNCHS
Girona, Spain	Building a city plan	UNCHS
Glasgow, Scotland	Housing, health, and poverty in Glasgow	UNCHS
Graz, Austria	ECOPROFIT-Graz	UNCHS
Katowice, Poland	Sustainable Katowice agglomeration project	UNCHS
Lancashire, UK	Green audit	ICLEI
Lanzarote, Spain	Well-planned tourist resort	UNCHS
Leicester, UK	Environment city	UNCHS
Lillehammer, Norway	Green games (1994 Olympics)	UNCHS
Linz, Austria	Citizen participation program	ICLEI
Lublin, Poland	Local initiatives program	UNCHS
Malaga, Spain	Programs for improving the urban environment	UNCHS
Merton, UK	Sustainability indicators	UNCHS
Neuss-Allerheiligen, Germany	Environment-friendly urban development	UNCHS
Oslo, Norway	Community participation in environment improvement	UNCHS
Poland	ECO-tickets	UNCHS
Povel, Germany	Local solution for a global challenge	UNCHS

Table 9-4 200+ Examples of Good Urban Environmental Practice: Supporting Sustainable Development (*Continued*)

City or country	Practice or process	Source
	EUROPE/MIDEAST (*Continued*)	
Qatar	Center for geographic information systems	UNCHS
Saudi Arabia	Ideas for improving living conditions	UNCHS
Solingen, Germany	Master plan in the spirit of sustainable development	UNCHS
Spain	Ecotouristic initiative	UNCHS
Stockholm, Sweden	Urban environmental planning	UNCHS
Tehran, Iran	Action plan for improving the living environment	UNCHS
Troyan, Bulgaria	Environmental action project	ICLEI
United Kingdom	Findhorn Foundation ecovillage project	UNCHS
Urdaibai, Spain	Ecological development	UNCHS
	LATIN AMERICA	
Cajamarca, Peru	Consensus building for a sustainable development plan	ICLEI
Havana, Cuba	Ideas for participative and sustainable development	UNCHS
Managua, Nicaragua	Productive home communities and local development	UNCHS
Mexico	Training for undergraduate urban planning	UNCHS
	NORTH AMERICA	
Canada	Ecoquest—reducing our ecological footprint	UNCHS
Canada	Ouje Bougoumou Cree first nation	UNCHS
Chattanooga, Tennessee	National center for sustainability	UNCHS
Chattanooga, Tennessee	Sustainability and smart growth in Southside	UNCHS
Chattanooga, Tennessee	Sustainable city program	UNCHS
Hamilton-Wentworth, Canada	Signposts on the trail to Vision 2020	UNCHS
Hamilton-Wentworth, Canada	Vision 2020: Sustainable community initiative	ICLEI and UNCHS
Jacksonville, Florida	Quality indicators for progress	UNCHS
New York City, New York	Greenpoint/Williamsburg environmental benefits program	ICLEI
Ottawa, Canada	Environmental conservation and management strategy	ICLEI
Portland, Oregon	Businesses for an environmentally sustainable tomorrow	ICLEI
Toronto, Canada	Healthy city project	UNCHS
United States	Green map system	UNCHS
United States	Interface's journey to sustainability	UNCHS
United States	Involvement of urban communities in brownfields redevelopment	UNCHS
United States	Third regional plan for New York tristate region	UNCHS
	SOUTH ASIA	
Ahmedabad, India	Innovative urban partnerships	UNCHS
Bangladesh	THRESHOLD 21 model	UNCHS
India	Engineering and participatory solutions for slum networking	UNCHS
India	People's participation program	UNCHS
India	Slum networking project	UNCHS
Mumbai, India	Sustainable urban development in Navi Mumbai	UNCHS
Surat, India	Preparation of inner-city revitalization plan	UNCHS
Surat, India	Urban governance in environment and public health management	UNCHS

Table 9-5 200+ Examples of Good Urban Environmental Practice: Reducing Risk and Protecting Natural/Cultural Heritage

City or country	Program	Source
	AFRICA	
Côte d'Ivoire	Gulf of Guinea large marine ecosystem project	UNCHS
Durban, S Africa	Metropolitan Open Space System	ICLEI
	EAST ASIA/PACIFIC	
Johnstone Shire, Australia	Cassowary conservation	ICLEI
	EUROPE/MIDEAST	
Barcelona, Spain	Revitalization of historical center	UNCHS
Belfast, Ireland	Commerce and conservation in partnership (harbor project)	UNCHS
Egebjerggard, Denmark	Skotteparken	UNCHS
Espoo, Finland	Education project on biodiversity	UNCHS
Frankfurt am Main, Germany	Green belt	UNCHS
Germany	Lebensgarten Steyerberg, e.V.	UNCHS
Madrid, Spain	Rehabilitation of historic center	UNCHS
Marseille, France	Risk management and prevention	UNCHS
Morocco	Planting trees for improving living conditions	UNCHS
Romania	Habitat and art in Romania program	UNCHS
Santa Cruz, Spain	Urban project for recuperation of historic city center	UNCHS
Segovia, Spain	Green plan for a world heritage town	UNCHS
United Arab Emirates	National man-made catastrophes	UNCHS
Valencia, Spain	Rehabilitation of old city	UNCHS
Xanthi, Greece	Changing city's image: The cultural face of sustainability	UNCHS
	LATIN AMERICA	
Cubatao, Brazil	Natural disaster control plan in Serra do Mar	UNCHS
Santos, Brazil	Prevention and reduction of geological risks on hills	UNCHS
Sao Paulo, Brazil	Guarapiranga project for rehabilitation of urban areas	UNCHS
Sao Pedro, Brazil	Integrated urban development and mangrove preservation	UNCHS
	NORTH AMERICA	
Ottawa, Canada	Community participation in open-space protection	ICLEI
Ottawa, Canada	Land-use development scenarios for Rideau Canal shoreline	UNCHS
United States	Integrated watershed management with participation	UNCHS
United States	Improving urban earthquake risk management	UNCHS
	SOUTH ASIA	
India	Innovative shelter delivery mechanisms for earthquake-affected settlements	UNCHS
India	Maharashtra emergency earthquake rehabilitation program	UNCHS

Resources and Exercises for Further Thought

Cities for Climate Protection

Up-to-date information on the CCP campaign can be obtained from its Web site at: http://www.iclei.org/co2/.

Unleaded Gas in Thailand

For more information about experience with removing lead from gasoline around the world, see:

ESMAP (Energy Sector Management Assistance Programme). 1996. Elimination of lead in gasoline in Latin America and the Caribbean. Washington, D.C.: World Bank.

Lovei, Magda. 1998. Phasing out lead from gasoline: Worldwide experience and policy implications. World Bank Technical Paper No. 397. Washington, D.C.: World Bank.

Lovei, Magda (ed.). 1997. Phasing out lead from gasoline in Central and Eastern Europe: Health issues, feasibility, and policies. Washington, D.C.: World Bank.

Walsh, Michael, and Jitendra Shah. 1997. Clean fuels for Asia: Technical options for moving toward unleaded gasoline and low-sulfur diesel. Technical Paper No. 377. Washington, D.C.: World Bank.

Singapore

A good historical overview of the development of environmental management in Singapore can be found in: ENV (Ministry of the Environment). 1997. Singapore—My clean and green home. Twenty-Fifth Anniversary Booklet. Singapore: ENV. A good non-governmental perspective on Singapore's environmental accomplishments and challenges is: Ooi Giok Ling (ed.). *Environment and the city: Sharing Singapore's experience and future challenges*. Singapore: Times Academic Press. Up-to-date environmental information can be obtained from ENV's Web site (www.gov.sg/env). More information on Curitiba, in English and Portuguese, is available from the municipality's web site (www .curitiba.arave.br).

Kumasi Strategic Sanitation Planning

In addition to the case study (Roche 1995), there is an excellent 1994 video on the Kumasi experience, entitled, "Strategic sanitation planning: The Kumasi experience." It is available from the World Bank/UNDP Regional Water and Sanitation Group for West Africa (c/o World Bank Field Office, B.P. 1850, Abidjan 01, Côte d'Ivoire; telephone 225-442-227), or from the World Bank/UNDP Water and Sanitation Program (c/o World Bank, 1818 H Street NW, Washington, DC 20433, USA; telephone 1-202-477-1234).

Zabbaleen

The Mega-Cities, Inc. publications cited in the text are excellent summaries of the Zabbaleen experience and were prepared with many of the key actors in Cairo.

Other Examples of Good Practice

In addition to the ongoing UNCHS Best Practices Award Program and the ICLEI case studies series, there are some one-off evaluations of successful urban environmental planning and management. UNCHS and UNEP prepared a review of efforts to manage the urban environment in over 50 cities in advance of the 1996 Habitat II Conference. Summaries of good practice for improving environmental information and technical expertise, environmental strategies and decision-making, implementation, institutional and participatory capacity, and use of scarce resources can be found in: UNCHS and UNEP 1996. Implementing the urban environment agenda. Nairobi: UNCHS and UNEP.

Moving from the global to the national level, a collection of "best practices" that covers environmental management and land development is: Rocky Mountain Institute, Alex Wilson, et al. 1997. *Green development: Integrating ecology and real estate.* New York: John Wiley & Sons. A summary of good urban and environmental planning experience in Florida can be found in: Read Ewing. 1996. *Best development practices.* Chicago: APA Planners Press.

At the thematic level, the Aga Khan Foundation determines an Award for Architecture every three years that has included urban environmental themes such as conservation and rehabilitation of historic heritage, environmentally friendly buildings, and urban greening. Contact information: Aga Khan Award for Architecture, 32 chemin des Crets-de-Pregny, CH-1218 Grand-Saconnex, Geneva, Switzerland; telephone 41-22-798-9391; fax 41-22-798-9070.

Exercises for Further Thought

1. To what extent can good practice in one locality be transferred and replicated in another city?
2. Obtain a "Best Practice" application from the UNCHS Web site (http://unhabitat.org/blp/), identify a suitable case study, and complete the application.
3. Beyond greenhouse gas reduction, what other global or transnational environmental problems might cities work together to solve?
4. Are there other examples of primate cities that have guided or stimulated national environmental policy as in Thailand? In countries without primate cities, what impact have local governments had on national environmental policy?
5. To what extent do windows of opportunity, like the 1991 fall in oil prices for Thailand, influence action on urban environmental issues?
6. Why aren't there more Singapores and Curitibas in the world?
7. How important is strong and stable municipal leadership, as in Curitiba and Singapore, for sustaining environmental improvement?
8. How applicable is strategic sanitation planning to cities where rigid technical standards are enforced (e.g., in most developed-country cities)?
9. When are subsidies for urban environmental services and infrastructure justified?
10. Beyond solid-waste management, where else is the informal sector active in providing urban environmental services and infrastructure?
11. What are some strengths and weaknesses of using multi-project, donor-supported programs to address neighborhood urban environmental problems?

References

Badshah, Akhtar. 1996. *Our urban future: New paradigms for equity and sustainability.* London: Zed Books, Ltd.

Briffett, Clive. 1992. The case for environmental impact assessment in Singapore. Paper presented at the 1992 Convention of the Institute of Engineers, Singapore. 28–30 May.

Chiu, Stephen, K. C. Ho, and Tai-Lok Lui. 1997. *City-states in the global economy: Industrial restructuring in Hong Kong and Singapore.* Boulder: Westview Press.

ENV (Ministry of the Environment). 1987. Clean rivers—The cleaning up of Singapore River and Kallang Basin. Produced by Information Division of Ministry of Communications and Information for Ministry of the Environment. Singapore: ENV.

———. 1992. The Singapore green plan: Towards a model green city. Singapore: ENV.

———. 1993. The Singapore green plan—Action programmes. Singapore: ENV.

———. 1997a. Annual report 1996. Singapore: ENV.

———. 1997b. Environmental controls in land use planning and building development in Singapore. Summary Report. Singapore: ENV.

———. 1997c. 1996 Pollution control report. Public Report prepared by Environmental Policy and Management Division. Singapore: ENV.

———. 1997d. Singapore—A sustainable city. Singapore: ENV.

———. 1997e. Singapore—My clean and green home. Twenty-Fifth Anniversary Booklet. Singapore: ENV.

———. 1997f. Singapore—Your window of opportunity to Asia's environmental business. Brochure. Singapore: ENV.

———. 1998. Annual report 1997. Singapore: ENV.

Field, Brian. 1992. Singapore's new town prototype: A textbook prescription? *Habitat International* 16(3): 89–101.

Foo, Kim Boon. 1993. Pollution control in Singapore: Towards an integrated approach. In C. Briffett and S. Lee (eds.). *Environmental issues in development and conservation.* Singapore: School of Building and Estate Management, National University of Singapore.

Foo, Tuan Seik. 1996. Urban environmental policy—The use of regulatory and economic instruments in Singapore. *Habitat International* 20(1): 5–22.

———. 1997a. An effective demand management instrument in urban transport: The area licensing scheme in Singapore. *Cities* 14(3): 155–164.

———. 1997b. Experience from Singapore's park-and-ride scheme (1975–1996). *Habitat International* 21(4): 427–443.

———. 1997c. Recycling of domestic waste: Early experiences in Singapore. *Habitat International* 21(3): 277–289.

Hin, David Ho Kim, Robert The Yoke Chong, Tham Kwok Wai, and Clive Briffett. 1997. The greening of Singapore's national estate. *Habitat International* 21(1): 107–121.

ICLEI (International Council for Local Environmental Initiatives). 1995. Limiting automobile use through integrated transportation demand management. Cities for Climate Protection Case Study No. 38. Toronto: ICLEI.

———. 1997a. Local government implementation of climate protection. Interim Report. Toronto: ICLEI.

———. 1997b. Local government implementation of climate protection. Final Report to the United Nations. Toronto: ICLEI.

———. 1998. Cities for climate protection campaign update. *Initiatives* 18, March.

Khan, Akhter. 1992. Orangi pilot project programs. Second edition. Karachi: Orangi Pilot Project Research and Training Institute.

Lee, Sing Kong. 1995. Concept of the garden city. In Ooi Giok Ling (ed.). *Environment and the city: Sharing Singapore's experience and future challenges.* Singapore: Times Academic Press.

Lovei, Magda, and Charles Weiss, Jr. 1998. Environmental management and institutions in OECD countries. World Bank Technical Paper No. 391. Washington, D.C.: World Bank.

Malone-Lee, Lai Choo, and Lan Yuan Lim. 1998. Urban planning in Singapore: Citizen participation and self-determination. Paper presented at the First International Conference on Quality of Life in Cities, Singapore. 4–6 March.

McNulty, Sheila, and John Parker. 1998. How to stop traffic jams. *Financial Times,* May 9–10, 7.

Mega-Cities. 1994. Zabbaleen environmental and development program. Urban environment poverty case study series. New York: Mega-Cities Project, Inc.

———. 1996. Environmental innovations for sustainable mega-cities: Sharing approaches that work. New York: Mega-Cities Project, Inc.

Mekani, Kirtida, and Heike Stengel. 1995. The role of NGOs and near NGOs. In Ooi Giok Ling (ed.). *Environment and the city: Sharing Singapore's experience and future challenges*. Singapore: Times Academic Press.

Murray, Geoffrey, and Audrey Perera. 1996. *Singapore: The global city state*. New York: St. Martin's Press.

PRD (Parks and Recreation Department). 1992. *More than a garden city*. Singapore: Toppan Printing.

PUB (Public Utilities Board). 1996. Development of water supply in Singapore. Paper presented to IWSA-ASPAC Conference, Hong Kong. November.

Quah, Jon. 1998. Learning from Singapore's development. *International Journal of Technical Cooperation* 4(1): 54–68.

Rabinovitch, Jonas, with Josef Leitmann. 1993. Environmental innovation and management in Curitiba, Brazil. Urban Management Program Working Paper No. 1. Washington, D.C.: World Bank.

Rabinovitch, Jonas, and Josef Leitmann. 1996. Urban planning in Curitiba. *Scientific American* March: 46–53.

Roche, Robert. 1995. Case study: Kumasi sanitation planning. Case prepared for World Bank Training Course on Urban Environmental Management. Washington, D.C.: World Bank.

Sayeg, Philip. 1998. Successful conversion to unleaded gasoline in Thailand. World Bank Technical Paper. Washington, D.C.: World Bank.

Taira, Koji. Urban poverty, ragpickers, and the "Ants' Villa" in Tokyo. In McQuade, Walter. 1971. *Cities fit to live in and how we can make them happen: Recent articles on the urban environment*. New York: The MacMillan Company.

Tan, Tah-Chew. 1995. Environmental excellence: The Singapore experiment and experience. Paper presented to UMP/WHO

Conference on Urban Environmental Health, Johore Bahru, Malaysia. May.

USAID (United States Agency for International Development). 1990. Ranking environmental health risks in Bangkok, Thailand. Office of Housing and Urban Programs working paper. Washington, D.C.: USAID.

———. 1992. Unleaded gas program: Awareness, risk assessment and public/private partnerships in Thailand. In *Success stories of urban environmental management*. Collection of Case Studies prepared by USAID Regional Housing and Urban Development Office/Asia.

Wee, Yeow Chin. 1993. Coping with nature and nature conservation in Singapore. In C. Briffett and S. Lee (eds.). *Environmental issues in development and conservation*. Singapore: School of Building and Estate Management, National University of Singapore.

You, Nicholas. 1998. Learning from the best: New paradigms and tools for a decentralised city-to-city co-operation. *The International Journal of Technical Cooperation* 4(1): 49–53.

Acknowledgments

Helpful comments and suggestions for the Singapore case study were received from: Clive Briffett of the Nature Society and the National University of Singapore; Billy Chew and Michelle Tan of the Singapore Ministry of the Environment; Mrs. Chew Wai Chan of the Singapore Public Utilities Board; Chan Lai Leng of the Ministry of Communications; Waheeda Rahim of the National Parks Board; Foo Tuan Seik of the National University of Singapore; and Tang Puay Ling of the Singapore Urban Redevelopment Authority. Useful advice on the Zabbaleen case study was provided by Dina Fakhry of Environmental Quality International (Egypt).

CHAPTER 10

The Frontiers: Conclusions and Conundrums

Chapter Outline

- Principles for sustaining urban development in the twenty-first century
- Practical lessons learned for planning and managing
- Tensions and false dichotomies
- What we still need to know
- References

This final chapter draws some conclusions about planning and managing cities in a more environmentally sustainable way in the twenty-first century. It also highlights areas of concern and uncertainty for the attention of scholars and practitioners alike. Conclusions are drawn about both principles and lessons for planning and management. Areas of concern involve tensions and false dichotomies for the urban environment, while uncertainty is addressed in a section that identifies what we still need to know.

Principles for Sustaining Urban Development in the Twenty-First Century

Principles for urban environmental planning and management can be distilled from Chapters 2, 3, and 4, as well as from literature that explicitly seeks to guide cities towards more sustainable paths. In summary form, the key principles for sustaining urban development in the twenty-first century are:

- *Address fundamental problems.* While priorities will differ across cities, planning and management should focus on improving environmental health, reducing pollution, and conserving resources while minimizing wastes, developing capacity for urban environmental planning and management, reducing vulnerability to hazards, and protecting natural and cultural heritages.
- *Deal with underlying causes.* Addressing fundamentals rather than symptoms requires a focus on the key culprits: lack of public awareness and participation; inadequate governance; poor policies; and insufficient knowledge.
- *Design with nature.* Many ecological concepts can be used to help incorporate the environment into urban development: Examples include the interconnectedness of problems from

Table 10-1 Conventional versus Ecological Design

Issue	Conventional design	Ecological design
Key criteria	Economic return	Human and ecological health
Form	Standard approaches are copied around the globe	Designs respond to the bioregion and local culture, needs, and conditions
Energy	Bias toward nonrenewable fossil fuels and nuclear energy	Bias toward renewable energy and reduction of greenhouse gases
Materials use	High degree of waste, with air, water, and land degradation	Emphasis on reuse, recycling, ease of repair, flexibility, and durability
Time horizon	Short-term	Long-run
Spatial scale	Focus on one scale	Consider interrelationships and integrate across scales
Relationship with environment	Design is imposed on nature for better control; nature is hidden	Design works with nature as a partner; nature is visible
Knowledge base	Narrow disciplinary focus	Integrate across disciplines
Decision-making	Top-down and expert-driven	Participatory

Source: Summarized and adapted from Van der Ryn and Cowan 1996, 26–28.

the local through the global level, nutrient recycling, the importance of diverse systems, variations between city and environmental boundaries, carrying capacity, synergy, and urban metabolism. These concepts of ecological design are quite different from conventional design principles currently in use (see Table 10-1 for comparison).

- *Share, adapt, and replicate successful approaches.* Communities and cities should document what works; learn from others; select or modify planning and management techniques appropriate to their needs and conditions; and apply successful approaches and lessons from elsewhere (this is a message from Chapters 7, 8, and 9).
- *Humanize cities.* Seek approaches that make nature visible, improve accessibility to natural spaces, encourage people to walk and interact, and increase the aesthetic appeal of the built and natural landscape (derived from Lyman 1997 and Van der Ryn and Cowan 1996).

Figure 10-1 Urban greening in a slum community, Jakarta, Indonesia.

Practical Lessons Learned for Planning and Managing

Chapters 5, 7, 8, and 9 contain a rich set of lessons for guiding practitioners to plan and manage their cities in a more sustainable fashion. Local environmental action planning will be more successful if the following lessons are internalized:

- *Start with the problems of the poor and vulnerable.* Because many urban environmental problems disproportionately affect low-income communities, women, children, the elderly, and the disabled, planning should disproportionately address their needs.

- *Involve stakeholders.* Planning and implementation of LEAPs requires political commitment, bureaucratic support, expert advice, and the participation of those concerned with and affected by environmental problems.
- *Use clear sets of criteria, objectives, and indicators.* Criteria should be applied to strategically rank problems and select priority solutions; objectives and quantifiable targets should be established so that cities specify where they are going; and indicators should be monitored and evaluated so that cities know whether they are achieving their vision of sustainability and environmental quality.
- *Find least-cost solutions.* Select appropriate and affordable technologies, incorporate environmental costs and benefits, and conduct appropriate economic analyses. Then, develop cost-effective solutions that pay their way.
- *Recognize and build capacity.* Realistic options should be pursued that are consistent with existing capacity; capacity should be expanded by developing institutional innovations, seeking partnerships with other stakeholders, improving municipal finances, using special opportunities, applying leveraging strategies, networking among cities, and strategically using external support.
- *Institutionalize the environmental dimension.* Environmental considerations should be integrated into the standard procedures of government, the private sector, voluntary organizations, and individuals through capacity building and public awareness measures.

These lessons can be applied within the framework for local environmental action planning that is developed in Part 2 of the text (Chapters 5 through 7).

Lessons learned for the day-to-day management of environmental problems in cities include:

- *Pursue win-win solutions.* Use management instruments and approaches that solve two or more problems at the same time or that deliver positive economic *and* environmental benefits.
- *Use a combination of instruments.* Management instruments, such as regulations and economic incentives, should be combined in the most effective package to achieve a clear set of management objectives.
- *Empower stakeholders.* Implement solutions that provide stakeholders with the resources to assess and solve their own problems, to participate in decision-making and implementation, and to improve governance.
- *Internalize the elements of good governance.* Management decisions should help realize the principles of subsidiarity, transparency and increased awareness, accountability, participation, and partnership.
- *Implement and learn over the long term.* Many environmental problems require sustained attention over a long time period to be solved. Solutions do not always work in their original form. So, a longer implementation period also allows for experimentation, learning, and adjustment.
- *Use the market as well as nature.* Management solutions should incorporate consumer preferences, opportunities for involving the private and informal sectors, affordability, full-cost recovery, the possible need to subsidize low-income groups, and linking environmental improvement with the development of economic opportunities.

Tensions and False Dichotomies

There are a number of tensions that have been identified in the field of urban environmental planning and management. Some are legitimate while others are false dichotomies. Tensions worthy of attention include: short versus long-term considerations; trade-offs between environmental, economic, and social concerns; complexity versus simplicity; and urban versus rural concerns. False dichotomies include analysis versus process; centralized versus local approaches; and integrated versus sector-specific solutions.

Governments typically have limited political horizons that favor short-term solutions, while many environmental problems require a longer period of sustained attention. There is also a time horizon tension regarding the distribution of costs and benefits. If benefits are too far in the future while costs are immediate, it may be difficult to garner public support. An example is local responses to climate change: Communities must make sacrifices now, but the benefits of reducing global warming, while uncertain, are likely to occur in the medium or long-term (OECD 1996). The implications are that solutions to environmental problems should yield some politically attractive short-term benefits as well as some immediate economic or social returns.

Rapid economic development and growth policies have long been associated with negative environmental and social impacts. Conversely, municipalities may resist implementing environmental policies that could drive off jobs and industries to other cities. From the social perspective, it is often the well-off who benefit most from environmental and economic development policies (e.g., with better access to often-subsidized water, sanitation, and waste collection services). The implication is that environmental strategies for cities must complement economic development and efforts to improve social equity. This calls for win-win-win solutions (for the environment, the economy, and the poor) such as incentives to attract environmentally friendly enterprises, improvements in providing water supply and sanitation services, better public transportation and traffic management, and energy efficiency in homes and industries. Even with all-win solutions, cities face budget constraints that necessitate tradeoffs between options. Thus, there is an additional need to focus on the most urgent and highest-priority solutions that yield multiple benefits.

A tension can arise between the need for simple and complex solutions. The public and politicians may be more amenable to a few easily understood answers, while experts can stress the importance of comprehensive solutions. This argues for a process that prioritizes problems while developing a sophisticated understanding of their underlying causes. Then, the complexity of the response to a limited number of critical problems can be geared to the nature of each problem. Two other implications for urban environmental planning and management arise from this tension. First, decisions and choices must involve political and social considerations as well as technical factors (Cohen 1995). Then, more complex solutions that resolve more than one problem along with simpler options might be pursued.

The final tension is between cities and their hinterlands: Resource consumption and waste generation are intense in urban areas, but more often than not the negative impacts of resource production or extraction and waste absorption are felt in rural areas. The alternatives for diminishing this tension include internalizing the cost of urban externalities using market mechanisms, pursuing self-reliant urban development, and redesigning urban areas so that they are more compact and resource-efficient. Haughton (1997) suggests a fourth path: balancing the needs and rights of rural and urban areas equitably by regulating flows of environmental value and compensating for damages. This would require implementing LEAPs that had governance, regulatory, and market mechanisms for both urban and rural areas.

Moving to the false dichotomies, environmental planning and management in cities can be plagued with an unnecessary tension between analysis and process. Certain stakeholders will prefer an emphasis on substance, while others will be more concerned with procedures for making decisions. In fact, analysis and process must go hand in hand. The process of identifying and ranking priority problems must be informed by good analysis. Similarly, the results of consultative and planning processes can help set the terms of reference for ensuing analysis. If a tension exists, it is the need to strike a balance between the findings of sound analytical studies and the concerns of various stakeholders that may not necessarily reflect the findings of experts (Bartone et al. 1994). This balancing is one of the main outcomes of informed consultation.

A second unnecessary tension is that between integrated and sector-specific approaches. We have seen how many environmental problems cut across sectors, jurisdictions, and media. However, the real world is rarely organized along environmental lines. The way out of this dilemma is to analyze problems and develop strategies using an approach that is cross-sectoral, inter-jurisdictional, and multimedia. However, implementation usually works best by carrying out sector-specific solutions through existing institutions. Implementation can be enhanced through partnerships and coordination under the guise of a citywide or regionwide action plan that is agreed to by key implementing authorities.

A final false dichotomy is whether to pursue solutions in a decentralized or centralized way. Decentralized approaches enable more public participation, accountability, and attention to local conditions. On the other hand, the desire for a central force to deal with problems between people and the environment goes back to the Malthusian concern about population growth with declining resources, and has been taken up again with concern for global environmental problems (OECD 1996). In reality, no level of government or society has the full set of powers, funds, and skills to solve urban environmental problems. Ideally, the principle of subsidiarity should be followed. However, each level of institutions will have comparative advantages. Central government, for example, is best suited for establishing minimum environmental standards, national environmental policy objectives, and environmentally sound macroeconomic policies. A regional authority is often most appropriate for environmental problems that spill over jurisdictions or that have ecological rather than administrative boundaries. Coordination and partnerships between different levels will ultimately be needed to fully realize sustainable approaches to urban development.

What We Still Need to Know

A number of knowledge gaps exist that need to be filled through additional research and evaluation of practice. These include one general conundrum concerning leadership, followed by sets of three uncertainties each for urban environmental planning and management.

The examples and cases cited in this text provide many instances of good practice, but they usually involve one problem or approach; there are few cities that exemplify good practice across sectors, problems, and institutions. Why are there not more cities like Singapore, Curitiba, and Chattanooga? One possible answer is that these cities have benefited from strong, innovative, and consistent political leadership. In fact, when one digs more deeply into most of the examples in the text, there will almost always be at least one public and/or private entrepreneur that has made things happen. Entrepreneurship has also been identified as one of the key elements of successful urban development in the United States (Garvin 1995).

Often, this visionary leadership has been encapsulated in a single person, for example, former prime minister Lee Kuan Yew in Singapore and former mayor Jaime Lerner in Curitiba. Lerner, an architect and past president of Curitiba's urban research institute, had a number of special advantages, including the time to develop approaches for sustainable urban development, the creativity to seek win-win solutions, and the political will to carry out unpopular decisions (see Box 10-1). This translated into public support that allowed him to be reelected twice, and for his policies to continue in effect even after he left office.

If leadership is a critical element for successful design and implementation of urban environmental actions, then several research topics are worth exploring in order to deepen our understanding of this phenomenon. Effective environmental and urban leaders cannot be cloned, but it may be possible to enhance the background conditions that lead to their emergence.

BOX

In 1972, Mayor Jaime Lerner of Curitiba, Brazil, was poised to close a major downtown street and turn it into a pedestrian corridor. This was to be the first step in a plan that would integrate land use, public transportation, and road development in order to reduce congestion and pollution.

This decision was developed and discussed during a series of meetings with stakeholders. Two groups were strongly opposed: Shopkeepers along the street feared that they would lose business, and motorists did not want to start down the slippery slope of reduced access and mobility. Mayor Lerner decided to act despite this opposition. First, vehicle flows were restricted to parallel streets, with only parking allowed on what was to become the pedestrian street. Then, one night, the mayor ordered municipal workers to close off the street. The next morning, enormous sheets of paper were unrolled on the street and children were invited to paint watercolors. This effectively blocked motorists who had threatened to ignore the traffic ban and drive on the street.

Both opposition groups were proved wrong. After an initial decline, business along the street actually improved, and real estate values increased. Motorists have benefited from reduced congestion, faster travel times, and the option of leaving their cars at home in favor of a highly efficient public transportation system. Mayor Lerner also benefited from these and other decisions that involved political will and decision-making. He was reelected to office twice and he maintained an approval rating of 70 percent.

Box 10-1 Leadership and urban environmental management.

Source: Rabinovitch with Leitmann 1993; Rabinovitch and Leitmann 1996.

Entrepreneurial leaders are risk-takers who are motivated by a perceived high probability or high payoff of success. How can an enabling environment be created to reduce risks and stimulate more entrepreneurial activity to resolve urban environmental problems? Potential entrepreneurs also need the time, space, and resources to develop their ideas and mobilize coalitions. What role can be played by forms of support such as incubators that have accelerated software and hardware development in Silicon Valley? Finally, what role will increased environmental awareness and improved governance play in forming future generations of urban leaders?

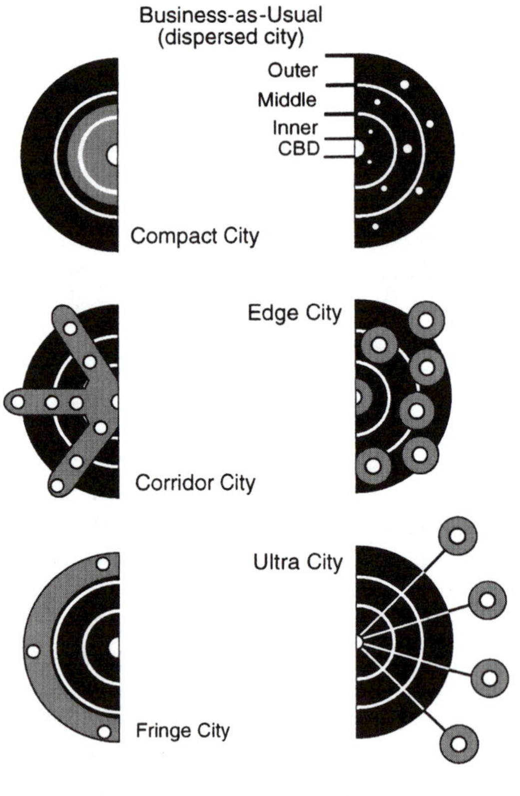

Figure 10-2 Possible urban forms for environmental investigation.

SOURCE: Newton 1997, 9.

Research for Planning

Three concepts merit further investigation in order to improve urban environmental planning: (1) ideal city form; (2) knowledge about the impact of problems; and especially (3) information about the potential importance of climate change for cities. Planners and urban activists often have a notion of what the ideal city should look like in the back of their heads, and this can affect the way that objectives are set, problems are defined, and options are selected. Is there a city form that is optimal for the environment? Conventional wisdom calls for a compact city where infrastructure and service delivery costs are lower, fewer resources are used for travel, and consequently pollution per capita is less than in a more dispersed city. Conversely, urban sprawl is linked with increased air and water pollution, loss of open space and prime agricultural land, and destruction of natural habitat (Sierra Club 1998).

There are, however, several different forms for urban development, as summarized by the simple diagrams in Figure 10-2. Modeling work in Australia (Newton 1997) suggests that residents of compact cities can be more exposed to concentrated air pollution; corridor cities turn out to be the optimal form, at least as far as air pollution is concerned, because of their low energy use and residential exposure patterns. In addition, the move toward urban compaction may face a set of economic, technical, and political barriers that make it unachievable (Breheny 1997). So, the research questions are twofold: (1) for a given urban setting, what city form will yield the best environmental outcomes (e.g., reduced pollution, improved environmental health, and more efficient use of resources)?, and (2) if there is an optimal urban form for the environment, how can it be achieved?

The second planning concept for further research is that of knowledge gaps. In most cities, there is at least one environmental problem, if not many, where the dynamics, extent, and magnitude of the problem are unknown. Either data do not exist or have not been collected and analyzed. This limits the ability of an informed consultation process to fully consider the range of problems for ranking and follow-up action. Thus, investigation is needed to fill the knowledge gaps by: (1) conducting primary research on unexplored problems; (2) developing an understanding of the cause-effect relationships behind the problem; (3) analyzing data to determine the extent of the problem (e.g., which groups of people and ecosystems are most affected); and (4) assessing the magnitude of the problem in terms of health, economic, and ecological impacts. This work will need to be done on a city-specific basis because each urban area will have its own set of knowledge gaps, and each unexplored problem will vary between cities according to dynamics as well as extent and magnitude of impacts.

One knowledge gap that potentially affects all cities on the planet is that of global warming. Coastal cities may be adversely affected by sea-level rise necessitating investment in protective measures, increased maintenance costs for water and sewerage infrastructure, and the relocation of exposed populations. All cities could experience both negative and positive effects related to changes in temperature and rainfall. These changes would affect crop production, water production, the incidence of fires, human health related to temperature change, energy demand, and energy supply (White and Whitney 1992). Uncertainty concerning the urban impact of global warming can be reduced through research on: (1) the extent and magnitude of impacts, updated as new information about global warming becomes available; (2) coping strategies for mitigating probable impacts, with a particular emphasis on low-cost options for developing cities; (3) design options for new settlements that are better suited to handle the effects of changing temperature and rainfall; and (4) policies, programs, and projects (e.g., the Climate Change Initiative in Chapter 9) that can reduce urban emissions of greenhouse gases.

Research for Management

Three research questions can be posed for urban environmental management: (1) within a city, who will pay for improving environmental quality, and how?; (2) within an ecosystem, what is the scope for regional environmental management?; and (3) around a city, what management measures can be taken to bolster food security? The implementation of environmental management options will require additional financial resources. These can be mobilized within a city through reallocation of the existing budget, transfer of some costs to the private sector, new taxes and charges, and so on. They can also be obtained from outside the city via central government transfers, borrowing on the capital market, loan guarantees, and grants from foundations or other donors. Research questions might include: What is the best mix of financing options for a particular city? To what extent can costs be fully recovered—or will subsidies be required for certain investments? Who will bear the costs of financing (e.g., polluters, high-income neighborhoods, other cities, other levels of government)?

Next, because many environmental problems have their own borders, what are the prospects for management on an extra-municipal basis? Regions that encompass cities might include air and watersheds; immediate ecosystems such as forests, basins, or plateaus; or larger ecoregions such as one of the 21 critical ecoregions identified by the Sierra Club for North America. Thinking about regional management of urban environmental problems (e.g., Atkinson 1992, Pivo 1996, Dyck 1998) has been exploratory and needs further development. Promising areas for research include: (1) what are the regional boundaries for environmental management that surround major cities?; (2) what are the political and jurisdictional constraints as well as opportunities facing

(a)

(b)

Figure 10-3 Urban food security in Lusaka, Zambia, and Singapore.

regional management of areas that transcend municipal and even international borders (as in the case of Canada and the United States for the Pacific Northwest bioregion)?; and (3) what are the most effective forms of governance for environmental regions?

Finally, the Worldwatch Institute has identified water supply and food security as two of the major threats to sustainable urbanization (Brown 1998). Water and food scarcity will increase the cost of living in cities and could slow the pace as well as quality of urbanization. We already possess a good deal of knowledge about water supply and demand management. However, less is known about urban food systems and the option of enhancing urban agricultural production in particular. One commentator concludes that:

> *The awareness that most academics, planners, and city officials have of food systems and foodsheds today is comparable to their awareness of environmental issues 30 years ago—something just starting to become visible on their radar screens (Dahlberg 1998, 26).*

Additional research could yield valuable information on: (1) developing measures to provide a degree of security against supply disruptions and rising prices; (2) lowering barriers to urban agricultural production, such as constraints on access to resources, inputs, and services (UNDP 1996); and (3) expanding general awareness about the existence and dynamics of food systems and foodsheds.

A Concluding Note

This text is really about a paradigm shift. Box 10-2 suggests that changing peoples' mindset is the most effective way to change a system's goals, rules, and feedback structures. Urbanists have worked for too long without considering the environmental consequences of urban development. Environmentalists have persisted in a rural or global focus without understanding the critical urban and local dimensions of problems. Urban environmental planning and management is a means of bridging these gaps, introducing change in systems, and modifying behavior toward more sustainable cities in the twenty-first century.

Mindsets are probably the hardest thing to change—and thus the lowest feasible point to intervene in systems. That does not mean we should not try all the same. Thomas Kuhn's advice about paradigm shifts suggests that we should:

- Emphatically and continuously stress the inadequacy and failings of the old paradigm.
- Similarly advocate for the comparative advantages of the new paradigm.
- Support advocates of the new paradigm in places of public visibility and power.
- Work with change agents and open-minded people rather than wasting time with reactionaries.

We look forward to working with you in the new century!

BOX

If cities are sets of systems (ecological, economic, political, social, etc.), then systems theory might tell us something about the most promising ways forward. Donnella Meadows, a system analyst famous for her environmental work with the Club of Rome, concludes that the nine most effective places to intervene in a system (and their urban applications) are:

1. ***The mindset or paradigm.*** **This is the source of a system, from which goals, rules, and feedback structures arise.**
2. ***The goals of the system.*** **Incorporate environmental goals in the system and change will ripple through the succeeding intervention points.**
3. ***The power of self-organization.*** **Develop new institutions, information flows, feedback loops, material stocks and flows, and/or market rules.**
4. ***The rules of the system.*** **This includes incentives, punishments, and constraints.**
5. ***Information flows.*** **Increase the transparency of environmental decision-making, raise awareness, and close knowledge gaps to support the stakeholder feedback loop.**
6. ***Driving positive feedback loops.*** **Intervene sooner rather than later to reduce the growth of self-reinforcing negative impacts (such as a potential epidemic) and avoid system collapse.**
7. ***Regulating negative feedback loops.*** **Environmental management objectives, a monitoring system, and response mechanisms or properly functioning markets that internalize costs.**
8. ***Material stocks and flows.*** **Urban spatial form, the layout, and technologies for environmental infrastructure and services, and buffers to absorb flows of waste.**
9. ***Market rules.*** **Parameters such as subsidies, taxes, and standards for urban environmental services and problems.**

Box 10-2 Places to intervene in systems.

SOURCE: Meadows 1997.

References

Atkinson, Adrian. 1992. The urban bioregion as "sustainable development" paradigm. Paper presented to International Workshop on Planning for Sustainable Urban Development: Cities and Natural Resource Systems in Developing Countries, Cardiff. July 13–17.

Bartone, Carl, Janis Bernstein, Josef Leitmann, and Jochen Eigen. 1994. Toward environmental strategies for cities: Policy considerations for urban environmental management in developing countries. UMP Policy Paper No. 18. Washington, D.C.: World Bank.

Breheny, Michael. 1997. Urban compaction: Feasible and acceptable? *Cities* 14(4): 209–217.

Brown, Lester. 1998. The future of growth. In Lester Brown, Christopher Flavin, and Hilary French. *State of the world: A Worldwatch Institute report on progress toward a sustainable society.* New York and London: W. W. Norton & Company.

Cohen, Michael. 1995. Finding the frontier: Posing the unanswered questions. In Ismail Serageldin, Michael Cohen, and K. C. Sivaramakrishnan. The human face of the urban environment. Environmentally Sustainable Development Proceedings No. 6. Washington, D.C.: World Bank.

Dahlberg, Kenneth. 1998. The global threat to food security. *Urban Age* Winter: 24–26.

Dyck, Robert. 1998. Integrating planning and sustainability theory for local benefit. *Local Environment* 3(1): 27–41.

Garvin, Alexander. 1995. *The American city: What works, what doesn't.* New York: McGraw-Hill.

Haughton, Graham. 1997. Developing sustainable urban development models. *Cities* 14(4): 189–195.

Lyman, Francesca. 1997. Twelve gates to the city: A dozen ways to build strong, livable, and sustainable urban areas. *Sierra* May/June: 29–35.

Meadows, Donnella. 1997. Places to intervene in a system (in increasing order of effectiveness). *Whole Earth* Winter: 78–84.

Newton, Peter. 1997. Urban infrastructure: Reshaping cities for a more sustainable future. Report to the Australian Academy of Technological Sciences and Engineering. Melbourne: Commonwealth Scientific and Industrial Research Organization.

OECD (Organization for Economic Cooperation and Development). 1996. Innovative policies for sustainable urban development: The ecological city. Paris: OECD.

Pivo, Gary. 1996. Toward sustainable urbanization on Mainstreet Cascadia. *Cities* 13(5): 339–354.

Rabinovitch, Jonas, with Josef Leitmann. 1993. Environmental innovation and management in Curitiba. UMP Working Paper No. 1. Washington, D.C.: World Bank.

Rabinovitch, Jonas, and Josef Leitmann. 1996. Urban planning in Curitiba. *Scientific American* 274(3): 46–53.

Sierra Club. 1998. *The dark side of the American dream: The costs and consequences of suburban sprawl.* San Francisco: Sierra Club.

UNDP (United Nations Development Programme). 1996. Urban agriculture: Food, jobs and sustainable cities. New York: UNDP.

Van der Ryn, Sim, and Stuart Cowan. 1996. *Ecological design.* Washington, D.C., and Covelo, California: Island Press.

White, Rodney, and Joseph Whitney. 1992. Cities and the environment: An overview. In Richard Stren, Rodney White, and Joseph Whitney (eds.). *Sustainable cities: Urbanization and the environment in international perspective.* Boulder: Westview Press.

ANNEX A

Environmental Data for the World's 35 Largest Cities

This annex presents a set of available data relating to the urban environment for 35 cities that are estimated to be the largest in the world by the year 2015. As you will see, many data are missing, which indicates the magnitude of the task ahead.

Unless otherwise noted, the data are for the year 1993. The primary source for this information is data drawn from the UNCHS indicators program as summarized in: WRI et al. (World Resources Institute, United Nations Environment Programme, United Nations Development Programme, and World Bank). 1998. *World resources 1998–99: A guide to the global environment*. New York: Oxford University Press. Additional information was drawn from: Girardet, Herbert. 1996. *The Gaia atlas of cities: New directions for sustainable urban living*. London: Gaia Books Limited.

Data	Bangalore	Bangkok	Beijing	Bogota	Bombay	Buenos Aires	Cairo
Socioeconomic:							
1995 population (millions)	4.8	6.5	11.3	6.1	15.1	11.8	9.7
2015 population (est.)	8.0	9.8	15.6	8.4	26.2	13.9	14.4
Urban density (persons/ha)	246	—	—	194	603	—	—
Crowding (persons/room)	2.8	3.2	1.2	1.5	4.2	1.3	1.5
City product (1993 $/capita)	264	—	—	1790	275	—	—
% poor households	12	—	—	23	17	—	43
Infrastructure (% of households with):							
Water	47	—	—	99	55	—	89
Sewerage	35	—	—	99	51	—	91
Solid waste collection	96	—	—	94	90	—	65
Electricity	82	—	—	99	90	—	99
Resource use:							
Water (L/capita/day)	93	—	—	176	127	—	—
Solid waste (kg/capita/day)	0.4	—	—	0.6	0.5	—	0.5
Pollution:							
% wastewater treated	68	—	—	—	10	—	98
Air quality (1990)*	3	3	1	5	3	7	—
Cars per 1000 population	130	—	—	52	51	—	59
% work trips by public transit	46	—	—	75	79	—	58
Ambient noise level (1990)*	4	7	4	4	5	3	7

	Calcutta	Chengdu	Delhi	Dhaka	Istanbul	Jakarta	Karachi
Socioeconomic:							
1995 population (millions)	11.9	4.3	9.9	8.5	7.9	8.6	9.7
2015 population (est.)	17.3	7.8	16.9	19.5	12.3	13.9	19.4
Urban density (persons/ha)	—	—	—	—	—	—	—
Crowding (persons/room)	3.0	—	2.4	3.1	1.6	3.4	3.3
City product (1993 $/capita)	—	465	209	219	—	2843	—
% poor households	—	—	17	54	—	9	—
Infrastructure (% of households with):							
Water	—	99	57	80	—	15	—
Sewerage	—	37	40	44	—	0	—
Solid waste collection	—	—	77	50	—	84	—
Electricity	—	100	70	74	—	99	—
Resource use:							
Water (L/capita/day)	—	273	133	119	—	188	—
Solid waste (kg/capita/day)	—	0.9	1.2	0.1	—	2.6	—
Pollution:							
% wastewater treated	—	37	69	55	—	16	—
Air quality (1990)*	1	—	1	—	—	1	9
Cars per 1000 population	—	39	205	7	—	68	—
% work trips by public transit	—	—	53	—	—	38	—
Ambient noise level (1990)*	4	—	5	4	7	6	9

* Relative scale: 1 = worst; 10 = best

Data	Kinshasa	Lagos	Lahore	Lima	London	Los Angeles	Madras
Socioeconomic							
1995 population (millions)	4.2	10.3	5.0	6.7	7.6	12.4	6.0
2015 population (est.)	9.4	24.6	10.0	9.4	7.6	14.2	9.2
Urban density (persons/ha)	208	194	37	264	—	—	296
Crowding (persons/room)	—	5.8	4.5	2.3	0.6	0.5	2.9
City product (1993 $/capita)	—	—	428	673	—	—	204
% poor households	70	66	30	29	—	—	19
Infrastructure (% of households with):							
Water	50	65	84	70	—	—	34
Sewerage	3	2	74	69	—	—	37
Solid waste collection	0	8	50	57	—	—	90
Electricity	40	100	97	76	—	—	82
Resource use:							
Water (L/capita/day)	45	70	194	211	—	—	70
Solid waste (kg/capita/day)	1.2	0.3	1.2	0.5	—	—	0.8
Pollution							
% wastewater treated	3	2	0	5	—	—	0
Air quality (1990)*	—	—	9	—	7	3	—
Cars per 1000 population	25	4	45	49	—	—	102
% work trips by public transit	61	54	16	65	—	—	42
Ambient noise level (1990)*	—	7	8	7	8	6	8

	Manila	Mexico City	Moscow	New York	Osaka	Paris	Rio de Janeiro
Socioeconomic:							
1995 population (millions)	9.3	16.6	9.3	16.3	10.6	9.5	10.2
2015 population (est.)	14.7	19.2	9.3	17.6	10.6	9.7	11.9
Urban density (persons/ha)	148	—	—	72	—	109	136
Crowding (persons/room)	3.0	1.9	1.3	0.5	0.6	0.8	0.8
City product (1993 $/capita)	2134	—	5100	30,952	—	35,060	5850
% poor households	13	—	15	16	—	—	19
Infrastructure (% of households with):							
Water	95	—	100	100	—	100	95
Sewerage	80	—	100	99	—	98	87
Solid waste collection	85	—	100	—	—	100	88
Electricity	86	—	100	—	—	100	100
Resource use:							
Water (L/capita/day)	—	—	555	466	—	212	299
Solid waste (kg/capita/day)	0.7	—	0.8	1.7	—	1.3	1.1
Pollution:							
% wastewater treated	—	—	100	100	—	45	23
Air quality (1990)*	6	2	3	5	9	8	8
Cars per 1000 population	94	—	138	232	—	426	177
% work trips by public transit	40	—	85	51	—	40	67
Ambient noise level (1990)*	4	6	6	8	4	6	7

* Relative scale: 1 = worst; 10 = best

Data	Sao Paulo	Seoul	Shanghai	Shenyang	Tehran	Tianjin	Tokyo
Socioeconomic							
1995 population (millions)	16.5	11.6	13.6	5.1	6.8	9.4	27.0
2015 population (est.)	20.3	13.0	18.0	7.7	10.2	13.5	28.9
Urban density (persons/ha)	—	—	—	—	—	—	—
Crowding (persons/room)	0.8	2.0	2.0	2.5	1.3	1.2	0.9
City product (1993 $/capita)	—	—	1832	—	—	—	—
% poor households	—	—	—	—	—	—	—
Infrastructure (% of households with)							
Water	—	—	100	—	99	—	—
Sewerage	—	—	58	—	—	—	—
Solid waste collection	—	—	—	—	—	—	—
Electricity	—	—	100	—	100	—	—
Resource use							
Water (L/capita/day)	—	—	271	—	—	—	—
Solid waste (kg/capita/day)	—	—	0.8	—	—	—	—
Pollution							
% wastewater treated	—	—	58	—	—	—	—
Air quality (1990)*	7	3	7	1	1	5	7
Cars per 1000 population	—	—	32	—	28	—	—
% work trips by public transit	—	—	—	—	—	—	—
Ambient noise level (1990)*	6	7	5	6	5	5	4

* Relative scale: 1 = worst; 10 = best

SOURCES: Crowding, air quality, and ambient noise level (Girardet 1996); all others (WRI et al. 1996).

ANNEX B

Resources for the Urban Environment

The most extensive collection of information and links about the urban environment on the World Wide Web can be found at the Urban Environmental Management home page, www.scitech.ac.jp/uem/. A major list service (listserv), Ecocity—Sustainable Urban Development, is available at listserv@searn.sunet.se. For U.S. cities, Tools for a Sustainable Community is an online guide for financial resources, technical assistance, and other support (www.iclei.org/la21/onestop.htm).

Information

Air Pollution

Global Environment Monitoring System (GEMS/AIR): Information and techniques for urban air pollution monitoring and management.

UNEP/DEIA
P.O. Box 30552
Nairobi, KENYA
Web: www.unep.org

URBAIR: Assists Asian cities with the design and implementation of policies, monitoring, and management tools to restore air quality.

c/o World Bank
1818 H St. NW
Washington, DC 20433 USA
Tel: 1-202-458-1598
Fax: 1-202-522-1664
E-mail: jshah@worldbank.org
Web: www.worldbank.org

General

Center of Excellence for Sustainable Development: Provides consultation on sustainable development for communities in the United States and links them to relevant public and private programs.

U.S. Department of Energy
1617 Cole Boulevard
Golden, CO 80401 USA
Tel: 1-303-275-4826
Fax: 1-303-275-4830
E-mail: sustainabledevelopment@hq.doe.gov
Web: www.sustainable.doe.gov

New Ideas in Pollution Regulation: Web site that offers state-of-the-art information and publications on environmental management.

Web: www.worldbank.org/nipr

Office of Sustainable Ecosystems and Communities: Promotes community-based environmental protection through ecosystem planning for local governments.

Web: www.epa.gov/ecocommunity

Organization for Economic Cooperation and Development: Publishes environmental and urban documents primarily focusing on industrialized countries.

2, rue Andre-Pascal
75775 Paris Cedex 16 FRANCE

Tel: 33-1-4524-8200
Fax: 33-1-4910-4276
E-mail: sales@oecd.org
Web: www.oecd.org

Urban Environmental Management: A clearinghouse of information on the Web for the urban environment.

Web: www.soc.titech.ac.jp/uem/

World Resources Institute: Publishes a range of environmental reports, including a biannual guide to the global environment that includes urban environmental indicators.

1709 New York Ave.
Washington, DC 20006 USA
Web: www.wri.org

Worldwatch Institute: Produces a magazine and publications on many environmental topics, including energy, transportation, water, pollution, recycling, infrastructure, and economics.

1776 Massachusetts Ave. NW
Washington, DC 20036 USA
Tel: 1-202-452-1999
Fax: 1-202-296-7365
E-mail: wwpub@worldwatch.org
Web: www.worldwatch.org

Indicators

Cities' State of the Environment: Facilitates access to environmental information for decision-making and awareness-raising in cities.

Longum Park Technology Centre
P.O. Box 1602 Myrene
N-4801 Arendal NORWAY
Tel: 47-370-35650
Fax: 47-370-35050
E-mail: grid@grida.no
Web: www.grida.no/prog/global/citysoei/index.htm

Community Indicators Network: Information and links to U.S. cities that have developed indicators of their long-term health and sustainability.

One Kearny St., 4th Floor
San Francisco, CA 94108 USA
Tel: 1-415-781-1191
Fax: 1-415-781-1198
E-mail: besleme@rprogress.org
Web: www.rprogress.org

Urban Indicators Programme: Global networking facility for assessing progress that cities are making in meeting the aims of the Habitat Agenda and Agenda 21.

UNCHS (Habitat)
P.O. Box 30030
Nairobi, KENYA
Tel: 254-2-623184
Fax: 254-2-624264
E-mail: guo@unchs.org
Web: www.unchs.org/guo

Infrastructure and Technology

Environment and Municipal Online: Group of online communities for professionals in water/wastewater, pollution control, public works, and solid waste industries.

Web: www.environmentonline.com

Public Technologies, Inc.: Develops, tests, and disseminates innovative and sustainable environmental solutions that protect natural systems, improve public health, and encourage economic vitality (mostly in the United States).

E-mail: wood-lewis@pti.nw.dc.us
Web: pti.nw.dc.us/env.htm

Journals

Cities: International journal of urban policy and planning that covers environmental issues in both the developed and developing world.

The Boulevard, Langford Lane
Kidlington, Oxford OX5 1BG UK
Tel: 44-1865-843000
Fax: 44-1865-843010
E-mail: amkirby@ccit.arizona.edu

EcoCity Journal: Regularly reports on sustainable community issues.

485 Leatherfern Place
Sanibel, FL 33957 USA
Tel: 1-813-472-1450
Fax: 1-813-472-2625

Environment and Urbanization: The premier journal devoted to environmental issues in cities; published by International Institute for Environment and Development.

3 Endsleigh St.
London WC1H ODD UK
Tel: 44-171-388-2117
Fax: 44-171-388-2826
E-mail: david@iied.org
Web: www.iied.org/human.html

HABITAT International: Journal of contemporary urban issues facing cities around the world; regularly includes articles with an environmental focus.

Dept. of Urban & Regional Planning
611 Taft Dr.
Champagne, IL 61820 USA
E-mail: choguill@uiuc.edu

Journal of Urban Design: Scholarly journal on theory, research, and practice in urban design, development, and the environment.

Carfax Publishing Limited
P.O. Box 25, Abingdon
Oxfordshire OX14 UE UK
Tel: 44-1235-401000
Fax: 44-1235-401550
E-mail: sales@carfax.co.uk
Web: www.carfax.co.uk/jud-ad.htm

Journal of Urban Technology: Publishes articles on the effects of new technologies on urban environments.

Carfax Publishing Limited
P.O. Box 25, Abingdon
Oxfordshire OX14 UE UK
Tel: 44-1235-401000
Fax: 44-1235-401550
E-mail: sales@carfax.co.uk
Web: www.carfax.co.uk/jud-ad.htm

Local Environment: Academic journal that reports on international experience with local environmental management.

School of Urban Development
South Bank University
London SW8 2JZ UK
E-mail: b.evans@sbu.ac.uk

Planning: Regularly contains articles on urban environmental planning and management, with a U.S. focus.

122 S. Michigan Ave., Suite 1600
Chicago, IL 60603 USA
Tel: 1-312-431-9100
Web: www.planning.org

Third World Planning Review: Often contains articles focusing on urban environmental issues in developing countries.

P.O. Box 147
Liverpool L69 3BX UK
Tel: 44-51-794-2235
Fax: 44-51-7086502

Urban Age: Global forum to promote the exchange of ideas, knowledge, and information about cities.

World Bank, Room F4K-256
1818 H St. NW
Washington, DC 20433 USA
Fax: 1-202-522-3223
E-mail: mbergen@worldbank.org

The Urban Ecologist: Forum for reporting and comment on sustainable cities.

Urban Ecology
405 4th St., Suite 900
Oakland, CA 94612 USA
Tel: 1-510-251-6330
Fax: 1-510-251-2117
E-mail: ueedit@aol.com
Web: www.urbanecology.org

Urban Ecosystems: International journal devoted to scientific investigations of the ecology of urban environments and their policy implications.

Subscriptions:
Chapman & Hall
Cheriton House, North Way, Andover
Hampshire SP10 5BE UK
Tel: 44-1264-342-713
Fax: 44-1264-342-807
E-mail: chsub@itps.co.uk
Web: www.wkap.nl

Natural and Human-Induced Hazards

Awareness and Preparedness for Emergencies at the Local Level: Produces newsletters, technical guides, and other publications to help communities prevent or mitigate disasters that threaten life, property, or the environment.

Industry and Environment Unit/UNEP
39-43 quai Andre Citroen
75739 Paris FRANCE

International Decade for Natural Disaster Reduction: United Nations effort to make people aware of what they can do to make themselves safer from natural disasters.

Palais des Nations
1211 Geneva 10 SWITZERLAND
Tel: 41-22-798-6894
Fax: 41-22-733-8695
E-mail: idndr@dha.unicc.org

Urban Agriculture and Greening

Cities Feeding People: Expertise and information on sustainable urban agricultural systems, including food and water security and wastewater reuse.

International Development Resource Center
25 Albert St., P.O. Box 8500
Ottawa, ON K1G 3H9 CANADA
Tel: 1-613-236-6163
Fax: 1-613-567-7749
E-mail: lmougeot@idrc.ca

Natural Resources Systems Programme/Peri-Urban Research: Research and documentation on optimizing the use of peri-urban natural resources.

Natural Resources Institute
Chatham Maritime
Kent ME4 4TB UK
Tel: 44-1634-883111
Fax: 44-1634-883959
Web: www.nri.org

Urban Planning and Management

Capacity Building for the Urban Environment: Research and documentation program on approaches to building local capacity for environmental management in developing countries.

Institute for Housing and Urban Development Studies
P.O. Box 1935
3000 BX Rotterdam NETHERLANDS
Tel: 31-10-402-1523
Fax: 31-10-404-5671
E-mail: e.frank@ihs.nl

URBANET: International data bank of expertise and information on urban management and regional development.

Postfach 51 80
65726 Eschborn GERMANY
Tel: 49-6196-791629
Fax: 49-6196-796104
E-mail: postmaster@gtz.de

Urban Management Programme: Conducts research and issues publications on the urban environment as well as urban infrastructure, land management, poverty, and municipal finance.

UNCHS (Habitat)
P.O. Box 30030
Nairobi, KENYA
Tel: 254-2-623225
Fax: 254-2-624264
E-mail: jochen.eigen@unchs.org

Water and Sanitation

International Environmental Technology Center: Facilitates transfer of environmentally sound technologies for freshwater resources in cities of developing and transition countries.

2-110 Ryokuchi Koen, Tsurumi-Ku
Osaka 538 JAPAN
Tel: 81-6-915-4590
Fax: 81-6-915-0304
E-mail: rmeganck@unep.or.jp
Web: www.unep.or.jp

UNDP-World Bank Water and Sanitation Program: Conducts research and produces publications on affordable water and sanitation options for developing countries.

c/o World Bank
1818 H St. NW
Washington, DC 20433 USA
Tel: 1-202-473-0693
Fax: 1-202-522-3228
Web: www.worldbank.org

Urban Development and Freshwater Resources: Produces information on water resource management for cities in coastal regions and small islands.

UNESCO-CSI
1, rue Miollis
75732 Paris, FRANCE
Fax: 33-1-4568-5808
E-mail: csi@unesco.org
Web: www.unesco.org/csi

Networks and Associations

American Planning Association: The largest U.S. organization working for better-planned communities. It has a wide range of publications and services, including information about the urban environment.

122 S. Michigan Ave., Suite 1600
Chicago, IL 60603 USA
Tel: 1-312-431-9100
Fax: 1-312-431-9985
Web: www.planning.org

CITYNET: Supports networking of cities in the Asia/Pacific region through documentation and dissemination of urban practices and provision of specialized expertise and information.

International Organizations Center
Pacifico-Yokohama
1-1-1 Minato Mirai, Nishi-ku
Yokohama 220 5F JAPAN
Tel: 81-45-233-2161
Fax: 81-45-223-2162
E-mail: mariko@citynet.imasy.org.jp

European Sustainable Cities and Towns Campaign: Supports European cities and towns to promote sustainability at the local level.

Web: cl24.uwe.ac.uk/fbe/euronet/campaign.htm

Healthy Cities Programme and Network: Technical assistance and information exchange to promote health as a goal for sustainable development at the local level.

c/o World Health Organization
20, Avenue Appia
CH-1211 Geneva 27 SWITZERLAND
Tel: 41-22-791-3559
Fax: 41-22-791-4127
E-mail: goldstein@who.ch
Web: www.who.org

International Association for Impact Assessment: Develops local capability to anticipate, plan, and manage sustainable development.

P.O. Box 5256
Fargo, ND 58105 USA
Tel: 1-701-231-1006
Fax: 1-701-231-1007
E-mail: rhamm@ndsuext.nodak.edu
Web: iaia.ext.nodak.edu/iaia

International City Management Association: U.S.-based network documents and disseminates information on good urban environmental and other management practices.

777 N. Capital St. NE, Suite 500
Washington, DC 20002 USA
Tel: 1-202-289-4262
Fax: 1-202-962-3500
Web: www.icma.org

International Council for Local Environmental Initiatives: Connects interested cities and towns to support sustainable development; provides information and support for local Agenda 21s, climate protection, and urban environmental policy.

City Hall, East Tower, 8th Floor
100 Queen St. West
Toronto, ON M5H2N2 CANADA
Tel: 1-416-392-1463
Fax: 1-416-392-1478
E-mail: iclei@iclei.org
Web: www.iclei.org

International Society of City and Regional Planners: International association of urban planners that has sponsored a number of activities related to environmental planning.

Mauritskade 23
2514 HD The Hague NETHERLANDS
Tel: 31-70-346-2654
Fax: 31-70-361-7909
E-mail: isocarp@bart.nl
Web: www.soc.scitech.ac.jp/isocarp

International Union of Local Authorities: Largest association of municipalities with an emphasis on sustainable urban development.

39 Wassenaarseweg
2596CG The Hague NETHERLANDS
Tel: 31-70-324-4032
Fax: 31-70-324-6916
E-mail: iula@iula-hq.nl

International Urban Planning and Environment Association: Network of planners that sponsors a biennial symposium on urban planning and environment.

P.O. Box 800
9700 AV Groningen NETHERLANDS
E-mail: upe@frw.rug.nl
Web: www.frw.rug.nl/upe.html

MEDCITIES: Network of Mediterranean cities to develop environmental programs through exchanges, technical cooperation, training, and environmental audits.

Palais du Pharo
13000 Marseille FRANCE
Tel: 33-91-551763
Fax: 33-91-554736

The Mega-cities Project: Transnational network of civil society, business, government, media, and academic leaders in 20 of the world's largest cities to share and implement urban innovations.

915 Broadway, Suite 1600
New York, NY 10010 USA
Tel: 1-212-979-7350
Fax: 1-212-979-7624
E-mail: nyc@megacities.org
Web: www.megacities.org

Metropolis: World association of megacities that holds regular meetings and maintains a focus on the urban environment.

61, rue de Babylone
75007 Paris FRANCE
Tel: 33-1-5385-6262
Fax: 33-1-5385-6269
Web: www.metropolis.org

Sustainable Cities Project: Network to incorporate environmental objectives in European urban development strategies.

Urban Environment Unit/DG XI
European Commission
Tel: 32-2-296-8702
Fax: 32-2-296-9554

Sustainable Communities Network: Provides resources and case studies to help create healthy, vital, sustainable communities.

1794 Columbia Road NW
Washington, DC 20009 USA
Tel: 1-202-328-8160
E-mail: concern@igc.apc.org
Web: www.sustainable.org/index/html

Tree City Initiative: Network that links arboriculture, forestry, ecological landscaping, horticulture, project management, and city planning.

Graf-Kirchberg-Strasse 26
89257 Illertissen GERMANY
Tel: 49-7303-43776
Fax: 49-7303-42114
E-mail: 100441.3577@compuserve.com
Web: ourworld.compuserve.com/homepages/G_kuchelmeister

United Towns Organization: International association of cities with a greater presence in French-speaking countries; maintains a focus on sustainable urban development.

22, rue d'Alsace
92532 Levallois-Perret FRANCE
Tel: 33-1-4739-3686
Fax: 33-1-4739-3685

Urban Environment Forum: Network for exchanging knowledge about urban environmental planning and management.

P.O. Box 30030
Nairobi, KENYA
Tel: 254-2-624205
Fax: 254-2-623715
E-mail: uef@unchs.org

Financial and Other Assistance

Developing-Country Cities

Institute for Sustainable Communities: Promotes sustainable development, environmental protection, and participatory democracy in Central and Eastern European cities.

56 College Street
Montpelier, VT 05602 USA
Tel: 1-802-229-2900
Fax: 1-802-229-2919
E-mail: isc@iscvt.org
Web: www.iscvt.org

Local Initiative Facility for Urban Environment (LIFE): Promotes local-local dialogue and action to improve the living conditions in low-income urban communities.

Management Development and Governance Division/UNDP
One United Nations Plaza
New York, NY 10017 USA
Tel: 1-212-906-5028
Fax: 1-212-906-6350
Web: www.undp.org

Localizing Agenda 21: Multiyear support for medium-sized cities to develop their Local Agenda 21.

UNCHS (Habitat)
P.O. Box 30030
Nairobi, KENYA
E-mail: raf.tuts@unchs.org

Managing the Environment Locally in Sub-Saharan Africa (MELISSA): Technical assistance program that supports local environmental action planning in African cities.

CSIR-Environmentek
P.O. Box 395
Pretoria 0001 SOUTH AFRICA
Tel: 27-12-349-2870
Fax: 27-12-841-3158
E-mail: melissa@melissa.org
Web: www.melissa.org

Metropolitan Environmental Improvement Program: Pilot program that funds innovative solutions to environmental problems in Asian cities; also produces publications and maintains a network.

c/o World Bank
1818 H St. NW
Washington, DC 20433 USA
Tel: 1-202-458-2726
Fax: 1-202-522-1664
Web: www.worldbank.org

Municipal Development Program: Support to African municipalities and national associations of local authorities, including training, policy research, and policy advocacy.

c/o Economic Development Institute
1818 H St. NW
Washington, DC 20433 USA
Tel: 1-202-458-2726
Fax: 1-202-522-1664
Web: www.worldbank.org

Public-Private Partnerships for the Urban Environment: Promotes collaboration between the public and private sectors to solve urban environmental problems in developing countries.

UN Development Program
One United Nations Plaza
New York, NY 10017 USA

Tel: 1-212-906-5767
Fax: 1-212-906-6973
Web: www.undp.org/undp/ppp

Sustainable Cities Initiative: Supports demonstration projects based on citizen participation to achieve a balance of economic, environmental, and social concerns.

Center for Environment/USAID
1601 N. Kent St., Room 409
Arlington, VA 22209 USA
Tel: 1-703-812-2484
Fax: 1-703-875-4384
E-mail: vgary@g.env.up@aidw.gov

Sustainable Cities Programme: Helps to improve environmental planning and management capacity in the public, private, and community sectors in low-income cities.

UNCHS (Habitat)
P.O. Box 30030
Nairobi, KENYA
Tel: 254-2-623225
Fax: 254-2-624264
Web: www.unchs.org

UNDP-World Bank Water and Sanitation Program: Supports projects to develop affordable water and sanitation options for developing countries; works through a series of regional offices.

c/o World Bank
1818 H St. NW
Washington, DC 20433 USA
Tel: 1-202-473-0693
Fax: 1-202-522-3228
Web: www.worldbank.org

All Cities

Institute for Local Self-Reliance: Provides assistance to communities interested in becoming more self-sufficient.

2425 18th St. NW
Washington, DC 20009 USA
Tel: 1-202-232-4108
Fax: 1-202-332-0463
Web: www.ilsr.org

Sister Cities International: Can pair cities to provide support for urban environmental planning and management.

120 South Payne St.
Alexandria, VA 22314 USA
Tel: 1-703-836-3535
Fax: 1-703-836-4815

ANNEX C

Training and Research Institutions

Training

Center for Sustainable Communities: Offers a ten-session online tutorial to help communities become more sustainable.

E-mail: common@u.washington.edu
Web: weber.u.washington.edu/~common

Centre for the Urban Environment: Offers an M.Sc. in urban environmental management as well as shorter courses for professional development.

P.O. Box 1935
3000 BX Rotterdam NETHERLANDS
Tel: 31-10-402-1523
Fax: 31-10-404-5671
E-mail: e.frank@ihs.nl

Centre of Human Settlements: Postgraduate studies on housing, building, and planning with scarce resources and pressing environmental constraints.

Catholic University of Louvain
Kasteel Arenberg
B-3001 Louvain BELGIUM
Tel: 32-16-321371
Fax: 32-16-321984
Web: www.asro.kuleuven.ac.be/onderw/pgcgen.htm

Economic Development Institute: Offers short professional training seminars on urban environmental and pollution issues, urban air quality management, urban and industrial environmental management, and building local environmental capacity.

World Bank
1818 H St. NW
Washington, DC 20433 USA
Tel: 1-202-473-6394
Fax: 1-202-676-0977
E-mail: abigio@worldbank.org
Web: www.worldbank.org/html/edi/edien.html

Interconsult Academy: Offers a training program on local environmental management, Agenda 21, and sustainable development.

Kopmanna-gatan2
SE-652 26 Karlstad SWEDEN
Tel: 46-54-187515
Fax: 46-54-187530
E-mail: infor@interconsultacademy.se

London School of Economics and Political Science: Offers one-year M.Sc. on "Cities, Space and Society" that covers planning for sustainable cities.

Dept. of Geography and Environment
Houghton Street
London WC2A 2AE UK
Tel: 44-171-955-6089
Fax: 44-171-955-7412
Web: www.lse.ac.uk/depts/Geography

Pratt Institute Center for Community and Environmental Development: Offers a one-year certificate program for staff of community-based nonprofits and related public agencies.

379 DeKalb Ave., 2nd Floor
Brooklyn, NY 11205 USA
Tel: 1-718-636-3486
Fax: 1-718-636-3709
Web: www.picced.org

Research Triangle Institute: Offers scheduled courses in a "Sustainable Cities" curriculum that include urban environmental management, reinventing governance, and water utility management.

300 Park Drive, Suite 115
Research Triangle Park, NC 27709 USA
Tel: 1-919-541-1234
Fax: 1-919-541-6621

University of Canberra: Offers Master of Urban Management that covers urban and environmental policy and planning in low-income cities.

Centre for Developing Cities
P.O. Box 1
Belconnen ACT 2616 AUSTRALIA
Tel: 61-6-201-2633
Fax: 61-6-201-5034
E-mail: lrn@design.canberra.edu.au
Web: www.cities.canberra.edu.au

University of Virginia: Offers M.A. in the Department of Urban and Environmental Planning with a concentration in environmental planning.

School of Architecture
University of Virginia
Charlottesville, VA 22903 USA
Tel: 1-804-924-6442
Web: www.urban.arch.virginia.edu

Urban Environmental Management Center: Provides education to Asian students in urban environmental planning and management to promote the development of sustainable cities.

Asian Institute of Technology
G.P.O. Box 2754
Bangkok 10501 THAILAND
Tel: 66-2-524-5033
Fax: 66-2-516-2126
Web: www.hsd.ait.ac.th/uem.htm

Urban Environmental Training Materials Program: Develops and tests guidelines on urban environmental management and action planning.

Division of Urban and Rural Programs
GTZ, Postfach 5180
65726 Eschborn GERMANY
Tel: 1-49-6196-791339
Fax: 1-49-6196-797153

Water, Engineering and Development Centre: Maintains training (including distance learning) and research programs on water supply, sanitation, urban infrastructure, and environmental management.

Loughborough University
Leicestershire LE11 3TU UK
Tel: 44-1509-222885
Fax: 44-1509-211079
E-mail: wedc@lboro.ac.uk
Web: www.lboro.ac.uk/departments/cv/wedc

Research

Center for Urban Policy and the Environment: Seeks to bridge the gap between communities and government by empowering communities and people to control the quality of their lives.

Purdue University
342 North Senate Avenue
Indianapolis, IN 46204 USA
Tel: 1-317-261-3000
Fax: 1-317-261-3050
Web: www.spea.iupui.edu/cupe

Cornell Urban Environment and Poverty Program: Promotes research and proposes policies on the intersection of poverty, environment, and urbanization.

107 West Sibley Hall
Ithaca, NY 14853 USA
Tel: 1-607-255-4331
Fax: 1-607-255-6681
Web: www.research.cornell.edu/vpr/centerdir/urbanenviro.html

European Academy of the Urban Environment: Creates and disseminates knowledge about the urban environment in European cities through workshops, conferences, research, and reports.

Bismarckallee 46-48
D-14193 Berlin GERMANY
Tel: 49-30-895-9990
Fax: 49-30-8959-9919

International Centre for Sustainable Cities: Conducts action research to promote sustainable urban development through pilot projects in developing-country cities.

555 West Hastings St., Suite 1150
Vancouver, BC V6B 4N5 CANADA
Tel: 1-604-666-0061
Fax: 1-604-666-0009
E-mail: icsc@direct.ca

International Institute for the Urban Environment: Organizes seminars and publishes books, reports, and guidelines on the urban environment, generally focusing on European cities.

Nickersteeg 5
2611 EK Delft NETHERLANDS
Tel: 31-15-262-3279
Fax: 31-15-262-4873
E-mail: urban@theoffice.net

Local Government Environmental Assistance Network: Offers research service to help local governments in United States to resolve difficult questions related to environmental issues.

Web: www.lgean.org/

Southeast Asian Centre for Environmental & Urban Management: Conducts research on materials and energy flows, trend analysis, lifestyles for low environmental impact, urban fabric, technology, and environment.

Institute Sultan Iskandar
Universiti Teknologi Malaysia
Mail Bag 791
80990 Johor Baru
Johor, MALAYSIA

Stockholm Environment Institute: Conducts research and issues publications on household environmental problems, analytical methods, and urban sustainability.

Box 2142
103 14 Stockholm SWEDEN
Fax: 46-8-723-0348
E-mail: seihq@nordnet.se
Web: nn.apc.org/sei/

Sustainable Cities Initiative: Funds research on urban and environmental sustainability through the Engineering and Physical Sciences Research Council.

Web: www.susx.ac.uk@units/gec/cities.htm

Urban Environmental Management Research Initiative: Network of urban planning researchers who use the Internet to exchange information on the urban environment.

Department of Social Engineering
Tokyo Institute of Technology
2-12-1, Ookayama, Meguro-ko
Tokyo-152 JAPAN
E-mail: hari@soc.titech.ac.jp
Web: www.soc.titech.ac.jp/uem/

Index

About the Author

Josef Leitmann, Ph.D., is a senior urban planner at the World Bank where he specializes in urban and environmental management. This book was written while he was on leave as a visiting professor of city and regional planning at the Middle East Technical University in Ankara, Turkey. Its preparation was enriched by his work on local environmental management with UNCHS/Habitat, the International Union of Local Authorities, and the World Wildlife Fund's Turkish affiliate. Leitmann is on the International Advisory Board of the Centre for the Urban Environment in The Netherlands. He earned his doctorate in city and regional planning from the University of California at Berkeley and a Master's degree in public policy from Harvard.